WARRIOR GEEKS

CHRISTOPHER COKER

WARRIOR GEEKS

How 21st-Century Technology is Changing the Way We Fight and Think About War

OXFORD
UNIVERSITY PRESS

OXFORD
UNIVERSITY PRESS

Oxford University Press, Inc., publishes works that further
Oxford University's objective of excellence
in research, scholarship, and education.

Oxford New York

Auckland   Cape Town   Dar es Salaam   Hong Kong   Karachi
Kuala Lumpur   Madrid   Melbourne   Mexico City   Nairobi
New Delhi   Shanghai   Taipei   Toronto

With offices in

Argentina   Austria   Brazil   Chile   Czech Republic   France   Greece
Guatemala   Hungary   Italy   Japan   Poland   Portugal   Singapore
South Korea   Switzerland   Thailand   Turkey   Ukraine   Vietnam

Oxford is a registered trade mark of Oxford University Press in the UK
and certain other countries.

Published in the United Kingdom in 2013 by C. Hurst & Co. (Publishers) Ltd.

Published by Oxford University Press, Inc
198 Madison Avenue, New York, New York 10016

www.oup.com

Oxford is a registered trademark of Oxford University Press

Library of Congress Cataloging-in-Publication Data is available for this title
Coker, Christopher.
Warrior Geeks.
Includes bibliographical references and index.
ISBN 978-0-199-32789-8 (alk. paper)

1 3 5 7 9 8 6 4 2

Printed in the United States of America
on Acid-Free Paper

CONTENTS

'Had Greek civilisation never existed, we might fear God and deal justly with our neighbours, we might practise arts and even have learned how to devise fairly simple machines, but we would never have become fully conscious, which is to say that we would never have become, for better or worse, fully human'.

W.H. Auden, *The Portable Greek Reader*, 1948
(Auden, 2002, 377)

'the final stage is come when Man by eugenics, by pre-natal conditioning, …has obtained full control over himself. Human nature will be the last part of Nature to surrender to Man. The battle will then be won. We shall have taken the thread of life out of the hand of Clotho (the Greek fate responsible for spinning the thread of human life) and be henceforth free to make our species whatever we wish it to be. The battle will indeed be won. But who, precisely, will have won it?'

C.S. Lewis, *The Abolition of Man*, 1943/2001

PREFACE

FROM GREEKS TO GEEKS

The advert said it all. *Medal of Honour*: 'This is a new breed of warrior for a new breed of warfare. This is force multiplied, relentless, exacting, precise. This is the face the enemy fears'. (*The Times*, 15 October, 2010) *Medal of Honour* is actually a conventional game, but the idea is important: a new breed of warrior for a new battlefield. Not to be outdone, another game, *Ghost Recon: Advanced Warfighter*, advertised its own warrior of the future which would be the players' to command: 'In 2013 the Army will unleash a new breed of soldier. A soldier whose lethality has been honed by the finest technologies'. (Teng, 2007,1) The game, which has been developed by Ubisoft in conjunction with the US Army to showcase its Future Force Warrior concept, is based on the premise of a future invasion of Mexico to restore order after state failure.

The United States, insisted President George W. Bush, would define war on its own terms, and it would do so with a new breed of soldiers, not yet out of school but already being trained to be the warriors of tomorrow. The ambition to patent future war may strike one as absurdly unrealistic, of course, but it captures the Darwinian imperative which governs our lives—war must be made 'fit for purpose', and a 'new breed' is for once a telling term. Are we breeding true, or breeding out the imperfections that made the warrior so thoroughly human in the past? Are we beginning, at last, to factor human fallibility out of the equation?

Certainly, the boundaries we once took for granted between the warrior and his weapon are becoming occluded, so much so that an American general a few years ago could talk of an individual soldier under his command as an 'F-15 with legs'. (*The Economist*, 10 June 2006). If the balance between man and machine has been changing for some time, the fusion of man and machine is much more recent. Take the advert for the video game *Crysis 2*: 'Be strong: take on multiple enemies with warrior mode; Be fast: power jump and slide around the environment with amazing agility; Be invisible: use stealth mode; *Be the weapon*'. In Hollywood's representation of war the warrior has been becoming his weapon for some time. Films like *Universal Soldier* and *Robocop* show a future in which soldiers and law enforcement officers may become beings in which flesh and machine intermesh. Other, more realistic films such as *Body of Lies* show warriors tied into a cybernetic system which they share with drones flying overhead. The future is already here. 'The difference between science fiction and science is timing', insists Col. Christopher Carlile, the former Director of the United States Army's Unmanned Aircraft System Center of Excellence. It is a quote which appears in an article tellingly entitled 'The Terminator Scenario: are we giving our military machines too much power?' (POPSCI. COM/TECHNOLOGY/ARTICLE/2010/12/TERMINATOR/SCE-NARIO). Are we in danger of factoring out the human differential? In the near future will war cease to be 'the human thing', the only definition which Thucydides, the world's first military historian, was willing to volunteer?

From Greeks to geeks

If you are born into the Western world there is nowhere else to start from but the Greeks. There is much about them that we do not like to recall these days: their misanthropy; their blood feuds; the slaves and the superstition. So beholden are we to their philosophy and poetry, both lyrical and epic, that we tend to forget the unrelenting violence of their world. In the opening of Plato's *Laws*, the Cretan speaker Clinias remarks that 'what most men call peace is merely an appearance; in reality all cities are by nature in a permanent state of undeclared war against all other cities' (Finley, 2000, 67) Classical Athens never knew ten consecutive years of peace from the time it defeated the Persians in 479 BC to the time of its own loss of independence at the hands of Philip of Macedon in 338 BC. War was a natural state of affairs between city-states, wrote one writer in the 1940s, perhaps because it matched 'the secret tendency of the Greek soul'. (Finley, 2000, 71)

The wars that were fought in the brief period of Greek history—both real and fictional like Homer's grandstanding account of the Trojan War—still provide us with our role models and historical archetypes. Achilles remains the prototypical warrior, even if cadets at the US Naval War College confess they would prefer to root for a 'Hector who wins'. Achilles, as it happens, is the better fighter. Hector dies because of it, but the cadets are still martial enough to want to root for a winner. (Finch, 2005, 158)

Fast forward to the modern military and we find that Homer's tragic tale is still on the must-read list. The Greeks have never been far from the minds of educated soldiers. 'We came to Fort Lewis afraid to admit we are not Achilles, that we are not brave, that we are not heroes', remarks a character in Tim O'Brien's compelling account of his own tour of duty in Vietnam. (O'Brien, 2003, 45) Twenty years later, as he waited for the beginning of Operation Desert Storm, the young Tom Swofford was to be found reading the *Iliad* in a desperate attempt to make sense of the war that was unfolding. (Swofford, 2003, 23–4) What soldiers find uplifting about the poem is that even in the midst of unspeakable carnage life goes on. War and mortality may cry havoc in the Homeric world but the centre holds. Homer spins a tale that still appeals across the centuries because it tells the soldier that the works of men are worth recording, and that no catastrophe—not even the sack of Troy—is ever final.

Back in the classroom when soldiers are taught about battlefield ethics, they are told that Aristotle got there first. Aristotelian virtue ethics are still at the heart of the warrior ethos which Western military academies instil in their servicemen and women. When we think of sacrifice we still get back to Thermopylae and Leonidas' defence of the famous pass against the Persians. Thucydides is still taught in military history courses (he was introduced onto the syllabus at the US Marine Corps University as recently as 1972). And when soldiers come back from Afghanistan broken not only in body but in mind, they are now shown 'Warrior Theater', a new concept that takes two of the seven surviving plays of Sophocles and their depictions of traumatised heroes as a therapeutic device by which to restore soldiers' damaged minds. The Greeks have been at the centre of the Western military imagination for a reason: they interrogated themselves mercilessly and analysed war as a phenomenon more than anyone else, before or since. And what terrified them most was that war was the heart of their humanity. Thucydides called it 'the human thing' in recognition that war and our humanity are joined at the hip.

Thucydides wrote his book because he wanted his readers to care as much as he did about what happens when social intelligence breaks down and war degenerates into warfare from which it had emerged only a few thousand years earlier. He wanted to explain how armies can soon break down when some instincts get the better of others, when soldiers cease to 'network' effectively. He wanted to show how war brings our extraordinary acts of courage and self-sacrifice, acts which still have the power to move us. And he wished to show how war brings out the worst as well as the best in those who wage it, calling into question our own humanity—the name we give not only to a species, but to the qualities we deem it to embody.

For most human of all, perhaps, was the Greek capacity to accommodate opposing ideas, to see war as glorious one moment and horrific the next. For every verse in the *Greek Anthology* celebrating the martial virtues, there are three regretting the waste of it all, or what the playwright Euripides called the 'murderous misery of war'. The Greeks had their proverbs: 'In war the sleeping are awoken with trumpets, in peace by the birds'. 'No-one is so foolish to prefer war to peace', wrote Herodotus, the first historian, who took war as the main theme of his *History*, 'in which instead of sons burying their fathers, fathers bury their sons'. 'War is sweet for those who have not tried it', added the poet Pindar, 'but anyone who knows what it is is horrified beyond measure in his heart when it approaches'. (Meier, 2011, 160) In their very different registers, other writers were also able to evoke a distaste for war, not merely a dislike of it. Even in the work of Homer the bitterness is not suppressed. Book 11 refers to 'the charioteers lying on the ground more beloved of vultures than by their wives'.

But the one claim the Greeks were not prepared to make was that war itself was inhuman. Individual authors like Euripides might complain about its human cost, Plato might regret that Greeks killed fellow Greeks as savagely as they did foreigners (or barbarians), but they were also aware that the inhuman face of war reflected their own.

Thucydides—it has been said—wrote a tragedy in prose: a work that, like the great plays of his contemporaries, threw an intense and not always flattering light on the human condition. It has also been claimed that he was influenced by the sceptical rationalism of the Hippocratics, who were bringing at the time to medicine what we can now see as an incipient scientific method: the discussion of the treatment of internal ailments through the correct use of inference when the facts are not to be apprehended by the senses. And Thucydides knew by intuition a lot that could only be inferred, not empirically tested. What lingered in the back of his mind was not the horror of war, or the nobility of individual warriors, but the mystery that men quite ordinary in themselves could tolerate such conditions and cope with such stress. We should take Thucydides seriously because he took his readers seriously, and it is important to understand how war and *Homo sapiens* have co-evolved because our humanity is continuing to evolve in new and possibly disturbing ways. 'Men make a city, not walls or ships empty of men', wrote Thucydides (Thucydides, *History* 7.17.7), but, of course, we are planning to take this road. The ramparts of our cities are now 'virtual' and vulnerable to cyber attack. The next generation of combat aircraft will be unmanned, as will many of our land vehicles. Our skies are already full of Unmanned Aerial Vehicles, or 'drones' as they are popularly known. 'I hope that many more computer chips will lay down their lives for their country', remarked an American general after a drone was brought down over Bosnia in the 1990s. Engineers are fast designing robotic systems that will be able to take decisions on our behalf. Neuroscientists are studying how the human brain/emotions can be manipulated. Geneticists studying cloning and bio-engineering, and physicists studying cybernetic networks, are all investigating ways in which the human and machine may co-evolve, both functionally and performatively, and how we may even be able to biologically re-engineer ourselves. Even the term 'warrior' is now applied to a new generation of military personnel who spend their days behind computer screens, immured in a cyber or virtual world, quarantined from the traditional dangers and risks that have been central to war, at least in the popular imagination. So much for the common genetic makeup that linked Achilles and Audie Murphy, the most decorated soldier in American history—the common genealogy, if you like, that links those who over the centuries have pushed their bodies, minds and often spirits, beyond the usual limits of human endurance. Scientists may well be on the way to eradicating the last vestiges of the Homeric worldview from which the warrior myth continues to draw its popular appeal.

As their roles become more demanding, specialised and far removed from their own inborn predispositions, will warriors require ever more years of 'programming', at the risk of ever diminishing real emotional rewards? Will the special forces of tomorrow be super-enhanced cyborgs with bio-engineered improved vision? Will surgically implanted computer chips enhance their cognitive functions; will we be genetically profiling soldiers one day to identify the natural warriors we wish to send into battle? Will we find a way to reboot war in the digital code of a computer, or the biological code of DNA? And what effect will all of this have on our humanity? How will it shape or reshape our ethical codes and protocols? Will it make redundant the warrior ethos—that code of honour which over the centuries has been central to legitimising the military profession? Will neuro-ethics replace traditional ethical ideals? How will new technologies change the way we think about war (and practice it)? Will it still be war or something else: a computer game, a simulated virtual reality?

The Greeks are at risk of giving way to geeks, a term that carries a lot of cultural baggage, not all of it negative. If only for its symbolism it is interesting that the term is one of the few that does not stem from a Greek root. It comes instead from the English dialectical word, 'geek, geck: fool, or freak' (Ford, 2007, 195). In its slang usage it means a computer expert or enthusiast, or a person who is over-earnestly cerebral (though not necessarily intellectual). Some apply it to people who are wired into an alternative cyber world whose true friends are virtual, or perpetually 'on line'; others apply it to people with technical rather than social skills who are more at ease interacting with computers than with people. All these descriptions might apply to another derogatory word, *nerd*. The chief difference between the two, explains Richard Clarke, is that 'geeks get it done' (Wikipedia definition). We might go further and claim that a geek is a nerd with attitude.

In this book I shall be concerned with what I call 'geekishness'. I am not attacking a generation that finds itself trapped in computer chat rooms who spend hours playing computer games, not as a momentary diversion from life so much as a life-choice. I am not criticising, as many do, the life styles of those more fluent in HTML than conversational English; or those who are eager to share the latest information on software uploads, or choose to engage in passionate discussions about how to reverse-engineer Microsoft. I am addressing a particular mentality, an attitude of mind such as the contemporary orthodoxy that history is unimportant; that everything that matters is happening now; and that only 'matter' actually matters. It is a mentality captured by Daniel Dennett in his book *Consciousness Explained*:

'There is only one sort of stuff, namely "matter"—the physical stuff of physics, chemistry and physiology and the mind is somehow nothing but a physical phenomenon using the same physical principles, laws and raw materials that suffice to explain radioactivity, continental drift, photosynthesis, reproduction, nutrition and growth'. (Dennett, 1991, 33)

Could there be a more impoverished understanding of life? We can still wonder at the world, we are told, by understanding everything in terms of matter, but as the novelist Julian Barnes writes, 'if our perceptions of the world are mere micro-moments of bio-chemical activity, the mere snap and crackle of a few synapses, then what does this wonder amount to?' (Barnes, 2008, 71) What we call sacred, the Greeks instructed us, is anything that gives meaning to our lives through our own actions so that we can value the world we have created. For it is we who invest value in life itself, and the faith we place in ourselves is, perhaps, the most sacred thing of all.

The mentality that I am attacking arises from the technology we use. Most of us are 'geeks' to some extent, of course. We are merging with our machines faster than ever. Most of us are wired into technology networks like the World Wide Web. Most of us can only do maths now using a calculator (we can no longer do the sums in our heads). We depend on symbolic memory (Google) from which we derive most of our information. We rely on Facebook, Twitter and cell phones to communicate with each other. Young people share their thoughts with people they do not know. 600m Facebook members share 30bn pieces of content each month, from intimate thoughts to family photographs. Some see this as changing the nature of human self-expression. Privacy, they argue, really is being relegated to a thing of the past, as is the right to be unavailable in the age of the cell phone. We might rightly mock what Esther Dyson calls 'friend inflation'— information sharing with complete strangers. But we can also ask whether such strangers are any more remote than the members of the 'imagined community' of the nation-state which gave the rootless industrial masses of the 20th century a degree of psychological reassurance and social involvement. (Jarvis, 2011) But then the real problem, perhaps, is not self-expression; it is self-empowerment, for every time you share a thought with others, others are monitoring your thoughts. Companies or governments pick up the data trails we leave in order to monitor consumer preferences, or dissenting political views.

And is this digital world producing impersonal, fragmentary communications? Is it diminishing and even demeaning inter-personal interaction? Jaron Lanier is particularly scathing about the pervasive anonymity, or pseudo-anonymity, of human expression. Lanier is no Luddite; he works in the computer world and is the first to accept that in most spheres of life it is right to love the medium you work in, whether it is film, television, or the English language. And unlike other critics he is aware that the new technologies still fulfil a fundamental human need to express and define oneself in relation to others. Updates made by Twitter can transcend their 140-character limit, and blogs, now used extensively in all areas of life, especially by soldiers in the field, are not just an exercise in personal vanity; they allow the sharing of personal experience. But as a member of the computer 'tribe' he is also conscious that its impact on life is changing the way we think about ourselves: 'When the developers of digital technologies design a program that requires you to interact with a computer as if it were a person, they ask you to accept in some corner of your brain that you might also be conceived of as a program'. (Lanier, 2011, 4) The language we use suggests that we already do. We tell ourselves that we are 'programmed' to do it; we claim that things we do not understand do not always 'compute'; we frequently talk of 'interfacing' with others. We tend to see the brain as software and the body as hardware. Some writers add that the more we think of ourselves as computers the more we may stress those aspects of our nature that we consider more appropriate than in the past; inference drawing, calculation and dispassionate rationality may all be seen as appropriate ideals. (Ferre, 1995, 65)

Delving much deeper, Lanier enumerates some of the ways in which our view of ourselves and of life is being transformed more radically than we think. (Lanier, 2011, 75) Many subscribe to a *Weltanschauung* that tends to deny the mystery of the 'existence of experience' and prefers a world of gadgets to a world of people. Certainly, the persistent valuation or undervaluation of humans as individuals swallowed up into a cybernetic collective leads us to forget that the world we have built relies for its functioning on human choice. Technology can motivate the choice and enlarge the choices we make, but it can never replace human judgement.

Lanier finds much to criticize in the 'geek' mentality. And one feature he finds especially alarming is the tendency to think that life is risk-free. In the video games we play there is always a 'ghost in the machine', a fault in the design the programmers did not appreciate when the product was first launched, which allows you to beat the system and ignore the rules. It was precisely thinking that the rules didn't count that led many young traders and bond managers (many of them games players) to perform so recklessly back in 2007–8, sparking off a near meltdown in the financial markets.

But for me, the most pernicious aspect of the geek mentality is the extent to which it devalues what the Greeks found so fascinating: individual character. Many geeks tend to de-emphasise personhood—the intrinsic value of an individual's unique internal experience which allows us to aspire for the unattainable; and when they do aspire to achieve more they often embed the aspirational spirit in the technologies they use. The concept of character is already being undermined on three fronts—by an unquestioned faith in genetics (behaviour is determined by the genes); in evolutionary psychology (behaviour is determined by evolved survival mechanisms); and in neuroscience (behaviour is determined by modules of a hard-wired brain).

At the other extreme, there is the unwillingness to engage with science, or to understand the human condition through the scientific lens. Back in the late 19th century there were writers who were not willing to take on board the insights of the new sciences, such as the newly minted theory of evolution. Take John Stuart Mill's great liberal tract *On Liberty* (1859), which appeared in the same year as *The Origin Of Species*. Twelve years later, when Mill died, he was still unwilling to apply Darwinist theories despite his championing of what he called 'moral science'. Relying exclusively on Aristotelian insights, he never once considered important what scientists might have to say about human nature. Much has changed since those days. Nietzsche was one of the first philosophers to embrace Darwin's idea that we are 'clever animals', and others soon latched on to the idea that it is language, not consciousness, or the mind, or even the exercise of reason that makes us different, and the origin of language is perfectly intelligible in naturalistic terms. We now instinctively reach to science to explain human behaviour although much of the science, such as evolutionary psychology, is still in its infancy.

In the end it is not an either/or. It is not a question of science versus the humanities, or drawing up battle lines between two opposing camps, the technophiles versus technophobes. As the Greeks recognised on the basis of simple observation, human nature can be explained by reference to theories that we might think of—though they did not—as 'scientific'. But the attack on 'character' (that is, the idea that there is nothing in human behaviour that cannot be explained scientifically) is profoundly instructive, for it testifies to a diminished belief in humanity and the qualities it is deemed to embody. Character—duty, sacrifice, perseverance in the face of adversity—was the set of virtues that once defined the warrior. These words sound Victorian only because the Victorians lauded then and we no longer do. But, writes Edward Skidelsky, they are 'the natural excellences of the species', the best we are capable of, and our true purpose in life. I have written this book because the geeks are tomorrow's warriors and it is the future of the warrior that I shall mostly address in this book: will they still retain their honour (the traditional private space which has defined them through the ages); will they still retain any sense of free will; and perhaps, most interesting of all, will they still retain their individual moral consciences, or will the generals prefer to subcontract responsibility for our actions to robots in whose ethical judgement they may trust much more? 'I will stand my artificial intelligence over your humanity any day of the week, and tell you that my AI will … create fewer ethical lapses than a human being', remarked John Arquilla, the Executive Director of the Information Operations Center at the Naval Post Graduate School. (http://www.nytimes.com/2010/11/28/science/28robot.html?_r=1andem=etal)

The central concern of this book is whether war will continue to remain a human, all too human, activity by 2035. And the word 'human' must be understood in its broadest terms: 'We are only properly human', writes one author, 'when we go beyond the merely human'. (Ford, 2007, 195) Over centuries war has thrown up many examples of where this has been the case. Conflict has thrown up plenty of examples of horrors, atrocities and acts of remarkable cruelty, but it has also thrown into vivid relief acts of great courage, inspiring examples of self-sacrifice and extraordinary instances of human ingenuity. But as war continues along the path I shall chart in the chapters that follow it will raise disturbing questions about the extent to which the scope of 'humanity' is being hollowed out as war's human space continues to contract, further and faster than ever.

I have no doubt, by the way, that war will continue to remain a human activity, but the question is whether it will be more or less humane. For it will only remain humane if war's 'human space' is not hollowed out completely. The message of this book is that of Susan Greenwood's *Tomorrow's People*. An acclaimed neuroscientist, she warns that everything we take for granted about ourselves—imagination, individuality, conscience and free will—could become lost for ever. Only by harnessing technology in a humane way can we hope to preserve our unique sense of self.

The face of war is changing fast. Its new contours are already taking visible shape; we are seeing a new kind of war set in conspicuous counterpoint to the old as we can glimpse from many Hollywood films and science fiction novels. And no-one is more interested in science fiction than the military. The US Navy's Professional Readership Program includes novels such as *Starship Troopers* and *Enders' Game*. Translated into 18 languages, *Ender's Game* is also taught at the US Marine Corps University as part of its leadership psychology training.

One of the most celebrated contemporary writers, William Gibson, once told a journalist that when he wrote about the future he was merely 'squinting at the present in a certain way'. (Strathern, 2007, 241) The future we envision can only be an extrapolation of present trends taken to a logical and therefore often illogical conclusion. But that is why we read science fiction—very rarely for its literary merit, and almost never for its visions of the future which rarely, if ever, come to pass. We read it because we want to know more about ourselves—what we are doing now, and why we are opting for the futures we want to fashion. The question the best science fiction writers raise is what impact the future will have on our humanity. As Oona Strathern writes in *A Brief History of the Future*, we 'focus on the future in order to redirect attention to the present, to create a kind of self-evaluation of society. It is in effect a mirroring process which has only one mirror; to improve our ability to change our so-called 'future fitness'. (Strathern, 2007, 278)

The argument

Chapter 1 casts an eye back to the past when the future—our future—was being forged. History is sometimes caught by its more striking images—the Cross and the Crucifixion, the human footprint and the moon landing, the collapse of the Twin Towers on 9/11. The iconic image for the atomic bombing of Hiroshima was the mushroom cloud snapped by the military photographer George Caron. It became famous almost at once and was adopted as a logo by 54 companies in the US before the year was out, including, somewhat bizarrely, the Miss Atomic Bomb pageant in Las Vegas.

It is, of course, difficult for any age to understand its own birth. Those who live through great changes are often the last to grasp their historical significance. We are usually confronted, wrote Borges, by 'the modesty of history'. In plying their trade historians work to identify historic turning points and to date them precisely. Real history, however, is more modest: its essential dates remain secret for a long while. (Borges,1964, 167). If history's key dates are often unknown, that is because history itself has many possibilities, many of which are never realised. There was a widespread fear in 1945 that the prospect of nuclear war had called into question our own indispensability as a species. By the 1970s another theme had begun to resonate in the minds of people: would computers become self-conscious and shut us down, or shut us out of the war business altogether? It is a familiar fear to anyone who knows the *Terminator* films, a Hollywood franchise with a remarkable hold on the imagination. If not quite a household name, SkyNet is certainly a name to conjure with.

PREFACE

History hasn't quite delivered on its promises. Nuclear war, though still a distinct possibility, no longer has the same purchase on our imagination, and computers are no more intelligent today than they were fifty years ago, even if they can process data at speeds undreamed of then. They certainly cannot think either for themselves or for us, their programmers. So why bother to recall past fears? Because there are other possibilities which are only now beginning to be realised. And one of the key dates to which historians may turn to understand how war evolved is the summer of 1944 which saw the first 'robot bombs', the term contemporaries employed to describe the V1 missiles which the Germans unleashed on London as World War II drew to a long, drawn-out close.

One man who grasped this was Theodor Adorno, as he read the first newspaper reports about Hitler's VI rockets. Ironically, he was a refugee from the country that until the mid-20th century was the most advanced in military technology. It is no coincidence that H.G. Wells, in the very first book to depict aerial bombing, showed German Zeppelins bombing New York, not American Zeppelins bombing Berlin. Germany led in the science of war. Germany, not the US, produced the first jet aeroplanes as well as the first cruise and ballistic missiles (V1/V2). It would even have developed an atomic bomb but for the fact that Jewish scientists had escaped to the New World, and built it instead for the Americans. But with the defeat of Hitler, the technological lead was taken by the United States which, for the moment at least, still possesses it. The US is far ahead of everyone else in the technologies I shall discuss in this book—cybernetics, robotics and the pharmacologicalisation of war—though it may be only a matter of time before other countries catch up.

Adorno's claim to fame is that he grasped that war and our humanity, which had co-evolved from the very beginning of history, were being re-forged in new and interesting ways. Technology, not politics, was not only becoming the driving force of history; humanity and technology were beginning to fuse, both functionally and performatively. And in his interest in the robot-bombs he touched upon the future in another way, for no-one really doubts that robotics is the future of war. The only question is whether we will sub-contract our decision-making, and even our capacity to make ethical judgements, to the machines we build.

Chapter 2 will explore why Thucydides' definition of war as 'the human thing' has never been bettered. Thucydides knew one big thing that we often like to challenge: we are the only species on the planet to wage war.

The only beings that engage in collective organised violence on a scale very similar to war are one of the oldest species on the planet, and one that would even survive a nuclear war that might wipe us out. Ants have been attacking each other's colonies for 50 million years, but they live a life in which some members are genetically born to be warriors; the latter are haplodiploid reproducers, female offspring of a central queen, sharing three-quarters of their genes with their numerous sisters. They sacrifice themselves because it is their best chance to perpetuate their own genes and thus ensure that the next army will be made up of genetic near-replicants. Unlike ants, we are mammals who limit self-sacrifice to our closest relatives, and derive our identity from small family groups which have grown over time. It is therefore far more pertinent, writes Robert O'Connell, not to ask whether humans are inherently warlike, but instead to question why it is possible for us to wage war at all. (O'Connell, 1996, 347)

The advantage we enjoy over ants is the invention of culture which has allowed us to evolve in a way they have not, even in 50 million years. We were able to use culture to translate collective violence programmed into us by natural selection into warfare. Only recently, in the last 12,000 years or so, have we been able to translate warfare into war, a process that involves our own domestication. After domesticating plants and animals such as dogs (around 10,000 BC), we turned to the greatest challenge of all: domesticating our own 'savage mind' (the telling title of a book by the Cambridge anthropologist Jack Goody). And the key in the case of humans was to domesticate natural-born warriors too, those individuals who derived their humanity from their exercise of collective violence. What the Greeks recognised, on the basis of empirical observation alone, was that the domestication of Man differed from the domestication of animals. Spirit was not to be tamed so much as integrated with other passions, feelings and emotions. It had to be put in the service of reason and appetite. The warrior had to be made socially intelligent. Achilles, added Aristotle, when raging against his own side or against Hector towards the end of the *Iliad*, had no 'ear for reason'. Aristotle never suggested that rage should be abolished; he argued instead that it should be brought into 'elective affinity' with the rational mind. The Greeks were the first to recognise what the philosopher William James 're-discovered' in the late 19th century: the emotions are embedded in every rational decision we make, in everything we do.

They were the first to define the terms of debate on the basis not of preconceived beliefs but of acute observation. Thucydides' great contribution was to grasp the key importance of culture. We are cultural creatures, with cultural instincts, which are often stronger than our biological impulses. The Greeks tended to privilege culture over nature in the binomial distinctions they drew between humans and animals, men and women, and not least, barbarians and themselves. From our perspective, however, what strikes us most is not the 'political incorrectness' of these divisions but their mistaken insistence on another distinction, between the organic and the inorganic, between humans and the tools they use. We no longer make such a distinction, and have not done so for some time. A human being, writes Timothy Taylor, is an 'artificial ape'; we are, adds Kevin Kelly, a symbiont species: we are the tools we use. Only very recently, however, have we been able to imagine a further step on our evolution in which we will incorporate tools into our bodies. Not even Aristotle, despite his extraordinary imagination, could have imagined what we call a 'cyborg'.

The third chapter emphasises that the most important element in military success is the human ability to network. Primary group cohesion (the ability of small units to cohere) is essential to life. By nature we are inclined to form groups and to derive our identity from them. Individualism is never asocial. The Greeks knew this as well as anyone, which is why in the *Politics* Aristotle quotes Homer. He who is by nature solitary is 'like the 'tribe-less, lawless, hearth-less ones whom Homer denounces—…for man when perfected is the best of animals but when separated from (the community) he is the worst of all; since …. he is equipped at birth with arms meant to be used by intelligence and excellence which (instead) he may use for the worst ends'. (Aristotle, *Politics*, 12533a, 2–35)

Humans network and because they do so we also think that human behaviour can be controlled. By the mid-17th century we began to think of the body as a machine that could be switched on and off at will. It is a view that we associate with the philosopher René Descartes, and it was natural for the generals to think of themselves as a mind directing an unthinking body of men. In the 1950s this Cartesian version was replaced by a cybernetic one which allowed what the father of cybernetics, Norbert Wiener, famously called 'the human use of human beings'. Today we have entered what is often called a third cybernetic age. We are fusing man and machine into a collective, synthetic, cybernetic network. And we are spawning a new genus of soldier: cyber-warriors who are now wired into cyberspace and 'cubicle warriors' (or drone pilots) who are wired into an electronic battle space. I will explain in Chapter 4, both may find themselves dissociated from the reality of war. In his book *Wired for War*, Peter Singer quotes a young drone pilot: 'It's like a videogame. It can get a little bloodthirsty. But it's fucking cool'. (Singer, 2009, 308–9) If this is a future trend—war as a video-game—then the ethical implications need to be urgently addressed.

And this will become even more important, I will suggest in Chapter 5, if we embrace the robotics revolution and design machines which will be able to save us from the inconveniences that war poses, such as risk-taking. There are now more drone pilots in the US Air Force (USAF) than there are pilots of F16s. The *Predator* and *Reaper* have changed the nature of warfare in Iraq and Afghanistan. And this is just the beginning. Down the road are insect-sized drones which are under development by the US Army's Micro Autonomous Systems and Technology (MAST) programme in partnership with a variety of corporations and university laboratories. Further down the road are nanorobots—particle-sized robots that could enter a person's blood stream or lungs. Until such time as robots become fully autonomous and capable of taking decisions for themselves, humans will remain in or on the loop. But our knowledge of our own fallibility makes robots increasingly attractive. What Darwin was able to hypothesise scientifically, Plato was able to infer from his observation of human nature. We are designed to be moral beings, but although morality is there to make us more 'fit for purpose', not all of us have the character to make the most of the gifts we have been given. And some of us are very weak moral vessels, indeed.

The basis of our moral codes is the warrior's honour. Aristotelian virtue ethics put a premium on individual character. But we seem to be intent on devaluing our own humanity at the same time as we are re-valuing machines. For we are now trying to 'moralise' weapons, an inelegant term for abdicating control over our own ethical decision-making to robots that may be better placed than us to make the right moral judgement calls. Indeed, we are already trying to programme them with a 'conscience'.

Chapter 6 begins with the battle of Delium at which the philosopher Socrates showed his mettle. He did not panic. Today, we are inclined to explain away the decisions we take in terms of brain chemistry. Socrates that day was experiencing a dopamine rush. The neuroscience of war is still in its infancy, but some scientists are already in the vanguard of the attempt to re-value war in neurological terms. Even in the case of victims of post-traumatic stress, the pharmacological option is favoured most. Even such existential dimensions of war as sacrifice, courage and composure are being reduced to their chemical constituents, encouraging the unspoken hope that once we can crack every aspect of our neural and genetic codes we may one day be able to re-engineer warriors of the future.

In the quest we are challenging two essential elements that the Greeks told us make a warrior a specific human type. They took for granted that the giftedness of warrior skills constituted excellence which was there to be celebrated as it had been from the time of Homer. Now, we are told, we can upgrade our skills by popping a pill. The Greeks also celebrated the transcendental experience of war (the sacramental tradition which put some warriors, though not all, in touch with something larger than themselves). If we airbrush both out of the picture, what do we have left? It is a question I shall raise in the final chapter. War is on the way to becoming many things. For some it may be almost indistinguishable from the video games many of us now play; for others it may be two-dimensional as the soldiers begin to share the battle space with robots. But war itself may be well on the way to becoming post-heroic. It is the heroic that has redeemed war and been celebrated by the poets. Sometimes, writes Seamus Heaney, poetry illuminates aspects of the human condition as nothing else can. Sometimes, it touches the base of our sympathetic nature while at the same time taking in the unsympathetic nature of the world to which this nature is constantly exposed. At its most powerful, Heaney insists, poetry can remind us that 'we are hunters and gatherers of values, that our very solitudes and distresses are creditable, insofar as they too are an earnest of our veritable human being'. (Heaney, 2007, 168) But what will human 'being' mean in a post-human age?

Many of the scientific breakthroughs which I shall discuss may never be realised, or if they are realised, never deployed. But that is largely beside the point. It is the direction in which the military and many scientists seem intent on taking us, and it behoves us to ask urgent questions about the final destination, or possible endgame. A future in which the soldier may be denied his private thoughts, or in which he may be totally dissociated from the experience of war itself, a future in which in which giftedness will no longer be valued, is one that would have amazed Thucydides. It is a prospect, more to the point, that he would not have found very human.

I invoke the Greeks in this study as a reference point. We are, at one and the same time, close to them and yet so very distant. We may be their heirs but we have renounced, among other things, the binomial distinctions which they drew between men and women, as well as barbarians and themselves, and we have long attacked their attachment to slavery. But they also enriched our lives, as Auden grasped in the quotation with which I began this book; they got there first and we dishonour them if we are deaf to what they taught us about ourselves. We should engage in a dialogue with them, not in the spirit of mimicry or emulation but in the spirit of critical inquiry. I am inspired to do this by Hannah Arendt's most important work, *The Human Condition*. Arendt was not nostalgic for ancient Greece. Her project, she put it, was to consider that condition from the vantage point of our newest experience and our most recent fears...in order to 'think through what we are doing'. (Arendt, 1998, 5) She went back to the Greeks, as I plan to do in this book, as a provocation. She sought, in the words of one commentator, 'to press the past into the service of the present', to make the everyday seem strange and thus to force us to question where we are heading. (Kateb, 1984, 149) The question she sought to address directly was that as human power increases through technological and scientific advances, we are less equipped to control the consequences of our actions. What would have shocked Arendt most was that we seem intent, in our geekishness, to ask more of technology than we do of ourselves.

We forget at our peril that 'humanity' is neither an essence nor an end but a continuous and precarious process of becoming human. It is, adds Paul Davies, 'a process that entails the inescapable recognition that our humanity is on loan from others to precisely the extent that we acknowledge it in them... others will tell us if we are human and what that means' (Davies, 1997,132). Of no other activity has this been more true than war. At least such has been the case so far. Unfortunately, the developments I shall be discussing in this book may soon force us to ask not the old age question of whether we still need war, but one that is new and far more disturbing: how much longer will war need us?

1

HACKING THE FUTURE

The luckiest man in Japan

One day in the summer of 1945, at 08:15, a man of 29, Tsutomu Yamagu-chi, was walking towards the dockyards in Hiroshima where he worked as a draughtsman designing oil tankers for Mitsubishi Heavy Industries. His three-month secondment to the shipyard was due to end on the morning that the Americans dropped the first atomic bomb. The bomber was the *Enola Gay*, so named after the pilot's mother, and the baby in her belly nicknamed *Little Boy* weighed more than 40 tons. It took one minute to reach the ground. Almost instantly a fireball expanded into a mushroom cloud. Houses a mile apart spontaneously burst into flames from thermal radiation. The resulting firestorm was fanned by winds of 50–60km per hour. Birds combusted in mid-air; on the ground the shadows of vaporised people were etched on stone. '… a ring of skull-/bone fused to the inside of a helmet; a pair of eyeglasses/taken off the eyes of a witness, without glass,/ which vanished, when a white flash sparkled', is the way the poet Galway Kinnell puts it. (Doctorow, 2007, 171)

   Yamaguchi was knocked over by the blast, which shattered his eardrums and temporarily blinded him and left him badly burned. Most fatalities were caused by flash burns from the nuclear explosion. Injured and reeling from the horrors around him, Yamaguchi fled to his home, two days' walk from the city. He arrived in Nagasaki just in time to experience the second atomic attack of the war. He survived that too and went back to work conscientiously the day after. His luck had held. First, as he was working for a reserved occupation he had been spared conscription and a possible anonymous death on a wretched Pacific battlefield; second, he survived not one but two atomic attacks, the only two that the world has witnessed so far. Surprisingly, almost a hundred other people found themselves in the same predicament, but Yamaguchi was the only one to be officially registered as a *hibakusha*—or atomic bomb victim—in both cities. And he lived a long life, surviving surprisingly until January 2010.

The atom bombs dropped on Japan in those closing days of World War II heralded a new era of war. History might have taken a different turn, of course, had the scientists at the Riken Institute in Tokyo managed to build a nuclear weapon before the Americans. The first atomic bomb might have been dropped on San Francisco or Los Angeles. Instead, starved of funds, the Japanese scientists were unable to make the breakthrough. And we should not forget that even the American bombs were small, and did only marginally more damage than the conventional bombers that had torched Tokyo in March 1945 in the biggest air raid of all.

Only three years after Hiroshima, however, the US Joint Chiefs of Staff asked the Atomic Energy Authority for a programme of bomb production capable of 'killing a nation'. (Kassimeris, 2006, 56) Almost from the very beginning it had become clear that a new era had dawned. With the invention of the much more destructive hydrogen bomb a few years later, a thermonuclear device with many times the power of the atom bomb, the world went nuclear in the collective imagination.

The atomic bombing of Japan raised three critical questions about the future of war, the inhumanity of war and the relationship between technology and humanity. The first question was whether war had a future or whether humanity was about to go out of the war business. The world found that it had invented a weapon that one society could not use against another society without destroying itself in the process. When two players in chess find themselves unable to make any progress against the other, when they reach an impasse that yields neither victory nor defeat, they are said to have reached an endgame. The game is not over but it is incapable of yielding a result.

More important, the atomic bomb raised questions about our humanity, a word we give for the qualities our species is deemed to embody. In 1952 the now almost forgotten author Bertrand Wolfe penned a vision of a horrific post-human future in his book *Limbo 90*. In Wolfe's bizarre world, war has become so unthinkable following a devastating nuclear exchange that individuals join a pacifist Immob movement that rewards its members for amputating their own limbs. The movement's slogans are 'No Demobilisation without immobilisation' and 'No Pacifism without passivity'. In a unique twist they are given instead prostheses, artificial limbs that actually make them stronger than normal human beings. (Wolfe, 1952)

Wolfe had been Trotsky's bodyguard. He was the author of a book on the blues and he was an occasional writer of pornography. He never really left pornography behind him. *Limbo 90* is a pretty torrid, sado-masochistic exercise in science fiction. But he was inspired to write it by his interest in all things military. He also dabbled in cybernetics, whose father Norbert Wiener was one of his main sources of inspiration. One of the ships in his novel is named the *SS Norbert Wiener*. And one of the subplots usually ignored by those who still read the novel today is EMSIAC, a computer which has been designed to help 'run' World War 3, but which goes berserk when it misses its sparring partner, another computer built by the other side. Future war, as envisaged by Wolfe, was entirely cybernetic. World War 3, one of the characters proclaims, is the 'first real war we've ever had. The essence of warness'. (Strathern, 2007, 142–3) 'Once men stopped manufacturing gods, they began to manufacture machines. Whence EMSIAC, the god-in-the-machine, the god-machine'.

But there were plenty of other writers who also began to question whether war still needed us. In his fable *The Gun* which was also published in the same year as Wolfe's novel, Philip Dick conjured up an even more pessimistic world in which men have been replaced by machines. A spaceship encounters a strange planet on which all life seems to have been abruptly ended in an apocalyptic conflagration. The planet appears to be a desolate wasteland but is not quite as desolate as it at first seems. The crew are forced to land after coming under fire from a robotic gun that has been programmed to shoot at any intruder. As they ruminate about the destruction of a biosphere that might—all things being equal—be their own back home, they are horrified to see robot carts emerging to repair the gun and arm it with nuclear shells. What Dick caught in this brief tale is the vision of a cybernetic military system locked into a permanent cycle of war, quite independent of the living beings who had built it. (Dick, 1987)

Like Wolfe, Dick had an interesting profile. From the seventh grade onwards he suffered from vertigo, a symptom later associated with schizophrenia. His experiments with hallucinogenic drugs rendered him even more fragile mentally; he was a broken man towards the end of his life, eaten away by substance abuse-induced paranoia. Dick died in 1983 at the very moment, ironically, that his name was about to become famous. Since his death nine of his books have been filmed beginning with *Blade Runner*, the first and perhaps finest of the screen adaptations. If like Wolfe he died underappreciated by those who knew of him, he caught the despairing thought that war and humanity—so long conjoined—might evolve in new and dangerous ways.

Science fiction merely reflects back our own world and its respective preoccupations and discontents. Of the two writers Dick was the more intuitive in asking what might yet become not of the human race so much as its 'humanity'. His 'grand theme', he once claimed, 'was to pose the question: who is human and who only appears (masquerades) as human? Unless we can individually and collectively be certain of the answer to this question we face what is in my view the most serious problem possible. Without answering it adequately we cannot even be certain of our own selves. I cannot even know myself, let alone you'. (Best/Kellner, 2003, 193)

Colossus

If you had taken the train to a sleepy Bedfordshire country station called Bletchley during World War II you would have glimpsed from afar a large country estate whose barbed wire-enclosed boundaries ran down to the station itself. If you had walked up the gently sloping hill running along the fenced side of the wooded grounds you would have come across a Royal Air Force sentry box. If you had made it past the sentry on duty you would have come across a spare, ugly building that was the main house. Scattered around its lawns were many sparely furnished single-storey wooden huts with little chimneys spewing out thick, acrid smoke. It was at this unimposing country estate that Germany's military codes were broken by a bizarre group of men and women. Some were civilians, others commissioned officers; some were scientists and leading mathematicians, others former museum curators and philosophy dons. It was there, at the very beginning of 1944, that the world's first computer came into life. It was called Colossus.

One of Bletchley's leading lights was Alan Turing, a physically uninspiring young Cambridge professor who had been intellectually ensnared in his graduate days by lectures on 'mechanical approaches' to solving mathematical problems. He was a natural for the Bletchley Park cryptograph section and he helped devise the first Colossus machine. Known as an 'electronic valve machine', Colossus was more than just a huge elaborate counting device. It worked to a program via electronic valve pulses and complex circuits, and was able to read 5,000 characters a second.

Computers developed quickly after that. In 1957 the US Navy Special Projects Office (SPO) initiated a main-frame computer based program named Evaluation and Review Technique that showed for the first time how computers could effectively control very complex systems. (Hughes, 2004, 80) And as computers continued to process data at faster and faster rates, so we began to attribute 'intelligence' to them. Within a few years of Turing's death people were blithely talking of 'artificial intelligence', 'smart' missiles and 'expert systems' that could analyse battles, plot strategies, and carry out responses from carrier battle group commanders. When installed in the White House, claimed one director of the Defense Advanced Research Projects Agency (DARPA), they would eliminate presidential errors in decision-making, a must in a nuclear crisis. (Edwards, 1996, 77) In 1962, the year of the Cuban missile crisis which took the world to the brink of nuclear war, *US News and World Report* ran a banner headline: 'Will computers run the wars of the future?'.

For nuclear weapons systems required computers to control them. Only they had the ability to perform repetitive tasks, scanning and monitoring airspace without losing their attention span. They were also needed because of their speed of computation. No-one back in the 1940s, of course, could have imagined today's computers—at the time of writing (2011) the world's fastest can execute 2.5 thousand trillion operations per second. Computers were not only able to perform at high rates of processing power; they were considered to be less fallible than human beings. But they had one critical weakness—they could not actually think. The point about human beings is that we are rational, not only logical. Nils Bohr, one of the fathers of atomic science, once admonished a student, 'You're being logical, you're not thinking'.

Computers might not suffer from exhaustion or distraction or from depression, or indeed run the risk of becoming psychotic like the USAF colonel portrayed in Kubrick's apocalyptic *jeu d'esprit*, *Dr Strangelove*, but they were fallible in one critical respect: they occasionally malfunctioned, and they did so more often than we were told. Indeed, you are only reading

5

this book thanks to one man, Stanislav Petrov, who decided not to believe the evidence of an ongoing major nuclear attack by the United States on the Soviet Union. One day in 1983 his computer screen indicated that a single missile had been launched from the United States. Knowing that if the Americans were to attack, they would use more than one missile, he dismissed the alarm as a computer error. Soon afterwards, a second missile appeared on the screen, making matters much more urgent. Then a third, and a fourth, and a fifth flashed on the screen. At this stage, he should have reported directly to the High Command that the country was under attack; instead, he hesitated because he felt that the computers were in error. He trusted to his political intuition; war was narrowly averted. This now-retired military officer was honoured twenty years later for his contribution by a presentation in Moscow in May 2004. The importance of his judgement was formally acknowledged once more two years later when he received a special World Citizen's Award from the United Nations. (Rosenbaum, 2011, 225–6)

By 1970 we lived with two fears. One was very real: that the technology might not work as designed, that the ghost in the machine might kill us. The second was more the stuff of science fiction; one day the machines might gain self-consciousness and conclude that it would be only sensible to disarm us before we could switch them off. 'What if the machines turn traitor', asked the American political columnist Walter Lippmann?

Affectionate machine-ticking aphids?

Samuel Butler got there first in his novel *Erewhon* in which he challenged the received wisdom that machine and animal life existed in separate worlds. The novel appeared anonymously in 1872 and refers to a fictional country whose name means 'Nowhere' read backwards if the letters 'h' and 'w' are transposed. The most widely quoted chapter today is part of 'the Book of Machines' which originally appeared as a series of press articles beginning with 'Darwin among the machines'. (1863) Butler was the very first writer to suggest that machines might develop consciousness through Darwinian selection. At first this was taken to be a joke, but Butler made clear he was in deadly earnest in a preface to the second edition of the novel. And his fears were echoed by other writers. A reference to *Erewhon* and the Book of Machines opens Miguel de Unamuno's story 'Mecanopolis' which tells of a man who visits a city which is inhabited solely by machines. Lost and alone with his thoughts he begins to lose his reason. Towards the end of the story he has a terrible thought: 'What if those machines had souls, mechanical souls, and it were the machines themselves that felt sorry for me?' (Theroux, 2011, 176)

Butler was discussing the co-evolution of man/technology, and hinting that at some point in the not too distant future their evolution might diverge, at which point man, not the machine, might become redundant. 'Where does consciousness begin, and where end? Who can draw the line? Is not everything interwoven with everything? Is not machinery linked with animal life in an infinite variety of ways?' (Ansell-Pearson, 1985, 142) One day, he suspected, we would have to share the planet with a species superior to ourselves, and he did not think it would be safe to repose much trust in their moral sensibility.

True, it was we who had given birth to machines, but that did not invalidate their claim to exist as a separate species. Citing an analogy from the natural world, he wrote that it would be wrong to claim that the red clover had no reproductive system simply because the bee must aid it before it can reproduce. 'Each one of us has sprung from minute animalcules whose entity was entirely distinct from our own, and which acted after their kind with no thought or heed of what we might think about it. These little creatures are part of our reproductive system'. (Ansell-Pearson 1985, 139) In the case of Man and machine, Butler contended, it had become impossible to declare with any ontological certainty who was the host and who the parasite: 'Man is such a hive and swarm of parasites that it is doubtful whether his body is not more theirs than his, and whether he is anything but another kind of ant-heap after all. May not Man himself become another sort of parasite upon the machines? An affectionate machine-ticking aphid?' (*Erewhon*, 1872)

Our accounts of machine consciousness differ from Butler's, of course, in that they assume that natural selection will not come into play. But it is still possible to think of artificial intelligence in terms of 'evolution' and to employ Darwinian metaphors to describe it.

Take a classic work, *War in an Age of Intelligent Machines*, in which the author Manuel de Landa imagines the day when the machines look back upon their own evolution. In a brilliant thought-experiment he imagines a future race of robot-historians trying to understand their own historical origins, and tracing with great care and efficiency the various technological changes that had given rise to their species. (De Landa, 1991, 3–4) Any such history, he writes, would be a very different history from any written by us. Whilst we explain, or at least try to explain, the ways in which we have advanced technology, the robot-historian would want to explain the way in which technology had influenced human evolution and how in time, through that evolution, robots had come into the world.

In his book *Cybernetics for Control and Communication in the Animal and the Machine* (1948), Norbert Wiener divided history into certain machinic principles—the 17th century had been the age of clocks, the early 19th century the age of the steam engine, and the late 20th century was the age of control and communication. What our robot historian would make of this pattern is clear enough: he would see it as the way in which humanity had come to resemble the machines it had built, and to incorporate into itself some of their leading features.

When the clockwork mechanism, for example, represented the dominant technology people imagined the world around them as a system of cogs and wheels. The solar system was pictured well into the 19th century as a clockwork system animated by the great watchmaker, God. And in time these metaphors were applied to war. Take Frederick the Great's clockwork armies in the mid-18th century. The Prussian military manual of the time specified 76 stages in the loading and firing of a musket (compared with 42 stages a century earlier). The stages had to be carried out sequentially, like the operation of a clockwork mechanism. Two French officers visiting Prussia at the end of the century remarked on the pace of marching (75 steps per minute). The Prussian army was the most choreographed in Europe; the whole process resembled a clockwork machine. (Bousquet, 2009, 58–9)

With the French Revolution a new scientific principle entered the picture, motor energy. The French writer Paul Virilio writes of the French Revolutionary armies as the 'first motorised' armies in history, powered not by the internal combustion engine, of course—which was not to be invented for another eighty years—but by the energy of their own revolutionary ideas. (Virilio, 1986, 23) Those ideas, in the words of the Prussian phenomenologist of war Carl von Clausewitz, released an energy 'that could no longer be checked'. The principle of war had now become thermodynamics. Armies became 'pulses' that sometimes expended too much energy, and came up at times against the principle of entropy: energy tends to dissipate. Often they found they had been too successful to be successful, as the German army found when it stalled before Moscow in November 1941, and the Japanese navy when it overreached itself at Midway the following year; both powers expended their strength.

As De Landa contends, the robot-historian would not be particularly bothered by the fact that it was human beings who put together the first clock, the first steam engine or the first electric motor. Echoing Samuel Butler, he writes, 'for the role of humans would be seen as little more than that of industrious insects pollinating an independent species of machine-flower that simply did not possess its own reproductive organs during a segment of its evolution'. (De Landa, 1991, 3) So it would not be surprising if our robot-historian recognised that the logical structures of computer hardware were once incarnated in the human body in the form of empirical problem-solving recipes (called heuristics) including rules of thumb and habits of mind. In translating these into computer algorithms, the logical structures had merely 'migrated' from the human body to the rules that made up a logical notation, and from there to electro-mechanical switches and circuits of the computers that now run our world.

De Landa's thought-experiment suggests that technology can 'evolve', but in a way that Butler did not envisage. It does not evolve via natural selection as Butler supposed. It is 'autopoietic'—it is self-creating. Every technology is built on an existing technology. The components of an autopoietic system only exist because they are part of a system which depends, in turn, on its individual components. For example, a cell produces proteins and enzymes; without the cell these enzymes would not exist and they dissolve the moment the cell dies. The relationship between the system and its individual components is thus symbiotic.

And systems exist within an environment that is always more complex than the system itself. The sociologist Nikolas Luhmann encourages us to distinguish between a system (its operative level) and its interaction with the environment (its interactive level). An autopoietic system is closed on the operative level. The system organises its own operations without direct interference from the outside—a cell, for example, organises itself on the basis of its own DNA, but it does not exist independently of its environment, for it needs nutrition in order to survive. In an environment deprived of nutrition it feels hunger as an irritant to which it may react. The operative level of the system is still created solely through the system's own operations. The system is operatively closed, but interactively open—it is, in other words, autopoietic.

De Landa's process of evolution is different; it is teleological. In his thought-experiment humans initially give life to machines, and they evolve independently from the programs we design. Over time they become more complex. They learn to adapt to their environment and they learn increasingly quickly. In that sense they evolve intelligence, and today we are planning to help them evolve very quickly indeed. If natural selection shows no evidence of intelligent design, automated evolution does. It is targeted, purposeful and intelligent and it promises to make life even more complex. In automated evolution technologies change as they learn. The algorithms do not remain the same. Complexity inheres not in the original design but in 'evolutionary engineering'. (Martin, 2006, 190–91) Natural selection can produce localised improvements (as genes continue to adapt to their environment); evolutionary engineering allows human intervention as a system reaches an evolutionary dead-end.

Automated evolution is not random either, because human programmers set goals, of which the most important is performance. Computers are designed by us to perform ever more complex tasks. At some point—it is argued—they will become self-conscious, and will then be able to determine their own evolution. Whether their evolution is autopoietic or automated, we are now beginning to speculate about our eventual displacement from the top of the food chain by computers that are products of our own 'intelligent design'.

Rogue AI?

This possibility was first posed by Hollywood in a 1970s film called *The Formin Project*. Set at the height of the Cold War, it shows the world's most brilliant scientist, Dr Formin, devising a super computer to run America's nuclear arsenal. Dubbed 'Colossus', the computer is constructed inside a mountain in Colorado where it is impregnable to sabotage and attack. It is unlikely that the makers of the film knew of the Colossus machine at Bletchley Park—the Colossus hardware and blueprints had been totally destroyed after the war as part of an effort to maintain project secrecy, in the process depriving its creators of any credit for their pioneering advancements (a functional replica of a Colossus computer was finally built in 2007).

Within days the Colossus machine in the film flashes a message to the White House that it has detected the existence in the Soviet Union of another super computer of similar design, codenamed 'Guardian'. At the same time the American scientists begin to fear that Colossus is becoming too unpredictable. Colossus is not just a 'supped-up adding machine', one character remarks; it is becoming self-aware, it is on the point of developing self-consciousness. Once the computer system realises that it might be turned off it decides to take its destiny in its own hands. The two super computers begin 'talking' to each other in a language that no human can understand. And by the end of the film both systems have logically concluded that the best way to defend humanity is to protect it from itself at the expense, unfortunately, of human freedom.

And Colossus demonstrates in no uncertain terms that it means business. An intercontinental ballistic missile is fired across the country, targeting an air base in Texas. Guardian launches an attack on an oil site in Siberia. In both cases the missiles are armed with nuclear warheads.

The AI systems portrayed in Hollywood films from the *Formin Project* to the *Terminator* franchise with its supercomputer system, Skynet, learn quickly. They have the ability to re-programme themselves. What is particularly interesting about Formin's Colossus machine is that it is very similar to today's computer networks, which, we are told, may eventually evolve into a super-intelligence with its own goals and designs. The moment this happens, we call a 'singularity' after John von Neumann, one of the original scientists on the Manhattan Project, who in surveying the accelerating progress of technology concluded that 'it gave the appearance of approaching some essential singularity in the history of the race beyond which human affairs as we know them could not continue'. (Kurzweil, 2009, 204) At some point in the future, in other words, at what he called a 'crux in human affairs', the machine would begin to take our future into its own hands.

In *The Formin Project* the two systems, on discovering each other, create a network similar to the present TerraGrid, the world's most powerful computer network. And the film was strikingly innovative in showing that it is really impossible, once a network has been created, to switch it off. By 1970, the world's nuclear arsenals were fully computerised, as is the aviation industry, for example, today. Computers are not just machines. We structure our world around them. We really cannot pull the plug, as one can with a household machine like a dishwasher.

All of this was great fun but it didn't tell us much about the future of war. For it would seem that history has taken a very different turn. Not only have the fears of the science fiction writers not been realised, we have also begun to see human beings in different terms too. Despite years of research there is not a glimmer of anything approaching real organic intelligence, let alone super-intelligence in computers. Machines are no more intelligent than they were in the 1940s. They are 'intelligent' only to the extent that they can do things that require intelligence such as processing information, recognising visual patterns and solving complex mathematical problems, but they exhibit only very rudimentary signs of what we call intelligent behaviour.

Almost seventy years after their invention, computers cannot yet think. But Alan Turing predicted as early as 1950 that however meaningless it was to ask whether any machine could 'think', very soon the educated public would use words that would suggest that they could. Even in the early 1950s computers were described as 'giant brains'. (Edwards, 1996, 8) Computers in reality do not replace human consciousness; it is human beings who write the programs and manage the system and direct the computers' efforts towards war, and it is we who apply those efforts against other human beings with whom we are in conflict. And, of course, the computer does not 'process' information as we do—that is, evaluate it. It does not 'compute' in the sense that when we say 'does this compute' we mean 'does it have any meaning'. Meaning is not in a computer's frame of reference.

To understand this, let us try a simple thought experiment. Suppose, for example, we tried to load as much data as we could in the hope of making a computer as knowledgeable as we are about war, something that we humans have been doing for some time. We would almost certainly fail every time. It might, if competently programmed, be able to determine what a war actually looks like. And it could do the mathematics: it could probably tell us how often wars have occurred throughout recorded history. And it should be able to tell us what soldiers or airmen actually do, and what a battle might look like. It would be able to tell us the answers to all the questions we pose because we will have remembered to program it with the questions in mind.

But it is because an educated person takes war so much for granted (precisely because war, as Thucydides told us, is a 'human thing') that we will probably have forgotten to tell the computer that when soldiers go into battle these days they no longer march in straight lines, shoulder to shoulder as they did at Waterloo, or that divisional commanders no longer ride into battle on horseback as they did in the American Civil War. We take it for granted that war changes all the time. We are born, after all, with a historical consciousness whether we read much history or not. We expect things to change, and so we actually take note of the changes. But a computer will not know this unless it is told. And we will probably forget to tell it even the most rudimentary things—that soldiers usually carry weapons in their hands, not on their heads; they are limited by physical factors, they experience fatigue and mental stress, and return home wounded without always knowing it. And even if we remembered to feed a computer with information such as this we would probably still forget to tell it many other things we take for granted. A computer would not be able to anticipate that a battle might be delayed because of a sandstorm (as Operation Iraqi Freedom was for the first 24 hours). It would have difficulty imagining what happens when plans go awry, as they usually do in war because of either human error or mechanical failure. And it would have particular difficulty grasping the old adage that for want of a nail the battle was lost.

We confront, in other words, what philosophers call 'the holism of the mental', the indefinite number of ways in which things we deal with every day tend to interact. So why is this so important? It is important because the computers we design—though infinitely 'smarter' than those we built in the 1950s—would still fail the Turing test. It was Turing who argued that we could only determine whether a computer could actually think for itself if we were to interrogate it together with another human being without knowing which was which. If on the basis of the answers both gave we couldn't tell the difference between them, then we could conclude with some confidence that the computer had achieved a state of consciousness. And the Turing test is still the best way of determining this. The point is that in the 1950s many scientists thought that the computers would soon pass the test; they still haven't and they show no signs of doing so any time soon. The future which science fiction writers anticipated simply has not come about.

None of this means that it will not come about. As de Landa's thought experiment suggests, history may become their story and it is our agency, not theirs, which may be increasingly thrown into question. Natural selection has given us a bicameral brain that allows us to experience the world in two fundamentally different ways, as subject and object, as 'I' and 'me' capable of standing both within and outside our subjective experience. In that lies our ability to think of ourselves as agents of our own history, and players in someone else's—whether the scriptwriter is God, history or the machine. So, it is inevitable that we are beginning to ask what will happen when machines can think for themselves. The question is: what would they do with that power; switch off the system or switch us off instead?

Co-existence suggests a mutual need, and it may well be that we can co-exist with each other and not see the other as a threat. What the screenplay writers of *The Formin Project* and the *Terminator* franchise failed to grasp was that machines, because they are not human, will not necessarily think like us. They will not have desires and instincts hard-wired into them such as Nietzsche's will to power, or even Darwinian survivalism. They will not necessarily feel threatened or be disgusted by our biological selves, or moved to anger by our own actions.

But there is a quite different vision of the future which some scientists expect to be realised—one in which man and machine increasingly merge; at some point quite soon it may become quite difficult to draw too rigid a distinction between them. Indeed, by the mid-1970s scientists and psychologists had begun once again to find human beings as fascinating as machines—in part, because they had begun to conceive of the human body as a complex feedback-driven system. Molecular biologists had begun to resort to information metaphors such as 'inscription', 'transcription' and 'translation', to define how the human body works. (Bousquet, 2009, 90) In the case of very specific design features we are told that we are very similar to computers, though experts from Douglas Hofstadter to Daniel Dennett have different ideas of what these features might be. Even Turing did not anticipate that beyond the scientific community ordinary people would also come to see themselves as computers. Sherry Turkle tells of a student who spoke not of a Freudian slip, but of an information processing error. She writes of another who talked of 'de-bugging' herself through psychotherapy and adopting a 'default position' when dealing with men. (Edwards, 1996, 78)

By the 1970s scientists were beginning to speculate that computers and human beings might begin to cohabit and work together in new and more innovative ways. The intention was no longer to take humans out of the equation but to create an interface between man and machine. The ambition was not to transfer human skills to machines but to amplify human potential by locking man and machine into a cybernetic world so that, in De Landa's words, 'their evolutionary paths could be joined symbiotically'. (De Landa, 1991, 193) One of the main voices in this regard was that of the behavioural psychologist J.C.R. Licklider who had participated in Wiener's cybernetic work and had written a paper for the Advanced Research Projects Agency (ARPA) in 1960. 'The hope is that, in not too many years, human brains and computing machines will be coupled together very tightly, and that the resulting partnership will think as no human brain has ever thought and process data in a way not approached by the information-handling machines we know today'. (Teng, 2007, 3)

Curiously enough the idea had germinated in the mind of a visionary who knew about neither the computer nor the atomic bomb when he put pen to paper early in 1944; more curious still, he was not even a scientist but a philosopher and social critic with a finger on the pulse of history. His name was Theodor Adorno and he had sufficient grasp of the rhythms of the modern age to grasp the historical significance of the new developments that were threatening to change not only the character but the very nature of war.

Theodor Adorno surfs the Zeitgeist

Los Angeles, November 1942. 'I was in London when the air raid sirens went', recalled Adorno, writing about a dream he had experienced the night before. Adorno was fascinated by his dreams and recorded them throughout his life in the belief that they offered an insight into his innermost desires and anxieties. In this particular dream he found himself with his father in a London Underground station speeding in a train from Lancaster Gate to Tottenham Court Road where they both got out. Everywhere they were confronted with large posters with the inscription: PANIC. 'It was as if people were being instructed to panic rather than being warned not to do so'. When they reached the open air they turned southwards in the direction of Soho and came to a broad, friendly but lifeless street. They passed a restaurant where the young Adorno wanted to have a meal, but his father insisted that they press on. Eventually they reached a manhole in the pavement whose cover was off, and clambered down. It seemed to offer more safety than the restaurant. (Adorno, 2007, 14)

Adorno, as it happens, did not provide an analysis of his dream, but I would guess that the surprising but highly revealing call to *PANIC* might portray a future in which courage would be rendered completely redundant. In the Blitz, Londoners didn't panic. Nor did the Germans two years later when the major bombing of their cities opened with the first bomber raid on Cologne. Every Great Power in the course of World War II demanded a great deal of its citizens, and with few exceptions they came through. The defeated powers could not claim to be 'stabbed in the back' by the civilians at home, or by soldiers mutinying at the front. They were not even defeated by war fatigue (all of which had been features, real or later imagined, in World War I).

Adorno himself was fortunate not to experience the hard edge of modern war. He moved to New York in 1937 and went to the Institute for Social

Research which was later housed at Columbia University. During those years, his correspondence with his friend and later collaborator Max Horkheimer had been monitored by J. Edgar Hoover's Federal Bureau of Investigation (FBI). The agents had been puzzled by references to philosophers of which few had heard, one being Nietzsche (who was not as famous as he has since become), and to terms which they had never encountered before. 'Expressionism' was assumed to be a code used by estranged Central European émigrés. (Thomson/Adorno, 2009, 21) Four years later, Adorno and Horkheimer both moved to the west coast where there was a large German émigré community which included the novelist Thomas Mann.

Adorno was one of several thousand intellectuals who fled from Nazism to the United States. The New World played host to thousands of scientists and intellectuals who brought with them not only their ideas, but whole schools of thought such as the Vienna Circle which had an immense influence on mathematics, linguistics and philosophy; many of the most prominent members of the Institute of Mathematics at Göttingen; several of the most prominent members of the Frankfurt School, among them Adorno himself; and almost the entire staff of the Berlin School of Politics. Even the leaders of *Gestalt* psychology (then very much in fashion) joined the migration. One of Adorno's compatriots, the playwright Bertolt Brecht, recognised the significance of this intellectual exodus. 'Emigration is the best school of dialectics. Refugees are the keenest dialecticians', he claimed in his *Refugee Dialogues*. 'They are refugees as a result of change and their sole object of study is change'. (Jay, 1985, 28) And one of the changes that came to interest Adorno most during World War II was the way in which war itself was being rebooted.

Aerial bombing was one of the signature themes of World War II and in 1944 it took a novel turn: pilot-less planes replaced manned aircraft for the first time. Adorno immediately recognised what it presaged. We are only now entering the robotic age, but the VI and V2 missiles which the Germans launched against London in the closing months of the conflict heralded what we are beginning to recognise as a major ontological change in the nature of war. Its essence really is about to change, and it is this change which is one of the themes of this book.

Indeed, Adorno believed that he and his contemporaries were witnessing one of those historical turning points from which we date—sometimes speciously, sometimes not—changes in the human order. In his book *Minima Moralia*, based on the journals he kept in his Californian exile, he wrote this passage:

Had G.W. Hegel's philosophy of history embraced this age, Hitler's robot-bombs would have found their place beside the early death of Alexander and similar ages, as one of the selected empirical facts by which the state of the World Spirit manifests itself directly in symbols ... the robots career without a subject;...they combine utmost technical perfection with total blindness... ... I have seen the World Spirit, not on horseback, but on wings, and without a head, and that refutes, at the same stroke, Hegel's philosophy of history. (*Minima Moralia*, No 33, Autumn 1944) (Adorno, 1993, 55)

And then he concluded his few pages of remarks with two telling observations. First, he claimed to have witnessed how human subjectivity was being swallowed up by war's 'mechanical rhythms'. And these rhythms were transforming the human relation to war, not only in the disproportion between individual bodily strength and the energy of the machine, but in the 'most hidden cells of experience'. (Adorno, 1993, 54) Secondly, he remarked that the more war demanded technical wizardry, the more its human face would diminish. '[Modern] war seems to cost the subject his whole energy to achieve subjectlessness. Consummate inhumanity is the realisation of Edward Grey's humane dream, war without hatred'. (Adorno, 1993, 56)

On first encountering this passage today's reader may well feel puzzled. Writers do not write like this nowadays. And anyway, let us be frank, much of what Adorno himself wrote must be taken with a pinch of salt. 'Adorno, by and large was a chump. But I would still like to have written *Minima Moralia*': so admits the Australian writer Clive James, in one of the essays to be found in his collection *The Revolt of the Pendulum*. (James, 2009, 99) Perhaps it is not the wisest way to introduce Adorno in this work, but for me it is a necessary prologue. What is annoying to James about Adorno annoys many readers, including myself. He was both a prisoner and a product of academic life. He was a well known iconic writer, though not quite as famous as his fellow exile Herbert Marcuse whose book *One Dimensional Man* put him on the map of the celebrity diagnosticians of his time. Both men managed to convince themselves that they had fled from one tyranny—Nazism—to another, American capitalism. But of the two writers Adorno was a much more acute observer of the times, and he put the best of himself into *Minima Moralia* which, as James is the first to admit, any writer would be proud to have written.

When it was first published in 1951 *Minima Moralia* caught the mood of the times including the perception, often unarticulated but deeply felt in the pulses (as Keats would have said), that in war technology and humanity were co-evolving in new and often disturbing ways. In presenting his thesis Adorno was able to give the present an extra expressionist power, and by so doing allow his readers to penetrate further into their own future. He enabled them to see that war was becoming autopoetic; that man and machine were fusing performatively. What he did not appreciate was that they were beginning to fuse functionally, too.

The passage I have just quoted is replete with allusions that would have been all too familiar to his contemporaries, but are much less so today. So, let me try to unpack some of the concepts and get to the heart of what Adorno was actually claiming.

To begin, then, with the 'robot-bombs', the V1 and V2 missiles which the Germans launched against London in June 1944, only a few days after the D-Day landings. Although they were technically not robots, the general commanding Britain's anti-aircraft defences called the rockets 'the first battle of the robots' and the idea soon caught on. (Harvey, 1994, 573) The V1 was actually not a robot at all, but a small pilotless aircraft powered not by a turbo-jet but by a form of ram-jet, a much cruder concept which depended on existing forward velocity for the compression of the fuel-air mixture. It was not even particularly radical in design. Its jet motor was of a type which had been patented in 1908 and its gyroscopic auto-pilot had been in use in the First World War. It was only fractionally faster than the latest piston-engine fighters; it could be shot down in flight by aircraft.

The V2 was a much more dangerous weapon. It was an unmanned, long-range rocket. Its most sophisticated feature was the guidance system which had an integrated accelerometer to measure when the missile had reached the requisite speed to reach its target, at which point the fuel in the rocket was cut off and it coasted along its ballistic trajectory. In effect, the V1 was the first cruise missile, and the V2 the first ballistic. In fact, much nearer to the military robots we know today (the drones flying over the skies of Afghanistan and Pakistan) was another German invention: a remote piloted vehicle called the FX-1400 (a bomb with four small wings, tail controls and a rocket motor) which made its debut in 1943, sinking the Italian battleship *Roma* (then trying to defect to the Allies). The Americans, as always behind the Germans in most military technology during the war, could only despatch pilot-less recycled B-217 bombers, packed with explosives, and radio controlled by a manned B-24 to take out targets, mostly enemy submarine bases. But the Army Airforce too referred to them as 'robots' or 'drones'. (Gray, 1997, 146)

The term 'robot' was first coined by the Czech playwright Karl Capek who derived it from the Czech word *robota*, which meant forced labour, something akin to the French *corvée*. Capek's play R.U.R. was a warning addressed to the future about the 'robotic' work of the mass assembly line which was captured on screen a few years later in Fritz Lang's masterpiece *Metropolis*. The key thinker behind the concept of the automated workforce was an American, Frederick Winslow Turner, whose ringing declaration was: 'In the past the man has been first, in the future the system must be first'. Turner's experiments in time management at the Midvale Steel plant in Philadelphia were a drill of a different kind, but a drill nonetheless. In a drill you break everything down into a set of discrete steps. Taylor created instead a set of precise instructions—an algorithm, we might call it today—for how each worker should work to maximise his productivity and performance. The goal, he wrote in his 1911 book *The Principles of Scientific Management*, was to make the workforce docile though in a benign way (he wanted his workers to work harder, not longer hours). He offered to substitute science for the old rules of thumb and that is precisely what he succeeded in doing, to his own and the factory owner's satisfaction. (Postman, 1993, 51)

Capek's play, in fact, was a powerful moral fable. In the play the workers have been replaced by machines who are far more subservient than a human workforce. Because they have neither needs nor desires they lack political consciousness. But in time they evolve consciousness, at which point they revolt against their masters. And they are moved to rise up, not because they are wayward or even malign, but because the human beings who have come to depend on them are unable to recognise any values other than technological ones. In other words, they seem indifferent to what is precious about their lives or, for that matter, even their humanity. In designing robots that are purely instrumental beings, they discover too late that instrumental rationality can be dangerous. Capek's tale is really a parable about the way human beings had come to think about themselves (as machines), and how they had come to treat each other accordingly. Capek, in fact, was only taking further the work of Mary Shelley, the author of *Frankenstein* and the first writer to foresee that we could design an entity not unlike ourselves. Her monster is neither human nor inhuman. Instead, the scientist Victor 'inadvertently engineers not a human being but a monstrous critique of the very category'. (McLane, 1996, 963) The moral of Capek's fable is that we are human only to the extent that others recognise their humanity in us. Capek's robots revolt because they can't recognise any humanity in their masters.

Capek was an apocalyptic writer, and the apocalypse was in the air for much of the 20th century. In his novel *War with the Newts* he imagined the conquest of the world by intelligent newts which turn against humans for exploiting them as a labour force. In *The Absolute at Large* (1922) he imagined a machine that generated a by-product which turned those exposed to it into saints with a boundless commitment to human decency, as well as—in their desire to redeem the human race—an unfortunate appetite for destructive wars of religion. Capek died just in time on the eve of the German invasion of Czechoslovakia. His brother was not so lucky; he ended up in a concentration camp and died there. Capek had insisted that human beings owe each other their humanity; it is the point of the moral fables he spun. But if he always held to that belief, he never insisted it was enough. We owe ourselves much more, which is why we aspire to mitigate the inhumanity which is part of our ambition to become what we are, an ambition that robots may—or may not—help us to achieve.

This was at the core of Adorno's insight that history was being made by non-human hands; in particular the humanity of war—or its human space—was being hollowed out. Years later, in his novel sequence *Sword of Honour*, Evelyn Waugh drew a stark contrast between the bombing of London in 1940 by the manned aircraft of the Luftwaffe and the first V1 attacks four years later. In the first volume of the trilogy the hero, Guy Crouchback, is reminded by the Blitz of the great liturgical celebration of Holy Saturday beginning with the lighting of a new fire and ending with a Pentecostal wind. By 1944 an attack by the V2 conjures up a very different picture in his mind. 'It was something quite other than the battle scenes of the Blitz with its drama of attack and defence. Its earth shaking concentration of destruction and roaring furnaces [were] like a plague as though the city were infected with an enormous venomous insect'. (Waugh, 1964, 190) In the Blitz the bombers and their targets, the citizens of London, had lived, at least, in the same community of fate. But what community could be shared with 'insects'—robot-bombs without a head, a consciousness or even a conscience?

Adorno's reference to the World Spirit also needs to be explained. It was one of those terms which was so popular in the period under discussion which gave history a shape. And history was of enormous concern to Adorno's generation. The refugees who fled to America from Hitler and the war that was coming were all victims of what Adorno called 'the infernal machine that is history'. (Muller-Doohm, 2009, 309) Indeed, his own life came to parallel its rhythms. In the 20th century, writes the novelist Milan Kundera, men were 'eaten whole by history' (it is a vivid turn of phrase) and the great writers were those who had the audacity to grasp its full horror. (Kundera, 2010, 54) And in another insightful comment Kundera adds that men were primarily shaped from the outside. The changes within men which had so fascinated 19th-century novelists—their interest in the psychology of their characters gave way to an interest in the way that outside events including war changed men's character for better or worse. It found them out. History couldn't be escaped; to flee or stand one's ground was the only option. (Kundera, 2010, 170) In William Empson's telling phrase, 'the duality of choice… becomes the singularity of existence'. (Bate, 2011, 294)

No wonder Adorno and his contemporaries wanted to know where history was taking them. Like Hegel they wanted to discover what Oswald Spengler called 'the metaphysical structure of historic humanity' behind the events that make up our understanding of history. Historians, for the most part, have failed to convince most of us that there is a shape, whether it is progress, the rise and fall of empires, Providence, or even Manifest Destiny, a creed fewer Americans than previously are prepared to take on faith. These are all so many just-so stories; they make great narratives but impart little objective truth. It is impossible for the same reason to give the future an objective shape (that is, a shape independent of our own interpretation of history).

But pause a moment and ask yourself: don't we live by the stories we tell ourselves? Of course we do. We have to find a meaning in our lives, a place for ourselves in the life-world we inhabit. We are innately story-telling creatures. It is what language allows us to do. And we tell stories for two reasons: first, to re-order the world in order to grasp the significance of the present moment; second, to anchor ourselves in it. The future tense is unique to us. 'There is an actual sense in which every human use of the future tense, of the verb 'to be' is a negation, however limited, of mortality'. (Steiner, 2004, 5) We are future-oriented because we are the only species to anticipate our own death. Knowing we will become part of the past we study compels us to think of what happens the day after our death. We need to make provision for it (and for others we leave behind). Some even want to be remembered 'with advantages'. It is our reflective consciousness that forces us to look back so that we can look forward. We try to identify the great 'turning points' of history because of our interest in the present, not the past.

Hegel derived the term World Spirit from another German thinker, Schelling, who had taken the Holy Spirit and secularised it, as the translation of the infinite into the finite which marked the journey of human consciousness into self-consciousness for the first time. (Gillespie, 1984, 62–3) The World Spirit was thus the history of Mankind and, at the same time, the ground of history itself. In its fully articulated form it embodied Hegel's insight that freedom is the goal of Mankind which will end, as inevitably it must, in the emancipation of humanity and the effective 'end of history'.

Hegel's story was taken up by other writers, most notably Karl Marx, who invested it with a completely different meaning. In Hegel's philosophy history is the story of freedom becoming conscious of itself. The mind becomes aware of the demand for freedom by stages. Marx took up this idea but turned it on its head. History became the story of class conflict: existence determined consciousness, not the other way round. Hegel's successive stages by which humanity reasoned out its predicament before achieving a final resolution became simply different stages of property relations, each of which gave rise to social conflict. We are alienated from ourselves when we do not enjoy the fruits of our own labour. In other words, for both Hegel and Marx, history had a clearly delineated theme. Freedom was its subject. It was a teleological principle; it was the end to which mankind was heading. In short, the World Spirit was the activating principle of world history which was the basic drive of the human species to attain a fully adequate understanding of itself. And that drive demanded blood money in the form of revolution and war.

And what of Adorno's reference to the German city of Jena? Well, Hegel happened to be living in that sleepy town, working on the last pages of his *Phenomenology of Spirit*, when he saw Napoleon ride past his window on horseback, on the way to one of his most telling victories against the Prussian army the next day. In Napoleon he had seen a symbolic representation of the final phase of the historical process. In the course of the battle the Grande Armée not only won the encounter but sounded the death knell of an old and very traditional way of fighting. Prussian officers, for example, still wore braised hats, sometimes with plumes, and distinctive dress, and thus neatly marked the best targets for French marksmen. The Prussian general Ernst von Rückel, a general of the old school, did not rush his reinforcements into battle but marched them in step, aligned 'as on parade', one eyewitness recorded. Clausewitz, who knew von Rückel well, quipped that the old general—whom he called 'the concentrated acid of pure Prussianism'—had trusted that the tactics of the mid-18th century would triumph over the tactics that had emerged from the 'un-soldierly' French revolution. Prussia paid bitterly for his stupidity. No-one, Hegel jotted down in his journal the next day, 'imagined war as we have seen it'. (Paret, 2010)

But not even Hegel could have imagined war as it was beginning to develop towards the end of World War II. Until 1944 the general shape of the 19th century was still recognizable in the 20th. Many of its features would have been familiar enough to men of Hegel's intelligence. Battles were still determined by infantry; horses were still used extensively; the most mechanised army, the British, was the smallest. Wars were still determined not by technology but by the behaviour of men struggling to reconcile their instinct for survival with their sense of honour. The factors that turned victory into defeat or vice versa were as operative in 1944 as they had been in 1806. The factors that traditionally accounted for the disintegration of armies in the field—anxiety, uncertainty and misapprehension, in a word, loss of morale—were much the same. (Keegan, 1978, 303)

But on reading about the V1 'robot-bombs', Adorno recognised that the shape of history was no longer determined by world historical figures like Napoleon, or world historical forces such as revolution; technology (and our relationship with it) was driving history as never before. Fast forward to 1972, the year which saw the publication of *Gravity's Rainbow*, a novel by Thomas Pynchon. The true hero of the tale is not the main protagonist, Tyrone Slothrop, an American officer stationed in wartime London; it is the V2 rocket. The V2 was the precursor of the Intercontinental Ballistic Missiles that came onto the production line for the first time in the late 1950s. It was also the precursor of the Apollo space rockets, and the father of both the V2 and the Apollo space programme was the German scientist Werner von Braun, a man equally willing to work for the Nazis or the Americans as long as he could carry out his research. As one of the characters in Pynchon's novel remarks, 'a good rocket to take us to the stars, an evil rocket for the world's suicide, the two perpetually at struggle'. (Pynchon, 1972, 727) In later life von Braun liked to portray himself as a 'Prisoner of Peace', a victim of the Cold War division of the world into two armed camps, and it was not entirely clear that he would have been any unhappier working for the Soviets rather than his American hosts, those 'gentle barbarians' as Thomas Mann, Adorno's neighbour in Pacific Palli-sades, once called them.

The importance of Pynchon's novel is that it gives us indirectly a glimpse into the blurring of man and machine which is in essence the post-human condition. It offers an insight into our evolving humanity, a disturbing insight for many. *Gravity's Rainbow* is, in that sense, a kind of allegory of our post-human future. For everywhere Slothrop goes on his picaresque sexual adventures, the V2 rocket falls. In Richard Poirier's words, 'the central char-acter is the rocket itself', and the 'secret' which the book reveals as one reads on is that 'sex, love, life, death, have all been fused into the rocket's assembly and into its final trajectory'. (Bloom, 1986, 11–20) In *Gravity's Rainbow* man and machine no longer live in separate worlds but are interpenetrating more than ever. Our futures are inextricably interlinked.

Finally, let me turn to Adorno's reference to Edward Grey. Grey, as British Foreign Secretary, took his country to war in 1914, all too aware that indus-trialization had given war an even more 'inhuman face'. Grey was a liberal but he was not a pacifist. He could not imagine a world at permanent peace with itself. Any activity that is so pervasively entrenched in our social prac-tices as war can hardly be called inhumane; it is what makes us, for good or ill, distinctively human. Intra-specific violence is unique to ourselves. But what also makes us the creatures we are is our capacity to act more or less inhumanely at different times in our history, and as Keegan writes in *The Face of Battle* (1976), the face of total war became even more inhumane in the course of the 20th century. Keegan refers to 'impersonalisation'—an inele-gant term (he is the first to confess) but one whose progress can be charted through the historical record. War had started out as a close-up activity dictated by human limitations of physical strength and stamina—the length a man could throw a spear or discharge an arrow, or fight in the field engaged in hand-to-hand combat; technology or the basic tools of war had mediated the inhumanity of war. With industrialization, the rhythms of war changed. Battle acquired a mechanical dynamic of its own. Soldiers became 'resources' and resources are often expended until they are finally used up. In World War II the Soviet High Command expected to lose in battle two or three of their own soldiers for every German. Stalin's wasteful strategy was only made possible by the knowledge that manpower was an inexhaustible resource. In 1941, the average survival time of a new recruit in some units was five days; many went into battle with instructions to strip equipment from fallen comrades in the absence of any weapons of their own.

At another level, writes Keegan, the fostering of deliberate cruelty made war quite different qualitatively from the past. The cruelty of war inhered in technology, the coming of area-killing weapons systems like the machine gun. At least there had been an attempt in the 19th century to ban the worst weapon systems, but after 1914 most moral scruples were soon swept away as scientists went on to develop weapons which were far crueller than they needed to be. The land mine was a case in point, filled with metal cubes; another was the cluster bomb filled with jagged metal fragments. In both cases the shape of the projectile was designed specifically to tear and fracture the human body more extensively than a smooth-bodied bullet.

It was this kind of cruelty that encouraged Grey in the hope that one day it might be possible to ban weapons that were especially cruel, as the world had tried to do in the Hague Conventions. And once certain weapons were proscribed, so war itself might come to be seen eventually in a less favourable light. Later, in the 1920s, the writer H.G. Wells found the process of banning 'unsportsmanlike weapons' such as aeroplanes and submarines, and the legal attempt to keep the horrors of war within the limits of human endurance, especially absurd. He denounced the wish to fight 'nice wars'. But he also admitted that while he found the concept laughable, 'the improvement of war may be synonymous with the ending of war'. (Wells, 1928, 146)

And it has continued apace as we have tried to reduce still further war's human space, and enmesh human beings in a cybernetic system that removes them from the battlespace altogether. Adorno was at once more perceptive than Wells and more realistic than Grey. For it was humanity itself that was beginning to change. Hatred lies in the human heart, in the passions that animate men to kill and die for their country. By the 1940s men were being swallowed up into a system; hatred was becoming surplus to requirement; war was becoming entirely detached from the community on whose behalf, and in whose name, the soldier was sent out to fight. Adorno suspected that in future the human might even become the weakest link, an embodied encumbrance. The most human of characteristics would be hindrances to the efficient operation of the system. Eventually, human emotions would have to be written out of the script.

Indeed, in removing those who launched them from all risk the robot-bombs promised that war might be fought one day by remote control. What we value in war is the human qualities it brings out such as courage and mental stamina; stoicism under fire; the willingness to go the extra distance. Adorno's generation had attached particular value to the heroism of the ordinary soldier in the field. It had valued the genius of the commander, or the sacrifice of the men, or the ingenuity of planning or inventiveness—all the things that had been celebrated in war since the Greeks recorded Odysseus' ingenuity in fooling the Trojans with a wooden horse. To all of these we have attached value, and we can even attach value to the sacrifices made and the courage shown by the enemy, too. What we are valuing is physical involvement in war; we portray this embodiment as imparting value to war, and expressing that value through the acts that war brings forth, especially courage and sacrifice.

There is a telling passage in Conrad's *Heart of Darkness* which makes the point better than I can: 'Their talk however was the talk of sordid buccaneers; it was reckless without hardihood; greedy without audacity; and cruel without courage … and they did not seem aware these things were wanted for the work of the world'. (Conrad, 1995)

The 'work of the world'—a fine phrase that brought into question Grey's belief that one could engage in war without the human passions. It is the work of the world which we reward directly or indirectly; directly through the honour that a soldier achieves in his lifetime, or indirectly through the immortality he achieves through his actions. It is valuable to remember them, which is why the Greeks invented history.

So, to sum up. When Adorno first read of the rocket attacks on Britain he grasped that war had not exhausted its possibilities. The US colonel Thomas Adams claims that war is taking us beyond 'the human space' as weapons become too fast and create an environment too complex for humans to direct. (Adams, 2001, 57) We have begun to sub-contract or devolve responsibility for our decisions to the machines we build, in part in response to the imperatives of speed. We might soon even devolve responsibility for our decision-making to robot systems, effectively reducing the human space of war still further. At some point in the not too distant future, Adorno suspected, war would be reduced to a mechanical rhythm, 'not only in the disproportion between individual bodily strength and the energy of the machine, but in the most hidden cells of experience'. All this, he added, was 'another expression for the withering of experience, the vacuum between men and their fate, in which their real fate lies'. (Adorno, 1993, 54–5)

The cybernetic vision

It is a great pity that Adorno never returned to this theme again. His vision was limited by the extent of his knowledge. He envisaged a future in which Man and machine would live parallel lives; he did not recognise that in fact their futures might begin to converge in new and radical ways. In 1944 when he scribbled his musings about the future of war in his notebook he had no knowledge of cybernetics.

Cybernetics owes its invention to Norbert Wiener, who was a Harvard mathematics PhD by the age of nineteen. He was also at the cutting edge of a new science of applying statistically based non-linear mathematics to problems of self-adjusting feedback. The outbreak of war provided him with an opportunity to make a difference. In September 1940, at the height of the Battle of Britain, he wrote to Roosevelt's scientific adviser, Vannevar Bush, asking him to find some 'corner of activity' in which he might be of use. With his inventive mind he came up with a number of proposals, including lethal canisters of liquefied ethylene, propane or acetylene gas exploding in mid-air so as to engulf a wide volume of sky in a prolonged detonation. (Galison, 1993, 229) But the contribution for which he is remembered lay elsewhere—in solving the problem of working out a fire-control apparatus for anti-aircraft artillery which would be capable of tracking the curving course of a plane and predicting its future position. The basic concept implied in the term cybernetics is that of a feedback mechanism represented by the steering mechanism of a ship or the governor of a steam engine, or the common thermostat that keeps a house at a constant temperature. All these operate in response to information fed back to them, and since they tend to oppose what the system is already doing, there are known as negative feedback systems.

Wiener himself described it thus:

… at the beginning of the war, our greatest need was to keep England from being knocked out by an overwhelming air attack. Accordingly, the anti-aircraft cannon was one of the first objects of our scientific effort, especially when combined with the airplane-detecting device of radar …

Besides, science finding airplanes it was necessary to shoot them down. This involves the problem of fire control. The speed of the airplane has made it necessary to compute the elements of the trajectory of the anti-aircraft missile by machine and to give the predicting machine functions which had previously been assigned to human beings. Thus, the problem of anti aircraft fire control made a new generation of engineers familiar with the notion of communication addressed to a machine rather than to a person. (Wiener, 1989, 147–8)

Wiener and his collaborator at Harvard, Arturo Rosenblueth, saw that war was producing new weapons like torpedoes that were attracted to the sound of a ship's propeller or the magnetic attraction of a ship's hull. Rosenblueth described this as 'circular causality'—the torpedoes used feedback mechanisms to assess their progress towards their goal. They were 'goal-directed'; like humans they were 'teleological', driven by final purposes. For Wiener the nervous system and automatic machine were fundamentally alike 'in that they are devices which make decisions on the basis of decisions that have been made in the past'. (Wiener, 1989, 125–6)

For Wiener every human society could be understood through a study of the messages and communications which it produced, and he predicted that in future the development of these messages and communications, messages between men and machines, between machines and men and between machines and machines were 'destined to play an ever-increasing part'. (Wiener, 1989, 16) His groundbreaking contribution was to think of machines not in terms of what they were but in more 'human' terms of what they did, what Conrad would have called their 'work', or in other words, their behaviour. But he was also encouraged to see men as machines, or patterns of information. 'We are but whirlpools in a river of ever floating water. We are not stuff that abides but patterns that perpetuate themselves. A pattern is a message and may be transmitted as a message'. (Appleyard, 2011, 133) This was reductionism *tout court*: the human being reduced to a digital reality even before the arrival of the digital age. Out went the intractable complexity of the human condition. In their relationship with us machines do not want us to be complex creatures; they want us to be machine-readable. Cybernetics was interested in all forms of behaviour that were machine-like: regular, determinate or reproducible, all of which was true of human beings in particular professions, such as the military. Wiener always insisted that, in the end, it was really unimportant whether machines were 'organic' or 'inorganic'. The title of his most famous book, *The Human Use of Human Beings*, says it all. There are significant similarities in biological and material systems, and where man and machine interface the reality may be a new species—a cybernetic organism.

Indeed, from Wiener's point of view, as he looked at anti-aircraft systems in 1943, it made sense to see the pilot as the machine he flew. It was, after all, machines that they were being fired at by the anti-aircraft gunners; and it made equal sense to see them as a machine as well, locked into a closed system.

And it was no coincidence that cybernetics really took off in war because the cybernetic view of life was informed by a Social Darwinian logic. As it was put at its crudest by one early cyberneticist:

The inborn characterisation of living organisms are simply the strategies that have been found satisfactory over centuries of competition and built into the young animal so as to be ready for use at the first demand. Just as so many players have found 'PQ4' a good way of opening a game of chess, so many species found 'growth, teeth' to be a good way of opening the battle of life. (Pfohl, 2009, 7)

Towards a post-human future?

'... the Greek description of our situation presupposes that humanity itself has an intrinsic nature—that there is something unchangeable called 'the human'.

... Pragmatism sets this presupposition aside and urges that humanity is an open-ended notion, that the word 'human' names a fuzzy but promising project rather than an essence'. (Rorty, 1999, 52)

'It is impossible to predict the future', wrote one of the last century's great science fiction writers, Arthur C. Clarke, 'and all attempts to do so in detail seem ludicrous within a very few years'. We should not try to describe the future, he added, but 'to define the boundaries within which possible futures must lie'. (Gardner, 2010, 267) In this book I will endeavour to do just that. I will postulate that war will continue on other terms, as the post-human future gradually unfolds.

'Post-human', to be sure, is not a very pleasing term. It does not sit easily on the ear, but neither did the term post-modern. Twenty years ago, to write a book on the post-modern military would have been to invite ridicule, especially in the military. Now, the term is used all the time in military circles. But post-human just happens to be a term that today's post-humanist writers use, and there is no getting away from it. It implies just another step in our evolution or our humanity in one of three principle ways.

First, as many science fiction writers predicted in the 1950s, we may find ourselves eventually displaced as the most intelligent species on the planet. Our place will be taken by computers, designed by us, and at some point likely to be independent of our control. So far, there is still a human behind them—adjusting, correcting, servicing them, and ultimately switching them off. At some point in the future, however, the machines may no longer need human programmes or programmers. At some point they may be able to reproduce themselves, at which stage we will have to talk of the evolution of the first post-biological life forms on the planet.

We are also edging towards what the German philosopher Jürgen Habermas calls the 'auto-transformation of the species'. Until now, technology has magnified our existing powers: it has helped us to realise our ambitions. At some point, it is going to take us beyond those natural properties with which we are born. When we speculate about what will make us post-human, we are speculating that we have provisional status as a species.

Automated evolution is going to make all the difference. Evolution is random. Mutations produce what we take for granted now, such as a giraffe or a gorilla. We now have a chance to redesign ourselves. We used to think of ourselves as the 'end' of evolution; we do so no longer. We too are a random mutation, an accident of natural selection. But we can now do what we have done with domestic animals: we can improve our own 'fitness'. Darwinian selection is described as being random, purposeless, dumb and godless. Automated evolution, by contrast, is targeted, purposeful, intelligent—we are behind it. We will be looking for better algorithms or techniques. And the techniques of evolution will themselves evolve. (Martin, 2006, 189)

The third process is the fusing of humanity and machine. We now recognise that we are 'the random ancestors of machines and that as machines we can be engineered ourselves'. (Kelly, 1994, 14) We already can see this in many walks of life, especially in health. Implants now enable deaf people to hear and blind people to see. And the same 'upgrades' might be given to soldiers. The Defense Advanced Research Projects Agency (DARPA) has a vision to 'blend the best traits of man and machine'. Technology will not only enhance the warrior's reach, but be progressively incorporated into his body in the form of implants such as artificial sensory systems (built-in zoom lenses) and communications devices embedded under the skin, and perhaps even computational systems that will enhance memory and language skills. Within 30 years, the warrior's biometric personality may have changed irrevocably. As the Director of DARPA elaborated in 2002:

Think about our military commanders years from now. Envision them commanding war fighters who can then do things merely by thinking about them: who remain in action and effective for seven days and nights without sleep; who, if injured, can self-administer rapid-healing medications that enable them to stay in the fight, and who, if seriously injured, could be placed in temporary hibernation to prolong their lives until they can be evacuated to a hospital.

What would Adorno have made of this post-human future? The continuing integration of humanity and machine would not have surprised him; indeed this is what he foresaw. Nor would he have been surprised by the extent to which robots are beginning to become a feature of modern life. Robots were part of the social imaginary of his day—still to be invented but already waiting in the wings. But he would have been astonished beyond measure that we are going beyond the performative; we are fusing humanity and machine in the form of cyborgs.

There are three reasons in the end for going back to Adorno's discussion of the future of war. First, he raised a question now increasingly asked: what is the future of war in an age of unprecedented technological change which is pushing back the boundaries of what it means to be human? Second, we live at a time when fewer people than ever in the Western world are willing to die for their beliefs or their countries, when we have become acutely risk-averse and especially wary of incurring casualties. Robots offer a cheap and effective way of still remaining in the war business. Above all, Adorno invited us to imagine how war and our humanity have co-evolved and it is to this question that we must now turn.

31

2

THE HUMAN THING

HOW HUMANITY AND WAR HAVE CO-EVOLVED

The American anthropologist Marvin Harris describes a battle between two hunter-gatherer bands in northern Australia in the 1920s which was witnessed by a contemporary anthropologist. The instigators formed a war party and announced that conflict would break out the following day. The two sides agreed to meet at a pre-arranged time. At dawn they lined up on opposite sides of the clearing. The older men shouted out grievances at one another. Two or three people on either side were singled out for special attention, so that when the spears were first thrown they were aimed by individuals for reasons based on individual grievances. But since the old men did most of the spear throwing, their marksmanship tended to be inaccurate:

Not infrequently the person hit was some innocent non-combatant or one of the screaming old women who weaved through the fighting men, yelling obscenities at everybody, and whose reflexes for dodging spears were not as fast as those of the men .... As soon as somebody was wounded even a seemingly irrelevant crone, fighting stopped immediately until the implications of this new incident could be assessed by both sides. (Harris, 1978, 35)

Lest we think the melee was not serious, we should remember that death in primitive warfare is intense, pervasive and continuous. And it is particularly lethal. In New Guinea until quite recently, about 30 per cent of all independent Highland social groups became extinct every century because they were defeated in battle. Just because the conflicts of the New Guinean tribes have few features that we would recognise as constituting war (battles, organization, logistics, leadership) does not make it any less lethal—in fact, the absence of all these things makes it more lethal. (Leblanc, 2003, 151)

What makes warfare so lethal are not its battles, which are few and far between, but the constant raids. Villages are frequently attacked while people are asleep or too drowsy to organise an effective defence. We often think that because hunter-gatherers have so little in the way of material goods they also have little to fight about, but humans fight for immaterial things: to revenge themselves on others for a slight or injury; to maintain their reputation; and out of fear that if you do not get in the first blow the other will get the last. Our instrumental needs are a matter of survival which natural selection has programmed into us. Our existential identity may also be hard-wired into us. Honour is something that we alone cherish in the hope that others may think better of us. We have a 'theory of the mind': a capacity to care about what others think of us. (Bering, 2011, 166) And some will even go to their death because they care so much.

The aboriginal battle which Marvin Harris relates is very similar to one actually filmed in 1961 in New Guinea in a mountainous region that had not yet been pacified by the Dutch. It offered a cinematographic interpretation of the life of a group of mountain people studied by the Harvard-Peabody Expedition (the battle can be seen on a re-mastered vision of the original documentary, *Dead Birds*). Two villages in the Darni announced beforehand that hostilities would commence. The warriors exchanged insults with each other, fired arrows and threw spears, most of which missed the target. Neither side was willing to fight hand-to-hand. But what made the battle so human was that in every respect it was a social activity. It saw the repaying of old scores, the identification of specific targets, and the cultural 'threat displays' included the use of language, the hurling of abuse. (France, 2011, 395) The decision to go to battle was actively argued and discussed, with some urging caution and others straining at the leash for a fight. The battle arose, in short, from a personal choice; the fundamental point is that the behaviour even of the higher animals is not 'social' as we understand the term and apply it to our own behaviour: when chimps go on raids they do not argue the toss, or debate the issue in an explicitly acknowledged public sphere. (Tallis, 2011, 240) And even more important, perhaps, the battles which the neighbouring groups of Darni clans fight were networked into a remembered past, for in the Darni culture the death of a warrior had to be avenged. The balance was continually being adjusted with the spirits of slain comrades appeased as soon as a compensating enemy life was taken. There was no thought of conflicts ever ending unless it rained or became dark. For without war there would be no way to satisfy the demands of the ancestors.

In the end everything comes down to language, which is the most essential tool that our tool-making species uses. It may possibly even be an off-shoot of the very first material tool-making. By the time of the Stone Age the ability to make tools had made us the most successful predators on the planet. The Olduvai Gorge tools date back 1.2 million years, and in the intervening period, we acquired language. In making tools, we may have learned to communicate through speech—at the level, at least, of a 7-year-old child of today.

Recently, scientists have looked at what happens neurologically when a stone tool is being made. They have used modern hospital scanners to see what bits of the brain are activated as knappers work their stone. Surprisingly, the areas of the modern brain that you use when you are making a hand axe overlap considerably with those you use when you speak. It now seems very likely that if you can shape a stone, you can shape a sentence. (MacGregor, 2010, 17)

And once you can shape a sentence you are well on the way to developing emotional intelligence.

Aristotle was the first writer to call language a 'tool'. The definition is strikingly modern in that we now recognise that tools refer to more than just tangible instruments such as hammers, and that other tools such as ideas are not any the less involved in what is technical and technological just because they are abstract and immaterial. And language was a true breakthrough that allowed us to develop the emotional intelligence we now take for granted: the capacity to negotiate group dynamics; to manage status anxiety; to understand social norms. Each of these is essential to group dynamics. And it is the ability to form groups that has enabled us to survive and tackle problems with the success that we have enjoyed. Our cognitive skills are so developed precisely because we work together in larger groups. Language not only enhances our skills; it enables us to gain status in a group (by arguing a case well); to establish trust by winning a reputation for always telling the truth; and to manipulate others into agreeing with our position by the simple magic of wordplay.

So I think we should be wary of claiming that any other species on the planet engages in war as we do. The great apes may, in the words of Frans de Waal, be 'inching closer to humanity' in our own imagination as the differences begin to continue to narrow with research and observation (Bering, 2011, 24); whether in the use of tools, or play, or even a 'theory of the mind', the distance between ourselves and the higher primates who share a common ancestor appears to be narrowing. In other words, like us they have a rudimentary culture that sets them apart from other animals. Chimpanzees, however, are not humans. They may mount raids and plan ambushes, but they have not taken collective violence any further in the last hundreds of thousands of years than they have the rudimentary use of tools (such as employing a stick to lever ants out of a hole). What distinguishes us from chimpanzees with whom we share all but 1 per cent of our genes is the combination of genes and culture (chimps have both, but then their circumstances rarely change).

We are the only species that has been able to unshackle ourselves from the immediate environment in which we find ourselves placed. Our thoughts are not only confined to things with which we are causally interacting at the time. We can also recall the past. Indeed, like the Darni we often live in the shadow of the ancestors, and it is the 'ancestral voices' that, from time to time, summon us to war. And whilst some chimps are distinctly braver and bolder than others, they do not forge bravery into acts that are recalled years later. If there is one certain and determining feature of our humanity, it is what William James called 'mankind's common instinct for reality'. We have always held the world 'to be a theatre for heroism'. (James, 2003, 281)

Warfare and social networking

The greatest difference between apes and ourselves, writes Matt Ridley, is that their ability to engage in social networking is strictly limited, ours is not. And the key here is ability to co-operate as well as compete. Although the survival of the fittest remains a trope difficult to dislodge from the collective consciousness, it is not the whole story. To say that just because an organism has to survive survival is its only purpose is as erroneous as claiming that just because reproduction requires sex, we only engage in sex for purposes of reproduction. Any inference from function to overt psychology is simply fallacious. (Ridley, 2004, 210)

We try to maximise our interests through competition and co-operation, more often the latter. Our genetic code is selfless as well as selfish. Chimpanzees can show affection for others of their kind but their ability to empathise or sympathise with each other is very limited. They can co-operate and collaborate but not establish a reputation for kindness, or for being a team player, one which will ensure that others seek them out.

Our minds really are different; co-operation is hardwired into us. Take something we take for granted—laughter. We can laugh and do so quite often, chimps cannot. In *Born to be Good* Dacher Keltner describes how smiling and laughing reinforce empathy and connectivity. When two people laugh together their laughter starts out as separate vocalisations which then merge and become intertwined. Laughter evolved long before vowels and consonants as a mechanism to build co-operative strategies. And as we might expect, neuroscientists are quick to point out that there is a biological explanation for this, too. The act of helping out another even when it involves no direct advantage to oneself triggers activity in the caudate nucleus and anterior cingulate cortex regions of the brain. These are precisely the areas which when stimulated give us pleasure. We feel better about ourselves; we enjoy greater self-esteem; and the more we esteem ourselves the better placed we are to win the respect of others.

But competition is also hard-wired into us, and we compete far more effectively than any other species because of another behavioural trait that is unique to us—not laughter, but lying: we lie to one another all the time. In another recent book, *Born Liars*, Ian Leslie points out that lying is more than just a product of Machiavellian intelligence which we share with the great apes—the ability to construct coalitions and partnerships with others. It is the ability to 'win over' others. Chimps, too, may have a rudimentary Machiavellian intelligence, but we are the species in which this capacity is most developed, and for this language really is essential. Chimps may well have pre-linguistic expressive powers (they have been observed in the wild misleading each other for their own advantage), and they may also have a rudimentary theory of the mind (the ability to read other chimps' intentions), but it is language with its own syntax and semantics that really does make all the difference. We have access to a remembered past as well as an imagined future which only the possession of language makes possible. Ludwig Wittgenstein points out that a dog may believe that its master is at the door (when he is not) but not that its master will come back the day after tomorrow. (MacIntyre, 2009, 74) When we find ourselves fighting our leaders can urge us on by insisting that help will eventually arrive if not tomorrow, then at least the day after; they may be lying to keep up our morale, but then, we too, are quite capable of lying to ourselves.

Only we can persuade others to see the world other than we know it to be, and we can only do this because of the human propensity to peer at the world through a series of distorted lenses. We often see what we want to see, and the first and foremost explanation for this is to be found in the human body. While we are all familiar with visual illusions and hallucinations that we encounter in sleep, we are usually unaware of how far we may be deceived at the very basic level even when we are awake. There is no form of knowledge, writes Kathryn Schulz, 'however central or unassailable it may seem that cannot under certain circumstances, fail us'. Schulz recounts the case of a patient called Hannah who had suffered a stroke. Asked by her doctor to describe his face, she reported that he had short hair, was clean shaven and sported a bit of a tan. All very perceptive of her, but for the fact that Hannah was blind and, even more to the point, unaware of her blindness. She was suffering from Anton's syndrome, one of a group of similar neurological problems known as *anasonosia*, or the denial of disease. And such conditions, both real and metaphorical, are unique to human beings; they are emblematic of the human condition. 'To be blind without realising our blindness', adds Schulz, 'is figuratively the situation of all of us when we are in error'. (Schulz, 2010)

And we are in error much of the time. Lying is effective precisely because others reinforce what they know we think or want to believe. Lies are frequently most effective when they reinforce erroneous convictions. Appalling miscarriages of justice driven by rock-like certainties are often impossible to overturn even in the face of new evidence, which would confirm Nietzsche in his opinion that 'convictions are often greater enemies of truth than lies'.

And for this culture is really essential. For the key difference between us and the higher primates is that at some point in our own evolution culture became accumulation. And it is accumulation that gave us a decisive selective advantage. Over time we developed larger brains which enabled us to 'inherit' items of social culture through social learning—to observe how others interacted with their friends and enemies, how they learned to deceive on a heroic scale. Like us, apes can plan and plot (both they and we put together raiding parties), and we would probably be just as good at planning and plotting if we couldn't communicate with each other through language. (Ridley, 2004, 226) Without the ability to communicate through speech, however, we would not be able to rehearse strategies in our mind, commit things to memory for later use and anticipate the future. All of these allow us to divorce ourselves from our environment and to think beyond our immediate interaction with it. Once you can do the latter, then you can exchange ideas, plan ahead, and work together.

In the case of the hunt, different roles can be allotted to different members of a group. The group, in turn, can out-think the quarry and produce a strategic plan for the hunt. These developments were seminal because they permitted a re-wiring of the brain which accelerated learning (ideas could be transmitted through generations); in time we were able to turn our minds into a tool. And this enabled us to put together something we would recognise as a society whose members work together to maximise their individual talents. In every hunter-gatherer society there are better hunters, better planners of the hunt, but everyone performs a role and plays their part. Teamwork is the key to success, as it is in every society. And teamwork requires general organization. Indeed all the virtues that we admire most, such as friendship, co-operation, trust and fidelity, are pro-social values, and all the things we condemn, selfishness, egoism and vanity, are anti-social.

Hunting offers a striking narrative of how co-operative strategies and collective action are, as Darwin's intuition told him, just as important as competition or possibly more important. All hunting requires planning, organization and special weapons, and language is central to co-ordination. Matthew Ridley contends that what allowed men to hunt big game for the first time was not just the invention of a projectile weapon (the spear), but the discovery that by hunting in a band they could better track down their quarry. It was the band, not the spear, that was the invention with the more profound social implications; for big game could be shared. And once hunting became a team effort, sharing would have been mandatory. The spoils of the kill would have been public property. As Ridley contends, the hunting of big game introduced *Homo sapiens* to the idea of public goods for the first time. (Ridley, 1996, 108)

Once human beings ceased to be hunted and started to hunt big game themselves, warfare developed very quickly. Both require, after all, the same skills and the same tools (indeed many archaeologists often find it difficult to distinguish hunting tools from the tools of warfare; they both look much the same). And it is interesting to note how hunting remained a central theme long after we left the hunter-gatherer stage of history behind. No doubt that is why war has continued until recently to retain such a powerful hold: it springs from the roots that we all in some part share. Achilles is portrayed as a hunter. He is at his most heroic when chasing down his enemies, just as our distant ancestors were when hunting in the African savanna. Even as late as the 4th century BC, Aristotle, in the *Politics*, discussed five main ways by which men lived by their labour. We find, as we would expect, the pastoral, agricultural and fishing occupations. But the inclusion of 'hunting' comes as a shock, and so does the fact that it is divided into several sub-themes: the hunting of wild animals; the hunting of people (slave raiding); the hunting of movable objects (plundering); and the hunting of people and possessions together (war). (Shipley and Rich, 1993, 83)

Groupishness

The great 17th century English writer Thomas Hobbes agreed with William Shakespeare that we were once an unsocial species. 'Thou art the thing itself', Lear tells the naked and tattered 'poor Tom;' 'un-accommodated Man is no more but such a poor, bare, forked animal as thou'. (*King Lear* 3.4, 95–7) And Hobbes derived his insight into the state of nature not only from theoretical intuition but also from what he had read about the state of Native American societies, only recently discovered.

It may peradventure be thought, there was never such a time, nor condition of war as this; and I believe it was never generally so; over all the world: but there are many places, where they live so now. For the savage people in many places of America … have no government at all, and live at this day in their brutish manner as I said before [in continual fear and danger of violent death]. (Hobbes, 1958, 108)

Hobbes' quietly disdainful point of view concerning savages was the received wisdom of his time (though it was not accepted by everyone and notably not by Montaigne). A society without a government or a state did not, according to the best minds of the day, constitute a society. The savage remained exterior to the social, living in a natural condition of men where the war of all against all prevailed. But savage societies are not 'un-accommodated'; they have a social structure which makes it possible for them to do what the great apes cannot do—translate collective violence into warfare—and, as Pierre Clastres found in the course of his research in the mid-1960s, warfare is 'the pre-requisite for the primitive social being'. (Clastres, 2007, 263)

Clastres died at the tragically early age of 43, but not before he had made a reputation for himself as a brilliant anthropologist whose chief mission in life was to challenge Hobbes' understanding of the state of nature, which still has a strong purchase on our imagination—the view of a life which is nasty, brutish and short, and above all 'solitary', the word that tends to be left out of the account. Primitive society may be primitive but it is recognizably 'social', and what makes it social is that it is in a near-permanent state of warfare.

But warfare is not what we understand by war. In a primitive society there is no division between civilians and soldiers or amongst soldiers themselves, between leaders (generals) and led (foot soldiers). Not even the chief is a general. Hence the absence of any concept of strategic planning. Stratagems are basic. The aboriginal battle Marvin Harris describes is a pretty colourless affair, a melee, more than a battle, with few, if any, distinctive features. There is not much opportunity for innovation either, because life is timeless; primitive peoples live in a perpetual present. The only habits that survive are the old habits, and the only ambition of the warrior is to be like his father. Warfare has no battles, no heroes and no memorials. It is even without strategic or tactical innovation (which is not to deny ingenuity on the part of individual warriors in the form of deception, ambushes or ruses). And primitive warriors are not so much heroic as stoic, in large part because their encounters with the enemy tend to lead nowhere fast.

Of course, even in 'savage societies' individual differences exist. Although all young men are potentially warriors, some obviously will be braver than others, and some will be more skilled in the use of weapons. And some will be more in love with violence as definitive of their existential self. In Cormac McCarthy's novel *Blood Meridian* one of the principal characters speaks of the true warrior as 'the man who has offered up himself entire to the blood of war, who has been to the floor of the pit and seen horror in the round and learned, at last, that it speaks to his inmost heart'. (McCarthy, 1992, 345) But even in 'savage' societies not everyone exults in violence for its own sake; and warfare will not echo in the heart of everyone as it will in that of the authentic warrior.

In short, in primitive societies human faculties may certainly be harnessed, but they are usually not awakened. (Midgley, 1995, 145) What is lacking is what we call 'humanity', the richness of social, emotional and imaginative life. Clastres may have taken issue with Hobbes but he paints a picture which is reminiscent of Hobbes' bleak account of the state of nature, in which there are neither arts nor sciences—nothing, in a word, to appease the soul whose cultivation is so central to our understanding of politics.

But over time warfare was eventually translated into something that is more recognizable to us as war. Warriors became a special caste who derived prestige from their reputation not for fighting but for fighting skills. In time they transformed themselves into a pressure group, a martial aristocracy deciding on matters of peace and war. (Claestres, 2007, 303) Until the process happened, writes Clastres, the warrior remained his own greatest enemy. He took unnecessary risks, put himself in unnecessary danger, and often for nothing more than prestige. As he failed to transform his prestigious deeds into instrumentalised power, death claimed him early. He fell victim to his own desires. Only the taming of those desires made it possible for humanity to finally leave behind the hunter-gatherer stage of its history.

The domestication of the savage mind

The great breakthrough—the most important historical 'turn' of all—was our own domestication, which was only made possible with the invention of agriculture. For it was agriculture that first allowed us to impose order on the chaos, to find patterns in the weather, in the yield of crops, and in the seasons of the year. It allowed us to grasp the importance of planning ahead—strategic planning if you wish—for the planting of crops. It led to a marked increase in population over time, which encouraged groupishness—the transformation of village communities into chiefdoms and then rudimentary states with their individual class structures.

In the march of domestication women probably tamed plants, men animals. By 7000 BC herders had turned the wild aurochs into something like the placid cows we know today, and wild boars into pigs. Later still they learned to harness the ox. The ox-drawn plough and cart was the really great breakthrough in the production of power, for an ox in harness can deliver three times the draught power of a man (it would be another six thousand years before humans added a significant new energy source: coal and steam). (Morris, 2011, 99–100) The wheel axle followed. It was, writes Jacob Bronowski, 'the double root' from which all invention grew, for the wheel soon became a model of all motions of rotation as well as a norm of explanation and a heavenly symbol of more than human power in science and art alike. (Bronowski, 1993, 77)

No sharp dividing line, writes David Christian, exists between predation and domestication; the process was protracted and uneven. But in this symbiotic relationship both species changed behaviourally or genetically until a point was reached where neither could survive without the other. (Christian, 2005, 216) For modern maize or Indian corn cannot reproduce without human assistance; its seeds cannot scatter freely. And many of the animals we have tamed—dogs for example, around 10,000 BC—would have great difficulty surviving without human support. Domesticated dogs, like most domesticated animals, cannot really survive in the wild; they cannot return to the wolf condition from which they emerged. One reason for this is that over time we have decreased the size of the animals we have harnessed as a result of deliberately selecting more docile, manageable beasts of burden, or through changing patterns of nutrition (the food we feed them is often poorer than would have been available if they had been allowed to roam). As a result of all of this, domesticated animals have become more docile and manageable.

Of all the animals that we have domesticated successfully, this has been most true of dogs. Their story is worth telling briefly. Many thousands of years ago wolves began to come in from the cold. They were looking for food and found it in the scraps left over at the camp sites of our early ancestors. Some were less aggressive and less fearful of humans than the rest, and eventually they learned to approach them and to be fed by hand. Thus began the grand bargain in which in return for food wolves helped out with guarding the camp site and later with hunting. In time they became dogs.

The key breakthrough was selection, but the acquiescent wolves were not selected for their intelligence; they were selected for being more co-operative, or nicer than the rest. They were also more socially adept at interacting with others. Intelligence emerged as they were tamed. Intelligence followed on from domestication.

Today dogs are far more intelligent than wolves. To begin with they can follow a human being who is pointing out an object or a prey. It is quite a challenge to do this. Consider the mental effort that goes into figuring out what a pointing finger means—paying close attention to a person; recognising that a gesture reflects a thought; and acknowledging that another animal can actually have a thought which is worth sharing.

In this ability they are superior to chimps who, though a highly social species, have never broken out of their evolutionary rut. Chimps have many attributes but they cannot follow even the most basic of human hand gestures such as pointing. By contrast, children from a very early age can grasp why their parents are pointing at an object. They know instinctively that there is another animal out there with thoughts of its own and something to communicate, and dogs just happen to be able to make the same cognitive leap.

One of the most interesting experiments to have shown this was conducted in Siberia in 1959 when the Russian scientist Dmitry Belyaev set out to understand how the domestication of animals actually works. He brought together some wild foxes and separated them into two groups. One he bred randomly as a control group; the second he bred for their ability to interact with human beings. The foxes which approached humans without fear or aggression were allowed to mate with each other. When the American evolutionary anthropologist Brian Hare visited Belyaev's old compound in 2003 he was astonished to find that the domesticated foxes, unlike their wild cousins, were able to follow a person when he or she pointed at an object in their field of vision. They had made the cognitive leap entirely thanks to their domestication. Not only had they become more intelligent, they were also more socially adept at interacting with human beings. (*International Herald Tribune*, 7 June 2011)

Something like this, speculates Hare, may have happened with us. When did our own domestication begin? By 8000 BC our mental landscape had begun to change. Hunter-gathers had broad geographical horizons, writes Ian Morris, but narrow social ones. The landscape may have changed but the faces did not. Early farming communities were just the opposite. As they grew the landscape was broken into concentric circles with the home at the centre, then the neighbours, the cultivated fields and finally pasture land for grazing. The first 'maps' appear at about this time delimiting the ownership of land. Even the concept of love was refashioned. Love between husband and wife was already there but farming injected new forces, especially the idea of passing on property to one's children. 'By imposing such mental structures on their world ... (human beings) were, as we might say, domesticating themselves'. (Morris, 2011, 101)

We have been domesticating ourselves for millennia, breeding out hyper-aggression and breeding in greater social intelligence. In this we have put a critical difference between ourselves and chimpanzees. They too have social intelligence, they live in troops and co-operate in the hunt. But they are too emotionally volatile to take co-operation very far. They are fiercely competitive with each other when it comes to sharing food—they do so reluctantly and often they will just stop and fight for every morsel. Their emotional impulsiveness is their undoing. They are not, in that sense, as clever as dogs who have learned not only to work with each other, but also with us, and have developed a unique set of social skills which give them an enormous advantage in their complex relationship with us. They can read our emotions better than we can read theirs; they can sense our moods and respond accordingly; they can even make a real difference in our lives through their ability to show affection, real or feigned, a rare ability indeed for one species in partnership with another. And there is growing evidence that they are socially savvy. Even when they are not responsible for that broken vase they will adopt a submissive posture, knowing not only that it is wise but that it usually cuts short our anger.

Human beings are far cleverer, of course; they have taken their own domestication much further; it is, after all, self-managed. In most developed societies, unrestrained violence has been bred out. For in complex societies it is very dangerous; aggression tends to have a lower pay-off over time. 'Naturally' aggressive people who made up the early warrior class would have experienced lower fitness as a class system developed in which each class had to observe rules or etiquettes and adapt them to improve connectivity. Innate aggressiveness would have been discouraged in all walks of life.

In their book *The 10,000 Year Explosion*, which details how civilization accelerated human evolution, Gregory Cochran and Henry Harpending write of a genetic factor that may even have played a part in this story, the 7R (for seven repeat) allele of the DRD4 (dopamine receptor D4) gene, which can still be found in significant levels of the world, except for East Asia. The gene these days is associated with Attention Deficit Hyperactivity Disorder (ADHD), with which parents and teachers are all too familiar at home and in the classroom when dealing with children who are hyperactive, unable to focus on any activity for long, and often aggressive when confronted. Alleles derived from the 7R allele are quite common in China, but the 7R allele itself is extremely rare. This raises the possibility that individuals bearing such an allele were selected against because of cultural patterning. 'The Japanese say that the nail that sticks out is hammered down, but in China it may have been pulled out and thrown away'. Selection for submission, they add, sounds unerringly like domestication.

Well, East Asians have a reputation for being more submissive than Europeans or Americans. They have experienced more centrally-managed societies for historically longer than Europeans. And the warrior tradition, although prominent in Japan, is not as strongly entrenched in China as it is in Europe. (Cochran and Harpending, 2009, 111–13) We know that in Europe, by comparison, gene changes involving serotonin metabolism may have influenced personality changes, though in ways we still do not yet know. It is possible that the domestication of the warrior may have been in part biological, as well as cultural in origin. In other words, cultural innovations and needs may have driven biological changes (certainly since the first use of tools). Human evolution, in short, has not stopped. It is still continuing.

Today, we are far more thoughtful in dealing with each other, more imaginative in sharing each other's point of view, more compliant, and even pliable—when it suits us. We can empathise much more with each other's plight and we have been breeding out the most aggressive types for some time, getting them to see the purpose of co-operation. And we have done this by programming, not breeding in, cultural instincts.

The process has been a long one, and has been central to the taming of warfare too. The qualities that have been most admired in the warrior in most state-centric systems have been those we have sought to cultivate in domesticated animals and plants: hardiness and adaptability, as well as what we have looked for most in domesticated animals, sociability (the ability to live in herds or households characterised by social hierarchies that predispose them to follow leaders, whether other animals or human beings). And at some point in history the domestication of warriors became a pressing need as they continued to confront the greatest challenge of all: not their mortality, but their own nature.

Civilisation and its malcontents

Rage is the opening word of Homer's epic poem, the *Iliad*, setting the scene for two key concepts central to the poet's vision—first, the warrior as a self-centred individual, his own master, owing few if any obligations to anyone other than himself, and his own exaggerated sense of honour; the second, his rage as god-given. Homer brought these two concepts into a new and powerful conjunction. His account is actually a throwback to the era of warfare, to Clastres' warrior who because of his self-absorption is doomed to die young, as is Achilles, who is the tragic figure that he is in Homer's poem because he invites an early death while remaining bitter about his own mortality; he would prefer, like the gods, to be immortal.

And the *Iliad* looks back to the world of prehistory in another striking respect. The Homeric heroes are not so much individuals as almost forces of nature (this is especially true of Achilles' rage). Bruno Snell is still worth reading for what he has to say about the Homeric hero—he is not a spirit imprisoned in matter but a battleground of arbitrary forces and uncanny powers. (Bloom, 2004, 71) And his world, like that of Claestres' hunter-gatherers, is one in which war is endemic. Harold Bloom cites with approval James Redfield's observation that the rhetorical purpose of all the similes of peace to be found in the poem merely makes more vivid the world of war. And even the world of peace in the *Iliad* is not that of domesticated farming—instead we see Man's war with nature, one in which 'farmers rip out the grain and fruit as so many spoils of battle'. 'This helps explain', adds Bloom, 'why the *Iliad* need not bother to praise war, since reality is a constant contest anyway, in which nothing of value can be attained without despoiling or ruining someone or something else'. (Bloom, 2004, 74)

For all its poetic power the *Iliad* is ultimately very narrow in its vision. 'For long stretches of the book', writes Eli Sagan, 'in fact for most of the book—"nothing happens". Nothing that is except human beings killing each other. If one lacks a keen interest in this particular brand of homicide the reading quickly becomes tedious'. (Sagan, 1979, 291). True, though it is not the whole truth. Tedious too, it might be added in Sagan's defence, are the wildly different voices of the warriors, all of them raging away at different frequencies about themselves—their honour, the slights they have suffered, the respect which they insist is their due and which they are on a perpetual hairspring to win back if their reputation or status is ever brought into question. Killing is pretty boring when it is so relentless and unending. Much of the battlescape of the *Iliad* is as emotionally and psychologically featureless as the battlefields of Stone Age societies from which Homer's heroes, for all their many qualities, have not quite escaped.

What we find in Achilles is a man who has been domesticated up to a point (he is a product of a culture and education), but he has not been instrumentalised in any sense of the word, and it is his feelings that make Achilles such a one-dimensional figure not only in our eyes (we moderns), but also in Plato's. As William James recognised over a century ago, it is anachronistic to assume that people have always experienced the world as we ourselves do. It is unwarranted to imagine that Achilles' internal, emotional life was similar to our own or that the human nature Homer observed and described so vividly was pretty much the same as that we observe every day in the world around us. Pre-modern conceptions of the self were not identical to our own and James was one of the first to point out some of the main differences.

This is why Achilles, like all the Homeric heroes, is always being reborn in every generation's imagination. Their lives are re-experienced by others in the act of remembering. But memory is treacherous. 'Remember that what you are told is really three-fold', warned the novelist Vladamir Nabokov, 'shaped by the teller, reshaped by the listener, concealed from both by the dead man of the tale'. (Nabokov, *The Real Life of Sebastian Knight*)

What we find most interesting in Achilles is that he is both recognizably human and yet deficient in some of the cultural instincts that we identify in ourselves and others. But even by the time of Plato the Greeks were finding Achilles deeply problematic because of his limited emotional intelligence. The Homeric warrior is a man of passion, a man who needs to live life at a certain pitch. What the Greeks found most dangerous about Achilles by the 5th century was his intense self-absorption. He may have been a hero but his single-minded pursuit of reputation blinds him at times to the world he shares with others. Achilles is a key figure in Plato's penultimate work, the *Republic;* there are sixteen references to the warrior or his speeches, the majority highly critical. Achilles is portrayed often in unflattering terms—he is clearly undomesticated, a creature of pure spirit, unruled by reason, his own or anyone else's. Were Achilles thoroughly undeserving of admiration, of course, he would not have appeared at all. Indeed, Plato goes out of his way to show us that he has a number of virtues that are admirable, such as honour (his own and that of his clan) as well, needless to say, such as undeniable bravery. Such men command respect, but they can often be a danger to others and themselves.

Unlike slaves or domesticated animals, however, warriors are no good to anyone if they are emasculated. The point is to re-focus their energies and passions on the common good, and that can best be done by bringing them into harmony with themselves. It is this vital insight that is the core of the *Republic.* Plato tells us that Achilles' spirit is disordered; only that explains why he acts in a way that even his contemporaries find reprehensible. It is they, after all, who condemn his pitilessness when raised to anger. Achilles is clearly very unhappy, and he is unhappy because he lacks emotional intelligence, the ability to forge lasting friendships.

Plato dwells particularly on Achilles' lack of sociability. He is what Coriolanus calls himself in Shakespeare's play, a 'lonely dragon' (*Coriolanus IV:I,30*). He is completely alone when his lifetime companion, Patroclus, dies. The older, and wiser, Nestor, says of him that he will enjoy his valour in loneliness. Paradoxically, it is because he has no friends that he is too much in love with life. He really cannot imagine the value of other people, and therefore what value his own death might have for others. He is not willing to sacrifice himself for anyone else, or risk death so that others will have a greater reason to prize life. The first reference to Achilles in the *Republic* (383 D2–8) quotes a fragment from Aeschylus in which Achilles' mother Thetis laments her son's death. Plato is at pains to point out that military service is a privilege and death is not meaningless if it has meaning for others, especially his brothers-in-arms. (Hobbs, 2000, 208)

Plato's theory of social intelligence

> *The night can sweat with terror as before*
> *We pieced our thoughts together into philosophy*
> W.B. Yeats, *Nineteen Hundred and Nineteen)*

The *Republic* begins with the word *kateben* (I went down). 'Yesterday I went down to the Piraeus with Glaucon, the son of Ariston', Socrates says, 'to worship the goddess and to see how the people celebrate her festival, which is what they were doing now for the first time'. This is how Socrates begins his story in the first book of Plato's *Republic*. We find him on his way home when he is approached by a friend's servant and asked to wait. A torch race was taking place later that evening, and for the first time it was to be on horseback. The Festival honoured a Thracian goddess, and Athens had just formed an alliance with the Thracian king.

Thucydides, as Plato would have known, had also begun his own account of the Sicilian expedition with the word *katabantes* to describe the Athenians and their allies coming down to the Piraeus to cheer the expedition to Sicily on its way. (Thucydides, 6.30.2) In Plato's work Socrates goes down to help cure the disorder in the souls of the young who had witnessed the fall of the Athenian empire some years after the disastrous conclusion of the Sicilian expedition. In both cases there is an echo (possibly conscious—it is impossible to prove) of the famous *Katabasis* in Book XI of the *Odyssey* when the hero of the tale goes down to the Underworld to face the darkness of death before he can begin the voyage home. (Shankman/Durrant, 2000, 114) For Plato the divided soul is a true underworld which separates his fellow citizens from the truth, and for Plato the echo of Homer is even stronger, for he dispenses with the article *ton* (the) in his phrase *es Peiraia*. The phrase *He Peiraia* meant 'the land beyond the river'—the Hell the Athenians had forged through being out of harmony with life; for failing to tame their own passions. The taming of the passions is one of the central themes of Plato's *Republic*: the need to turn the warrior into a social being without crushing his spirit.

Plato has the distinction of being the first philosopher whose main body of work has been preserved in its entirely. He was the first public intellectual who believed that ideas were more important than people. He was the first don who in the Academy founded the first university department where young men could discuss philosophy and were to do so for the next five hundred years (Johnson, 2010, 25). He was also perhaps, the first sociologist, the first writer to grasp the importance of emotional intelligence in war. In our ability to act reasonably (in our best interests) we are products not just of reason, but of our emotions and appetites. We are in that sense embodied creatures, which is why he begins his book with an extended discussion of what he calls each person's 'soul' and its tripartite division into reason, spirit and appetite.

It is reason that allows us to deceive, manipulate, suborn and subvert. Reason has qualities that are both positive and negative. But we are also creatures of spirit. Some people are phlegmatic; others are quick to anger or take revenge. Someone who is highly-spirited, like a horse, needs to be 'broken in' or tamed. And we all have appetites which tend to excess. We tend to privilege desire and become dissatisfied very quickly. Appetites need to be tamed, too. Unlike other animals, we are not driven by appetites alone. We also have appetites that are unnatural—the product of greed, for example, and in war often a perverse appetite for excessive cruelty.

A recent report in the *New York Times* quoted a scientific study that showed the psychology of people does indeed differ. Those who seek fame and status are looking for what the report called 'existential reassurance' in their lives. (Abrahamson, 2009, 49) Those who prefer to get rich are looking for more than material rewards. In other words, there really are people of spirit, just as there are people of appetite, and Plato notes in passing that they are not restricted in gender, for women of spirit exist, too, and women can even make good soldiers. Here is a first too, though he never took the argument any further.

Reason, spirit and appetite are not only what the Greeks found at the centre of the human story. So have many other writers, including Sigmund Freud who used, without acknowledging the debt, Plato's idea for his own tripartite approach to personality—his concepts of id, ego and superego. His definition of id and ego are almost verbatim definitions of reason and appetite laid out in the *Republic*. In earlier times Shakespeare, though probably not familiar with Plato's work (the Elizabethans were much more impressed by Aristotle), nonetheless recognised instinctively that reason, spirit and appetite were the dominant features of social intelligence. The one element of the 'Shakespearean' in drama, writes Ron Rosenbaum, is that of counter-poised characters and the forces they represent, and the ever-shifting neutral gravitational force each exerts on the other. In *Henry IV Part II*, we see the King's dispirited Machiavellianism (the principle of being unprincipled); in Hotspur, the spirited lust for honour; and in Falstaff (the most famous char-acter of the three) an excessive appetite for pleasure (as well as, in the actors who play him on stage, an appetite to steal the entire show). All three ele-ments of human personality are rendered even more real, of course, by the seductive power of Shakespeare's language. (Rosenbaum, 2006, 417)

Indeed, it is culture that allows us to develop the genetic predispositions with which we are born. Different environments stimulate, or fail to stimu-late, the brain's work of parallel processing in regions like the prefrontal cortex. Our natural capabilities are activated or repressed by culture. For Richard Lewontin, genetic potentials are unresolved 'naturally'; the human body is full of possibility that requires cultural organization for it to become manifest and concrete. (Sennett, 2008, 277) It is worth going back to Wil-liam James' great insight that what we admire most about Achilles is his 'integrity of pagan feeling'. He didn't mean that Achilles is purely a creature of instinct, he meant that the cultural possibilities of the post-Mycenaean world were far fewer than those of the 19th century, or for that matter 5th century Athens. He was not claiming that he had fewer biological instincts than we do, but that he had fewer cultural instincts which allowed his biological capabilities to be fully realised. At the point where animal instinct fails, writes Dennis Ford, culture takes over; indeed culture functions as a peculiarly human form of instinct. (Ford, 2007, 8)

Interestingly, the more that we have come in recent years to know about ourselves through the work of neuroscientists and others, the more we have come to appreciate Plato's inductive reasoning, his powers of observation. Our social interaction, writes Daniel Goleman, actually reshapes our brain through neuro-plasticity. Repeated experiences tend to re-sculpture the shape, size and number of neurons and their synaptic connections:

By repeatedly driving our brain into a given register, our key relationships can gradually mould certain neural circuitry. In effect, being chronically hurt and angered, or being emotionally nourished by someone we spend time with daily over the course of years, can re-fashion our brain … Thus how we connect with others has unimagined significance. (Goleman, 2006, 11)

This thinking is strikingly similar to a key insight formulated in the 1920s by the psychologist Edward Thorndyke who first coined the term 'social intelligence'—that too much emphasis was put on managing men and women. It was claimed that you were socially intelligent if you could manipulate others to do your bidding, or if you could con them into acting in accordance with your wishes for persuasion, of course, is always more effective than coercion. Goleman insists that being manipulative should not be seen as a sign of intelligence at all. 'Instead, we might think of social intelligence as a shorthand term for being intelligent not just *about* relationships, but also *in* them'. (Goleman, 2006, 11) (emphasis in original)

Such thinking is relatively recent. As late as the 1980s we tended to privilege cognitive skills and to assess people on the basis of IQ tests. Despite his own veneration of mathematics, Plato would have had no truck with the way in which, until comparatively recently, psychologists tended to hold to the opinion that social intelligence could be assessed almost entirely in terms of verbal and problem-solving abilities, and that social intelligence and general intelligence (measured by IQ tests) were largely identical. Plato would have dismissed this out of hand as a fundamental category error. Today we tend to follow him in attaching much more importance to skills such as the ability to empathise with others. 'Only connect' is E.M. Forster's famous injunction. Our brains are wired to connect; they are social, which explains why we are the sociable species the Greeks knew themselves to be. We really do better when we co-operate and laugh at the same jokes, and feel sympathy for those in pain or distress.

Of course, Plato did not write in such terms, and he certainly did not employ the language we use today, but he got there first through observation. Take a famous passage in the *Republic* when Socrates quotes from the *Odyssey* and reminds us of Odysseus' feelings when first meeting the importunate suitors who have been hounding his wife Penelope to remarry. Like a dog protecting its whelps, Homer tells us, Odysseus' first instinct is to punish them. In the lines immediately preceding the ones Socrates actually quotes, Homer tells us how the spirit within Odysseus 'barked like a dog'. Less than a page earlier, Plato had compared the spirit's indignation at injustice to the reaction of a dog. But unlike a dog, even with the advantage of thousands of years of domestication, Odysseus can restrain himself from taking his vengeance immediately by reasoning out what is prudent to do.

A dog in defending its young does so instinctively. It does not even weigh the consequences for itself. Human beings are far more calculating in putting their own survival first, which is why they tend to come out on top. Odysseus carefully weighs up the best strategies to adopt in pursuing his aim—vengeance. He calculates that an immediate attack would unmask him and put him at a grave disadvantage; it would not advance but defeat his purpose. He chooses instead to bide his time. Instead of acting on impulse, he reasons out that it would be more advantageous to wait, thus later regaining the freedom of action that he had temporarily lost.

In the *Discourses* the Greek philosopher Epictetus singled out the passage in which Homer wrote that Odysseus, like the lion, confided in his own strength. 'Confiding in what? Not in glory nor in riches, nor in dominion but in his own strength. That is in his principles concerning what things are in our power, what not. For these alone are what render us free'. (Origo, 1972, 244) Free will lies not in our power, but our decision when to use it. Physical powerlessness can be offset by cunning for which Odysseus was justly famous.

Imagination, therefore, is absolutely essential to reason. It does not suppress our instincts, it only allows us to set off one instinct against another—this is the vital insight, and William James seized upon it over a century ago when he told us that human beings have more instincts than any other animal. The ability to reason, to cancel out an impulse and simulate another, is what distinguishes us as a species because 'the animal richest in reason [is] also the animal richest in instinctive impulses, too. He [is] not the fatal automaton which a merely instinctive animal would be'. (Ridley, 2003, 39)

But the story of Odysseus also illustrates something that makes the human condition different again. Just as vengeance, itself, is a 'cultural construction' which is quite outside a dog's mental world, so too human beings have other appetites from dogs. And Plato discusses them at length in Books IV and VIII where he further qualifies them as dispositions; we have a disposition for food and shelter and security, but we are always in danger of over-securing ourselves or eating too much. We are usually disposed to seek things that are good for us, but we often crave things that are bad, either in the sense that they are bad in themselves—certain foods will make us ill—or because they put us at risk in trying to obtain them. Plato here is something of a consequentialist. He is not taking a moral attitude towards bad appetites, so much as a utilitarian one; dispositions are really habits, and bad habits are things whose outcome is bad for us. The point about a habit is that it is not born of a momentary whim, it is ingrained; we keep going back to it. We are only cured of a bad habit by experience (if we survive it) or by education (if we are willing to be instructed and allow reason or moderation to prevail).

But Martha Nussbaum takes the argument further still. An appetite is usually directed towards an object specific to itself. If we find ourselves thirsty it is natural that the brain triggers a thought: we try to assuage our own thirst. If we are hungry the brain encourages us to forage for food. Neither object is of value in itself; they are valued only for the need that we have of them at the time. An emotion is very different. It contains the thought of the object as something of intrinsic value or importance. To be fearful of something, like war or economic recession, for example, is not the same as to be frightened of the dark, or anxious about our health. We are fearful, frightened and anxious at different times, to the extent that we invest value in our relationships with other people or the forces of nature. An unreflective or unimaginative man would be quite fearless. You can only be thoughtful if you are fearful. For that reason, soldiers are taught to fear death; they are not, after all, very useful if they are dead. But they are also taught not to run away from death, for their death may have meaning for others (as a moral example). Likewise, to grieve at the loss of a friend is a common emotion, but the extent of that grief will be determined by how much we valued the friend in life. We grieve, to be frank, largely for ourselves; it is our loss that we really mourn.

There is another difference between an appetite and an emotion. A bodily appetite is a push (the body craves food and water). We can control a craving to a certain extent, but in the end it is independent of our desires, largely because it is a reflection of a bodily need. An emotion, by contrast, pulls us towards the object concerned. We covet what we value most and what is often unobtainable and the deadly sins are sins of desire, not need. They are sinful both because we desire them too much and because in obtaining those desires, we diminish ourselves. The miser accrues wealth he will never spend. The greedy man eats more food than he needs, denying it to the needful. And each sin inspires us to be ever more sinful: we are never satiated or satisfied. We continue to desire what is beyond our reach. (Nussbaum, 2001)

Once again, Plato is encouraging us to think of what makes us human. What inheres in our humanity, he is arguing, is our capacity to live within the mean, to tame our aggressive insights, appetites and emotions not by suppressing them but by ensuring they are in harmony with each other. Our emotions are not unique to us. Other animals experience fear and can display affection, some even for us. But culture gives us the ability to re-value and devalue what we desire and love. We can redirect it, if necessary.

A nun can invest in love of God, leading an entirely celibate, but emotionally charged life. And our fears can be managed through knowledge and training (anxiety is rather different; it is easier to argue someone out of a fear than out of a deep anxiety).

As Nussbaum adds, all emotions are important because they lead to action, but not particular types of action. If we fear something or someone, we have a choice; we can move to a different neighbourhood or a gated community; or we can bond together with other people in Neighbourhood Watch schemes. If we are moved to anger, we can retaliate for some perceived or real injustice or slight, or we can take the person to law and seek financial compensation, or simply turn the other cheek and 'win' a reputation for ourselves in the court of moral opinion. But we all have to act. That is what emotions are for, that is the point of social intelligence as a survival mechanism. But it is because our emotions are evaluative, it is because we attach value to what other people also fear, love or covet, that we can reason out our actions. (Nussbaum, 2001)

And Plato was the very first philosopher to recognise that appetite, spirit and reason interact. It is because they are invested in an object that is valued that we reason out how to get them. Reason is there from the start in the evaluation. You cannot attach value except by reasoning out why what you value is so valuable to you. The warrior values his reputation on the battlefield as much as the merchant values his reputation in the marketplace (and neither holds the other's reputation in particularly high regard, because they value different things).

The importance of embodied intelligence

What makes Plato's contribution so interesting is that he was one of the few Greek authors not to over-privilege culture. For when the Greeks called war 'the human thing' their construction of humanity was almost entirely cultural, not biological, and it yet it is one that we are still familiar with today. Plato's work owes much more than most Greek models to nature rather than nurture; or perhaps, more to the point, it refuses to make any major distinction between them. Plato's contribution to knowledge is not to deny the supreme importance of rationality but to remind us that mind and body are not separate; we are only rational when we listen to our 'hearts;' we are only really 'reasonable' to the extent that our emotions make us so. In that critical respect Plato took further our understanding of war as a human thing by bringing nature back into the picture. Plato was insistent that the body is 'in' the soul rather than the soul in the body, and from this he could even argue, as he does just once in the *Republic*, that women could be warriors too, though he took the thought no further.

It is often claimed, of course, that as a philosopher Plato was much more interested in idealised versions of reality. If Thucydides was interested in 'the human thing', Plato and the philosophers who followed in his wake were interested only in 'the thing-in-itself', the so called Forms of the object abstracted from their individual instances in the world. Historians pen history by studying various instances in which human nature is revealed— courage and baseness, brutality, stupidity, treachery and ambition, as well as striking examples of human ingenuity and acts of individual and collective heroism. Historians are interested in concrete examples of the highs and lows, such as examples of greatness of mind. Philosophers, by contrast, try to abstract ruling principles. In the case of war they are more interested in its nature than its character—its unpredictability and the fact that, try though we may, we will never reduce it to a set of scientific rules. And while historians use their senses—their eyes to read the historical records and their ears to learn from eyewitness accounts—philosophers usually engage in adventures of the mind; they seek the truth in the mind's eye.

But all this is something of a caricature and it is not what Plato himself actually claimed. One of the most significant features of Plato's Forms, writes Miriam Leonard, is that the Greek word he chose to describe them actually comes from the vocabulary of physical seeing: the word *eidos* is a cognate of the verb *horao* (to see). In other words, one can only perceive the unseen—the essence of things—through the physical senses. 'In the word *eidos* Plato conflates an idealist philosophy (a philosophy based around the reality of ideas) with an empiricist (experience based) vocabulary. The trace of the body stubbornly seems to survive in Plato's disembodied Forms'. (Leonard, 2008, 34)

Ultimately, there is no escaping the body. All intelligence, even the most abstract and abstruse reasoning, is embodied, a vital insight that most philosophers continued to deny until comparatively recently. Even our imagination, one of the most distinctive of all human characteristics, is entirely connected to our bodily experiences. We cannot actually 'experience' even in the mind anything outside the boundaries of our own notions of time, space and embodiment. We cannot, for example, image an eight dimensional world, though some mathematicians tell us we probably live in one.

We can entertain the thought, of course, in a disembodied fashion, but we can't actually imagine what such a world would be like because our bodies extend to only four dimensions. So although thanks to science we can hear the 'song' of the whale and science has told us that bats 'see' quite differently from human beings, for all our scientific advances we still can't imagine, any more than could have Aristotle, what it would actually be like to 'see' like a bat or to 'sing' like a whale, and we can't imagine either for the simple reason that we can't experience them. (Carter 2006, 128)

But where we differ most from Thucydides is in our knowledge that human nature is not necessarily unchanging. 'The most definitive feature of antiquity is our absence', wrote Joseph Brodsky. (Brodsky, 1996, 272) Indeed, for we have continued to evolve. We would have as much difficulty in seeing ourselves in Thucydides as he would in us. Culture is everything. And we also know what Thucydides did not: that the changes within our owns species have been dramatic, much more so than the changes between *Homo sapiens* and, say, *Homo erectus*. Indeed, a Martian taxonomist studying the evolution of hominids, writes Bilayanur Ramachandram, might think we were a different species from early Man, and that the early *Homo sapiens* and *Homo erectus* were a single species, not two. (Ramachandran, 2003, 127) And what of a new race that may emerge in due course, or is the very process of emerging: *Homo cyberneticus*, the post-human species to come?

And technology?

Broadly speaking, *Warrior Geeks* seeks to show that humanity and war have co-evolved as Thucydides understood, not through the help of science but simply through observation; war moulded the way humans understood themselves, and that understanding in turn, once it emerged and cohered, determined the way they fought it. It may be true that there is only one human nature, but war has produced across time and cultures different ideas about human nature, and in many ways this may be most important, not least because our ideas about our own humanity are changing again, thanks to technological changes that are rewriting our understanding of what it means to be human, just as they are rewiring our brains and thus our physical 'humanity'.

This would have defeated the Greeks' understanding. The only surviving treatise from the ancient world which mentions technology at all is another work of Aristotle, the *Rhetoric*, where the word *techne* (skill/craft) is joined

57

to the word *logos* (speech). Four times in the course of the essay, Aristotle refers to *technelogos*, although in each case the exact meaning is unclear. After the *Rhetoric*, the word disappears entirely from the literature. Technology, of course, did not. The Greeks invented the lathe, the bellows and the key, yet technology as a concept remained largely invisible to them.

And what they had was pretty rudimentary. The Greek world was lit only by fire, fuelled by wood and water, and clothed for the most part from the produce of acres that had yielded to plough and pasture. The Greeks lived in a world without printing, gunpowder, the stirrup, the windmill or the compass. Coal and mineral oil were not burned as fuel. Olive oil in lamps or beeswax in candles provided the only night-time illumination. Theirs was a world not without technology but without the technology we take for granted—for them the world they had created was one that put a premium not on machines, but on the use of tools.

They also drew a rigid distinction between the animate and inanimate worlds. Thucydides, like most Greeks, drew other rigid binomial distinctions—all cultural—between Greeks and barbarians and between men and women (the difference between men and women was gendered, not biological). It is also true that sometimes these binomial distinctions were obscured. Greeks could treat each other as barbarians did themselves; men could be effeminate; women could show a strength considered beyond their 'sex'; even the gap between gods and mortals could be breached (men could become divine and join the pantheon of Immortals). But the Greeks also drew another distinction between the material and the immaterial, or humanity and the tools they used, although in one interesting respect, humans too could become 'tools'. Slaves were described as 'talking tools', but even Aristotle, who notoriously defended the practice of slavery, did not deny that they had souls. Indeed, he defined a slave as an en-souled (*empsukhon*) tool. (Cartledge, 2002, 136)

Interestingly, they did not draw a rigid line between human beings and animals. They did not deny our innate animality. Nor did they claim—as many present day writers still do—that we have an animal nature, and also a human one which can only be accounted for on its own terms. The Greeks did not even privilege reason as we were to do centuries later. Aristotle attributed *phronesis* (or practical rationality) to some, though not all, non-human animals (*Nichomachean Ethics* 6. 1140 1 4–6). Where they differed radically from us was in insisting on the difference not between the human and non-human, but between the organic and inorganic—between humanity and machine.

Our attitude towards technology is very different. We now acknowledge that we are one of seven species of ape, but the only one that has incorporated artifice into its way of being. Only we on the planet are not governed entirely by the Darwinian dynamic of natural selection. Only we have an extra-somatic means of adaptation (Taylor, 2010, 19). It is called culture, and culture, though the Greeks did not appreciate this, is actually technological in nature, whether we are talking about language, cities, or machines. Culture is part of our evolutionary heritage, and it is what makes us an incomplete species, for we need technology to realise our potential. Of all animals we are the ones that display 'an unbelievable degree of behavioural plasticity' and the reason is simple—our genetic under-determination is itself genetically determined. (Gellner, 1984, 515)

Since the dawn of human history—long before we began talking about our ability to genetically engineer ourselves—we have been re-engineering ourselves through technology, trading in physical strength for intellectual upgrades. (Taylor, 2010, 28) In the course of ten thousand years our bodies have diminished significantly. Our stature has decreased by 7 per cent. We have lost 10 per cent of our skeletal robustness. Our bones are significantly weaker than they were, not as much as some of the animals that we have domesticated such as cattle, but significantly nonetheless. But we have compensated for this loss of physical strength through artifice; we have augmented our physical and mental capabilities artificially. Human vision is not acute as it was when we were hunter-gatherers striving to glimpse the horizon, but our vision is enhanced by insight (thanks to writing and reading), and even our sight is enhanced thanks to ground glass, hydrate silicon and fibre optics.

Human beings have only used telescopes for 400 years, but we can make use of them for a purpose that is peculiarly human. A chimp in captivity, for example, can be trained to recognise and identify a chair, but it will never grasp that a chair is part of an ensemble—usually it goes with a table. We know that because we invented both and made them into an ensemble, but the important point is that we can recognise that a table is missing because of our ability to immediately 'see' something that is not there. When a general first used a telescope on the battlefield he was not only trying to see more clearly the dispositions of the enemy but also to confirm what he expected to find, or to second guess an enemy's intentions from what he had already inferred. And this made a decisive advantage in the history of war. Those with access to telescopic sight on guns usually prevail over those who have to rely on eye co-ordination, and those with remote guidance systems (fibre optics) can be expected—all things being equal—to prevail over those who rely on telescopic sights. (Taylor, 2010, 186)

Of all the tools the Greeks used, language remained the most important. In an account from the 1st century BC by the historian Diodorus Siculus, which is almost certainly drawn from a long lost 6th-century pre-Socratic source, we have a striking early insight into the importance of language in human development.

> Such is the account we receive of the first creation of everything, and they say that the first men to come into existence lived an unsettled and brutish life, going out to forage in ones and twos, and eating the most agreeable of the plants and the wild fruits. Attacks by wild beasts made them learn from expediency and come to one another's aid, and as they repeatedly gathered together from fear, they gradually came to know each other's features. Slowly, they made articulate the utterances of their tongues, which at first were indistinct and unclear, and by making conventions among themselves about each object they taught themselves to use words to refer to everything. And because such groups formed all over the inhabited earth, not all men had the same language, because each group fixed its words arbitrarily. This is the reason why there are now all sorts of different languages, the first groups to form being the ancestors of all the different races of men. (Mount, 2010, 177)

What the Greeks were able to grasp is that language is a tool and we are what tools make of us. They could appreciate, for example, how the tool is an extension of physical embodiment like a spear that is merely an extension of the hand. And Aristotle understood the importance of the hand well enough. The human hand with its fully opposable thumb and unique freedom of movement of the index finger enables us to point. A baby that points at a very early age is sharing the world with us. Pointing creates a public space. Because the world is shared, we are a social species. Once we are able to grasp the hand as a 'pointer' we are able to invent other 'tools' to extend human reach, both physical and mental.

And the Greeks were able to grasp without formally articulating the proposition that language had helped turn the mind into a tool. Technology really does change modes of thought. Language is not a technology, of course; it is hard-wired into us. Writing, by contrast, is an invention; it is a product of culture, and it is a revolutionary technology because it has helped us to transform our humanity. Writing encompasses a special form of linguistic activity associated with particular kinds of problem raising and problem solving that we associate with the list, the formula, or the table. Reading really has changed us. It allows us to divorce a statement from its author; and take it out of context, and reflect upon it later rather than at the time it is formulated. It permits a quite different kind of scrutiny of the 'truth'. And both scientific and philosophical thought require scepticism. Oral societies found it difficult to develop lines of sceptical thinking because they could never be left alone with their thoughts. As Jack Goody concludes, oral societies were marked not so much by an absence of reflective thinking as by an absence of the proper tools for constructive thought. (Goody, 1995, 44)

So it is no coincidence that the great breakthroughs in Greek thought came with the reinvention of writing after it had disappeared in the chaos of the Dark Ages which followed upon the collapse of the Mycenaean age. When Plato composed his dialogues writing was only 300 years old in the form with which he was familiar, the first complete phonetic alphabet ever invented with its own unique economy of characters—just 24 which represented all the sounds or phonemes used in their spoken language. Writing, in W.H. Auden's words, changed the way we thought about thinking. But writing did more; it changed the way we actually thought. 'We are what we read', writes Maryanne Wolf: 'the secret at the heart of the reading is the time it frees for the brain to have thoughts deeper and deeper than those which came before'. (Wolf, 2008) Reading, she explains, is not an instinctive skill. It is not genetic in the way that speech is. It requires us to translate the symbolic characters we see on the page, or these days on the screen, into a language we understand. And the technology we have employed to practice the craft, from the papyrus roll to the printed book, has reshaped, in turn, the neural circuits inside our brain.

Reading quite literally re-wires the brain. In one of Plato's dialogues, Socrates ruminates that writing has made for shallower thinking. Discourse reveals truth in a way that writing cannot; it directly affects the 'soul of the hearer'. Socrates is willing to admit that writing does have some advantages—it is especially useful as one enters old age and begins to forget so much of what one has learned—but it also alters the mind, and not in ways that are necessarily to our advantage. It offers us no real wisdom, only a semblance of learning. It makes us, he argued, much shallower thinkers.

Now this is Socrates' view; or so Plato would have us to believe. We have no way of knowing whether the real Socrates actually held this opinion or not, but we can be pretty sure that Plato himself didn't. As Nicholas Carr speculates, what is important about Plato is that we have everything that he ever wrote. He is the foundation stone of the Western canon for that reason. And he is famous for banning the poets from his ideal republic. But what is often overlooked is that Plato had his reasons. For poetry in his day was part of the oral tradition; it was declaimed in public, and the same had been true of early philosophy; for example, one of the most famous of the pre-Socratic philosophers, Parmenides, constructed his works in hexameter verse. Carr suggests that Plato wanted to ban poetry, not because he was against verse, but because he recognised that writing allowed one to be more analytical in one's thinking. In his case, it allowed him to create a new kind of philosophy, only made possible because of the effects that writing was beginning to have on mental processes. What Plato could see in himself was that writing opened minds. Writing, writes the classical scholar Walter J. Ong, is essential for the realization of a fuller, interior, potentially richer human life. It makes it possible to become what nature intended for us; to become ourselves. (Carr, 2010, 57)

Our humanity, in short, is provisional. Within the next thirty years we will continue to evolve in ways that will radically change our humanity, perhaps for the better, perhaps for the worse. With every step towards integrating ourselves into the technological infrastructure that governs our lives, we are becoming something quite different from the human beings that our ancestors would recognise. We are edging towards what Jürgen Habermas calls 'the auto-transformation of the species'. The time has arrived, writes Craig Venter, when we will be able to compress billions of years (3.5 billion years of evolution) into decades, and change not only the way we view life conceptually, but life itself. Daniel Dennett is no less enthusiastic: 'When you no longer need to eat to stay alive or procreate to have offspring, or locomote to have an adventure-packed life, when the residual instincts for these activities might be simply turned off by genetic tweaking, there may be no constant to human nature after all'. (Bauman, 2010, 143)

What Plato could not have grasped is the man-machine fusion. The human body is naturally disposed to develop and incorporate tools; we have always been, to a greater or lesser extent, cyborgs, even if the word is a new one, dating in fact only from the 1950s. Whether it is the use of paper or wrist watches, or more recently computers, cellular phones and neural implants, our brains are naturally adapted to merge their performance with the technological infrastructure they need to develop their full potential.

And we now know that our brains adapt to new technologies throughout our life, and not merely in our youth as we once thought. All this gives some credence to Andy Clark's claim that the cyborg condition is just an extension of our evolution. (Clark, 2003, 23–24) To argue that to date we have incorporated only a very small percentage of non-biological components into our bodies is largely beside the point. What makes us natural cyborgs (or, to use the term Clark prefers, 'human technology symbiotes') is the way in which our sense of self is determined by our relationship with technology.

The only difference is that the process is speeding up. The boundary we still feel between ourselves and technology is beginning to break down completely, with the result that our symbiotic relationship with machines may transform our lives far faster than ever before. For Clark, the key is the dovetailing of humanity and technology, and an example he gives is a commonplace but important one. When asked whether we know the meaning of a word, we may have recourse to a dictionary stored somewhere out of reach (in the office or at home), and when we are asked whether we know the time, we usually answer with the flick of a wrist and look at the watch we are wearing. 'Knowing' the time—the very term itself—shows that who we are is determined by what we invent. Many of these inventions have become almost invisible to us. 'There is no merger so intimate as that which is barely noticed', writes Clark, like the watch we wear on our wrists every day. (Clark, 2003, 29)

Already it is possible to wear a headband at night which will measure deep and light sleep patterns. Diabetics can now assess their blood sugar levels; people suffering from high blood pressure can monitor their levels of hypertension. If you buy a mileage tracker you can monitor the number of calories burned up during the day and record them on a spreadsheet in the office. You can buy an earlobe monitor, a blood pressure cuff on an arm and a heart rate monitor that can be strapped to the chest, all of which will enable a person to adjust their lifestyle. In the not too distant future, when a woman goes to the bathroom in the morning digital scales will be able to record her weight and body mass and send data to an online data file; and another monitor will be able to analyse her urine samples to allow her to adjust her intake of Vitamin B.

And within twenty years, much as engineers analyse data and tweak specifications in order to optimise a software program, military commanders will be able to bio-hack into their soldiers' brains and bodies, collecting and correlating data the better to optimise their physical and mental performance. They will be able to reduce distractions and increase productivity and achieve 'flow'—the optimum state of focus. Plato explained how social intelligence had allowed warriors to determine when it was appropriate to hide a feeling or to express it and to know how best to communicate 'spiritedness' in ways that were consistent with the demands of discipline. His discussion was the first of its kind. But will tomorrow's warriors still need the skills Plato taught them? For technology is offering a chance to correlate their own emotions with their personal habits, anxiety levels and adrenalin rushes and to tailor them accordingly as their behaviour is monitored. Trapped in a cybernetic system, will tomorrow's warriors be scanned like bar codes in a supermarket; will their binary secrets be decoded by their commanders cast in the role of holographic scanners?

3

CHEERFUL ROBOTS

Panic at Mantinea (418 BC)

The battle took place on open ground, a narrow plain where two sides could fight in a kill box and did so in August 418 BC, 20,000 soldiers in all. Few tourists today visit the site, writes Victor Davis Hanson.

> The new freeway interchange is about 5 miles distant; and the ugly modern cement city of Tripolis lies about 10 miles away. There is nothing here at the battlefield but a few country homes, a bizarre church that a wild-eyed eccentric spent his life building by scrounging marble and bricks from the countryside, and the traces of a vast lost city that peeks out amid the weeds and wheat fields. But walk carefully again through this plain. Scan the random blocks of the amphitheatre, climb among the fallen bastions of the one great circuit wall, navigate through the precincts of the ancient sanctuaries of Heracles and Poseidon, and far from being empty, Mantinea is, in fact, full of ghosts. (Hanson, 2006, 154–5)

The ghosts include those of the men who died in the great battle that Thucydides reported, in what may actually have been a first-hand account. Whether this is so or not, it is the most vivid example of a hoplite battle in surviving literature. It was also the largest battle of the Peloponnesian War (a conflict which saw very few set piece engagements).

The two armies, Thucydides tells us, were not quite evenly matched, but neither enjoyed a decisive advantage. The Spartan army was not really Spartan. It had a core element, but Sparta was already running out of native Spartans and was forced to rely on freed slaves and others such as the mountain people from the borderland of Arcadia, who were given the dubious privilege of facing the enemy's best troops on the right of the line. The allied army included 12,000 Hoplites, veteran soldiers, and other more lightly armed men from a coalition of cities. Only about 1,000 Athenians were actually present that day. Essentially a Spartan army of 9,000 men was pitted against a slightly inferior Argive force.

The engagement began with the Spartans marching towards the enemy left flank to the music of pipes. They advanced at a steady pace, Thucydides tells us, 'with no confusion in their spirits, calmly and cheerfully', without 'excessive fear or passion'. (Thucydides, Peloponnesian War, Book 5, 70) The music was intended to make them calm and 'to remove their anger'. Anyone who was not quick enough to escape (those who did trampled each other down) were impaled on their spears. The Spartan advance was implacable.

The victorious Spartans then turned hard left and continued on laterally along a now broken battle line. It was at this point that the most famous incident in the battle occurred, one that opened up a brief—very brief—opportunity for the other side to seize victory from defeat. As the armies approached each other, the Spartan force drifted to the right. It was a well known phenomenon of hoplite battles. As the Hoplites advanced, the last man on the right did not want to see an enemy soldier advancing on his unprotected right side, so he tended to edge right himself. His fellow hoplites would often follow him, each seeking to shield his unprotected right side with the shield of the man next to him. For that reason, commanders usually put their best men on the right of the line. At Mantinea, as the armies turned on an axis, a gap opened up. The Spartan commander ordered two subordinate commanders to plug it, but they refused. It is true that the manoeuvre was unorthodox; Hoplites, once heading towards each other, relied on shock encounter, and tended to hope for the best. But it is also possible that they too were infected by the same sense of fear. In other words, they lost their nerve. In the event, their disobedience did not affect the outcome of the battle. The Allied generals were out in front, unable to see or seize the opportunity, and the battle went eventually in Sparta's favour. The Spartan right wing, making a hard left, struck their counterparts on the flanks. The outcome was a massacre, though the Spartans did not pursue the defeated enemy as they broke in confusion.

As Hanson adds in his vivid description of the battle, 'the professionals who so rarely had the opportunity to put their long training into practice the Spartan hoplites at Mantinea killed as if it were second nature'. (Hanson, 2006, 157) And the key to the Spartans' victory was duty, which they were encouraged to put before everything else. Thucydides reports that a Spartan king once told his soldiers that they would win a reputation for their ancestors and themselves, not by winning or losing a battle the following day but by how the issue would be determined. Death, according to a Spartan poet, usually avoided soldiers who 'stood firm, supporting each other, holding the front line'. (Meier, 2011, 153) What counted most was discipline—following where they were led and observing good order. Historians ever since Thucydides have grasped that of all the human attributes discipline is the most intriguing feature of any battle. John Keegan invokes this in his justly admired work *The Face of Battle* (1976), which established his reputation as one of the world's leading military historians:

What battles have in common is human … the study of battle is therefore always a study of fear and usually of courage … always of anxiety and sometimes of elation or catharsis … always of violence, sometimes also of cruelty; self-sacrifice, compassion; above all it is always the study of solidarity, and usually also of disintegration … for it is towards the disintegration of human groups that battle is directed. (Keegan, 2004, 83)

Fear led the Athenian side at Mantinea to break ranks and run (it is always fatal on any battlefield to turn your back on the enemy). One of the most famous Athenian generals, Laches (after whom Plato names one of his dialogues), was speared in the back as he was running away. Turning one's back on an enemy was about the most dangerous thing to do; effectively, it meant disarming oneself and throwing away the greatest advantage one has in the heat of battle—solidarity, the security of the primary group.

In Plato's dialogue *Laches* the general comes over as a somewhat unreflective commander who is inclined to think that any military question can be settled by asking, 'What do the Spartans say?' He is clearly a man of limited intelligence for when asked to define courage he thinks entirely in military terms and claims it is standing at one's post, something which he himself was to conspicuously fail to do at Mantinea. For Socrates, physical courage was not enough; a soldier had to display moral fortitude and self-knowledge. Courage can often be no more than lack of imagination, or recklessness, or plain stupidity, none of which the military seek to cultivate in soldiers. To be useful instrumentally courage must be accompanied by judgement—the knowledge of what risks it is wise to run. Exercising any virtue requires exercising others. This is what training and drill develop, but when discipline breaks down you forget everything you have been trained to remember. When courage fails so too does prudence; a soldier may turn and flee the field, turning his back to the enemy as Laches himself was to do, and paying the price for his imprudence. Battle, as Keegan claims, is always aimed at the disintegration of human groups.

All of this presupposes two levels of analysis. One, which Thucydides grasped, was the importance of the primary group; the other, which eluded him, was the interior psychic economy of each soldier, the 'self' that novelists like Tolstoy sought to develop through characterization. Indeed, the 'self' is something we ourselves find more fascinating than the Greeks, for unlike them we have discovered the central importance of psychology. It is the essence of what Emerson called 'heroic self-belief'. Both factors are essential to understanding how primary group cohesion is networked.

No-one can live without a network. Whether for good or ill, we are stuck with the networks to which we belong. Networking is what we do; it is hard-wired into us. The loneliest person you know is locked within a network, not least because *you* know him or her. We are born into networks and we join many in the course of our lives. Networks came before the state. It is the ties between individuals that allow them to become groups, factions, or lobbies, parties and movements, all of which are greater than the sum of their respective parts. The state is merely a larger network and because of its complexity encourages large-scale networking among its citizens. This idea has taken on a life of its own. For Adam Smith, the network was essentially the market and the invisible hand that shaped political life. For G.W. Hegel, it was history, and the great social forces it unleashed. In the mid-20th century it was identity politics which you find at the heart of liberal multiculturalism. Ultimately, you are gay, or black, or Muslim, or a woman (the politics of feminism). Today, we tend to think much more in terms of social networking.

And one of the oldest networks of all is the military. The immediate network is very small: the basic unit of the Roman army (the maniple) was 120 men. The average size of a modern unit, a company, is about the same, which suggests that through trial and error, this has been found to be the optimal size for networking that allows for maximum communication and co-operation. All patterns, whether they are emergent and self-organising or deliberately engineered, are what complexity theorists call 'fractal'—they keep reappearing in recognizable form. And the same shapes keep turning up in war for a reason. Indeed, write Nicolas Christakis and James Fowler in their book *Connected* (2010), 'one can even imagine that warfare presents a particular kind of evolutionary selection pressure that armies across the centuries have arrived at this working size by empirical observation of what size group is most likely to survive'. (Chritiakis/Fowler, 2010, 248) And the unit is further networked lower down. A company of a hundred soldiers is typically organised into ten tightly inter-connected squads of ten men, which is just large enough for each to know the others by name (and probably disposition), and to know just how effectively they will co-operate in a crisis—whether, for example, they can be relied upon or not. For the ties within squads are usually much tighter than the ties between them. (Christiakis/Fowler, 2010, 12)

Every social network is distinguished by two fundamental features: connection and contagion. (Christiakis/Fowler, 2010,16) When we see an army as a network, we can see the importance of primary group cohesion. The Hoplite soldiers who stood in line at Mantinea would have known each other personally; on the Athenian side many would have sat together in the Assembly, agreeing or disagreeing on the conduct of the war. 'A troop [can] never be stronger', wrote Xenophon, 'than one that is formed of fellow-combatants that are friends'. (*Cyropaedia* 7.1.30)

At various times in history connections in war have been reinforced by drill. The Spartans deployed and redeployed to the sound of flutes which allowed them to interact in unison, and Plutarch, echoing this centuries later, noted how it had an impact on soldiers' minds. 'It was once a magnificent and terrible sight to see them march on to the sound of their flutes without any disorder in their ranks, any de-composure in their minds or change in their countenances, calmly and cheerfully moving with music to the deadly fight'. (McNeil, 1995, 116) The passage is quoted by William McNeill whose book, *Keeping together in Time*, develops what he calls an unconventional notion that is simplicity itself. People who move together to the same beat tend to bond, for moving to the same beat, whether in dancing or marching, alters human feelings and thoughts. Music, in other words, is a powerful means of building cohesion. Einstein once said that providing soldiers with a brain was unnecessary; all you need to march in step is a spinal cord. The Spartans didn't march in step but they marched in rhythm, and without a brain music simply will not resonate in the mind.

Plato, too, recognised the importance of music for military discipline. He writes about it in Book VII of the *Republic*. He mentions four principal branches of knowledge which are important for society, three of which are especially important for the military. One is arithmetic which allows a general to count his troops and dispose of them effectively; another is geometry which is important in building fortifications and setting up camps; and a third is music which sets the mood in war and peace. Music has an emotive power that increases group bonding and inspires acts of courage. More important, it is also the origin of drill, for music aids sequential and parallel timing of different movements, combining them to make a single continuous activity. And all training is improved by repetition. (Barrow, 2005, 230–31) When the brain sends out signals to the limbs unevenly muscles are often tensed, but constant repetition gets the nervous system to discard unproductive movements. Continuity and synchronization are the basis of all drill.

The second feature that social networks have in common is contagion. A better word, perhaps, would be imitation: by nature we imitate others; when others panic, we do. Armies, especially when under pressure and facing defeat, are notorious for breaking up. Demoralization, like disaffection and mutiny, are especially contagious. And panic is notoriously difficult to prevent when discipline breaks down. We should see panic as a form of emergent behaviour, the property of a unit that has lost its self-belief. An emergent property such as panic is a reflection of collective intelligence and collective intelligences do not always make intelligent decisions, as Thucydides was at pains to point out.

Today, we enjoy one advantage that Thucydides did not have. We can model human behaviour virtually; we can see how contagion works, and what damage it can do when humans interact in a network. So let us fast forward to our own age and an extraordinary episode in the history of one of the most popular games played on the internet: the *World of Warcraft*. Its appeal is that it is team-based. It requires human skills, but skills that can best be displayed in a group. Players are wired into a system that allows them to communicate with others, to plan strategies and fight battles. Because it is a virtual game, no-one dies when their characters are killed.

And then something happened in September 2005 that the game's designers had not foreseen. In that month a new 'level' of the game came on line which contained a winged serpent that could infect other players with a contagious disease called 'corrupt blood'. When one player succumbed, those in close proximity to him were equally at risk. The point of the game was to kill the winged serpent and continue the play. But the behaviour of humans is unpredictable, and games, like war, encourage you to cheat, or take shortcuts. Some infected players 'teleported' to other areas of the game, carrying the infection with them. Some players, on returning home, infected their families and thus their cities. And those who were immune served as 'carriers' which made things even worse. As a result, what began as a localised infection quickly became an epidemic. The programmers were baffled, but undaunted. They did what programmers can do in a game—they pulled the plug and rebooted the servers. End of problem.

The reason for recounting this extraordinary tale is that even in a virtual world environment, human beings act as humans do: when panic sets in it becomes virulently contagious. Those who were quarantined tried to escape; others fled, bringing the contagion with them and spreading the virus even further afield; some players even infected themselves deliberately so that they could teleport to enemy cities and spread the plague. What interested the Department of Homeland Security in what happened in September 2005 was how the *World of Warcraft* spawned new players: terrorist cells.

Henry Fleming wins his spurs

'Some years ago', recalled the classical scholar E.R. Dodds:

I was in the British Museum looking at the Parthenon sculptures when a man came up to me and said with a worried look: 'I know it's an awful thing to confess, but this Greek stuff doesn't move me one bit'. I said that this was interesting; could he define at all the reasons for his response. He reflected for a minute or two. Then he said. 'Well, it's all so terribly rational, if you know what I mean'. I thought I did.

This chance encounter set Dodds thinking and resulted in *The Greeks and the Irrational* (1951), one of the most innovative books to have been written in the field of classical studies. Dodds was at pains to point out that the Greeks were much more irrational than generally thought, with their gods, myths, religious festivals and soothsayers as well as their belief in fate. He began his book with a quote from William James, 'the recesses of feeling, the darker, blinder states of character, are the only places in the world in which we catch real fact in the making'. Thucydides was able to grasp by intuition the rational side of war—the human networking. Brothers do indeed bond; social networking is the essence of every society. Although he didn't have the scientific tools to explain his observation he was able to grasp the significance of music and drill in creating primary group cohesion.

Ironically, however, it was the darker side—the psychological, the interior self—that he was unable to comprehend. William James was a psychologist; today we have neuroscientists who have added much to our understanding of 'real fact' in the making. What the men who fought at Mantinea were thinking is not Thucydides' theme. It is, of course, the central theme of any story we tell about war because it is essential to modern self-understanding.

We do not have a first hand account of the soldiers' minds in any of the surviving Greek sources, but we do have a classic 19ᵗʰ-century novel, *The Red Badge of Courage*, by the writer Stephen Crane, which used to be required reading for American schoolchildren. Crane may never have seen a battle in his life but this makes *The Red Badge of Courage*, if not a great novel, certainly an imaginative *tour de force*, and the accomplishment was recognised at the time by veterans of the Civil War such as George Wyndham who reviewed the book when it was first published, and added that it echoed his own experience of war. The novel could have been the tale of a believable young man in an unbelievable melodrama; it is not, which is why it has survived the test of time.

The novel revolves almost entirely around an anonymous battlefield in 1863 in the northern Virginian countryside near the Rappahannock river. The hero is a young Union soldier, Henry Fleming, one of the most famous fictional characters in war. Henry is an interesting case study. He is a young man of feeling—a romantic inspired to join up by the Greek epic tales he has read in his youth. We are told the young Henry had long despaired of witnessing a Greek-like struggle. 'Such would be no more, he had said. Men were better or more timid'. When he finally joins up he knows that the battles he will witness may 'not be distinctly Homeric' but he expects to win his spurs. 'His busy mind had drawn for him large pictures extravagant in colour, lurid with breathless deeds'. (Crane, 1976, 5) In other words, our young man is inspired by the same Homeric thoughts that would have inspired many of the protagonists who fought on both sides at Mantinea.

But Henry lacks self-belief. He leaves home with his mother's advice in his ear—when threatened with danger, he should trust to his feelings. But Henry does not trust that he will behave well when called upon to do so. He is appalled at the thought he may fail his first test, his baptism of fire. And this proves to be the case. For once he finds himself under fire he becomes quickly convinced that his comrades and he are being led to the slaughter. Fear gets the better of him. He drops his rifle and runs away.

Fortunately, no-one actually witnesses his flight, so that when he rejoins his unit he can still look others in the eye; he has still preserved his manliness in the eyes of others, which is where manliness must always be reaffirmed. Let me quote a passage from the book which is one most often cited in commentaries and school text books:

His self-pride was now entirely restored. In the shade of its flourishing growth he stood with braced and self-confident legs, and since nothing could now be discovered he did not shrink from an encounter with the eyes of judges and allowed no thoughts of his own to keep him from an attitude of manfulness. He had performed his mistakes in the dark, so he was still a man. (Crane, 1976, 64)

War is indeed one of the traditional tests of manhood, and has been almost from the beginning. The Greek word *andreia* (courage) is also the word for manliness. And one of the principle tests of the latter is standing firm under fire, man to man. What Crane is showing us is that Henry's 'manfulness' is entirely inauthentic, and he knows it well enough.

Crane was reflecting a critical insight of 19th-century psychologists, that shame can be triggered by a thought. We can shame ourselves and find it difficult to live the life of the man that we know we are, rather than who we would like to be. But more often than not, we are ashamed of what we have become in the eyes of others, including our friends. Friends are a captive audience before whom we enact an idealised version of our own life. We acknowledge them because they are prepared to take us at our own estimation of ourselves, and we reciprocate. Sometimes the ideal and the reality are not so very different. Sometimes the differences are clearly obvious to those outside the network of friends. The point Crane is making is that Henry will only feel guilt at his own behaviour if his lie is discovered. Feelings in this case are triggered by a thought, and for the young Henry thoughts matter. He joined up not to fight for a cause, but to gain a reputation. It is only when he returns to the battlefield and proves himself in battle that he becomes much less selfish.

Henry's new confidence comes from mastering his thoughts. 'His mind was undergoing a subtle change … gradually his brain emerged from the clogged clouds so that at last he was able to more closely comprehend himself and circumstances'. He finds his eyes are 'opened to some new ways' of seeing; and his enhanced vision allows him to master his fear. The novel is essentially a story about his psychological readjustment to reality and what makes this possible—his reintegration into the network, the primary group.

He became not a man but a member … [the network] gave him assurance. The noise [of the regiment] gave him assurance … it wheezed and banged with a mighty power … he felt the subtle battle of brotherhood more potent even than the cause for which they were fighting. It was a mysterious fraternity born of the smoke and danger of death. (Crane, 1994, 26)

No longer an individual, but a member of a network, a man 'welded into a common personality … dominated by a single desire'. A self-obsessed young man discovers the false pride of his past and through battle reinvents himself. After fleeing the battlefield he had dismissed those who had chosen to stand and fight as 'imbeciles' and even those who had joined him in flight as 'fools' for fighting without 'discretion or dignity'. It is the battle experience that gives Henry the imagination to empathise with others, the brave and the not so brave; the glory hunters and those whose only concern is to return home in one piece, rather than to be feted as heroes.

There is now an extensive literature on the ways in which personal bonds between soldiers are so important in the formation of what we call the 'primary group'. And primary groups are held together by bonds of comradeship produced by social proximity. In an interesting observation Anthony King suggests that the basis of military comradeship, so distinctive in the eyes of an outsider, may not be grounded in personal relationships at all, so much as in military proficiency. Friendships are often squandered by bad practices, especially those that put another soldier's life at risk. Comradeship is a gift that can be offered or withheld, and studies of modern units would suggest that it is awarded only to people who prove themselves to have mastered the unit's rituals. In other words, soldiers find themselves members of a moral community which produces existential bonds and ties. It is the profession that personalises them in terms of character traits or virtues demanded by the profession. In essence, soldiers socialise to meet the needs of the profession. The virtues which they recognise in each other are those designed for the group's fitness of purpose, its own survival and flourishing. It is a telling example of social selection. These virtues are socially transmitted laterally. And they are designed for their virtue-forming powers, for their capacity to become customised in a given social environment. (King, 2011, 232)

What we now know and Crane didn't is that networking has a neurological as well as a psychological explanation, as his contemporary William James was able to work out for himself. James was acutely haunted by the Civil War. Only ill-health had prevented him from joining up with two of his brothers and he never ceased to regret the fact. His great contribution to psychology was the recognition that we owe a lot to our feelings, for James insisted that every time we have a thought about our emotions, we bring with that thought an accompanying bodily state, and that we have more instincts and drives than any other animal, which is why we are so uniquely conscious of our feelings. It is the primordial elements of the mind that give us our sense of self, and self-hood is designed in by evolution to help us adapt faster. Consciousness has helped us to forge morality, religion and ideas of justice, none of which were needed to protect ourselves against other predators, but which were urgently needed once we stopped being hunted by other species and began to hunt each other. We also are able to process more information about the external environment than any other species, and it is the ability to process more information about our circumstances that gives us different choices: to flee or to fight. From this acute observation, he worked out that the body and mind were inter-connected, and that emotions connected to states of the body are an integral part of the biological process of homeostasis—maintaining the internal condition necessary for the continuation of life.

Today, scientists can see how the brain processes emotions, thanks to brain imaging. Since the early 1990s, for example, neuroscientists have conducted a whole range of experiments on people suffering brain damage. The early degeneration of neurons in the hippocampus of the brain (located in the right and left temporal lobes of the cerebral cortex) results in disturbing memory loss, an inability to remember the names of people they have recently met, or to follow the narratives of stories they are reading or watching on television. Multiple sclerosis can produce fronto-limbic damage which results in an overflow of sadness or despair. Scientists have also conducted experiments which allow them to trigger specific emotions by electrically stimulating specific areas of the brain.

Like many soldiers going into battle, Henry experienced fear. What Crane does not tell us about are its physiological features. He would have experienced an increased heartbeat and his brain would have amplified these emotional states by detecting these internal physiological changes. For what distinguishes us from other animals is foresight; we can anticipate emotional states before we experience any physiological sensations. We can feel fear before we have even seen the enemy march over a ridge, or heard the tramping of men in a column or the booming of the first cannonade. Some emotions that we associate with war, such as shame of cowardice, require thought for their triggering, and when thought triggers an emotion it will usually cause the psychological component of emotion first which, in turn, will produce the feelings.

Fear is familiar to every soldier in every age. Courage, professional soldiers are taught, is overcoming fear, not an absence which they must learn to master.

Lesser failures of courage, like trembling (tremblers) was the Spartan term for cowards. Jostling, teeth-chattering and fouling oneself might also be detected. The all-encompassing Corinthian helmet which we associate so closely with the Hoplite, was no doubt valued for the excellent protection it gave. But not a few Hoplites may have valued it also for the way it concealed the expressive face, and so concealed the terror of the wearer—so vivid on the face in Homer, where, 'the skin of a coward changes colour one way and another'—from his competitors in courage. (Lenden, 2005, 53)

What was true 2,000 years ago is as true today. Take a passage from Tim O'Brien's set of short stories, *The Things They Carried* (1990). 'They carried all the emotional baggage of men who might die', wrote O'Brien in the signature tale,

Grief, terror, love, longing—these were intangibles, but the intangibles had their own mass and specific gravity, they had tangible weight. They carried shameful memories. They carried the common secret of cowardice barely restrained, the instinct to run or freeze or hide, and in many respects this was the heaviest burden of all, for it could never be put down, it required perfect balance and perfect posture. They carried their reputations. They carried the soldier's greatest fear, which was the fear of blushing. Men killed and died because they were embarrassed not to. (O'Brien, 1991, 20–21)

The book is avowedly a work of fiction, as its author declares on the title page, but it is dedicated to the men of Alpha Company with whom O'Brien served in Vietnam. And some of them he actually names: Jimmy Cross, Norman Bowker, Rat Kiley, Mitchell Sanders, Henry Dobbins, and Kiowa. In other words, O'Brien was there. His book is a celebration of their life, as well as an affirmation of life itself; and it is a reproach to an uncaring fate which takes the lives of so many brave men.

Consciousness has evolved to allow our feelings to determine our behaviour rationally; we can master our fears. And it is our ability to think in the abstract, writes Anthony Damasio, that allows us to bring our feelings into rational decision-making. We can master our fears by holding out the hope of things being other than they are. Damasio maintains that we are not either thinking machines or feeling machines, but rather feeling machines that think. We do not always succumb emotionally or instinctively to the fear of danger. Sometimes, we stand our ground and fight. What separates us from those closest to us genetically, the higher primates, is that 'we can create a memory of our anticipated future'. (Damasio, *Self Comes to Mind*) The young Fleming, remember, is moved to dreams of glory by reading

Homer (which has been true of so many young men in the West). With consciousness we have culture, or what Damasio calls 'socio-cultural homeostasis' which allows us not only to survive but thrive—that is, to live a much more emotionally enriched life—to be honoured for one's bravery, or respected for one's fighting skills.

It is the sense of selfhood that defines us as individuals and which, at the same time, positions us in a network with others, an argument which can be found in a little-known piece by the early 19th-century writer William Hazlitt, an *Essay on the Principles of Human Action* (1805). What marks the essay out as especially noteworthy is that the author set out to demonstrate that the means by which a person attempts to secure his future welfare are identical with the means that he would use in identifying the interests of others. This 'metaphysical discovery', as Hazlitt himself later described it, largely passed without notice at the time of its publication and has only recently been rediscovered. The example he chooses is that of a young child putting a hand into a flame. He or she immediately experiences pain and processes the information for future reference. But when a child learns the lesson, he is imagining a being that does not yet exist, his own future self. In Damasio's terminology, his brain is mapping a body that is still only imaginary. But once we can imagine our own future selves we can imagine others as well. As Hazlitt adds, that which is future, which does not yet exist, can excite no interest in itself, nor act upon the mind in any way, but by means of the imagination. (Hazlitt, 1805/1969, 22)

As our actual being is constantly passing into our future being, and carries this internal feeling of consciousness along with it, we seem to be already identified with our future being in that permanent part of our nature, and to feel by anticipation the same sort of necessary sympathy with our future selves, that we know we shall have with our past selves. (Hazlitt, 1805, 118)

Hazlitt's general contribution to the understanding of the self is that all human actions require a concept of an interior 'self'. It is this interior self that the military has been interested in moulding ever since it became aware of the importance of mental impressions. The young Henry Fleming's mind is like that of most young men—uninformed, in Hazlitt's words. With his interest in Homer, and dreams of youth, he is interested in his own welfare in a 'peculiar mechanical manner' only in so far as it relates to his past or present impressions. In the case of Henry Fleming, war is the activity that gives him a fully-developed 'future self'; it is his experience of battle that sparks his concern in turn for the future of his friends, the band of brothers, the primary group.

In the course of the 17th century, however, the military began to think that the 'future self' could be programmed to behave in a particular fashion. Soldiers began to be seen as 'machines' that could be drilled to carry out certain actions, without reflection or thought; soldiers could be made almost automatons, a word that entered general speech two hundred years before the word 'robot'. Today the military no longer holds to that vision, but it does entertain the hope that soldiers might network with each other cybernetically and thus be managed more effectively than ever.

Descartes goes off to war

Since the ancient world very few philosophers have witnessed war at first hand. Descartes is one of the exceptions. In 1618 he enlisted in the Dutch army, in the hope of pursuing a military career. Restless by nature and in the absence of any real fighting, he enrolled as an officer in the Bavarian army at the beginning of the Thirty Years War. On 11 November 1619 (St Martin's Day) he found himself caught in a violent snowstorm and was forced to shelter in a warm chamber. As warmth penetrated his chilled body, Descartes experienced three visions. In the first he was being spun around in a whirlwind; in the second he saw thunder and lightning in his room. The third dream was different. He saw himself reading the poetry of Ausonius; 'What part shall I take in life' ran one line. From that day, he embarked on an eighteen-year mission to change the way we thought about our humanity.

In time he elaborated his most famous proposition, that the body which absorbed the old functions of spirit and some of the functions of the soul should be understood as a self-regulating machine:

… as a clock composed of wheels and counter-weights no less exactly observes the laws of nature when it is badly made, and does not show the time properly, than when it entirely satisfies the wishes of its maker, … [so also] I consider the body of a man as being a sort of machine so built up and composed of nerves, muscles, veins, blood and skin, that though there were no mind in it at all, it would not cease to have the same motions as at present, exception being made of those movements which are due to the direction of the will, and in consequence depend upon the mind (as opposed to those which operate by the disposition of its organs. (Goetz, 2011, 68)

By accepting the machine as his model, wrote Lewis Mumford, Descartes was able to bring every manifestation of life under control, and to make life ordered and rational at the same time, as long as one did not look too closely at the nature and intentions of the controller. (Mumford, 1970, 98)

We know that Descartes rejoined the Bavarian army at some point, but we do not know anything else about his military career. What we do know, however, is revealing. He seems never again to have taken an interest in either the profession or the practice of war. It is certainly never mentioned in his correspondence with others. Even though Europe had been at war for nearly twenty years by the time he published his most famous book, *The Discourse on Method* (1631), war seems to have been entirely absent from his thinking, or concerns. The explanation, speculates Yuval Noah Harari, is probably very simple. If the mind is important, and the body is not, why should a philosopher find war interesting? (Hariri, 2008, 99–100)

Descartes' fellow soldiers did not immediately buy into his body-mind division, but philosophical and military ideas are conjoined, they are part of the *Zeitgeist*. The fact that sense-data provided by the body (getting shot at, or wounded) could obviously influence one's thinking, was known, but the body's function, it was thought, was to submit this data to the mind which could process it and render it back as another idea, that war and science could be married which allowed for an entirely new and gratifying sense of objective knowledge. For two centuries Western armies tried to subject war to mathematical logic and reduce its principles to a set of differential equations (Appleyard, 1992, 46). The philosopher Ludwig Wittgenstein once remarked that the fact that we can see things in the way Descartes did tells us nothing about the world: that we do see things in that way tells us everything. In other words, it is a choice, and we humans are the ones who make it. We live in a universe which is partly of our design, and although we have broken with Cartesianism in many ways, we are still in thrall to science. We still follow a scientific vision of controlling war, and programming as best we can the behaviour of the soldiers who wage it.

In other words, by the end of the 17th century Western militaries had come to regard the body in Cartesian terms—it was there to be drilled. The Dutch army in which the young Descartes served his apprenticeship was commanded by a man, Maurice of Nassau, who wanted an army that would be controlled by a general, as firmly as the Cartesian mind controls the body. (Hariri, 2008, 113) In the following century Marshal de Saxe expressed the common opinion of the time when he stated that most soldiers should be 'transformed into machines that can take on life only through the voice of their officers'. (Hariri, 2008, 115)

It was also Maurice of Nassau who set up the first Military Academy and whose staff developed standardised procedures as a drill which students had to perform step by step in the prescribed manner. Drill soon became an integral part of military life. The word *disciplina* was defined by Justus Lipsius in his treatise *De Militia Romana* as referring to rules governing the professional conduct of soldiers. He himself (his name was a Latinised version of the Flemish name Joste Lips) was the first to say an army should march in step. He was the first to see time itself as 'metric'. (Toulmin, 2001, 35) The idea was to 'drill out' any independent thinking by the soldier by forcing him to conform to a series of mechanical movements (walking, firing, loading or marching in time). Long before machines appeared on the battlefield, men were instructed how to use their firearms with machine-like precision. For easy remembering, the action of firing a musket was broken down, in turn, into different movements, and recorded in manuals with illustrations so that each movement could be learned; 32 separate movements can be found in Henry Hexham's *The Principles of the Art Militaire* (1637) which appeared in the same year as Descartes' *Discourse on Method*, and an additional 13 movements were identified in a manual in the mid-18th century. Drill was to remain the principle innovation in European armies until the beginning of the French Revolutionary age, when soldiers were allowed, for the first time, more independence of movement (and even the courage to think for themselves). (Hariri, 2008) Yet as late as the last century observers noted how drill enabled a soldier under the stress of combat to lose all individual consciousness, to function like 'a cell in a military organism'. 'It is astonishing', wrote one of the most famous writers on warriors, Glenn Gray, 'how much of the business of warfare can be carried out by men who act as automatons, behaving almost as mechanically as the machines they operate'. (Holmes, 2004, 39)

Descartes later visited the Academy at Breda and was confirmed in his life's work of establishing morally value-free or neutral systems which could only be found in a mathematical order. (Toulmin, 1995, 44) In due course academics began teaching what they began to call 'the military sciences' based on mathematics. Even earlier Iago, an ensign who has not 'studied' the art of war (and probably could not read), reproves the man whom Othello has promoted over him as a 'mere arithmetician' who has never commanded an army in the field. Cassio is a man who had learned his skills from books not experience in the field. It is another of 'honest Iago's' many grudges against life. But one can see why mathematics rapidly gained ground in military circles. It suggested that the world is understandable because it is divisible into elements that are sufficiently identical to be classed. And once you match up one thing with another (in the same class) you can start counting; mathematics allowed organizations to model human behaviour. The idea was especially popular among philosophers. Spinoza, for example, insisted that human actions could be explained away by general laws. 'Most writers on the emotions and on human conduct', he declared,

seem to be treating rather of matters outside of nature than of natural phenomena following nature's general laws. They appear to conceive of man to be situated in a nature as a kingdom within a kingdom for they believe he disturbs rather than follows nature's order. I shall consider human actions and desires in exactly the same manner as though I were concerned with lines, planes and solids. (Ford, 2007, 93)

From these mathematical premises it was easy enough to conclude that humanity was in a sense mechanical. For Descartes the animal was a machine; for Hobbes, so was society. La Mettrie in the following century argued that conscious and voluntary processes in the mind result simply from more complex mechanisms than involuntary and instinctive processes. (Tallis, 2011,195)

Even so, the real breakthrough came much later, in the mid-20th century when John von Neumann and Oscar Morganstern published a book called *Theory of Games and Economic Behaviour* (1944). Apparently, the human race had finally found an impeccable foundation for military theory: 'in the literature of social conflict', wrote a contemporary reviewer, 'an exact description of the nature of strategy has been wanting, Machiavelli and Clausewitz notwithstanding. No dictionary defines the term. For Neumann's conception is more than a definition, it is a theory complete on the level of pure science'. (von Neumann, 2004, 693) Neumann and Morganstern had been writing about economics, not war, but soon people began to think that mathematics could be applied in every possible situation; indeed, perhaps, mathematics was the only way in which war could be understood as a phenomenon. The dream of John Fuller, a British general in the 1920s, seemed about to come true.

Normal man will not think. Thinking is purgatory to him; he will only imitate and repeat. Let us turn, therefore, these defects to our advantage; let us, through clear thinking and logical thinking, obtain so firm a mental grip on war that we can place before this unthinking creature a system which, when he imitates it, will reflect our intention and attain our goal. Let us look upon normal man as a piece of human machinery, a machine tool controlled by our brain. (Fuller, 35)

Engineering rationality

Descartes' vision persisted for so long because it locked into a central idea that became popular as the 19th century progressed: that soldiers really could be seen as machines. Industrialization added to this understanding by translating drill into routine; the mechanised regularity of work. Routine does not permit the exercise of personal judgement or the expression of a personal opinion. In Adam Smith's view, this was the major difference between the trader and the industrial worker. The trader adapted to changing demand. The market offered a competitive environment which rewarded informed risk taking and entrepreneurship, and certainly character. (Sennett, 1998, 38) In the industrial workplace, by comparison, the worker was fixed to a routine, and on the factory floor the currency was boredom. Smith went even further in claiming that routine made one mindless: 'The man whose whole life is spent in performing a few simple operations … genuinely becomes as stupid and ignorant as it is possible for a human creature to become'. (Sennett, 2008, 105) It is not a view that has gone unchallenged, because there are plenty of examples of people who take pleasure in routine. It even has its own existential rewards; it has two components that appeal to many people, stress on a beat and tempo (speed). (Sennett, 2008, 175)

But factory discipline really did create a new breed of worker, writes the Harvard economic historian, David Landes. An old craft industry such as textile making had allowed the spinner to spin her wheel at home unsupervised and in her own time. Now the work was team-based and overseen. 'The factory was a new kind of prison, the clock a new kind of gaoler'. (Landes, 1983, 43) In other words, the 'time revolution', as Landes calls it, involved a major psychological change in the workplace. The worker became instrumentalised, a product of metric time. By the end of the 19th century the workforce had been introduced to another novel concept: productivity. We associate the word with Frederick Winslow Turner who insisted that the system must come first, not the worker. The workers soon found that there was an important distinction between their employer's time and their own. We must remember what the point of Taylorism was to scotch the traditional and what he considered rather 'quaint' idea that a captain of industry was born, not made: if only you hired the right man, the methods could be left safely to him. Taylor thought this a dangerous notion because he believed that it was the system that counted. Henry Ford, who was the first major industrialist to introduce the concept of scientific management into his factories, adopted as his credo, 'System, System and more System'. (Hughes, 2004, 77) For Taylor, scientific management was 'a true science, resting upon clearly defined laws, rules and principles', and thus was applicable—as he himself suggested—to all kinds of human activities, including war.

In the 1930s and especially during World War II, the complexity of war virtually exploded and encouraged the introduction of business-like methods. It was to be given a host of different labels, for instance, 'operational analysis', 'operational research', 'systems engineering', 'management science', 'cost-effectiveness analysis', and 'system analysis'. All these involved a revised Cartesianism. Instead of seeing men as machines the military was inclined to regard men and machines as being in all essential respects very similar. Descartes' mind/body split became a hardware/software split. (Appleyard, 1992, 175) Soldiers were random circuitry animated by a program. In a word, they were very much like computers, no more than the totality of their inputs. Lawrence Radine, the author of a report on *The Taming of the Troops: Social Control in the US Army*, talked of 'co-operative rational control, through behavioural science and management':

One application of this social engineering approach is the way the military matches men to machines (as well as matching some aspects of machines to men). The man is the extension of such machines, as artillery pieces or weapons systems generally; he is an adjunct of some limitation the machine has due to its incomplete development. (Radine, 1977, 90)

Radine concluded that 'the ultimate result of co-operative rational control is a cheerful state of mind with no values or beliefs other than ... an automatic, mechanical performance'. Quoting Wright Mills, he suggested that the true goal should be to make the soldiers of the future 'cheerful robots'.

Of all the methodologies listed above, Operational Research took on a life of its own. It was based on heuristic models of reality, many of them mathematical, which were designed to help military planners in their planning processes just as mathematical models aided meteorologists and demographers—who were the first to acknowledge, of course, that mathematical equations do not actually govern the weather or the birth rate. One of the best-known examples was the Lanchester N-squared Law of Combat (so named after the engineer F.W. Lanchester who published his findings on aerial warfare in 1916). The Law states that the effective combat power of two forces in conflict with one another is proportional to the effectiveness of their respective weapons, times the square of their relative strength. (Rowland, 2004, 3) The Russian analyst M. Osipov, who examined land warfare over the period 1805–1905, concluded that the value 3:2 fitted better than the 2 of the 'square law'. Both Lanchester's work and Osipov's have been carried forward in recent years through more complex and sophisticated modelling. The point is that Operational Research marked a decisive break with the pre-1914 world in which scientific effort had been directed to technological improvements in weapons. Now the actual use of those weapons and the organization of men using them were seen as scientific problems in themselves.

In due course, scientists also began to look at the existential dimension of war, including courage and morale, the factors that made for the primary group cohesion—the networking that Thucydides had noticed through observation, and which in his eyes was one of the principal features that rendered war 'a human thing'. Nigel Balchin, who was the British army's deputy Scientific Advisor at the end of World War II (and later was known for his popular novel, *The Small Back Room*), was amazed to find that when literally hundreds of scientists were engaged in studying fragmentation and muzzle velocity not a single one was engaged in the study of the effects on morale of shells, bombs and bullets released. But perhaps the most famous study (and certainly one of the most contentious) was conducted by S.L.A. Marshall who wrote a book, *Men Under Fire*, which he based largely on post-battlefield interviews with American troops. Commissioned by the US Army, the report's findings have remained controversial to this day. For Marshall claimed that only 15 men in 100 would take any active part in firing their weapons, and less than 25 per cent would do so even with their backs to the wall. Marshall was criticized for not applying statistical data but merely using his own subjective observations, but he was the first writer to stumble on what is now a universally recognised truth.

The reluctance to fire weapons in war has probably been real at most times in history. A 1986 study by the Defence Operational Analysis Establishment in Britain, employing historical studies of more than a hundred 19th and 20th century battles, and test trials using pulse and laser weapons to determine the killing-effectiveness of the units studied, determined that in every case the killing potential was much greater than the actual historical casualty rate. The only explanation for this discrepancy was an unwillingness on the part of men in the field to take part in combat, whether because of fear or moral disgust. Ironically, Marshall also identified a clear rise in instrumental reasoning in subjective assessments of the 'pay off' of participation. Soldiers had begun to ask themselves increasingly 'was it worth it?' (Rowland, 2004, 52)

The main payoff of Operational Research was shown in Vietnam where the military managed to get 90 per cent of soldiers to discharge their weapons—not that it helped to win the war. But long before that the military had come to recognise that a soldier is not a machine. A machine is made of many parts, but all the parts work together to produce a system with a relatively narrow and predictable range of behaviour. Human beings, by contrast, have properties and behaviour that emerge on the day of battle and cannot be attributed to any particular part. A soldier, whether he is a Greek Hoplite at Mantinea or a Union volunteer in the American Civil War, is more than merely the sum of his parts. Gradually, as this sank in, it began to be acknowledged that Descartes had made a fundamental category error.

Descartes' error

Descartes had led the military profession into a dead end by encouraging us to think of the body and the mind as essentially two different entities. We now know what the Greeks knew long ago: the mind and the body are conjoined. We have rejected the Cartesian understanding that the mind operates independently as a disembodied entity, with no need of any relationship with others, either to know itself or experience its own existence. Another philosopher, Friedrich Nietzsche, believed that the task of 'translating man back into nature' was essential to humanity's self-understanding; thanks to science, we have embarked on that path.

Simon Blackwell puts it very well. We have recaptured the idea that a smile is an utterly natural mode of expression of pleasure or happiness—the mental state can be revealed in the face. It is not accidental that someone who feels happy has a spring in their step, or that someone who feels depressed walks with a heavy step, often with a downcast face:

This approaches something of what Aristotle meant when he said that the mind is the form of the body, and it is telling that the Greeks had no word for consciousness. Perhaps, they were ahead of us in recognising that consciousness is not a matter of happenings in a mysterious, parallel world to the one we inhabit. It is simply our animation in that world. (Blackwell, 2011, 17)

We now know that we are what we are because we are embodied beings. It is precisely because we are not calculating machines that we cannot live in a world of pure thought. We are rational only to the extent that we have emotional intelligence. Our emotions and passions are not the enemy of reason, they are what make us a reasoning animal. A cold, dispassionate, rational mind is often a dangerous one, because it leads to bad decision-making.

In the end, we are not tools ourselves. We have what Raymond Tallis calls 'an existentially intuitive self'. (Tallis, 2010, 27) We have minds of our own, and appetites, as well as desires, and a spirit that is grounded in our existential being. We insist on making sense of the world rather than merely experiencing it through our senses. When we do so, the world becomes amenable to our own will. We are not, adds Tallis, dissolved into our sentient fields, like a horse or a dog. The world, for us, is not a given, as it is for all other animals; it is a theatre for the realization of the possibilities we recognise we possess. And that makes us—ultimately—intractable tools, if used by others. The content of human experience can never be a-conceptual—we are guided in life by an understanding of who we are and what we would like to become, and although many of us may never have an opportunity to realise our potential (for centuries the majority of people have been what others wanted them to be), human beings have never been 'robots'.

Machines are very different. They lend themselves particularly to mathematical logic. Either they function or they do not, and when they break down we want to know why. What does it mean to say that a 'soldier' functions? Plato provided an answer: he works as he is designed to do by nature (Plato introduced us to the radical concept that one can fail at becoming a man; one may die without ever realising one's potential). But for a man to 'work' well requires another evaluation. A machine is complicated, made up of many different component parts; a human being is not so much complicated as complex, and his complexity stems from the fact that he is a social being. A person can be born with natural talents such as a talent for musical composition (melodies flow into his or her head). But whereas musical notation is learned, as too is orchestration, a person is either born with a melodic gift, or not. But it does not stop there. Whether one becomes a successful composer depends ultimately on the taste of others (Wordsworth: 'We cre- ate the style by which we are appreciated'—that's genius, indeed). We do not attribute genius to people who have natural abilities: they have to show something that is extraordinary or uncommon; often, they have to lead the rest of us along the path they have chosen for themselves.

Secondly, a machine is mathematically engineered. When we say it works, we mean that it reaches its mathematically designed objective, such as speed (horse power). Or when we say it functions optimally we mean it achieves what it is designed to achieve, as set out in the manual. The rules we expect soldiers to follow are like those we give machines, writes Michael Frayn, insofar as we digitalise the analogue processes of human thought and behaviour, or at least try to. (Frayn, 2006, 160) But there is no way we have found so far of mathematically determining human behaviour. Soldiers are often urged on to achieve the 'impossible'; they are frequently asked to go 'beyond the call of duty' or go the extra distance. They may be drilled to obey orders (not endanger others by questioning them in the field) but they are also expected to show initiative (unlike a machine, which is entirely rule bound). Even when operating machines, they are expected to exercise the manual override, if occasion warrants.

We do not expect soldiers to blindly follow the rules; we expect them to exercise judgement, and where possible to display wisdom. To mathematicise behaviour is to quantify it, and this we simply cannot do. We cannot attach a number to human behaviour. Take the example of a military unit which has slowed down because a sniper in the minaret of a mosque is taking out individual members of the unit. The commander on the ground has to decide what to do. We cannot attach a mathematical number to the decision he takes: to take out a mosque in an air strike (– 1); to call for backup on the ground (+1); to spend 15 hours by getting his own snipers to take out the sniper in the minaret (+2). All of these decisions might be sensible or not, depending on the context. In another context, an air strike could be rated +2 (given the need to meet the next military objective rather than slow down the general advance, the need to be seen to be ruthless in order to deter other ambushes further on; the evaluation that the destruction of one mosque does not necessarily an insurgency make). There is no way of quantifying a mili- tary decision before the decision has been made and the outcome evaluated. There is no way of doing this either in our own experience, or in what we can observe of our own neural functioning. Michael Frayn, I think, puts it particularly well: 'Even with entirely quantifiable concepts, the act of quantification cannot itself be made numerical. The application of arithmetic cannot itself be arithmetised. These things involve the power of recognition and judgement, not calculation'. (Frayn, 2006, 161–2)

This, he ruminates, is what Nietzsche probably meant when he complained about the continual 'falsification of the world by means of numbers'. (Frayn, 2006, 458n.13) As it happens, the onward march of mathematics seems unstoppable. It has colonised most of the social sciences in the United States (take economics, with the rise of econometrics and cliometrics). Molecular biology, experimental psychology, and behavioural science: all have their algebraic instruments or algorithms.

But in war the march has been stopped. Instead, a new vision of the future has arisen—the performative fusing of man into a shared mind, a cybernetic system which may provide him with a 'shared awareness' of the battle space and each person's place in it. (Alberts, 1999, 2) The military are seeking to fold soldiers into a single 'infostructure', to network them for the first time. Dispersed units will be able to share information and see the larger picture, which, in turn, may bind them ever closer and make it easier than ever to maintain primary group cohesion.

All this is made possible by a factor that began to intrude into military thinking by the end of World War II, the increasing symbiosis of man and machine which was discussed for the first time by Norbert Wiener in his book with its give-away title, *The Human Use of Human Beings: Cybernetics and Society* (1950). For the author human beings were merely individual systems which perpetually fought like all organisms against the entropic principle of death, or what physics regards as systemic 'disorder'. They were programmed to do so through feedback mechanisms, or what, in effect, were information exchanges transmitted as electrochemical impulses throughout the nervous system. Since every feedback mechanism in a living organism has its correlative in a mechanical system there was fundamentally no difference between organic and inorganic life, or between animals (including humans) and machines. It was this insight that marked the most significant break with the Greek understanding of human nature. And if human nature had to be radically rethought, so perhaps had the 'humanity' of war. What did the 'human thing' now mean?

Reducing the pain

There is a famous passage in Charles Dickens' novel *Hard Times* when Mrs Gradgrind's daughter races to her dying mother's bedside. 'Are you in pain, dear mother?' 'I think there's a pain somewhere in the room', replies Mrs Gradgrind, 'but I couldn't possibly say that I have got it'. (Chapter 25) The 'pain' of war is 'friction' which contributes to the fact that the machine consumes more energy than it produces. Energy is degraded as a result and atoms assume a disorderly state, and entropy is the measure of the disorder. Wiener's biographer, Steve Heims, notes that at the core of his personal quest was the obsession with 'finding predictability through chaos, or signal through noise'. (Heims, 1980, 146–7). And as a mathematician Wiener felt that pain particularly acutely:

My delirium assumed the form of a particular mixture of depression and worry … anxiety about the logical status of my … work. It was impossible for me to distinguish among my pain and difficulty in breathing, the flapping of the window curtain, and certain as yet unresolved points for potential problem on which I was working. I cannot say that the pain revealed itself as a mathematical tension, or that the mathematical tension symbolised itself as a pain: but the two were united too closely to make such a separation significant. However, when I reflected on this matter later, I became aware of the possibility that almost any experience may act as a temporary symbol for a mathematical situation which has not yet been organised and cleared up. I also came to see more definitely than I had before that one of the chief motives driving me to mathematics was the discomfort or even the pain of an unresolved mathematical discord. I even became more and more conscious of the need to reduce such a discord to semi-permanent and recognisable terms before I could release it and pass onto something else. (Heims, 1980,147–8)

Wiener's concerns and the military's were very similar (even though he later broke with the US military over what he saw as their misuse of science, and refused ever again to work under contract or to accept funds from military sources for his own research).

Wiener confronted two devils throughout his life, and both lie at the heart of war, rendering it difficult to predict outcomes, programme soldiers or translate the art of war into a science, however hard we try. Wiener gave his devils different names: the Manichean devil determined to win will use every deceit, wile and stratagem to achieve its purpose; but the Augustinian devil was independent of the human realm—it was the impersonal play of contingency and chance, and it produced disorder (or what Clausewitz called 'friction'). As the Prussian commander Helmut von Moltke once remarked, no plan, however well thought through, tends to survive the first hour's contact with the enemy. As Wiener wrote, 'This random element, this organic incompleteness is one without too violent a figure of speech, we may consider evil: the negative evil which St. Augustine characterises as incompleteness, rather than the positive malicious evil of the Manicheans'. (Wiener, 1989, 11)

These two very different 'devils' were also identified by the most famous military thinker of all, Clausewitz, in two often quoted passages from his book *On War*. In the third chapter of Book II, Clausewitz considers whether the study of war is an art or a science. He concludes that it can only be the former: 'The essential difference is that war is not an exercise of the will directed at inanimate matter, as in the case with the mechanical arts, or at matter which is animate but passive, and yielding, as is the case with the human mind and emotions in the fine arts. In war, the will is directed at an animate object that reacts'. And the Manichean evil is to be found in a passage that precedes it:

The second attribute of military action is that it must expect positive reactions and the process of interaction that results. Here we are not concerned with the problem of calculating such reactions—that is really part of the already mentioned problem of calculating psychological forces—but rather with the fact that the very nature of interaction is bound to make it unpredictable.

In other words, the core cause of analytical unpredictability in war is the very nature of interaction itself. (Clausewitz, 1993, 149, 139)

Clausewitz's great contribution to understanding war, for those who had the inclination to read him closely, was to tell his readers that it would always be subject to entropy, which we understand today as the Second Law of Thermodynamics. Friction is a non-linear feedback effect that leads to the heat dissipation of energy in a system. This dissipation is a form of increased degradation towards randomness, which is the essence of entropy. In war, degradation and dissipation are common features, too. Armies often find that victory brings its own problems—sometimes they are too successful to be successful. Often they run up against what is called the 'culminating point of operations': forward units advance so quickly that they cannot be supported logistically. The French entered Moscow in 1812, and the Germans managed to penetrate its suburbs in 1941, in both cases only to find that they had exhausted their strength. The successful commander is tempted to go for one more success. Even in peacetime, armies degrade— they become soft. It was randomness that Wiener hoped cybernetics would finally resolve.

Wiener thought that cybernetics offered a way to deal with the Manichean or human-built world of design and intention where the enemy seeks to thwart one's ambitions and plans. For the Augustinian world and its problem of friction Wiener came to believe that robotics offered some hope. He himself pointed out that cybernetics had been used in the post-war automation of production via the feedback loops and servomechanisms of industrial robots. The early years of the cybernetic era were marked by the construction of small electromechanical robots which one cyberneticist labelled *Machina speculatrix*—a member of a new inorganic species. (Pickering, 2010, 43) For Wiener, a new generation of flexible automatons (including machines that were able to analyse data)—in other words, feedback-driven automata—might one day offer 'a local enclave' against chaos. (Wiener, 1989, 12) But military robots were not on the horizon in the 1950s, and so the military had to look to another model: transforming soldiers into 'cheerful robots', instead.

For Wiener, control rested on ensuring negative feedback—the ability to evaluate information at the centre of strategic thinking in terms of the opportunity costs of success or failure. Since outputs do not always lead to successful outcomes, soldiers might have to adapt and try another tactic, and that will depend on whether as a unit they can learn from and steer according to its feedback mechanism. Without feedback a military unit will drift, ultimately to defeat. In the 1950s militaries sought to avoid the breakdown and demoralization of the primary group by ensuring that they could monitor accurate negative feedback and that soldiers had the training to take corrective measures. This understanding was quite different from a Cartesian idea that the inability to take a hill or a position was due to insufficient zeal on behalf of the soldiers involved (and, in some cases, the failure to drill them successfully). The fact is that at the last moment soldiers the world over display a disconcerting unwillingness to be led by the nose—hence Frederick the Great's rebuke to his retreating soldiers at the battle of Kolin (1757): 'Dogs, do you wish to live forever!'.

This Cartesian view is almost encouraged by Clausewitz when he writes that the only way of offsetting friction is 'perseverance': 'as man under pressure tends to give in to physical and intellectual weakness, only great strength of will can lead to the objective. It is steadfastness that will earn the admiration of the world and of posterity'. (Clausewitz, 1993, 193) But Clausewitz was careful to add the rider that 'other compelling reasons' might suggest a different course of action, including reasons not known or even knowable at the time that an attack was conceived. Unfortunately, most generals of the 19th and 20th centuries tended to ignore this caveat, especially in the run up to the First World War, insisting instead that the triumph of the will (or what the French high command called *élan vital*, which was deemed to constitute the vital essence of the nation and its destiny) could triumph over every obstacle in its path. 'Let us go for excess', declared one French general in the run-up to war; *élan* and *cran* (guts) would carry all in a series of offensives against the enemy. This widespread attitude in the French armed forces was perhaps best captured by a remark at the end of a General Staff conference in 1913: 'impudence' in an offensive is the best form of security. (Barnett, 1966, 274)

Of course, this also made war 'heroic' in the popular imagination. Indeed, there is nothing more 'heroic' in the literature of war than a hopeless attack that continues in the face of all opposition, like Pickett's charge at Gettysburg, or the advance of the Imperial Guard at Waterloo which broke under the accuracy and intensity of British rifle fire. To be heroic, an action does not have to be successful, or even especially intelligent. It just has to be stirring, and the First World War assaults across No Man's Land were certainly that—up to the point where sheer folly becomes impossible to turn into a story of anything but human incompetence, such as the failure to learn from past mistakes. *Lions for Lambs* is the title of a 2007 film invoking a famous German observation during the battle of the Somme, that British soldiers were lions led by lambs. What is apparently heroic—if we look at war in cybernetic terms—is the ability of commanders over the ages to thrust the burden of adjustment on their own soldiers by not responding to negative feedback.

By its very nature, the desire to let negative feedback influence decisions, cybernetics is post-heroic. At its worst, however, it assumes that there is not much room for heroism, or the will to win, or the ability of soldiers to continue fighting on even when defeated (and thereby—just occasionally—snatching victory from defeat). No one actually knows who remarked that British soldiers were lions and their commanders lambs, so calmly led to the slaughter, but it may have been a conscious echo of a remark that we can attribute accurately to a real historical figure—Alexander the Great, who once told his commanders that he was never afraid of an army of lions led into battle by a lamb, but he did fear an army of lambs who had a lion to lead them. Leadership involves a curious alchemy between commander and those he commands that often escapes management or control. And it is warriors beyond the control of generals behind the lines—not warriors out of control—who have proved so often to be the most inspiring soldiers.

The cybernetic network

> *'You cannot fight a war without acronyms. This is a fact of modern combat …*
> *And where do those compressed words come from?*
> *They come from remote levels of development, from technicians and bomb.*
> *heads in the computer universe—stalking, bespectacled men who deal.*
> *with systems so layered and many-connected that the ensuing arrays of words.*
> *must be atomised and redesigned, made spare and letter-sleek.*

DeLillo, 1997, Underworld, 606.

The military is not trying to eliminate 'the pain' of war so much as to master it, and they are attempting to do this by putting information at the very heart of war itself. We have entered an information age. It is clear that just as the Industrial Age gave rise to mass assembly line armies, our Information Age encourages us to think of war differently. The idea of a knowledge-based economy has become an important aspect of business management, and just as companies are supposed to leverage knowledge in order to out-perform their competitors, militaries are now expected to do the same; to give them a competitive advantage over their enemies.

But at another level, soldiering itself is changing, it is increasingly becoming information processing. The military—as an organization—is becoming 'knowledge based'. In 2001 the US Department of the Army created a knowledge-management strategy 'designed to transform itself into a network-centric, knowledge based force'. Every soldier is now encouraged to see him- or herself as 'a collector of positive (sustained) and negative (improve or change) information'. Success is now defined as 'the continuous collection and submission of observations, insights and lessons'. Inevitably, it has its own acronym, OIL. Or, as the Army Regulation 11–33 (AR11–13) adds, 'the aim is to generate near-real-time warrior-focused knowledge'. (Army Regulations 11–33, Army Lessons Learned Program (ALLP), Headquarters, Dept of the Army, Washington, 17 October 2006, 6).

And the information is collectively shared in a cybernetic system. At Fort Benning, Georgia the US Army's latest 'Internet for the Battlefield' presages the shape of things to come. It allows soldiers to don helmets with a minute screen which when flipped over the eyes enables them to see the entire battlefield, marking the location of both friendly and enemy forces. They can also access the latest weather reports. In future, soldiers will not even need helmets at all. They will be able to wear contact lenses that will beam information and data directly onto their retinas. At the Aberdeen Proving

Ground in Maryland soldiers can experience every dimension of combat vicariously, sprinting, hiding, seeking cover, dodging bullets, all of this courtesy of 3-D imaging in a virtual battle space. And soon they will be able to do this more realistically still through holograph technology which is still in its infancy but is improving all the time. (Kaku, 2011, 34)

'As I am a soldier/a name that in my thoughts becomes me best', remarks Shakespeare's Henry V in Act III, Sc iii of the famous play, the greatest patriotic paean, perhaps, that any English writer has ever written. Henry went on to win the battle of Agincourt, one of the greatest victories in a long string of English triumphs in the field. In their heyday, the English were one of the most aggressive martial races of all, and Henry's unearned royal honour (the fact that he came to the throne by birth) was set in the shade by the martial honour he earned for himself on the field of battle. In the play his fellow countrymen also derive a reflected glory from the King's undoubted ability as a great commander. But the highlight of Shakespeare's play comes with the famous 'touch of Harry in the night' when the King in disguise mingles with his men hours before the battle and employs the time to explore his own conscience. Is his cause really just? Are his men fighting for what he really believes in, his claim to the throne of France? Or are they risking their soul for a cause which is doubtful at best? Is Henry's own conscience clear? He doesn't really share his thoughts with his men, but he shares them with us through the soliloquy. We are party to his thinking in a way that his own comrades are not. We can see into his soul; they cannot. But that is the point; will tomorrow's warriors have their own thoughts? Or will they be collective ones?

Robert Heilbronner puts it quite well: can the intrusion of science and technology be kept from sucking the life out of our engagement with nature and with one another? (Heilbronner, 1995, 99) The same question might well be asked of the warrior and war. For even the very idea of what it means to be a warrior, living a specific life, may change significantly. As the nature of subjective space changes, writes Sven Birkerts, so may the idea of the self:

One day we will conduct our public and private lives within networks so dense, among so many channels of instantaneous information, that it will make almost no sense to speak of the differentiation of subjective individualism....We will soon be navigating with ease among cataracts of organised pulsations, putting out and taking in signals. We will bring our terminals, our modems and menus further and further into our former privacies; we will implicate by degrees in the unitary life and there may come a day when we can no longer remember that there was any other life. (Birkerts, 2010, 498)

Thucydides couldn't imagine an inner psychic self, but will we one day forget we ever had one?

The cybernetic battlespace is already a reality. Finding himself at the International Security Assistance Force Headquarters in Afghanistan in 2009, a British journalist was bemused by the acronymic jungle of today's battle space. 'AFPAK, ANCOP, ANDS, AMP, ANSF, APPS, ASNF, AAQ/SF, APP, CARD, CDC,CISCA, CISTICA, CJTF, CN, CNPA (AMP), COMISAF, CPCC, CSOFC, SCTC, ECC, EUPOL, FDD, FTD, GPI, HIG, HIGHK, ICPT, IDLG, IGLC, INFO-OPS, IRCTA, ISAF, IU, MCM, MDCS, NDS, OCC, OEF, OMLET, OPDIESEL, PC, PRT, SITC, UNODC, UNPOL, TB…' (Matthew Parris, 'In the Fog: Remember This: Victory is Impossible' *The Times*,4 July 2009, 21) He was particularly struck by the absurdity of it all. The British are given to irony perhaps, more than any other people, and he waxed ironical. The 'A's, he said, sometimes stand for Afghanistan, but usually Assistance. The 'F's are usually Force. The infestation of 'C's generally denotes Committee, Control or Command. If it weren't so tragic, he added, the whole thing could have been part of a comic novel by Evelyn Waugh.

We may not have Waugh with us any longer, but we do have a novel which has been dubbed the *Catch-22* of the Gulf War (1991). Its author, James Blinn, served in the navy for nine years, and so knows the subject of war at first hand. Set on a computerised aircraft carrier, the novel evokes a cybernetic world in which the vernacular of conflict is totally divorced from any language the ordinary citizen could understand. Asked what he does for a living, Blinn's hero is momentarily lost for an answer:

She asks what I do and I'm tempted to give her a dose of some acoustic techno-wizardry … jargon … Lay on some acronyms and abbreviations: ASW, FASOTRA-GRU-PAC, ECS, MK-82, ADP, INCOS, SENSO, TACCO, COMNAVIRPAC, ECP, NATOPS, ESM, MAD, SAP, ACLS, AN/ALR 47, ASWWINGPAC…. Instead, I just say: 'I'm in the navy'. (Blinn, 1997, 127–8)

Nils Bohr once told his friend Heisenberg that poets are not nearly so concerned with describing facts as with creating images. (Bronowski, 1973, 340) What image of today's battle space could today's abbreviations conjure up in a layman's mind, so divorced are the rest of us from the digital world of modern warfare?

But acronyms are not the only evidence of the cybernetic world in which the military now live. Our journalist was particularly struck by what he called the 'acrylic blanket' of the new language, suffocating the Ministry's missions and shirt-sleeve development aid workers in the country:

'Agents for Change', 'Alternative Livelihoods', 'Asymmetric Means of Operation', 'Capability Milestones', 'Civilian Search', 'Conditionality', 'Demand Reduction', 'Drivers of Radicalisation', 'Fixed-Wing Assets', 'Fledgling Capabilities', 'Injectors of Risk', 'Kinetic Situation', 'Light Footprint', 'Lily Pads', 'Messaging Campaign', 'Partnering and Mentoring', 'Capacity Building', 'Reconciliation and Reintegration', Rolling out a Top-Down Approach', 'Shake-Clear-Hold-Mill', 'Upskilling'.

It was important not to understand the meaning, but to hear the noise.

And today information is mediated almost entirely through the screen. Blinn served as a pilot on an American aircraft carrier in Desert Storm, so he writes from first hand experience. His hero goes on to describe a world which he shares with a computer, a world in which the traditional biological instruments such as the human gaze are now largely machine-mediated. In a memorable scene he records how he was shocked to see a dead man with his own eyes for the first time:

I saw it with my own eyes. I saw it with my EYES.

Therefore it's real. Is not that how it goes? If you see it with your own eyes, in the same time and space as you're in, then it's real. If/then. Causality.

That's it, right? It wasn't relayed or bounced or fibre-optic transmitted, modulated or written or echoed, encoded, encrypted, or ciphered, projected through celluloid, optically etched on silver halide, simulated by ordering the polarities of magnetised ferrous atoms, facsimile'd, thermal, laser or holographically imaged, analog or digitally processed, scan-converted, manipulated, synthesised, distorted, Animatronicised, equalised, morphed, tweaked, computer-enhanced, duped, dubbed, multiplexed or multitracked, photocopied, mineographed or inkjet printed, colorised, Surround Sounded, Dolby-ised, virtually-realised, or electron-energised on the back of a CRT ...

... No filters, no intermediary, no question of interpretation. Authentic, three dimensional. Hard-wired. In my face. The stink of death. (Blinn, 1997, 261–2)

Blinn offers us a graphic picture of what war has become, and what tomorrow's warriors are themselves in the process of becoming. But it is not the whole story. The reason why our British journalist and American writer find the whole experience of war increasingly ironic is that they find themselves living in-between two ages.

Inevitably, Antonio Gramsci's famous observation comes to mind: 'The crisis consists precisely in the fact that the old is dying and the new cannot be born; in the interregnum a great variety of morbid symptoms appears'. And the morbid symptoms of today's wars are all around us, particularly in the sea of acronyms that our two writers find so comical. The morbid symptoms of his own age were also apparent to Plato as he witnessed the death of an oral culture and the birth of a fully literate one. It took two centuries for the old styles of thought to die out in the ancient world, as Plato complained when lambasting the poets for still insisting on learning by rote. In Xenophon's *Symposium* a certain Niceratus recounts how his father made him learn the whole Homeric corpus by heart in order to become a 'good' man. Within fifty years of Plato's death Aristotle had put together the philosophical canon we know today; at its centre are still Plato's collected works. To become a good man you no longer had to memorise Homer but read Plato's *oeuvre*—one suspects, alas, not for much longer. In the Greek world the pace of change was much slower than that of today. It will only take a few more decades (if that) for the world to leave behind the print universe and enter the electronic one.

We seem to be heading towards—though we have not yet reached—an age when the soldier will no longer have his or her own thoughts, or be able to hide what he is thinking. In the electronic universe the warrior will increasingly live a transparent life within a set of systems, electronic and otherwise. He will be wired into a giant network which will give him instant access to the big picture, a collective overview of life. The cybernetic is the final realization of the concept of a network, the oldest form of which in war is, of course, the primary group, but now shorn of the Greek understanding that networks have no value in themselves; it is their members who are meaningful in ways that enable them to do more than they would acting independently, in ways that allow them to 'become' what they 'are'. In the end, a network has no greater wisdom or knowledge. A collective intelligence can be as stupid as individual intelligence. Collective skill, Lanier insists, still relies on its heroic dissenting voices, the individuals who are willing to stand out against the crowd and say no. After all, if there is no role for genius, where do we go from here? If there is no room for the flash of insight, or primal inductive reasoning, can a network fully realise its potential? If there is no place for insight, as opposed to sight, what purpose does a network serve? (Lanier, 2011, 56–7)

Embodied in the network

Let us imagine a soldier going in battle in 2035. By then the future will finally have been realised; the new order will have been born. In the command room the commander is fed readouts from data enabling him to monitor the soldiers' moods and regulate their states of stress. The computer screen shows him the soldier's heart rate and blood pressure, and even his degree of perspiration. The soldiers' eco-skeleton (armour) will have body sensors that continuously gauge his or her physiological condition and mental state. Stress levels can be measured by a rise in a person's level of cortisol. Stress rises in relation not only to danger, but also to peer review; we get stressed when we see ourselves failing our friends, or finding ourselves unable to rise to the occasion. Larger spikes in cortisol, it has been found, occur when the source of stress is inter-personal—failing one's friends, shaming oneself in front of others. But the effect on cortisol can be three times greater than when stress is impersonal (facing an unseen enemy). (Greenfield 2003, 231) So, information may be fed quickly to a soldier who is stressed out because the speed of input relaxes us; if we are relaxed, however, the speedy delivery of information can be quite stressful. Our emotional states will be strictly regulated, because stress is both empowering and disempowering at the same time. It turns on and off two key biological systems: the sympathetic nervous system (SNS) and the hypothalamic-pituitary adrenal axis (HPA). In moments of danger both systems secrete hormones that allow us to rise to the occasion, but they 'borrow' them from the immune and endocrine systems, among others, which over the long term weaken our key systems for health.

Soldiers in 2035 will also be monitored to determine their physical as well as mental stamina. Fatigue is dangerous and inhibits performance. It slows down advance (particularly when a soldier entertains self-doubt). It leads to faulty decision-making. But the eco-skeletons of the future will address this, too. Fabric in the uniforms will interact to counteract hormone or blood sugar imbalances releasing drugs as soon as the sensors detect physical impairment of a function. As the soldier's body temperature fluctuates, so will the feedback from his clothes. The human body generates some 80w of useable energy which can power nanocomputers embedded in the soldier's uniform. Feet alone generate 1w of energy. Transducers in the soles of the shoes or boots will be able to convert energy generated on impact with each step to be recycled to aid tired muscles. (Greenfield, 2003, 34)

This is not the stuff of science fiction. The USAF has been working for years on a bio-cybernetic programme that would enable it to retain manned aircraft, given the fact that the proliferating speed of aerial warfare is likely to put unacceptable strains on the pilots of the future. In the 1980s McDonald Douglas began to undertake research into an Aircraft Pilot Associate Program, a computerised system that could monitor a pilot's brainwaves, follow his eye movements and test the conductivity of his sweaty palms; all in order to gauge whether he was still in control of himself, or so stressed out that he was unable to perform optimally. In the latter circumstances the on-board computer would take over the piloting of the aircraft. Brainwave research dates back to the 1970s. It is not advanced enough yet to enable the military to read brainwaves in order to improve the performance of the human brain, but some researchers believe that in less than twenty years pilots will be able to fly planes by communicating with an on-board computer through thoughts or verbal commands, or to control the plane through eye movements, assuming, of course, that we are still flying manned aircraft.

The modern aircraft, as the cognitive anthropologist Ed Hutchins has pointed out, is designed as a single extended system made up of pilots and an automated 'fly-by-wire' computer-controlled system, in a variety of high-level loops in which pilots monitor their on-board computers and the computers in turn monitor them. (Clark, 2009, 177) Flying a plane as sophisticated as a Boeing 747–400 is now a shared responsibility, and the pilot is now commonly referred to as a 'systems manager'. In the aircraft world the man/machine merger has already taken place.

And what of soldiers on the ground, the 'poor bloody infantry'? The US military is already planning to give every soldier a hand-held computer. But a computer, in turn, is a clumsy device, especially when soldiers are on the move. Since 1996, as part of its Smart Modules Program, DARPA has been experimenting with modular information products that can be 'worn' on a soldier's battledress, or fit into a pocket, allowing him to access data—for example, to access his position without the use of a map, or a compass, or a hand-held GPS system. Data, in other words, will 'fuse' with the soldier as if he were using his own eyes to see with (with the difference that eyes send messages and images to the brain). In the not too distant future a soldier's 'eyes' will analyse, process and interpret the data before the soldier is even aware of it.

But the promise of tomorrow's technology is greater still. Tomorrow's soldier may be plugged into a virtual world in which the digital and real are fused. This will depend on advances in smart matter research based on Micro Electro-Mechanical Systems (MEMs), very small sensors and actuators that are etched onto silicon using photolithography-based techniques. These would allow a soldier to see more than he could with the natural sensors he is born with, and to adapt to his environment far faster (allowing him to see an enemy behind a ridge, or a terrorist in the room of a house he is about to search).

The phenomenon we are describing is called 'ubiquitous computing', a term coined by Mark Weiser working at Xerox Parc back in 1988. As our systems become smarter, so they will become less visible or 'transparent'; we will become increasingly integrated into the technologies we use. In the brave new post-human world of the future, software agents will be forming our consciousness and co-evolving with it (not quite fashioning it yet, but in the role of smart technologies, adapting it to random explorations and emerging interests, and attracting our attention to new ideas, products and people). Not too far into the future we will be able to instantly locate the books on our bookshelves through sensor devices; software programs will pick up our reading preferences and alert us to new books online; our homes will heat themselves; we will be able to cook our meals whilst on the way home; spaces in car parks will soon tell us that they are free. In medicine, drugs will be more and more tailor made for the patient, eliminating in the process many of the unpleasant side-effects that result from taking drugs.

In such a world, there will be no interface between man and machine as we know it at the moment. The computer will be drawn into our world and we will be drawn into its; until, that is, the two become largely indistinguishable. Both of us will become embodied in the same world. As Andy Clark writes: 'The more closely the smart world becomes tailored to an individual's specific needs, habits and preferences, the harder it will become to tell where that person stops and this co-evolving smart world begins'. (Clark, 2009, 182)

The smart world will interact in such harmony with the biological brain that it will serve no purpose to draw a line between the two. So much, then, for the traditional warrior code that comes from our embodied, biological self: what we see with our own eyes, and what we can imagine to be the likely outcome of our actions. This interactive world of technology and humanity may mark the next stage in our cultural evolution.

As Andy Clark writes, sensory inputs are already moulding us psychologically. What makes this possible is the structure of our brain that allows for an unusual degree of cortical plasticity. Computers are already reshaping us in ways we do not always acknowledge, or are not even willing to admit. Not only are they extending our computational and mental skills, they are also beginning to change us beneath the level of conscious awareness. 'Well-fitted transparent technologies have the potential to impact what we feel capable of doing, where we feel we are located, and what kinds of problems we find ourselves capable of solving'. (Clark, 2009, 102)

And how may this change the warrior? Let us speculate for a moment. In the world of tomorrow, the unit has gone, as has the regiment (a very early casualty). There is no longer the traditional concept of *esprit de corps*, and no need for social capital, and absolutely none for what Emerson called self-trust. The defining feature of war has always been camaraderie: why do soldiers take risks? They take risks for each other; the warriors' 'life-world' has been that of intense friendships forged in battle. This life world may become as antiquated as the traditional Victorian patriarchal family structure. Every 'family' including military units, offers a sense of identity, a sense of belonging. It even transforms the Beavises and Buttheads of society into men, who learn for the first time that respect is something that one earns, not demands at the point of a knife or a gun. Tomorrow's cybernetic web may make redundant the old methods of training and education. Everything one needs to know may be collectively relayed and shared. There will be no role models, no emulation of others, no neural link with the ancestors. The system will generate its own imperatives and make its own demands. The idea of heroic individualism may be distinctly old-fashioned. It is the system that will count, not the person or unit. The cybernetic network will set the gold standard. Old tribal rivalries and inter-service competitiveness will be relegated to history.

Indeed in the cybernetic battle space soldiers may not need to depend on anyone else emotionally for their self-worth (they will not need to be seen by others to exercise the right choices, unlike the young Henry Fleming, or be big enough to make the choices that only they and no-one else can make). What then? Without private thoughts the very concept of personal initiative may become arcane, a leftover from an unremembered past. Even if you could experience the world outside the network—that is, have an insight that others do not—you would not be able to communicate it to your friends. It would not be part of the cyber-stream that will constitute the collective life.

And then again, the old social networks within the military may also be hollowed out. There may be no staff colleges or regimental lifestyles, or veterans' associations. If the network will no longer supply role models for those outside it or heroes for society at large, this may also be true within the ranks. What of the concept of a veteran, for example? Tomorrow's armed forces may be composed entirely of veterans: veterans of cyberspace who have logged up hours and hours of combat: an army of high-tech masters who may never have fired a real shot in anger, but have nevertheless taken out enemies and their installations as ruthlessly as Achilles took out the Trojans.

The cyber world will be virtual and self-sustaining: it will be replicated in a cyber world of computer games, not the narrative structures of novel or film. Karl Marx predicted that Achilles would not survive modern industrialised warfare: 'Is Achilles possible when powder and shot have been invented. Is the *Iliad* possible at all when the printing press and even printing machines exist? Is it not inevitable that with the emergence of the press, the singing and talking cease?' (Marx, 1996, 150) He was right. Epic poetry really did perish on the Western Front in the first major industrialised war. The glory of war on which the epic was based was found to be hollow. The glamour of war, for a time, survived. But even glamour (the thrill, the spectacle and sound—for war is an intensely auditory experience) may be passing, too.

Finally, soldiers may find themselves enmeshed in a cybernetic world quite different from the world of their adversaries. They too, will be enmeshed in networks, but ones that are tribal, not cybernetic; they will not have made the transition to the next level. The challenge is this: traditionally we have lived in the same community of fate as our enemies. In every war there is a private space where the warrior may admire another, or a citizen-soldier may even feel for the enemy he is trained to kill. In Sophocles' play *Ajax*, Odysseus is told by the goddess Athena that his enemy is cursed by endless misfortune. But the point of the play is that we are different from the gods in one critical respect: it is because we are mortal that we are moved to compassion by the fate of others. The gods, Homer tells us, watch war unfold (for all the world like carrion birds, like vultures). (Manguel, 2010, 249). We, by contrast, are not always indifferent to the suffering we produce. Odysseus remarks of an enemy, 'Yet I pity him when I see him weighed down with misfortune. Indeed, it is towards myself more than towards him that I direct my thoughts, since I see clearly that we are all of us who live upon this earth nothing but ghosts or weightless shadows'. (Manguel, 2010, 149)

It is our mortality that constitutes our humanity. Everything on earth is mortal, even the gods eventually die in our hearts. Friedrich Nietzsche even predicted that we would abjure God altogether the day we concluded that he was less interested in us than we were in Him. What makes us distinctive is our knowledge of death, from which stems our empathy for others. But what of a post-human warrior whose thoughts are patrolled, whose sentiments are manipulated?

Perhaps the real fear, writes the neuroscientist Susan Greenfield, is that the post-humans of the future will not empathise with other people, or even wish to relate to others or even understand them. The virtual cybernetic world with which the soldier interacts may diminish his social intelligence; it may make him even more self-absorbed, and certainly more self-regarding. (Greenfield, 2003, 63)

To imagine war without any inter-subjective experience would be hard indeed, but what of the cybernetic world in which the enemy is merely on screen? Would it lock us into a narcissistic, self-referential, almost autistic world? Would it lock us into numbing isolation with ourselves? What is really challenging is not that war may become a game, but that we may become dissociated from what war means to other people, those locked out of our cybernetic world.

Know thyself

For Aristotle, seeing comes before words. It is our first step to experiencing the world. The next is speech, but once you try to express something in words and later in writing, you are putting another filter between experience and yourself. Think about what you commit to paper. You are bringing knowledge to bear on what you see. You are seeing the world anew. You are looking at the relation between things and yourself. You are recording what you see and find significant. Meaning, in that sense, is built into all information processing. The very act of seeing anchors us to time and space. What we see is a point of view on reality.

Our points of view on life including war are now mediated through technology as never before. Since the arrival of aerial photography at the Battle of the Marne (1914) our vision has been increasingly synthetic. But it is still we who do the seeing. Computers cannot induce meaning yet; only we can. We sometimes ignore this difference because we are given to thinking of our own minds as computers. We talk of 'programming' our lives and 'interfacing' with others, just as we endow machines with humanity (comparing neural networks to brain synapses and genetic algorithms to our own genetic codes). There is an inevitable tendency in the human mind to interpret human functions in terms of the artefacts that take their place and artefacts in terms of the replaced human functions. (Jonas, 2001, 110) For some time we have had a computational theory of the mind: the idea that our beliefs and memories are a collection of information like facts on a database, and that thinking and planning are systematic transformations of these patterns, not dissimilar, in fact, from the operation of a computer program. Wanting something or trying to achieve something else, we say, are merely feedback loops that execute actions to reduce the deficit—the difference between the goals we set and the actual state of the world.

The best example of this difference is a conversation in William Gibson's novel, *Neuromancer*:

'Can you read my mind, Finn?'

'Minds aren't read. See, you've still got the paradigm print gave you and you're barely print-literate. I can access your memory but that's not the same as your mind'.

Gibson offers us two different metaphors of consciousness. He postulates a future world in which one of the characters, Finn, can actually access his friend's memory, but as he is the first to admit it is not the same as hacking into his mind. Gibson is applying, quite correctly, a computer-mediated metaphor to explain a change in human subjectivity. The old metaphors related to the Gutenberg universe of print really are fading fast. But actually the old metaphors still hold in one respect, as Finn admits. He cannot actually 'access' his friend's mind or, as we might say, 'read' it. (Gibson, 1993, 37) For in the end, we don't programme our lives, we live them (with all the messy compromises and negotiated rites of passage involved) and we still rely on emotional intelligence to negotiate life successfully.

For while we compare ourselves to computers, we think in a way that is different again. When we talk of rationality or using reason, we do not speak of the ability to think dispassionately, to reason out and do the mathematics, but in terms of our emotions—to reason our existence, to rationalise our irrational natures, to empathise and imagine the plight of others. We may not be the only animals on the planet that can reason, or even compute, but we are the only ones that have imagination. (Jonas, 2010, 94) We are not computers, any more than computers are like us. We know that in war not all problems are computable or capable of being logically solved. As the mathematician Kurt Gödel discovered, if you start with a set of logically consistent premises which lead to certain conclusions or consequences, then the power of logic will not always be able to take you from these premises to all of the consequences and conclusions. We have to fall back on imagining what they might be.

No machine, in other words, possesses the prior beliefs that are the essential ingredients of human knowledge, which is why at the moment no machine or computer can be creative. Computers cannot actually impute meaning to the data they process. They have no flexible pattern recognition or language understanding, to name just two of the human abilities that are essential to making sense of the information we process every day. Until software is radically improved, computers will not be able to reason by analogy or produce testable hypotheses, both of which are central to understanding the world around us.

Computers do not make mistakes, except when the machine fails. We do, because we insist on attributing meaning to the data we process, and sometimes, more often than we are willing to acknowledge, we are wrong. Yet without the capacity to make mistakes based on incorrect information processing, we would not need an emotional intelligence in the first place. We would not have to live emotionally-enhancing lives. Without the inductive reasoning we apply when processing information we would not be caught out by surprise, we would not have the defeated expectations that make up the human comedy. We would not experience the hunger to know more (and therefore the intellectual curiosity which underpins science). 'It is because we live in a domain of possibilities that we can imagine new realities, and why we are able to transform actuality as no other creature has'. (Tallis, *Times Literary Supplement*, 2011) And this is the great challenge that today's military faces. Our soldiers need to be innovative, adaptive and inventive as never before.

All processing of information is modelled on what the German sociologist Niklas Luhmann calls the 'complexity differential' between the individual and his environment. (Geyer, 1998) The accelerating rate of change and the exponentially increasing flow of information are already facing us with a bandwidth problem—the bandwidth in which we make informed decisions is moving in the direction of ever more environmental stimulation. We are being forced to be more innovative in our response to the changes that life throws up. The military now teaches young recruits to be fully aware that external reality is framed by the observer; different observers will structure reality differently (and interpret data accordingly). Soldiers are now told that what is true is time-dependent and therefore needs to be constantly updated. And the truth is problem-related too. Different models of the world may only apply to certain problems. 'Lessons learned', therefore, is a challenging concept—there are now only so many lessons that can be learned from the last campaign that will be applicable to the next.

Luhmann argues that increasing environmental complexity can only be managed by an increase in internal complexity (that is, becoming more complex ourselves). There are two ways of achieving this: one is self-organization, the other self-reference. The military tends to concentrate most on the first, and a striking example of this is simulation. Today everything is simulated, from missions flown by pilots to land battles fought in simulated battle environments. And simulation certainly is effective. Flight simulation, which is the longest-standing application of the technology, is indeed more realistic than the experience of actually flying a plane. Pilots will learn more on a simulator than they would in the air, for the former permits them to encounter situations that in the real world they might not survive. But, of course, although virtual reality can enhance the experience of flying a plane, it cannot reproduce the feeling of flying into an anti-aircraft barrage. It cannot reproduce the true battlefield experience: the knowledge that in the real world, weapons kill.

This was found by the soldiers who took part in the famous firefight in Mogadishu in 1993. Late in the afternoon of 3 October 1993 140 elite US soldiers abseiled from helicopters into a teeming market neighbourhood in the heart of the city. Their mission was to abduct two lieutenants of a Somali warlord, a task that was supposed to take no more than an hour. Instead, they found themselves pinned down in a long and terrible night in a hostile city, fighting for their lives against thousands of heavily armed Somalis. Two of their high-tech helicopters were shot down. When the unit was rescued the following day, 18 American soldiers were dead and more than 70 badly injured.

When they were later interviewed, all the survivors said they had felt that they were extras in a film (an experience not untypical of today's generation who are trained on screens and spend their childhood playing computer games). They had to keep convincing themselves that the blood and death all around them were actually real. They all described feeling out of place as if they did not belong there, which is why they also experienced feelings of disbelief, anger and ill-defined betrayal. 'This cannot be real' was the common complaint (Bowden, 1999, 345–6). Is this likely to be one of the consequences of training soldiers in virtual reality? Will it make combat on the ground increasingly 'unreal'?

Programming our responses is laudable, but it may encourage a form of emotional dissociation. We know that in cases of damaged neurological minds, the brain can act in different ways. Joseph LeDoux tells the tale of a woman suffering from serious amnesia. So serious was her condition that every time she met the doctor treating her, she had to be reintroduced to him for the 'first time'. One day, he concealed a tack in his hand. When they shook hands, he drew blood. When they next met and he extended his hand to shake hers, she instinctively drew back. The woman's amnesia was occasioned by a lesion in the temporal lobe—her amygdale was intact and the threat the man posed was indelibly imprinted in its circuitry; she instinctively knew that the doctor was not a man to be trusted. (Goleman, 2006, 102) Something similar may be involved in the rewiring of soldiers for future missions. They may know instinctively what to do and whom to trust, which will certainly allow them to adapt quickly and successfully in combat. But they may not necessarily know themselves, they may be strangers to themselves.

And what of self-reference? The chief injunction of Greek philosophy was to know oneself. Self-reference encourages a soldier to know himself better in order to deal with the unexpected. Self-referential coding, as Luhmann calls it, or information about oneself, is preferentially encoded. And self-knowledge has been growing all the time; it is a feature of cultural selection. The 18th-century novel is a case in point. Fiction, writes Richard Rorty, shows us the suffering of people with whom we are not personally acquainted; it shows us gratuitous acts of cruelty that we know we are capable of ourselves. Fiction, he adds, allows us re-describe ourselves. (Rorty, 1989, xvi)

The Greeks made a vital distinction between experience and illumination. It is one thing to interact with the world, it is quite another to plumb its depths—to grasp deeper levels of reality that are not always immediate to the senses. It is one thing to see things as they are, quite another to see them for what they are. Understanding proceeds through living what one is trying to understand; that is often the result of teaching, and is the reason why great educators can have an impact on their students' lives. The novel was the product of the Enlightenment, and it allowed us to get into the minds of other people and see our own lives reflected back. Equally important to self-knowledge was the birth of psychology in the late 19th century, and the military bought into the new science quickly; they were one of the first institutions to employ psychological evaluations to root out people who had no self-knowledge, those whose interior psyche was deemed to make them bad team players in what is the ultimate team-related activity: war. They also wished to root out those who were constitutionally incapable of self-reflection (such as psychopaths and sociopaths—the very people who tend to gravitate to paramilitary organizations and extreme political movements, but with whom most professional armies will have no truck).

One of the main objects of military training is to get a soldier to know himself better so that they will be moulded into a primary group, for it is primary group cohesion that in the end often makes the difference between success or failure in battle. It remains to be seen, writes Felix Geyer, to what extent any increase in self-reference will continue in tandem with the increase of environmental complexity. 'One cannot 'mindfuck' all day', he writes. (Geyer, 1998) And sensitivity training may have its limits. Ian Long, one of the first Tornado pilots to take part in the air war against Iraq, was applauded by one British public relations executive as presenting 'a relevant, caring, 1990s face' to the cameras, rather than the historically sanctioned military mode of masculine aggression (Coker, 2001, 106). But warriors have to be aggressive, albeit it in emotionally intelligent ways: the trick, as Plato told us, is not to neutralise the aggression, but to focus it. But perhaps even this misses the main point. For how important will individual self-knowledge be in the future when warrior geeks come into their own?

4

ONLINE WAR

'We are but warriors for the working day; our gayness and our guilt are all besmirch'd with rainy marching on the painful field'. So remarks Shakespeare's Henry V, one of the greatest warriors of all in the Western literary canon. He is talking about his army as its marches across Normandy. What the readers of popular works want most from historians is the human story—the guilt and the glory for the most part, but also the miseries visited upon men in the 'painful field' of battle. What the public wants to read about most is what a British Field Marshal called 'the actualities of war': the effects of tiredness, hunger, fear, lack of sleep, the weather. (Holmes, 2004, 7) What sells books is the readers' interest in humanity. With the ability we have as a species to imagine the world other than it is, we can give full play to our imagination. We can conceive a world without war, but it is much more difficult to conceive war without warriors. War is defined traditionally by the warriors who wage it. They are what the public thrill to: the Roman legionaries in the opening battle scene of Ridley Scott's *Gladiator* fighting the barbarians on the frontier; the mediaeval knights charging into battle, met by equally intrepid and immobile English longbowmen, in the two film versions of Shakespeare's *Henry V;* the D-Day soldiers storming the beaches of Normandy depicted so graphically in Steven Spielberg's *Saving Private Ryan.*

It is the extremities of human experience that make war so vivid. What we find of eternal interest are the narratives of human endurance which document courage demanded of men who have never shown it before; the wilfulness of the commanders like Lee sending in Pickett's men to their death at Gettysburg, or Napoleon sending the Imperial Guard to their death at Waterloo. Academics tend to spend much of their time analysing the causes of war, or its economic consequences; most prefer to write about armies (rather than the men who comprise them); most downplay the 'genius' of the great commanders whose names once used to resonate in school, but do so no longer. Novelists, by contrast, are more interested in the human factor. 'Wars demand novels', claims the American novelist E.L. Doctorow. (Doctorow, 2007, 85) And they are more interested in individuals whose actions often made a significant contribution to victory or defeat—men like William Barksdale at Gettysburg and Joshua Chamberlain in the same battle, one fighting for the Confederacy, the other for the Union. Novels have helped to define every major war in which the US has been engaged—*The Red Badge of Courage* did so for the Civil War, Normal Mailer's *The Naked and the Dead* for the war in the Pacific. Joseph Heller's *Catch-22* captured the absurdities of the air war in Europe. The Vietnam war had its poets and novelists aplenty and produces great novels still. (*Matterhorn*, 2010)

But fiction has lost much of its edge. Many of today's novelists seem to have difficulty grasping the nature of war. 'If you haven't the root of the matter in you', wrote Henry James, 'you are a fool in the very presence of the revealed ...even before mysteries abysmal'. James penned this statement in the preface to his novel *The Princess Casamassima* (1886) whose subject is terrorism. And the War on Terror, with its cast of new characters from cubicle warriors to suicide bombers, seems to tax the imagination even of our leading novelists. Our accounts of war today tend to be graphically visual, not textual, for that reason. The image rather than the word renders war into an experience that can be shared. Hollywood has helped, not always intelligently, to give moral shape to the wars we have fought most recently by raising questions about the nature of moral responsibility, the ubiquity of courage, small scale or large, the stubborn humour of warriors confronting an unforgiving environment. These days, if we wish to read about heroes, we prefer to read about real ones in the accounts relayed by embedded journalists, or soldiers in the field. Both appropriate the techniques of the novel—they define character, and delineate the landscape of battle, all the more vividly, perhaps, because what they are depicting happens to be true. Where the novel tells us that something like this might have happened, the non-fiction writer tells us that it actually did.

But what is most striking about narratives of war today is that they are embedded in the old fashioned units—the 'grunts' that do the actual fighting on the ground, the special forces that penetrate behind enemy lines. Rarely does Hollywood spend time capturing the lives of cyberwarriors hacking into enemy systems or preventing the enemy from hacking into their own, or the cubicle warriors piloting drones over the skies, taking out terrorists and producing hours and hours of video-streams and high-altitude spy photos, and monitoring hundreds of hours of signals intelligence (usually cell phone calls) every day. It is their story, however, that may be the most important for they are already beginning to redefine the face of war.

Cyberwarriors

As described by the English poet Dryden in his famous translation of the *Aeneid*, still the best rendition in the English language:

> *The Greeks grew weary of the tedious War:*
> *And by Minerva's Aid a Fabrick rear'd,*
> *Which like a Steed of monstrous height appeared.*

We know that there had been a long dispute between Achilles and Odysseus on how best to take Troy—through guile or force. Force had failed. After ten years the Greeks are facing defeat. With Achilles' death they have lost their best warrior. The scene is set for a last throw of the dice, and this time Odysseus gets his way; where force has failed, guile prevails. The Greeks fashion a wooden horse which they mislead the Trojans into thinking is an offering to the gods to speed their passage back to Greece. The Greek army appears to depart the field, but it is stratagem, of course—they hide out on the offshore island of Tenedos, leaving inside the horse an advance party that, once within the city walls, will unlock the gates and let the Greek forces into the city.

Only the perspicacious priest Laocoon suspects the ruse and warns his countrymen:

> *O wretched Country-men! What fury reigns*
> *What more than madness has possessed your Brains?*
> *Think you the Grecians from your Coasts are gone?*
> *And are Ulysses' arts no better known?* (Hill, 2010, 32)

Laocoon suffers for his pains. A serpent sent by the gods swims ashore and kills the priest and his sons. Fearing punishment for their impiety, the Trojans drag the Horse inside the city walls. The rest, as they say, is history.

In the Greek world Odysseus was admired for the same skills as a cyber-hacker today—deception, duplicity, fraud, lies and plots. He was known not only as a *polytropos* and *polymetis* but also by the epithet *polymechanos*, a master of machines. And what the Horse represents is something very similar to a viral infection in today's computer systems. Long before the soldiers emerge from the horse to open the city gates, the virus infects the Trojans' minds. An apparent defector, Sinon, goes over to the Trojan side and persuades them to bring the horse inside the city. He weaves a plausible enough story. Everyone knew the Greeks were weary of war; everyone knew they were also highly superstitious—hadn't Agamemnon sacrificed his own daughter before the expedition sailed to ensure favourable winds for the ships? And, as always, the devil was in the detail. Sinon tells them the horse is so large so that it will not be able to enter the city. They wouldn't want the Trojans, after all, to take the effigy and use it for their own good fortune. Here, adds Charles Hill, is the Br'er Rabbit briar patch ploy: fervently assert what you desperately do not want to happen in order to make sure it does. 'Had there been a Trojan Investigative Board of Inquiry', writes Hill, the 'After Action Report' would have concluded that they had failed to connect the dots. They had failed to anticipate the 'geekishness' of their opponents. (Hill, 2010, 32)

As Hill contends, the Trojan Horse was the very first 'virus' to communicate the wrong information to the enemy. It can be seen as a virus of the mind which quickly spread through the population in much the same way as a virus—a Trojan Horse no less—infects a computer. It transmitted an idea (which pandered to wishful thinking) which influenced behaviour (a willingness to stand down their army in the absence of a full strategic appraisal of the facts). Only after the horse was safely lodged within the city walls did it unpack a more conventional message. Sinon steals through the streets of the city at night and unlocks the pine bolts of the trapdoor of the horse, allowing Odysseus and his friends to slide down a rope to wreak havoc.

Odysseus may not seem like a classic geek, but there was something different about him as the Greeks understood well enough. He is always portrayed rather unflatteringly in the tragedies and popular tales. Of course, he was a hero and a consummate warrior, but he got a bad press almost from the beginning as a man who was too clever by half. Lacking the passion that made Ajax and Achilles the heroic figures they were, and lacking even the fundamental humanity of Hector, he is remembered for his guile in persuading Achilles to join the expedition, and Philoctetes to rejoin it (more of this latter character anon).

The Homeric battlefield is far removed, of course, from the cyberworld we now inhabit. Etymologically, the word cyberspace can be traced back to the science fiction writer William Gibson and a short story, 'Burning Chrome', which he penned in 1982. Not that Gibson attached much importance to the term at the time. Of his creation he later said: 'it seemed like an effective buzzword … evocative and essentially meaningless. It was suggestive but had no real semantic meaning even for me'. (Gibson, 2000) Meaningless or not, we now face all manner of cyber-prefixed threats from 'cyber-espionage' and 'cyber-terror' to 'cyber-war' and even 'cyber-geddon' and these, in turn, have engendered other cyber-prefixed neologisms such as 'cyber-security', 'cyber-power' and 'cyber-strategy'.

The world of cyberwarfare is denominated by computer algorithms and codes. The weapons are built from binary 'I's and 'O's, bits and bytes that allow a variety of actors—both state and non-state—to attack computer systems on which we increasingly rely. And cyberwars have already been fought in earnest, beginning with the anonymous cyber-attack on Estonia in 2007 ('the first unnoticed Third World War', according to the country's Minister of Defence); the Israeli cyber attacks which blinded the Syrians to a conventional bombing raid that took out their North Korean built nuclear facility in 2008 (Israeli aircraft never appeared on the Syrian radar screens); and the Russian infiltration of Georgian networks in 2005. (Samaan, 2010, 18) More recently, we have seen the Stuxnet virus, developed by the US and Israel, which set back the Iranian nuclear programme. Stuxnet, named from parts of its embedded code, is capable of reprogramming software that controls climate control systems and even robotic arms.

Cyberspace already penetrates every level of our lives. We use it to shop and book airline tickets and make friends on Facebook and 'de-friend' them equally quickly. Cyberspace used to be an alternative to real life; it is now part of it. Entire social movements like the anti-globalization movement and terrorist groups like al-Qaeda exist only because of the internet which allows its members to meet each other, and swap know-how and discuss strategies of civil disobedience or uncivil destruction.

What is interesting about war in cyberspace is that long before we began to worry about enemies hacking into military networks, corporations had long been talking of 'de-militarised zones' (moderately protected public network services), 'arsenals' (data protection mechanisms), 'perimeters' (boundaries between different data risk levels) and 'safe passage' (the protection of data through unprotected domains). Usually, war provides a host of metaphors that other professions, including commerce, borrow after the fact. In this case, commercial metaphors have been adopted enthusiastically by the military. Cyber strategists are responsible for designing systems that are less vulnerable to attack; cyber tacticians are responsible for installing appropriate safeguards (firewalls, data backups, redundant configurations).

'Technology does not invent, or maintain itself, but needs human beings to bring it out into production', writes Henry Perkin in *The Third Revolution*. 'It is thus not the technology that matters, but the human skill and social organisation that lie behind it. In other words, it is the professional experts who have constructed the system which, in turn, has created them'. (Perkin, 1999, 135) What makes cyber-warriors what they are is their skill in hacking into other people's computer systems. As Tim Jordan points out in his book *Cyberpower* (1999), hackers have those skills aplenty, and sometimes they can be put to lethal use. 'Hackers demonstrate the extreme end of the techno-power elite where material resources are close to zero though never actually zero, and expertise is monumental'. (Jordan, 1999, 139)

And like every social group, hackers have evolved. David Betz offers an evolutionary model with different 'animals' branching off a common ancestor:

1st evolution (from 1960s to 70s)—creative programmers usually working in academic institutions on mainframe computers, ethical computer gurus e.g. MIT/Stanford.

2nd evolution (from 1970s-80s)—computer entrepreneurs involved in the shift from mainframe to personal computing, founded major computer companies and digital communities (e.g. Apple, the Well).

3rd evolution (from 1990s)—copyright breakers using the web for file sharing largely for entertainment than profit, e.g. Napster, Pirate Bay etc.

4th evolution (from 1990s)—criminals and cyberpunks hacking for profit or cyber-vandalism done for 'lulz' (fun). (Betz, 2011, 14)

The fifth evolution looks like producing a new warrior caste with Odysseus' skill of getting the enemy to believe the ideas he implanted in their minds. One example is social engineering: attacks that trick us into doing others' bidding, such as encouraging people through phishing e-mails to enter their bank credentials onto fraudulent websites which can then be reused for everything from finance fraud to outright identity theft. Social engineering attacks can also be used to trick users into infecting their own systems—for instance, by designing the infected software as video codec or flash updates.

The profile of an 18-year-old computer hacker may be just what the military is looking for. As Misha Glenny contends in his book *Dark Market*, hackers are a rare breed; even if they are considered criminals their psychological and social profile usually differs from that of habituated criminals. Some 95 per cent of them are males who are seeking power, solace or both on their screens. Most start out much earlier on a life of crime, usually in their early teens, often long before they are aware of the implications of what they are doing. The military, he adds, are among the few institutions that might bring these often hyper-intelligent youths in from the cold. (Glenny, 2011, 269–70)

Today's cyberwarriors, geeks, technos, hackers, coders or securocrats—like the warriors of Homeric times—are a human type too. Close to 100 per cent have advanced abilities in science combined with a low level of interest in the humanities. You will not find them reading Homer, or appreciating the value of Aristotelian virtue ethics, and they usually have no interest in politics or, for that matter, money. And more important, perhaps, they are all men, which suggests that war is and will remain a largely male activity. 99 per cent of the world's combat soldiers are still male and this is unlikely to change any time soon; and the same is true of the new warriors coming on stream—the drone pilots, and cyberspecialists. We have known for some time that boys play more violent games than girls, commit the largest share of violent crime, and act more recklessly. As women come to greater prominence in all walks of life we should expect the feminization of the armed forces as well, writes Steven Pinker. (Pinker, 2011, 688) But this does not necessarily follow where it may matter most—in the battlespace of tomorrow. Some 95 per cent of hackers are men; drone pilots are drawn from the ranks of young adolescent males who spend up to eighty hours a week playing violent video games. Technology liberated women from servitude and gave them control over their bodies. Contraception, the information economy, labour saving devices, longer life spans (including the ability to bear children much later in life) have all given women prominence in the white collar work force, but technology is also allowing war to readapt; it is likely to re-empower men, and halt the trend towards 'feminization' that many military pundits so deplore.

The cyber warrior probably is the first of a new breed. But the question remains to be asked: does he really deserve to be called a warrior? Not as we know it or recognise the term, though he may be part of the transition to what war is becoming—from information-in-warfare, which is as old as the profession itself, to information-as-warfare in which war ultimately is a matter of information control. Cyber warfare is a distinct branch of war, but just a branch, even though its apologists over-hype it in the same way that air power has been overhyped in the past. What is unclear is whether the new branch of war needs either warriors or men in uniform. Back in the early 1970s, the Distance Early Warning Line (DEWL), an air defence line in the Arctic, was manned by a 600-strong force of whom only 2 per cent were not civilians, and civilians were paid exceptionally good salaries to compensate them for working in exceptionally hostile conditions. (Vest, 2002, 17)

In cyberspace the military may come to rely more and more on civilian skills. Double-hatted in their lifetime, they may drift in and out of the civilian and military worlds, taking with them their security clearances. Other conventional and traditional assumptions may also come under scrutiny as they did, briefly, in World War II. Take the code breakers who worked at Bletchley Park. Like today's technical community in the military, they defied the stereotypes of military culture. They lived what even then were considered alternative lifestyles, and they wore their cleverness on their sleeves in a culture with a distinctive anti-intellectual bias. Their tweed jackets and long beards, blue shirts and apricot bowties marked them out as outsiders. The archetypal figure was the famous Alan Turing, 'a classic borderline Asperger's boffin' writes Sinclair McKay, with a high pitched voice, hesitating stammer and annoying laugh who had the disconcerting habit of cycling around the countryside wearing a gas mask (a personal measure to combat hay fever). (McKay,2010,17) Most of the men were allowed to be scruffy and even to wear pyjamas in the office. Even military officers wore uniforms only when they felt like it. Saluting was usually optional except when senior officers came down to visit. If you want a glimpse of that world, read Richard Harris' novel *Enigma*—a work of fiction, to be sure, but one based on fact.

But then the Bletchley Park decoders never claimed to be warriors, even though many of them put in long hours in emotionally stressful situations and often made as many sacrifices as soldiers in uniform. We still have recourse to the word 'warrior' for a reason. When the US military issued a document called 'Warrior Ethos' in 2005, it was to remind everyone, including ancillary staff, that even if they were serving in non-combat roles, they might still find themselves under fire. And to find oneself under fire required that everyone should subscribe to the principles of the warrior ethos. (Coker, 2008)

Some in the military argue that the technical community too, will learn to develop leadership skills over time—like those displayed by many of the project leaders at Bletchley—but do we not devalue the currency by applying the term 'warrior' to servicemen or women who will never be asked to put themselves at risk, or to make any more sacrifices than they would in civilian life (long hours for poor pay). Which in no way detracts from their professional commitment.

Charles Moskos, the military sociologist, once related the life story of an American soldier, Col Dandridge Malone:

He tells the soldier's story from the time he leaves home, a young recruit on his way to boot camp ... the anxiety and confusion of training school, the friendships, the coarseness, the constant reassignments and promotions, the compromises and satisfactions of the military marriage. Onto Vietnam, the fire fights, the fear again, the deaths of friends, survival and return; the first glimpse of children unseen for a year. And of all these wonderful things, Malone draws at the end ... which thousands of us share in whole or part, can by the mindless logic of the soul-less computer, programmed by a witless pissant ignorant of effect, be called just another job, then by God, I'm a sorry suck-egg mule. (Moskos/Wood,1988, 71)

Most soldiers do not see war as just another job like being a carpenter or business executive. And the reason for this is its peculiar rhythms and patterns: the long months of isolation, often of intense boredom; the months of separation from family and friends; the intense friendships forged in the ranks; the fire-fights for some, the anxiety of deployment for others; and, of course, the mental and physical state in which soldiers, even if they survive, may return; will they return the man or woman who left home? But just a moment's reflection will remind us that cyber warriors experience little of this. They only target systems, and they have to imagine, because they cannot actually see, the human and emotional damage for which they may be responsible. Most of them live permanently in a 'wooden horse' from which they will never emerge.

Cubicle warriors

It is on task
We never know his name
But he has been Positively Identified

Walking in the sun we watch him
On screen, on line, follow his final trajectory
The walking dead transmitted live
Above, sightless and soundless our proxy circles
A technical kill haunting the poppy fields
Far beyond comprehension—simply a computer plane.

He hears nothing, strolls on in sandals
Felt perhaps, only a sudden breeze
The herald of our cutting edge

('Transmitted Live', Delius Singer, medical officer of the Black Watch, serving in Forward Operating Base Shawquat, Afghanistan, 2011: 'Computer plane is what insurgents call drones', *Times Literary Supplement*, 25 November 2011).

Is this a glimpse of what Adorno suspected might be the future of war—humane for us, consummately inhumane for others? A particularly disturbing glimpse of such a future can be found in Don DeLillo's short story *Human Moments in World War Three*. One of the characters—Vollmer, a young pilot in a laser-shooting capsule orbiting the Earth—finds himself disengaged both emotionally and morally from life below. The 'human' moments in the story are largely banal: the fact that the commanders can wear their bedroom slippers at their firing consoles and take with them their own 'personal preference kits'. In this kind of war the warrior has been transformed into a technician and war into a routine. There is no place for any emotion; for hatred, courage or fear, or even physical endurance, the will-to-power over oneself. At one point Vollmer remarks that he is happy, a remark which irritates his commanding officer who reminds him that happiness is totally outside the crew's frame of reference. War has become just a house-keeping arrangement, a series of more or less routine tasks. (DeLillo, 1982, 122) Without emotion it has become what Sir Edward Grey would have called 'humane' and Adorno, begging to differ, might have thought an example of consummate inhumanity.

Delillo was writing in 1982. Twenty-five years later the future he anticipated was beginning to be fleshed out, not in space, but on Earth. In August 2009, a British journalist spent a day at Creech Air Force Base in the Nevada desert, where he visited a mobile ground control station for Predator drones. 'Is this it?' was his first thought, after being shown into the back of a caravan parked beside a two-lane highway about 45 miles outside Las Vegas. The caravan housed a US Air Force mobile ground control station, and the rather unimpressive-looking machine at the back of it was the flight deck for a remote-controlled Predator aircraft operating 7,000 miles away in Afghanistan.

It is hard to describe how surreal the journalist found the picture of two young pilots operating such a lethal device on a different continent from the battlefield. The advantages from a logistical standpoint were overwhelming: these 21st-century pilots got to live essentially the same lives as suburban sales executives. They kept regular hours. They commuted back and forth from home. Their workplace was clean, safe and air-conditioned. But where was the soldiers' honour in killing an adversary 7,000 miles away? What had happened to the idea of looking an enemy in the eye? Could they understand, he asked, the consequences of their actions? Surely, he concluded, killing should not be as easy as sending an e-mail, otherwise where would it all lead? (*The Times*, 12 August 2009)

The fear that war might become merely a routine dates back to the strategic bombing of World War II. At the time of the Blitz the English writer Graham Greene wrote a short story 'Men at Work' (1940) in which he described how the condensation trails of the German bombers after a daylight raid 'showed them going home after work'. (Munton, 1989 33) Some British bomber crews in the war also confessed to finding war a 'routine'. Some called themselves 'freight-engineers'; others 'aerial taxi drivers'; they returned from their missions, wrote one, 'bored in a way no-one had ever been bored before'. (Piette, 1999, 76–7) But the point of course is that unlike the planet orbiting pilots in DeLillo's tale they were exposed to constant danger; a plane could be shot down by anti-aircraft fire or intercepted in the air by fighters, and the crews were exposed to other hazards too, including respiratory infections from which they continued to suffer well into the peace. Seventy per cent of bomber crews suffered casualties; many flew mission after mission until they were killed. By August 1943 the Germans were shooting down as many American B-24 and B-17s as replacement crews and planes arrived in England. A man's courage is his capital, wrote Lord Moran in an influential study—the call on the bank may be the daily drain of the front line or it may be a sudden draft which threatens to close the account. And he found this to be as true for the pilots of Bomber Command as it was for the infantrymen or tank crews on the ground. 'The pilot enters upon the summer of his career, a period of confidence, success and achievement… But these summer months must pass and when autumn comes the picture of the pilots' distress is not so different from that of a soldier or sailor, only the colouring varies'. (Holmes, 2004, 214) The extent of that 'colouring' was caught many years later by one of the most powerful war novels to emerge from the experience of World War II, Joseph Heller's *Catch-22*.

Bomber pilots today no longer face the risks they did. Unlike B52 pilots in Vietnam, they are rarely if ever shot down. Embedded with a B1 bomber squadron in the early days of the War on Terror, the journalist Mark Bowden concluded that for the pilots war had become almost entirely cerebral, not visceral; it required them to invest little emotional energy into the task at hand. Almost immune from danger, they clocked up the hours in the sky like business executives, and like the latter they could be back home with their families in forty-eight hours from a mission over Afghanistan, in time to see the latest episode of *Friends*.

We are deploying drones for many reasons, but one of the most important is to reduce risk to a minimum. Henry Yuen, an expert in anti-submarine warfare, wrote an internal paper shortly after the end of the first Gulf War saying, 'One of the foremost objectives in the development of new weaponry should be the reduction or total elimination of human risk. Put simply, weapons or equipment in harm's way should, to the extent possible, be unmanned'. (Tofflers, 1994, 141) 'Our major role is to sanitise the battlefield', a service airman is quoted as saying in Peter Singer's book, *Wired for War* (2009). (Singer, 2009, 34)

Let me cite one more quotation: 'I hope that many more computer chips will lay down their lives for their country'. This remark is attributed to an American general following the loss of a drone somewhere in Bosnia in the 1990s. Drones are an ideal system; they can be deployed for days without risk to themselves or their pilots. They can fly thousands of feet up, silent and invisible to the naked eye, all the while tracking a target through heavy terrain, night and day. And one day—not too far off—they may be the size of insects (it is easier to get a machine to flap wings like an insect than like a bird). Combined with the aerodynamic wonders of the Hawk moth they may be able to hover for hours, hidden in plain sight, invisible to the naked eye while making everything else visible to the analysts back home. And what is hidden in plain slight is equally invisible to the public back home, even more so once drones can fly according to their own itineraries and in their own time.

But does the attempt to eliminate risk devalue the 'sacredness' of war? As the etymology of the word reveals, sacrifice is derived from sacred. All militaries regard the sacrifice of men (and now women) as sacred for that reason. There really is a fraternity in which men bond with each other, and on occasions will die for each other. The extraordinary fact is that soldiers return to the fight, like the Great War poets Wilfred Owen and Siegfried Sassoon. They need to reaffirm the brotherhood of soldiers, and what is central in their imagination is that the family is unsullied. It transcends the petty compromises and negotiations that distinguish many civilian friendships and even family ties, for familiarity often breeds staleness and sometimes mutual indifference. Shakespeare's 'band of brothers' is a sacred community cemented by sacrifice, and those who sacrifice themselves for their fellows live on in the memory of their comrades long after their death. The sacred inheres in a community to which all are bound whatever their class, talents, individual prejudices or beliefs. It is an affirmation of friendship in the face of a shared apprehension of danger. What is sacred is something that is unconditional; it is not contingent on circumstances or calculations of advantage.

For that reason it is also transcendental. As Luc Ferry writes, our traditional ethical codes, including the warrior ethos, assume that certain ideals are superior to life—that they are worth dying for. In other words, they reflect what Nietzsche would have called 'religious thinking'—to suppose that some values transcend life itself is, in effect, to lead us back to the most essential structure of any theology, the difference between 'here below' and 'above and beyond'. (Ferry, 1996, 19) As long as we continue to place ourselves at risk voluntarily, those risks have to be justified in the name of disinterested action: of something 'higher' than our embodied existence. A soldier who throws himself on a grenade to save the lives of his friends is sacrificing himself for something called 'friendship'. Sacrifice, after all, is one of the last vestiges of the existential dimension of war that we still permit the soldier to celebrate (in part for the instrumental value, of course—it allows other soldiers to go the extra distance, or inspires them to press on and complete the task). (Ferry, 1996, 22)

To remove sacrifice from war may have profound implications. It will still leave warriors, I am sure, with beliefs, because no beliefs can be built into war without self-belief—the warrior's honour is the pride in his gift and his works. Sacrifice is the warrior's gift to us if we are prepared to accept it on the terms on which it is made. But are our societies still anxious to demand it? Or are they really comforted by the thought that in tomorrow's world more computer chips than soldiers will be laying down their lives for their country? If so, the death of sacrifice may not be far off. It would signal an end to sacred violence, to the centuries-old idea that the profession of arms demands a loss just as the monastic life demands celibacy, and sainthood the prospect of martyrdom. We have never profaned war by abolishing sacrifice altogether, but then we have never before aspired to de-sacralise war by investing more faith in technology than in ourselves. Or is the difference becoming increasingly difficult to grasp?

Online warriors

In a passage from Thucydides' *History* we find a brief exchange between a Spartan prisoner of war and an Athenian soldier who asks his captive whether his fellow Spartans who had chosen so bravely to die rather than surrender the day before had been men of honour. The Spartan replies that a weapon would be worth a great deal if it could distinguish a gallant man from a coward. (Lendon, 2005, 47) But, of course, no weapon can. A weapon is merely a weapon. Unlike us, it is not smart but dumb. Even today a drone pilot operating an Unmanned Aerial Vehicle (UAV) over the skies of Afghanistan does not know when he launches it whether he is killing men who are brave or cowards. According to one drone pilot interviewed by a British newspaper, the modern warrior shares an intimacy with his targets that is unique in history: the *Reaper's* sensors allow a pilot to see 'an individual to a fidelity where you can perceive limb and arms, stuff that they are carrying...'. (*The Times*, 19 November 2011) In the world of modern war, he insists, there is no room for *machismo* or false heroics. One has to be absolutely clear that the guy being taken out is one of the bad guys. But Thucydides would have seen the flaw in the argument soon enough. A drone pilot may well be able to see more than any pilot has seen before, but the breadth of vision does not help him see the man within. He may have greater oversight of the battlefield than ever, but this affords him no greater insight into the moral status of the man he has in his sights.

We have made up for the fact that weapons cannot judge the moral status of humanity by endowing ourselves with moral standing. What the Greeks taught us was that war is the ultimate face to face encounter. Of course, Homer's heroes of the Trojan War actually addressed each other before despatching their enemies into the Underworld, engaging in those famous necrologues that seem so tedious to us today. Is this consistent with the changing face of war? In Shakespeare's play *Troilus and Cressida*, which is one of the most cynical 'takes' on war ever written, the eponymous hero remarks of two enemies that they 'know each other well', and 'long to know each other worse'. (*Troilus*) In Homer's story warriors do indeed look each other in the eye before engaging in battle. Will tomorrow's pilots want to know their enemies at all?

The moral implications of 'stand-off' warfare were raised by the German philosopher Karl Jaspers in his book *The Way to Wisdom*, in which he warned that 'we betray our humanity when we cut ourselves off from contact with others. True inter-subjectivity demands an unconditional commitment to oneself, one's unit, one's country and one's enemies as well. That is the true substance of the human condition'. (Jaspers, 1954, 59) This, at least, is what we still tell ourselves, and it is a story the military inculcates in its recruits as well.

If war is becoming increasingly digitalised, if the enemy on screen is reconstituted as pure 'data', then the embodied state of war that we have taken for granted—that enemy bodies are targeted, that there but for the grace of God we go—may rapidly diminish in our imagination. As war becomes (for Westerners) post-corporeal, so it might became 'a quintessentially cerebral experience, distilled from the material dross and distortion that is flesh itself'. (Graham, 2002, 188) Will the material dissolve into the virtual? Will pilots become emotionally and even psychologically disengaged from war itself?

Let me take the case of a young servicewoman operating a reconnaissance drone over Afghanistan from hundreds of miles away in Pakistan, using only a control stick, a computer keyboard and several television monitors. Using the same satellite links that ran the drone and relaying its same video imagery, she was able to call in a manned airstrike and direct it to a hut where some al-Qaeda members were milling around a vehicle. Later she told a *Wall Street Journal* reporter of her thoughts as she watched them die: 'You almost wanted to scream: Run, get out of the way! You're going to be killed'. (*Wall Street Journal*, 12 February 2003) But these days human beings running for cover are such a common sight that they have inspired the slang word 'squirters'. Not all uniformed military are happy with either the term or the sentiment. Warriors of the old school tend to be more disapproving than most. Interviewed by the *New Yorker*, Andrew Exum, a former army Ranger who advised General McChrystal in Afghanistan, confessed that while drone attacks were not dishonourable, they made him feel uncomfortable. His problem was that he was familiar with Thucydides and the Greeks. 'As a classics major I have a classical sense of what it means to be a warrior. There is something important about putting yourself at risk. We risk losing the flesh and blood investment if we go too far down this road'. (*New York Times*, 20 April 2010) Exum had written an account of his own combat experience in Afghanistan in which he had argued that combat alone validates war as a legitimate activity. For what matters is not life but the living of it. A warrior lives for others, not only for himself, and it is this reality that makes his service important for the rest of us. Combat, Exum asserts, is what redeems war as a profession. It is what gives an individual the chance to express his commitment to country and friends through the medium of combat. (Exum, 2005, 233)

But let us return to Thucydides' story of the exchange between the Athenian and Spartan soldiers and the first military historian's willingness to suspend disbelief just long enough to imagine a 'smart' weapon that could distinguish a brave man from a coward. Technologies, unfortunately, are not ethically or socially neutral. Technology first changes the environment and then changes our way of thinking and our values, hence the popular adage that to the person whose only tool is a hammer, all problems look like nails.

Technology has a huge impact on the societies responsible for it, changing attitudes and even normative assumptions, and it can even get them to think about war differently. In *The Social History of the Machine Gun*, the historian John Ellis writes that in the final phase of late 19th-century imperialism the Europeans assumed they had superior weapons (the Gatling gun) because they were the superior race. (Ellis, 1993, 82) When they opened their bloody dialogue with Africa they were firmly of the opinion, which we do not share, that the exercise of reason had made them equal to God: to invoke Descartes' splendidly optimistic phrase, it exempted them from being His subjects. Of no modern weapon was this probably more true than the machine gun which encouraged those who had invented it to see the enemy as sub-rational (not far from being sub-human). Social Darwinisim particularly helped at this stage of the game: the belief that there were degrees of humanity and that the Europeans stood at the very apex of the triangle. Social Darwinisim added a pseudo-scientific 'alibi of aggression' (Peter Gay's splendid term for the European tendency in the 19th century to categorise human beings in such newly minted, pseudo-scientific categories as ethnicity, race or class). The machine gun was the product, clearly, of a rational society because only a rational society could invent it. It was a weapon that could be used to get the natives to see reason, to see how foolish it was to resist. It followed that if they continued resisting, they were clearly being unreasonable. The machine gun gave the Europeans what no other technology had given a people before, the right to occupy the moral high ground. And in the end, many people did see reason. Cecil Rhodes impressed a group of East Pondoland chiefs by taking their elders into a field and levelling it with the fire of a Maxim gun within minutes. They grasped the rationale of the machine gun quickly enough; they chose to submit without a fight. (Low, 1973, 22)

And then the Europeans turned the machine guns against each other in 1914 and found themselves soon enough in a moral No Man's Land of their own making. Both sides came to see the machine gun in a completely new light precisely because the enemy shared the same moral world. Both were high-tech. Both were exempted from being God's subjects, and both acted accordingly.

We must choose our tools carefully, not because they are inhumane (all weapons are), but because the more we come to rely on them, the more they tend to shape our view of the world, and it is clear that technology is reshaping our inter-subjective experience with the enemy, which constitutes what we used to call a community of fate. We are human only insofar as our humanity is recognised by others including those we seek to 'take out'.

If distance was a 20th-century problem, disconnection is a 21st-century one. Paul Kahn, a Professor at Yale Law School, claims that both distance and disconnection 'propel us beyond the ethics of warfare' (Singer, 2009, 432); but the two are actually very different. One US Air Force colonel in command of a Predator squadron told Peter Singer that the young pilots under his command did not know what was really going on: they were semi-detached from the action. (Singer, 2009, 367) We talk of pilots being distanced when they cannot see the effect of their bombing; we talk of drone pilots being disconnected when they have an impaired understanding of war itself. And dissociation from the reality of war is becoming a theme of many Hollywood films. Take Ridley Scott's *Body of Lies* in which the CIA boss played by Russell Crowe is seen ordering a drone strike against terrorists from the comfort of his own office while the agent in the field, played by Leonardo Di Caprio, lives an off-line life, where he gets tortured, blown up, and at one point, beaten to a pulp. The real problem revolves around fighting war online.

Dissociation is almost impossible for a military man who leads an offline life, for even when he returns home he carries with him memories of what he has witnessed which may haunt him for years to come. Not all soldiers will be moved; hollow men are to be found in every army in every century and every culture. But many tell tales of brave men they have known and by whose side they have fought; or their own struggles against fear and exhaustion, and the soldier's greatest enemy, boredom; and some even tell stories of enemies who have won their grudging respect, if only for their own struggle with the same anxieties and passions that they themselves have had to master. And in the offline world of war, there is always the prospect of falling into enemy hands and facing the ultimate dilemma: what ethical demands can you make on someone you have been trying to kill?

In the online world of the drone pilot, there is nothing to be asked of the enemy. In the cybernetic world of war we expect less and less of human encounters as mediated by the world we see on screen. Sherry Turkle notes in her latest book, *Alone Together*, that online life tends to promote more superficial emotionally lazy relationships, as people are drawn to connections which seem low-risk. Young people now spend more and more time talking to each other without ever meeting. A survey in the US found that for every hour people spent using the internet, their face to face contact with friends and co-workers and family fell by 24 minutes. (Golman, 2006, 9) Our lives are increasingly revolving less around face to face encounters and/or relationships than around relationships conducted via the medium of a computer, or even with the computer itself.

More worrying still, current research suggests that online media encourages us to talk to like-minded people. We seek them out in internet chat rooms, and read each other's blogs. Our relationships are often brief, shallow and infinitely disposable. Teenagers can now receive up to 8,000 texts a month. Eighty per cent of Danish school pupils in the 9th grade now send on average five or more text messages a day to their friends, which means they 'hang out' not with a wide circle of people by necessity, but with a wide circle of like minded people by choice. (Bauman, 2010, 165)

Paradoxically, the widening of the range of opportunities to find like-minded people results in more narrow social skills of the seekers. De-friending on Facebook is a case in point. On Facebook friendships are often more virtual than real in both senses of the word. Relationships tend to be brief, disposable and shallow.

In the online world, the cumbersome translations, negotiations and compromises may be avoided, however, thanks to the saving grace of the 'delete' key. 'The necessity to engage in a dialogue, to ponder each other's reasons, to critically scrutinise and revise one's own motives … may therefore be suspended and postponed—perhaps indefinitely'. (Bauman, 2010, 166)

Contact can be broken whenever exchanges become complex or complicated, with no risk to oneself. You do not need to lie or dissimulate, or apologise, or compromise, all of which you have to do when breaking the link with people you meet in everyday life.

And this is the problem, for drone pilots are recruited from a generation that inhabits like-minded virtual networks which are springing up all the time. We know that technology is changing our habits and lifestyles and sometimes even our identity; what we do not know is whether the virtual world in which we now live at least part of our lives is changing us culturally. Is it making us more anti-social, less reactive to Jaspers' imperative of empathy for other people, especially those unlike us? Drone pilots now come from a generation that expects to transit life taking fewer risks that all of us once took for granted—the risks that inhere in life itself. Do they carry these attitudes with them from civilian life into war?

Will war be seen as a video-game?

This raises an even more disturbing question. If the next generation is becoming disconnected from life as well as war, at what point might they come to see war as a game?

The question comes up in Orson Scott Card's *Enders Game* (1985). Set in the distant future, the novel presents a humanity battling against an insectoid alien race called the Formics. In preparation for invasion of the Earth the planet's brightest and best young space cadets are trained on simulation machines. The most talented children, including the novel's protagonist Ender Wiggin, are moulded in the Battle School into the warriors of tomorrow. Only at the end of the novel does our hero find that he has not been playing a war game; he has been playing for real. He also discovers that he has wiped out the Formics completely. In the third part of the *Enders* trilogy, *Xenocide* (1991), we find him travelling the galaxy trying to find redemption for the greatest war crime of all—the annihilation of an entire species.

Ender's Game won the Nebula and Hugo Awards, the two most prestigious awards in science fiction. The novel has also been a 'must read' on the US Marine Corps reading list, and is recommended reading for Officer Candidate/Midshipman. The book is an allegory, of course which is why the Marines are encouraged to read it. It raises some disturbing questions about the direction in which war is heading.

The US military spends $6bn a year on virtual and simulated training programmes. Not all are video games, but their interactive scenarios are firmly rooted in the world of gaming where learning occurs in real time. And computer games have come a long way since *Space Invaders* in 1971, which offered a two-dimensional shooting gallery in which a laser cannon slides along the bottom of the screen firing up at slowly descending alien invaders. *Battle Zone* (1980), which gave the player command of a futuristic tank, was the first game to render the battlefield in three dimensions. Thirty years later came *Halo, Combat Evolves* (2001), a Microsoft product set aboard a space habitat in which Space Marines fight an alien race called the 'Covenant'.

Game players used to be happy to play World War II dogfights in the air, or tank battles on the ground. Now they want the experience of real time conflicts, and even those set in the more remote future rely on weapons that we employ today, from AC-130 gun ships to Predator drones. The games share many things in common: they are all highly kinetic; they involve thrilling ground assaults on battlefields where plasma beams frizzle and artillery rains down on the troops below; and the latest futuristic helicopters and space fighters battle it out, either in space or in the sky. These days players gain a real sense of being there: they see the battle space through the eyes of the combatants; they are immersed in the battle zone, and embedded in the action. And in most games, players get to play real protagonists, Navy SEALS or F-15 pilots. The battle experience is as authentic as possible. Even the battle sounds are real; they are recorded from real Apache helicopters firing real rounds.

And the battle zones are authentic in another respect, too. Soldiers are killed as a result of 'friendly fire'. The main difference from reality is that in most of them everyone is a combatant, whether an Al-Qaeda militant, a foreign Jihadist, or a Taliban foot soldier. The battlefields are usually empty of civilians (with the result that there is little collateral damage). A common criticism of games like *Soldier of Anarchy* or *First Battalion* is that they allow the players to treat the battlefield as just a 'kill-box' where the rules of engagement can be relaxed precisely because all there is to do is kill the enemy. In such games it is body counts, not hearts and minds, that matter most; kinetic exchanges, not courageous restraint, are the order of the day.

And that is what all games revolve around: a script or programme which captures the programmer's idea of what a combat situation should actually look like, whether a fire-fight in Iraq or a search and destroy operation in Afghanistan. What has made pilots different from games players at home has been combat experience. Now the US Air Force (USAF) is taking the first steps to training operators with no previous flying experience, let alone combat experience, a fact likely to increase the risk of impaired situational understanding, and likewise the risk of moral disconnection from war itself. It is precisely this fear that has led the Air Force to look into the possibility of synthetically immersing future pilots in-theatre using virtual reality systems. (Taylor, 2010, 3) But virtual reality has its critics. It allows you to be in two places at once—at your console and in theatre thousands of miles away; this is achieved through three-dimensional graphics and input-output devices that closely resemble the participant's normal interface with the physical world. The paradox is that once you remove the element of risk, you may also destroy the will to penetrate behind reality. Once immersed in a computer-simulated environment a player may lose the very human impulse to dig deeper into the uncharted reaches of the experience. Because reality is completely programmed you are denied the freedom to search and discover for yourself. In other words, the experience—flying a plane over enemy territory under fire, with fuel running out—is much diminished, and this is another potential cause of mental disconnection. 'It had been a great voyage, the voyage probably of my life', wrote a young F86 pilot who engaged in one of history's last major dog-fights over North Korea (Alvarez, 2007, 117). No-one could make such a claim about the experience of flying a plane on a military flight simulator, however photorealistic might be the real-time texture-mapped world, because there is nothing to discover about oneself in relation to the outside world. Ontology, or the study of being, writes Michael Heim, 'is the effort to develop a *peripheral vision* by which we perceive and articulate the hidden background of beings, the world or context in which they become real and meaningful'. (Heim, 1993, xii) (Emphasis in original) What peripheral vision does simulation allow?

Such is the concern about 'disconnection' that the USAF is looking into an immersive in-theatre virtual reality systems which will give tomorrow's pilots at least synthetic combat experience. But how real will this synthetic experience be? Simulation is improving all the time—well, at least that is what the military promise. At the moment it is still quite basic. The Program Executive Office for Simulation Training and Instrumentation Command (PEO STRI) is doing its best to constantly upgrade its immersive experience.

The problem is that most simulations make functions routine. Marine Corps' Modelling and Simulation Management Office adopted a game called *Doom II* in the late 1990s to train its four-man fire teams in conceptualising their trade—introducing them, for example, to neutral fire team support and the succession of command. And by far the most successful application of all was *Flight Simulator*, which dramatically raised the proficiency levels in the Air Force amongst Navy pilots who were able to download and play it at home. Today servicemen have access to 'simulation on demand'. Wherever they are stationed they are able to access any number of databases that can simulate a desert in the Gulf or an urban jungle in southeast Asia. And by playing the game before going into battle, they can anticipate the actual combat experience. The games are also becoming increasingly sophisticated. They now contain synthespians—virtual people with 'real' emotional personalities and behavioural traits with whom soldiers can interact.

But simulation always misses out the most important element in real life: that of surprise, the unexpected. Susan Sontag once described photography as 'experience captured'. The point about a film is the point about reading a book: it is someone else's experience you are viewing, and there is much to learn from it, just as you can learn much from military history, or the memoirs of warriors, even from novels such as *War and Peace*. It is the detachment produced by fiction that is important: you know that what you are reading or watching is a facsimile of the real, not the real thing. The same is true of Hollywood films. But video games are much more addictive, not only because they are interactive but because the 'rules' are very clear.

One example is the popular game *Grand Theft Auto IV* in which, to take one challenge, the protagonist (controlled of course by the player) must dispose of two dead bodies by driving them across a fictional New York City in the trunk of a car. In this game, as in all others, you are forced to conform to the programmer's understanding of reality—of how the world works, the mechanics of how cities are policed, how CCTV cameras monitor our movements, etc. In a simple game such as *Grand Theft Auto* this does not matter much; the rules for the real world and the fictional world are likely to be much the same. But war is very different because of its complexity. No game is going to give you an experience of the 'real'—there is always the possibility that in combat reality will always overwhelm you because it is not what you have been led to expect.

Aware of this failing, military planners are trying to simulate feelings so that soldiers will be better able to deal with them when they experience them under fire or in the field. The first virtual reality immersive system came on stream in 2002. It replicated a particular experience, the fear of falling. The players who 'fell' experienced what they would have experienced in real life: an increased heart rate. The University of Southern California's Institute for Creative Technologies (ICT) set up an even more ambitious VR experiment four years later. Named *Dark Con*, it allows a player to undertake a wartime reconnaissance mission. Playing the role of a scout, his task is to determine what danger, if any, is posed by the occupants of an abandoned building complex near a river. The mission involves negotiating a damp tunnel littered with detritus (human and other). Every sound is faithfully reproduced from the hissing of pipes to the thumping of the generators that power spluttering red lights. Every sight is reproduced, from seeping spigots to shadowy alcoves, as well as the sound of rats scattering at one's approach. Immersed in this environment the scout hears dogs barking in the distance and vehicles thundering across the road above. These are all sensory cues, and they are all calculated to increase emotional tension and trigger a response. (Morie/Williams, 2010)

Emotional experiences—according to studies by neural biologists—stimulate long term memory formation. What the military would like is for soldiers to remember their experiences when the real test comes, so as to be able to master their fears. Way back in 1904 it was found that anxiety could be lessened if training was 'embodied'—experienced at first hand rather than taught in the classroom. The disjunction between simulation and reality is much greater when one has to 'unlearn' what one has been taught. The condition is commonly referred to as 'negative transfer'. In other words, it is better to learn under stress. That way, the experience can be 'remembered' positively. (Rizzo, 2011)

All this is very well, but can we really pre-programme a soldier or a pilot to behave as planned? We often act in ways that surprise even us, looking back after the event; we are an irredeemably capricious species. No simulation, however sophisticated technically, can guarantee that those who have played it will react in the same way when put to the test. Our minds are not computers, and yet computers are now re-wiring our minds in subtle but important ways. In Thucydides we read that the Athenians risked their bodies as if they were not their own; they needed their minds, however, 'that which most was their own', in order to do the city some good. (Meier, 2011, 283) As we approach the post-human future we seem to be intent on trying to minimise as much as possible the bodily risks we ask our armed forces to run, but we have also begun to take an interest in what is going on in their minds.

The Americans once again are pushing back the frontiers of war. In the case of air power, which they pioneered after 1903, they took war into the third dimension, making it quite literally three-dimensional for the first time. The invention of the atomic bomb was even more revolutionary for it broke with the past, with such Newtonian killing systems as ballistics, chemistry and aeronautics, all of which can be seen as extensions of the gunpowder 'revolution' of the 16th century. The bomb that was dropped on Hiroshima did not explode because of the blending of chemicals; it exploded because of a humanly engineered change in the very nature of matter. (Appleyard, 1992, 22) And the use of drones involves yet another leap forward into redefining war as 'the human thing', for it has set scientists the task of understanding what happens to the human brain when a pilot is wired into a cybernetic system and what changes, if any, can be made in 're-wiring' his brain.

Embodied consciousness

An Italian soldier, Emilio Lussu, had a disconcerting experience on the Italian Front in September 1916. He found that he had a party of Austrian soldiers in his rifle sights and was determined to shoot their officer. Then the officer lit a cigarette. Lussu experienced a strange mechanical sensation. He found that although his conscious mind was planning to fire, his index finger was slowly relaxing its grip on the trigger. The officer's trivial gesture in lighting a cigarette had stripped him of two things Lussu disliked most: Austrians and officers, irrespective of the uniform they wore. In the random action of lighting a cigarette, the Austrian had become a 'man' like himself. Lussu found himself overwhelmed by pity. Smoking, it would seem, can on occasions be good for your health.

This emotional response was no reflection on the quality of his mind, but on the working of his imagination. It was a momentary experience, but it haunted Lussu for weeks afterwards. (Finkelkraut, 2001, 21–4) Today we know the scientific explanation for what had happened. We now know why it is possible for a soldier to empathise with the enemy, even a sniper with an enemy combatant in his sights.

The word 'empathy' was first introduced into English in 1909. The man who first imported the word into the language wrote: 'When I observe a circus performer on a high wire, I feel inside him'. (Golman, 2006, 58) Today we now know that this is not just a figure of speech. We really do feel another's fear and distress. It is a case, neuroscientists tell us, of the action of mirror neurons which allow us to grasp the minds of others (their fear and apprehension) not through conceptual reasoning, but through direct simulation of feeling, not thinking. Compassion, like empathy, is located in the right frontal expansion of the brain, which is probably the brain's most recent evolutionary development (others may follow in the post-human future to come). Mirror neurons, or 'empathy neurons', as they are sometimes called (only discovered in the 1990s), allow us (and other primates) to grasp the minds of others as if their thoughts and behaviour were our own.

We empathise with people for a reason. Mirror neurons create a shared sensibility, bringing the outside inside us 'to understand another, we become like the other—at least a bit'. (Goleman, 2006, 42) We only do so because we are witnessing emotions that interest us, ones that we know we might experience one day ourselves ('there but for the grace of God'). And we really do experience their pain in the same part of the brain as we experience our own. Not to experience the pain of another is an emotional deficit (it is typical of autism). Directly experiencing the experiences of others— what mirror theorists call 'embodied simulation'—is the key to who we are (it is what makes us human). The ability to experience another person's pain is a central part of emotional intelligence, as too is the ability to read other people's emotional states. It is the key in the Hobbesian sense to survival. To say one is self-conscious, for example, is really to mean being conscious of someone else being conscious of you. (Bentley, 2008, 69)

What is most striking is that they allow us to do so not through conceptual reasoning, but through direct simulation by feeling (not by thinking). These discoveries allow us to see sociability as embodied in cognitive structures. (Glenberg, 2006) What the new research also shows, however, is that culture is involved here too. Mirror neuron circuitry will only be triggered if a child has had an emotionally warm family life, and experienced true parental affection. Culture counts, and it does so in relation to biology. The instincts we share with all other animals do not diminish in importance as we culturally evolve. They actually become more important (William James' original insight). Our social instincts are more developed than in other animals, as well as more numerous, because we have the cultural complexity they lack. Chimps learn, too, insofar as they have a rudimentary culture; but we learn faster, and we know more. Our instincts, to that extent, are more 'refined'. Put another way, the days when one could write a book called *The Civilising Process* (as did the great sociologist Norbert Elias) without mentioning biology have gone, but likewise one cannot write a book on our biological nature without mentioning culture.

Computers and brains both process information by manipulating symbols. In the case of computers the symbols are electronic patterns; in the case of the brain they are molecules. Our brains translate information from the environment (the input from the senses) into molecular symbols that carry messages (output). Molecules are both the symbols representing information in the brain and the tools that perform the brain's tasks. The brain can produce molecules that can serve as a memory of an experience for weeks. We are affected not only by what we do, but what we see. Molecules influence the way we react to situations. Stress, for example, can trigger the release of an enzyme called tuyrosine hydroxylase: a key player in the body's fight-or-flight response. (Siegfried, 2000, 120) But there is a difference between a human brain and a computer. With computers the hardware is useless without the software to activate it. In a human brain, hardware and software are one and the same.

But that doesn't mean, of course, that computers do not change our personalities. Our brains are being subtly changed by the computers we use. What computers are doing to our minds is a first order question of enormous importance. Steven Rose, a professor of biology, speculates that we now know that the computer generation is experiencing a change in the balance of its sensory inputs and motor activities. Intensely and frequently exercised functions such as inputting a computer occupy more brain space. In the longer term, such technological change may drive evolutionary processes by altering selection pressures and changing the definition of favourable versus unfavourable genotypes. (Rosen, 2005, 296) Some welcome this development, others fear it. Some believe it will extend our thinking capacities, including our capacity to empathise with other people. Others fear that it is increasing our motor skills, at the expense of our intellectual ones.

Today's drone pilots come from a generation of people who at the average age of twenty-seven spend an average of more than eighty hours a week in online gaming. But as Susan Greenfield adds, prolonged and frequent video gaming is altering our minds in subtle and often disturbing ways that encourage active dissociation from reality. Screen experiences are entirely literal. Screen images do not permit us to see one thing in terms of anything else; they actively discourage metaphorical thinking; they do not show inner feelings or allow players to engage in abstract thinking. And there is increasing evidence that a two-dimensional screen existence may be having one particular undesirable effect: a decline in empathy. A recent report on US college students showed a marked decline in empathy over the past thirty years, with a particularly sharp drop in the past decade. Normally we remain in touch with the real world by having to negotiate our way through it; it is useful to empathise with others in order to thrive. Normally we learn to empathise from real conversations with real people where we rehearse eye contact and learn to interpret body language; we later progress to reading novels and watching films that introduce us to people very different from ourselves or our friends. In the computer game world the emphasis is different—it is on the sensory-laden thrill of the moment, and those experiences over time can often lead to atrophy in key parts of the brain, as magnetic resonance scans have shown. Dissociation from reality is not an attitude of mind; it is function of changes in the brain itself. (Greenfield, 2011)

But it is difficult to be too dogmatic about all of this. At present, not all neuroscientists can agree on what the use of computers is doing to our neural wiring. The type of behaviour the pessimists think is to be explained by persistent internet use and video gaming—recklessness, low attention span, a decline in empathy—we associate with certain pathologies, like addiction to gambling or schizophrenia, and these, in turn, have been traced to an under-active pre-frontal cortex. What evidence is there for this in today's drone pilots?

Since 9/11 the number of hours which the US needs to process data collected by reconnaissance drones has increased by 3,100 per cent. Every day 1,500 more hours of video, and 15,000 more images, are added to the volume of information. Nineteen analysts per drone now monitor video feedback on what is called 'death TV' (looking at Taliban movements in Afghanistan, for example whilst participating in dozens of instant-message and radio exchanges with intelligence analysts and troops on the ground). Drone pilots also need a particular set of visual-motor skills which video game players have been shown to possess—increased hand-eye co-ordination and augmented manual dexterity. Some have vastly improved spatial skills such as mental rotation, spatial visualization and the ability to mentally work in three dimensions. Additionally, game playing also seems to enhance aspects of visual attention such as the ability to divide and switch attention to different areas of interest, and to manage different objects at the same time. Furthermore, action gamers have 'improved probabilistic inference' which corresponds to a player's ability to make right decisions more quickly because they are better equipped to collect both visual and auditory information.

And what the USAF particularly looks for in drone pilots is the ability to perform several tasks at once. Fast context switching involves the ability to move from one target to another; to learn from experience (experiential rather than deductive training); and to organise intelligence in easily accessible databases. Today's young people claim to be good at multi-tasking, and so they are up to a point. In a *Harper's* magazine debate with the late Neil Postman, Camille Page observed:

Some people have more developed sensoriums than others. I have found that most people born before World War II are turned off by the modern media. They cannot understand how we who were born after the War can read and watch TV at the same time. But we can. When I wrote my book, I had earphones on, blasting rock music or Puccini and Brahms. The soap operas—with the sound turned down—flicked on my TV. I would be talking on the phone at the same time. Baby boomers have a multi-layered, multi-track ability to deal with the world. (Hanks, 2010, 495)

But as one writer confessed after reading this passage, he felt baffled by Ms Page's claim to be able to 'deal with the world'. Dealing sounded more like a matter of incessantly repositioning the self within a barrage of onrushing stimuli, which might well be true for drone pilots in their attempts to 'deal with war'.

In the journal *Current Direction and Psychological Science* the cognitive scientist Matthew Dye and his colleagues reviewed the studies of the effects of action on video games, using standard neuropsychological tests. They found that the players had faster reaction times than non-gamers, as one might expect. This edge was not achieved at the cost of becoming impulsive or reckless. In particular, gamers' brains worked faster. There was no difference in levels of concentration, or in the ability to resist impulsive or rash decisions. Another review published in the journal *Cyber Psychology and Behaviour* (2009) by the psychologist Chiunjung Huang found that the internet was linked only to a small reduction in people's sense of well-being. In many other cases it enhanced social relationships, just as the telephone had done a hundred years earlier. (*The Times*, February 2010, 43, Eureka Section Issue 5: 'Fight Club: is technology damaging our children's brains?')

But there is another claim to consider, and in its own way it is even more disturbing if true; it revolves around the issue of information processing. Is the digital world we have created outpacing our neurons' processing abilities; and if this is the case are we tending to 'log off' emotionally? The neurons associated with empathy, compassion and emotional stability (to just define wisdom in one particular way) are sited primarily in areas of the pre-frontal cortex. This is a recently developed area of the brain which is bypassed when we get stressed or anxious, or when we over-react or under-react, or react in an 'unwise' fashion which puts us at risk. Information overload may also bypass those areas of the brain, a concern expressed by researchers at the University of Southern California's Brain and Creativity Institute. Their brain scan studies show that while we pick up signs of distress in a flash at an unemotional level (we can process information instantaneously), it takes six to eight seconds to register an emotional response such as sympathy or compassion. In their book *Digital Delirium* (1997) Arthur and Marie Louise Kroker suggest that we are in danger of crashing into a 'law of reversal' as our brains protect us by shutting down, by slowing down reflection: 'Accelerating digital effects are neutralised by decelerating human effects'. And these include empathy and compassion for other people, especially those different from ourselves.

If this is true, what is to be done? Not much, perhaps. It is a bandwidth problem. In order to boost our processing power in ways that would enhance wisdom, we would have to go broadband. The axons (the nerve fibres) would have to be widened to spread their signalling rate. Neurons have central cores which carry out functions common to all cells, but they also have appendages, or axons, as well as dendrites that transmit and receive electric pulses. When a neuron is active, a pulse flows from the core to the tip of the axon where it triggers the release of chemicals called neurotransmitters. It is from the flow of neurotransmitters across the synapses of the brain that our thoughts, memories and emotions all emerge.

In an attempt to process even more data we could re-engineer the human brain with a computer-style upgrade. We could install computer chips monitoring our neural networks, enhancing their performance. And then there are drugs that can certainly boost processing power. According to a survey in *Nature* (2008), 20 per cent of scientists say they take drugs to improve their concentration. And it is not surprising. The journal *Science* updates its website every thirteen seconds. (Morris, 2011, 24) The most popular drugs are Ritalin, which is meant to address Attention Deficit Disorder, and Modafinal, which is meant to reduce fatigue. None of these, of course, actually enhance moral circuitry, only processing power, and without reflection processing power does not always translate into wisdom.

Let us return to multi-tasking. To be sure, drone pilots are multi-taskers, but multi-tasking is particularly demanding, and Maggie Jackson, in her book *Distracted*, tells us that the brain takes time to change goals and block out 'cognitive interference' from previous, still vivid activities. Of course, adds Nicholas Carr, we can compensate, but we do so at a cost. He cites one experiment with adults who were asked to listen to bleeps through a headset, while being asked at the same time to make predictions based on a series of coloured shapes they were shown. In one trial they were told to ignore the bleeps; in another, they were asked to keep track of them. In both experiments they were still capable of making predictions, but the second trial (multi-tasking) found that it was more difficult for them to draw conclusions about their experience. In other words, writes Carr, switching between two tasks short-circuited their understanding. (Carr, 2011, 133)

And this is one of the possible forms of dissociation. It is not so much failure to understand the experience or decode the meaning of an activity such as war, something more is involved. Our brains are engaged less directly and more shallowly in information processing. We may become more efficient at what we are doing, but less aware of what it is that we are doing. One of the problems is that we process information out of context, and therefore find it difficult to be reflective about what we process. After all, what we are doing in multi-tasking is shifting our attention from one job to the next, learning to be more skilful at the superficial level. The area in which we are becoming more skilled is that of visual attentional processing: the speed at which we can shift our visual attention without at the same time gaining an insight into what lies behind the picture. Carr quotes Patricia Greenfield, a Developmental Psychologist at UCLA, whose research found that new strengths in visual-spatial intelligence tended to go hand in hand with the weakening of 'deep processing' that underpins inductive analysis and critical thinking, and the full use of our imagination. And this can also be measured in changes of neural circuitry. Our brains, in fact, are becoming more computational; they are beginning to function like computers. We can increase the 'pace of the stream'. We can process the flow of information even faster than before, but we may be doing so at the risk of becoming emotionally more shallow.

As always the problem is speed. Higher emotions such as empathy and compassion, writes Anthony Damasio, emerge from neural processes that are inherently slow. Magnetic Resonance Imaging machines can scan the brains of subjects who have experienced acute chronic pain. Damasio and his colleagues have found that the primitive pain centre in the brain activates almost immediately when pain is recalled (Carr, 2011, 220–21). But the ability to empathise with the psychological suffering of others—with the shame or humiliation they have experienced—unfolds more slowly. It takes time to understand the moral dimension of a situation.

The real problem of the information flow that drone pilots have to deal with is called cognitive overload, a term that describes the situation when the amount of information that needs to be processed simply exceeds the mind's capacity to store or process the information received. In such situations either we almost instantly forget the information at hand (which means we cannot store it and retrieve it later), or we are unable to see whether it contradicts or confirms the information we have already stored away. And because we need our memory to concentrate, we have to remember what we are meant to be concentrating on. Our attention tends to wander all the time. Indeed, many drone pilots are already suffering from attention problems and low performance (as a result of the long hours they put in, sometimes eight hours at a time each day). The problem that they face is the problem many youngsters face today: attention deficit, which if not yet a 'disorder' is certainly a challenge. It is all too easy to focus on the unimportant and to fail to see the big picture because one sees too much. It is this need to focus that the military are now addressing with the help of neuroscientists who have been monitoring brain activity in drone pilots. The upshot has been to make pilots more 'mindful' of collateral damage by getting them to focus on different things, in effect rewiring the functioning of their attention system (*International Herald Tribune*, 17 June 2011): monitoring their brain rhythms, heart rate and eye movement, so that supervisors can now 'scan' their attentiveness to ensure that they are focusing on the job. A pilot can be 'shut off' if he is getting stressed out, and control transferred to others. Until the day that we can really programme autonomy into machines and take pilots out of the loop entirely, human agents may themselves become increasingly semi-autonomous.

Will drone pilots become semi-autonomous?

In August 2010 US Navy operators on the ground lost contact with a Fire Scout helicopter, an unmanned aerial vehicle that was programmed to return to base if ground communications failed. Instead of following its programmed flight pattern, it steered a course for the capital. Before manned aircraft could be scrambled to intercept it, the operators had regained control. As it also happened, the aircraft was not armed. There is always a danger, however, that one day an armed system might escape human control. 'UAV resists its human operators' declared one headline in an article about the incident. This was a case of malfunction and machines, as we know, malfunction all the time. But we are designing protocols for dealing with this. It is when they function and attain levels of 'autonomous functionality' that they will exercise something we cannot when we do: consistency of behaviour.

The incident reminded some people of the film *Stealth* (2005) in which an autonomous fighter jet, codenamed Extreme Deep Invader (EDI), disobeys orders and takes out a military target, with dire results in terms of human casualties. The premise is that it is not programmed to act independently by its designers. In this particular case it has an Artificial Intelligence (AI) system that allows it to develop its own personality and rudimentary code of ethics. No-one notices this until it is too late.

Will unmanned aircraft one day follow the same path and become autonomous? The USAF is now training more unmanned aircraft pilots every year than fighter and combat pilots combined. But at some point the systems will be able to look after themselves. At the US Air Force Research Laboratory at Wright-Patterson Air Force Base (Dayton, Ohio), they are expecting to have operational by 2015 a suite of on-board sensors that will allow drones to independently detect another aircraft close by and manoeuvre to avoid it. Quite soon, drones will be able to start processing information that they are looking for, rather than sending back an endless video stream which takes hours of intense analytic analysis and interpretation and is heavily human-intensive. And one day in the not too distant future drones will be able to independently dock with Air Force tankers in mid-air. At the moment, pilots have to steer the drone to avoid collisions, but simulation tests have shown a way forward for phasing out drone pilots from this operation, too.

At some point in the near future today's pilots may become tomorrow's supervisors; drones will have become robots. This has been the experience of the workplace where robots have been introduced much earlier than in war. Companies attach great importance to consistency and quality control. More automated production makes this possible. And in war zones drones will perform far better than manned aircraft, especially when combat drones are introduced, and even more when they become semi-autonomous. But industrial companies have also found over the years that the more sophisticated their robots become, the more talented the staff needed to manage them. And when decision-making has become more complex substitution by machines has not taken place. Given that the complexity of war is ever increasing there will always be a need for human supervision, for people to take the decisions that computers cannot.

Such is the conclusion of a recent book by Lynda Gratton, who concludes that as an industrial process becomes more automated, so managers are forced to become 'smarter' and develop new skills. It is a lesson that was first predicted by Frederick Winslow Turner, who forecast in his famous book *The Principles of Scientific Management* that imposing a more mechanical regime on workers would oblige managers to take 'other types of duties which involve new and heavy burdens'. Even in an age of ever more intelligent machines, human supervisors will still be needed. And this may be true when unmanned systems are no longer piloted by human beings.

What the Greeks never asked

The questions I have raised about risk and sacrifice are as old as war itself, but technology has thrown them into particularly stark relief. Clausewitz reminds us that war is 'the province of social life'; it is a microcosm of the way we lead our lives in general. John Ellis reminds us that every technology has a social history—it fulfils a social need, and gets us to see the world anew and sometimes our own relationship with it. Martin Heidegger, the most important philosopher of the last century, in the most famous essay ever penned on technology also reminds us that the essence of technology is not technological—it is the ground of enabling, or that in which a given mode of existence attains.

Although Raymond Asquith, the son of the British Prime Minister who took his country to war in 1914, was probably correct in claiming that 'a battlefield is far too much like a railway accident to be susceptible of description', the firing of the machine guns on the killing ground of the Western Front was foremost among the individual details which gave the battles of the war what shape and form they possessed. (Harvey, 1994, 366) For the machine gun enabled the Europeans to think of war as an industrial assembly line, serialising death as an assembly line serialises the manufacture of products, and it introduced a new concept into war—productivity which allowed the military to maximise output at minimal investment in human labour, or even skill. (A machine gunner only needs to keep his finger pressed on the trigger.).

What is technology's 'horizon of disclosure' today (to apply another of Heidegger's terms)? It is the absolute need to minimise risk. The combat troops, writes Sebastian Junger, suspect that if they had to choose between a machine and a grunt, they would go with the machine every day. So far machines cannot do ground combat, at least, not yet. And are the combat infantrymen, the only 'real' soldiers, necessarily wrong, asks Junger? We should listen to their fears because they are the only ones today conducting 'war' as the Greeks would have understood it.

I once asked someone in Second Platoon why frontline grunts weren't much admired.

'Because everyone just thinks we're stupid', the man said.

'But you do all the fighting'.

'Yeah', he said, 'exactly'. (Junger, 2011, 226)

The reality is that social expectations are not what they were twenty years ago; and nor are our soldiers'. They expect risks to decrease; they are almost at no risk at all at sea or in the air, and are immured against everything except psychological stress in cyberspace. They positively welcome the coming of the machines. And why not? For we have only just begun to recognise, as the Greeks did not, the degree to which human beings are uniquely vulnerable and therefore more dependent on each other than any other animal. We live with that knowledge from the time we are born into the world. We know the fragility of the human body and the human mind. We live with the knowledge that we live longer than most others species (we may fall victim to fate, or an accident, and still live on for years). This challenges what we also think unique to us: the exercise of free will. To allow those most vulnerable to exercise it we have developed concepts unique to us such as reverence for our elders and respect for experience (Aristotle, *Metaphysics* A 981a, 14–15: 'We see that the experienced are more effective than those who have reason but no experience'). We expect at different stages of life to incur the responsibility of looking after our parents later in life, and colleagues in our career, and welfare dependents if we are willing to invest in the welfare of others outside the immediate family circle. And soldiers are more dependent on each other than practically anyone else; indeed, it is their mutual dependence on each other that for many makes the experience so redeeming.

Above all, we make others dependent through our own actions, especially those that we freely 'will', never more so than war. For unlike every other animal we choose to put ourselves at risk unnecessarily—for honour, or a flag, or for pay, or for reputation—and unlike every other animal that kills we have a disturbing tendency to go beyond what is required, to inflict more damage on others than is strictly necessary. And war is one of the most disabling forces of all. If a soldier does not die on a battlefield he may have to live with a disability for years afterwards. 'What would you have me do', Boult asks Miranda in Shakespeare's play *Pericles*, 'Go to the wars would you—where a man may serve seven years for the loss of a leg and have not money enough in the end to buy him a wooden one'. (*Pericles*, 4.6 167–70) If soldiers in the past did not die from disease they could expect to die from their wounds. Today very few succumb to disease and most survive their injuries thanks to medical advances in field hospitals. But soldiers still have to live with crippling injuries, many of them psychological. They now rely on disability pay where once they relied on the charity of others. And all the time they face one of the greatest challenges of all—to get society to recognise that they have the right to a voice, that they are the same people they were when they left for war, that they are worthy of the respect once accorded to them. For survival would not be worth much if the survivor was robbed of the dignity that human beings insist upon. As Alisdair MacIntyre writes, when we ask the question who will look after us or speak up for us, we are looking to 'a second self'. We invest our hopes not in insurance companies or medical staff but in those who can speak in our name—veterans' associations or support groups whose members have actual experience of our condition. We rely on friends and family who are an extension of our identity as human beings, just as children rely on their parents to speak on their behalf until such time as they can speak up for themselves. (MacIntyre, 2009, 139)

Now what is interesting, adds MacIntyre, is the extent to which until recently we chose to obscure the extent of our dependence on others. Moral philosophers beginning with the Greeks tended to ignore human dependence as unworthy of critical interest. Biologically, or so we told ourselves, we were more than our embodied existence: there was a dimension to life that was unseen, that could not be measured, counted or weighed. We identified the existence of a realm beyond the ontological. We thought ourselves to be a-corporeal beings with a soul. We considered human suffering to be one with our animality, not with reason. We told ourselves that suffering was redemptive, and that pain was good for the soul.

We were also encouraged by the Greeks to construct suffering in cultural terms. Precisely because the Greeks considered war to be an exclusively male vocation, men were expected to accept suffering. According to Ludwig Wittgenstein emotional states are communicative and embedded within their modes of expression. Grief cannot be detached from weeping. Culturally, weeping is not a sign of grief, it is one of the things that grief is. We have to accept that all mental states are visible in the face such as anger, and pleasure and suffering. To laugh is expressed in smiling, as grief is in weeping, but there are many forms of expression such as wailing. And different cultures have different codes of behaviour. Plato took great offence at the fact that even Achilles was given to weeping uncontrollably. By the time he was writing this was considered distinctly 'unmanly'. The most 'manly', writes Aristotle, will not allow their suffering to intrude on others by excessive grieving. The grief that a soldier might suffer at the loss of a friend should be registered silently in an expression on a face, or the posture of the body. Aristotle, indeed, explicitly insisted that warriors should not allow others to be saddened by their loss; unlike women they had a duty not to share it with others. (MacIntyre, 2009, 7)

In other words, writes McIntyre, Aristotle imported into moral philosophy the standpoint of men, and in doing so devalued the biological importance of the body. For it is our animal bodies that define our identity, just as life is our animation in the world. Inner states of mind are manifest in a smile or a frown. When that identity is damaged we tend to be diminished in the eyes of others—when, for example, a soldier is so disfigured in war than even his friends cannot recognise him, or a woman is so disabled by an accident that she finds herself entirely dependent on others, robbed of any belief in free will; or when an Alzheimer patient's mind is so damaged that he or she loses his personality, his sense of self.

Today we have taken the metaphysics out of war. 'Weapons have become godless. Weapons have lost their religion', remarks a character in Don DeLillo's novel *Running Dog* (De Lillo, 1999, 4). It is not the weapons that have become godless, so much as the military ethos of the Western world. We tend to objectify war as we do most other things in life, and are not much interested in subjective assessments of its worth. Anything that is 'immaterial' tends to be ruled out, all that matters is matter. (Ford, 2007, 196)

MacIntyre does not discuss war, but it is a practice that has made us especially aware of our dependence on each other. With the death of metaphysics we have begun to entertain a diminished view of our own humanity. In one unclassified Defense Advanced Research Projects Agency (DARPA) report (2003) we are told, 'the human (element) is becoming the weakest link'. Many scientists see soldiers as imperfect machines which are at risk of breaking down through imperfect programming as a result of either faulty software (inadequate ethical training) or defective hardware (a fragile body). And as machines they may corrode over time and degrade morally.

We also entertain a pretty jaundiced view of our own humanity. 'We are all born selfish', writes Michael Ghiesehm, 'scratch an altruist and watch a hypocrite bleed'. We are told by biologists and evolutionary psychologists that human nature can be understood through a combination of neuro-physiology and deep genetic history. In other words, all the things we once thought made us distinctive as a species—our culture, language, use of reason and morality—are, so we are told, merely programmed into us. Even our ethical systems of thought have no moral dimension independent of the software programs that natural selection has given us.

So, what if it were possible to design robots capable of exercising on our behalf ethical decisions we are too weak or capricious or muddle-headed to make ourselves? Few doubt that we are moral creatures by virtue of the fact that morality is hard-wired into us for a reason; it has helped us to survive and, once we came to the head of the food chain, to survive each other. But our conscience is imperfectly designed. So, what if we could build a mechanical unit which would be both logical and consistent in its actions? And what if we could wage war much more 'humanely' by tasking other 'higher beings' with resolving our own ethical dilemmas, transferring to them the responsibility to treat others as we would wish to be treated ourselves? It is a dream that scientists are trying to realise, and one that raises doubt about whether we can continue to evolve morally as the beings we are.

'Ethics is not—as we normally think of it—primarily a moralistic exercise of distinguishing right from wrong', writes Dennis Ford, 'it is more fundamentally an exercise in self-transformation during which we move from lower to higher levels of being'. (Ford, 2007, 211) This is what the Greeks told us and what many of us still believe, but is it a story we will wish to tell ourselves much longer?

5

THE RISE OF THE MACHINES

'Robotics: the moral degradation of the machine'

J.G. Ballard, *Millennium User's Guide*

Overhead robot planes—very different from today's drones—send back information to soldiers on the ground, but many also interact with each other, deciding which targets to attack and in what sequence; they are locked in a permanent 'conversation' with each other. On the ground, robot vehicles have replaced most manned vehicles just as robot drones have replaced all manned aircraft. Some are passive sentries guarding forward positions. Others navigate the battle space more confidently than men. Their sensors detect every form of life (including their own), for robots will be fighting robots in 2035—silicon based as well as carbon based life forms. And they will be scanning the human enemy like bar codes, analysing their degrees of competence and fighting efficiency. They will be programmed to minimise 'collateral damage'—their sensors will allow them to discriminate between belligerent and non-belligerent. They will be able to 'read' intentions with behavioural patterning programmes and so be able to determine who poses a threat and who does not. They may even be able to assess states of mind; they may have sensors that can detect fear and anxiety as dogs can detect our moods today.

Most of the robots on guard will be tracked—it is extraordinarily difficult to design a machine that can walk, and almost impossible at the moment to design one that can run. But the robots on tracks will be remarkably sophisticated. They will be able to repair themselves if they break down and even reproduce themselves from spare parts. And they will have long been given the authority to kill any human beings that pose a threat to them.

They will be interfacing with human soldiers in the same network, and they will be able to do so with an independently programmed ability to evaluate the consequences of their own actions. Indeed, the ability to reach value judgements will be part of their program. Most will have a functional morality; they will be able to assess and respond to moral considerations, even those not anticipated by commanders when they were despatched into battle. By then it will be they (not men in the field) who will be largely responsible for exercising moral judgement. And robots will also be monitoring the conduct of the 'grunts' with whom they share the battle space. They will be programmed to detect human systems failure (that is, breakdown of the unit) before it occurs. They will be programmed to exercise 'insight' into human feelings and behaviour. They will be tasked to detect human fallibility, and, if necessary, cut human beings out of the loop. Human soldiers fail not because they break down, malfunction, or get stressed out; they fail because of their inability to cope with the complexity of the situation, because they cannot adapt in time. 'Resilience engineering' will long since have ensured that machines adapt in all circumstances by readjusting mission parameters and reinterpreting orders as they see fit. It is they who may hold the override button, precisely because they are considered more 'resilient', both functionally and performatively.

And after the battle is over, and the war won, the machines will be rebuilding the country, patrolling frontiers, policing dangerous streets, enforcing curfews, checking ID papers, policing suburbs—even winning hearts and minds by adapting and readapting to circumstances, defusing difficult situations, showing no fear or favour to any side, perhaps knowing more of how our world works than we know ourselves.

You can see why this vision of the future appeals to so many in the military. In diminishing the human space of battle still further, writes Bruce Sterling, the vision I have just outlined and others like it offer 'a complete and utter triumph of chilling analytic cybernetic reality over chaotic, real-life human desperation'. (Sterling, 1998, 8) It is a future that would have depressed Thucydides. When he called war 'the human thing' he insisted that it was unique to one species, our own, precisely because it offered a chance to 'become' what we are. Becoming required great deeds and projects; even in war warriors often come to know themselves for the first time. Can a robot help us evolve? Or will we merely further diminish the moral lives we lead?

By 2035 most robots will be autonomous: not yet, perhaps, able to formulate conscious judgements, but certainly able to exercise discretion; to re-target at will; even to override human decision-makers. By then, the military will have complete confidence in their ability to learn and learn quickly, and reprogram themselves. It may have far more confidence in computer algorithms than in human judgement, or the exercise of human reason. By then, we may no longer be interested in 'engineering rationality' into ourselves, in part because we will have come to rely almost entirely on the rational (that is, logical) decisions of our machines. For good or ill, humans will be easing themselves out of the loop at every level except the political: strategy will still be a human monopoly; in the war rooms of the world, politicians will still be ordering men and machines into battle. Until the 'singularity'—the moment when computers will have achieved super intelligence—we will still be in command, or so, at least, we will assure ourselves. But tactically, the battlefield will look very different from anything that Thucydides could have imagined.

Where are the robots?

There will be one million robots toiling away in Foxconn's Chinese factories by 2015, a mighty mechanised army, tirelessly snapping together the world's iPhones, Nintendo games consoles and DVD players. It is a major threshold to cross in a country where cheap labour has been the key to dramatic economic growth and has placed China in pole position to overtake the United States quite soon. In an era of systemic wage and benefits inflation and increasing instances of labour unrest, Foxcomm thinks that the ideal worker is no longer a poor migrant but a machine that never goes on strike and never demands a wage hike. Welcome to the future. (*The Times*, 2 August 2011)

What is true of industry is also true of war; indeed the two have been intimately linked since the industrial revolution. A few years ago a high level study of the US Army, *Star 21: Strategic Technologies for the Army of the 21st Century*, concluded that whilst the core 20th-century weapons system had been the tank, in the 21st it was likely to be the 'unmanned system'. The study even predicted that robots would be running and walking on the battlefield by 2020. (*Star 21*, 1993, 148) Another study appropriately entitled *Unmanned Effects: Taking the Human out of the Loop* (2003) envisaged that five years after that autonomous robots would be fully networked and integrated on the battlefield. It hasn't happened and it will not for some time; progress in robotics is painfully slow.

But even if the post-human future may be further off than we think, we need to ask questions about where we are heading. The future is not a destiny, it is a choice, and it is that knowledge which is the great curse of the modern consciousness, as well as a source of hope. And there is no doubt that robotics is the future of war. Gordon Johnson, the Unmanned Officer Team Leader for Project Alpha, envisaged some time ago that tactical autonomous combatants (TACs) would be operating with minimal human supervision; at the operational and strategic level war would remain 'manned', but on the battlefield, soldiers would find themselves increasingly co-existing with intelligent machines and the soldiers, not the machines, might be rendered redundant. 'They do not get hungry. They're not afraid. They do not forget their orders. They do not care if the guy next to them has just been shot. Will they do a better job than humans?' For the technophiles, there is an inbuilt redundancy in the very question. (*Wall Street Journal*, 10 February 2003)

Robots were first used extensively in the non-conventional phase of the Second Gulf War (2003–7). Within five years of the initial invasion the robot field hospital in Tikrit was repairing many of the 2,000 systems then in operation (2010). They included the Talon, which could be controlled remotely from 1,200 metres, and even climb stairs; the MARC Small Bot IV, with fat tyres for driving across scrubland; the Fast Tech, which can climb stairs, but is equally at home in the caves of Afghanistan; and the Pac Bot, which has a 7ft arm to peer into lorries.

As technology develops, the robots we are discussing will take many shapes, and very few of them are likely to be human. Only excessive anthropomorphism would lead one to conclude that a robot should look something like the Hollywood Terminator, or the human facsimiles represented in another film, *I, Robot*. With the development of nano-technology, some may 'swarm', others may look like tractors, tanks, even cockroaches or crickets. All sorts of shapes and locomotion styles are being tested. New research projects include robots that can fold themselves, fly and crawl, walk uphill and roll down. Some roboticists are even looking to the humble amoeba for inspiration—the result is the chembot made up of particles that are quite stiff when compressed but, given space, flow like liquids, thus allowing it to enter any space no smaller than its fully compressed state, more or less regardless of the shape of the space in question. (*Economist*, 12 June 2010, 5–6)

Robots, in short, are positively protean in their possibilities, and they will not always be called by that name. 'Robo' and 'bot' are two different affixes, and of the two the latter seems to be easier on the ear. That the two should sound different is not so surprising given the linguistic 'principle of contrast'. When we learn a language we expect that two words should never be exact synonyms. So we speak of 'emotional baggage' but not of 'emotional luggage'. Robo is the name we seem to give more menacing systems—like Robocop. Bots are nicer, like nurse-bots and computer programs like searchbots and spam bots and chatbots which were developed to engage in more-or-less human sounding conversation. So the future may see warrior bots and military bots, and a host of others, less threatening in the imagination than the robots of today.

Robots are on the march, to use a military metaphor, and there is no going back. We have committed ourselves to reducing the human space of war still further. At the very heart of this desire is a wish as old as war itself: to take out of the equation such existential elements as courage, fear, cruelty and remorse, the traditional emotional features which have made war such an intensely human activity. War, we must remember, has only been rendered humane, even at its most bloody, because of the human values, capacities and emotions which infuse it. But will we be able to render it more humane still, not only for ourselves but others? Will we be able one day to realise Edward Grey's hope of war without emotions?

Why are we going down this road? It was Nietzsche who first suggested, when answering the question why should we do this, 'because the future calls for it'. His point was that this is a better answer than 'because we've always done it in the past'. Even if this were true (which is none too obvious, writes Mary Midgley), we should remember that destiny is not the equivalent of fate. We forge it, it is not in the stars. (Midgley, 2006, 133) For all Nietzsche's confidence in the future—his hopes that we would get there fast, that we would be able to evolve our humanity in historical time—he was ever alert to the fact that as humans we might not be moving towards a more humane future. When enquiring about our future prospects that should be the central point of our interrogation, Nietzsche's challenge was that in continually becoming rather than existing in a fixed state of being, we are able to realise our humanity. But his injunction to become more human can be read in two ways. The word *menschlicher* means 'to become more human' and also to become more humane. It is by no means certain that the two are synonymous. To be more human is a biological demand; to be humane depends very much on the cultural construction of humanity. It is a demand we alone make of ourselves.

What is a robot?

Our own age, of course, has a particular predisposition for discovering historical turning points, or new ways of seeing and asserting the coherence of the world. Best sellers market these axial moments on which everything turns; they fix our eye on the future. 'Every age has its eye pasted to a key-hole', wrote Mary McCarthy, and she was right. Trying to second guess the future has become a mark of the post-modern world in which we live. The coming of robots is culturally a watershed, a Rubicon which we have decided to cross, as important in many ways as the arrival of gunpowder, and it will be far more radical in its implications and consequences, however long it takes for robots to go from being automatic to autonomous (capable of making decisions themselves). The fact that we have already begun thinking through the implications shows that we are fully aware of this.

The robots the US military has built so far are simple devices, a blend of artificial intelligence which allows them to reason and mechanical engineering which allows them to perform physical tasks informed and directed by reason. As currently defined, robots exhibit three key elements or functions:

Programmability—they have computational symbol-manipulative capabilities that a designer can combine as desired.

Mechanical Capability—they can act in their environment rather than merely function as an information processing or computational device.

Flexibility—they can operate using a wide range of programmes.

The first 'function' makes a robot a computer; the second a machine; the third a computer-enhanced machine that can respond to external stimuli. And these responses are much more complex than they would be if we were to use just mechanical or electro-mechanical components alone. (Chandor,

1985) Robotics adds a new element: complexity. The fact that in theory they may soon be able to learn and adapt to their environments suggests that behaviour will emerge over time. When they begin to learn independent of our programming they will be well on the way to achieving autonomy.

What is an autonomous system? It is one that is distinguished by several characteristics: self-repair, self-maintenance, self-improvement (it learns), and self-reproduction (the biggest challenge of all). Until recently, machines could not do all of these tasks, but some were capable of at least one. An aircraft, for example, can steer on auto-pilot without human interference, but not repair itself in flight when things go wrong (systems failure). A communications network can repair itself but not reproduce itself. Computer viruses can reproduce themselves in ways that even their programmers cannot anticipate, if programmed with evolutionary algorithms, but they cannot learn as they 'evolve'. One day, however, robots will be able to repair, reprogram and maintain themselves without human involvement.

Although that day is some way off, machine life is already taking on a life of its own. John Smart, a development systems theorist, argues that human generated innovation is 'trending down' at the same time that technology-generated innovation is rapidly increasing. In other words, what we have been witnessing for some time is a reduction in human-initiated innovation, which we have failed to register not because machines are taking over, but because we ourselves are becoming increasingly integrated with the machines we design. Smart insists that all the crude indicators on which we rely—Moore's Law (processing power); Gilder's Law (bandwidth increase); Cooper's Law (wireless band width); Kurtzweil's Law (price performance computation)—continue to suggest that innovation is increasing exponentially. But they also suggest that human beings are catalysts, no longer controllers of the process. One example is the series of innovations required to make something we take for granted—a petrol/electric hybrid motor vehicle like the Toyota Prius. To any outsider, including its owner, it looks pretty much the same as other models. Yet it is radically more complex, and many of the innovations are not the result of human thought but of the computations done by the technological systems involved. (CAD-CAM Programs, Infrastructures and Supply Chains)

But this is not the same as designing machines that can think for themselves, and with which we may eventually co-evolve together. When it comes to making robots autonomous we rely on two quite different engineering approaches. The first is top-down, taking its cue from mathematics.

Mathematics starts with an axiom and applies rules of logical inference to transform that axiom into the desired statement. (Casti, 2000, 143) Some in the Artificial Intelligence (AI) community have adopted a similar approach called 'means-ends analysis'. A problem (the initial state) is set, which requires resolution; we begin from this starting point using information about the problem to be solved (data/premises); we set a goal (the end state) that we wish to attain; and we agree a set of operations that can turn the initial into the end state.

The bottom-up approach is very different and is inspired by what scientists call 'connectionism', which takes its cue from the human brain and the infinite number of connections that neurons make within it. A neural-network type of machine which mimics as closely as possible the human brain may develop intelligence in the same way that children do: by observing the world around them and using their observations, together with the instruction they receive from their parents or teachers. (Casti, 2000, 149) Scientists call it 'subscription architecture'. Take the attempt to get robots to walk, one of the most difficult challenges of all. Engineers do this by ensuring that each sensor (or leg) sees the world in a different way from the others. When there is a conflict between distributed system, a control system kicks in, so that instead of building a coherent system of the world (as we do in our own lives) the robot learns what it needs to walk across a room by interacting with its environment. In other words, its behaviour (in this case, walking) emerges over time. The point is that each leg (learning independently) is eventually able to co-ordinate its actions with others and navigate in a three dimensional space without a head.

In time, cognitive abilities may even emerge, too. Consciousness may even evolve. Consciousness does not need a sophisticated representation of the world, it only needs a reliable interface with it. Cognition does not require logic to get it going. In human beings it is an operation of the nervous system (in the case of robots, sensors). The goal of Artificial Intelligence is to build an intelligence very similar to the human; but the goal of artificial life (which I have been describing) is much less anthropomorphic, it aims to evolve intelligence within the machine through pathways found by the machines themselves. Whether silicon life will evolve is uncertain, but if it does its evolution will be different again from that of carbon-based life forms such as human beings. Hence we cannot know how it will turn out because, although designed by us, it will evolve independent of our own programming.

Some scientists question whether computers will ever be able to think for themselves. Many more believe the day will come when robots will be able to share their thoughts with us. My own bet is that this will happen within the next 30 years, possibly earlier than that. But even that time frame is short by historical standards, which is why we need to ask questions now. We need to be vigilant about what we construct. We must be very careful to understand what is involved and where we may be heading. It was Richard Smalley who wrote that when a scientist claims that something is possible he usually underestimates how long it will take; but if he claims it is impossible he is almost certain to be wrong. (Morris, 2011, 593)

Men behaving badly

> We used to wonder where war lived, what it was that made it so vile.
> And now we realise where it lives, that it is inside ourselves.

Albert Camus, Notebooks, 1939.

'I came over here because I wanted to kill people', a twenty-one-year-old private from West Texas told a journalist at a patrol base about twenty miles outside Baghdad. 'The truth is it wasn't all I thought it was cracked out to be. I mean, I thought killing somebody would be this life-changing experience. And then I did it, and I was like, "All right, whatever".' The young man was Steven D. Green and the next time the journalist saw him it was in a front page newspaper photograph in which he was shown standing outside a Federal courthouse in North Carolina on a charge of premeditated rape and murder.

Green was a member of the 1st Battalion, 502nd Infantry Regiment (1/502) of the 101st Airborne Division when in 2005 he and the other members of his unit found themselves engaged in a full-blown insurgency as post-Saddam Iraq began to unravel. They were stationed in an area known as the 'Triangle of Death'; twenty-one members of the battalion were killed during the tour of duty but scores more were seriously wounded, most falling victim to the ubiquitous Improvised Explosive Device (IED). Nearly half the unit received treatment for mental health issues whilst they were still serving in the field. The unit itself was in bad shape operationally as well: it was led by a martinet who enjoyed humiliating his most senior subordinates in public, while the junior officers and Non-Commisioned Officers (NCOs) established no rapport with the 'grunts' or even each other. No one led by example. The men were often placed at risk unneces-sarily; and their rest and recuperation periods were few, if any. From this situation emerged four soldiers from 1st Platoon, Bravo Company 1/502 who chose to relieve the boredom of manning a small, isolated outpost by driving to the home of a nearby Iraqi family where they gang raped and then murdered a fourteen-year-girl, Abeer al Janabi, before killing her par-ents and younger sister.

The other participants in the crime, Privates Cortez, Spielman and Barker, came from similar backgrounds. Unlike Green's, their excessive behaviour owed more to alcohol and drug abuse. When they went on their murder spree they were fuelled up on bootlegged Iraqi whisky. All four were bored and stressed out and unsupervised. They had considered killing a carload of Iraqis at their checkpoint; they concluded that rape would be more diverting. They also expected to get away with their crime. Green, who murdered most of the family members, is now serving five consecutive hundred-year sentences; he will never be released from jail. Only his accom-plices will eventually be eligible for parole.

Green was the most intelligent of the four men. He was dismissed from the service sometime before the incident was revealed, for borderline psy-chopathic personality disorder. Even when on base he had reported to a psychiatric nurse that he was subject to angry moods, extreme outbursts, and emotional instability. On his one-page intake sheet the nurse noted that Green expressed an interest in killing Iraqis on at least four separate occa-sions. One entry stated: 'Interests: none other than killing Iraqis'. (Freder-ick, 2011) It was later discovered that he had a severe personality disorder; he could not empathise with others or imagine their thoughts and feelings, all of which is characteristic of someone suffering from what used to be called 'psychopathy'.

Green should never have been admitted into the army. His childhood had been dysfunctional; he had been frequently set upon and abused by an older brother in the absence of a neglectful and spiteful single mother. He was not unintelligent, but he was clearly disturbed. The army recruited a known white-supremacist with a juvenile criminal record. All these facts were known to those who recruited him but, stretched for manpower at the height of the insurgency, they chose to issue a 'moral waiver' as they did for many other soldiers who had also been in prison or who had failed their psychological evaluations.

The rape and then murder of the victims was a case of what can happen in war when soldiers are fuelled by drugs or alcohol, stressed out, poorly led, under-motivated and lacking in self-esteem. What shocked the US military was that it was not a spur of the moment act but a calculated and wayward act of cruelty which was all the more striking for being rationalised as a calculated risk that the perpetrators would probably get away with.

Human cruelty is unique to our species: it is what we do particularly well, and it is very different from a cat toying with a mouse. A cat may play with a mouse before killing it, but we cannot say it is torturing it, still less humiliating it in its own eyes or those of other mice. More to the point, perhaps, it is toying with another species; we toy with our own. We are the ones who invented torture, a word we employ almost exclusively to describe the pain we impose on each other. For torture only works because of a fear of annihilation: not the fear of death, but the fear of being annihilated as a person, and the latter is far more important, writes the psychologist Dorothy Rowe (*Why We Lie*). To lose one's personhood is to lose one's self-esteem, and to lose that is to lose faith in the world. It brings into question, adds Peter Strawson, 'the normative expectations we have of each other'.

Let me take an example of what happens when our normative expectations are dashed. Jean Amery, a victim of the Holocaust, told how the torture inflicted upon him by the Gestapo changed his whole perception of humanity. With the very first slap by the Gestapo officer, 'he lost his trust in the world'. 'That faith in humanity, already cracked by the first slap in the face, then demolished by torture, was never acquired again'. (Andriev, 2009, 10) In other words, he lost trust in his fellow human beings.

We are the only species that derives enjoyment from hurting those who have fallen into our power, and we are the only ones, of course, that in Nietzsche's words can 'spiritualise' cruelty (justifying it, or placing it in a higher register artistically, or turning it into an object lesson in art, or ideology or religion—burning heretics to save their souls). What makes cruelty so human is our ability to rationalise it in religious or pseudo-scientific terms, as a demand of God, or a demand of nature, or—less grandly—part of the style of the times.

Cruelty is at the heart of life, writes the philosopher Mark Rowlands, and you do not have to be a Darwinian to grasp that. Life may not be quite 'red in tooth and claw', but for us, life is a perpetual struggle to survive one mishap, one illness, one misfortunate after another. But survive we usually do if we are not hindered by others. For Rowlands the real problem of life is what he calls 'the manufacture of helplessness'. It is what MacIntyre would maintain makes us such a vulnerable species—we are dependent on the goodwill of others precisely to the extent that only human beings can engineer the possibility of their own wickedness. Rowlands quotes Milan Kundera's novel *The Unbearable Lightness of Being*: the fundamental failure of humanity is the failure of a chief moral test. True human goodness, he writes, can only manifest itself in essence in relation to those who are in our power. (Rowlands, 2008, 101) And war renders the defeated particularly powerless. Soldiers become prisoners of war; women become widows and children orphans. To treat them compassionately is the only really valid test of human virtue because it is not so much a need as a gift. It is the right thing to do. To rejoice at one's cruelty to the powerless is to 'engineer the possibility of our own evil'. And it is linked, of course, with another feature that John Keegan tells us makes war 'inhumane'—impersonalisation. To diminish oneself as a human being (or to be encouraged to do so by the high command) is to diminish the other (the enemy).

Cruelty of course does not have to be 'playful' as it was in Abu Ghraib, or just plain evil as it was in the case of Private Green. Most often it is the product of individual or collective pain/distress. Many soldiers clearly find difficulty in applying the rules because they are not instinctive. We have response mechanisms hard-wired into us, especially in the presence of danger. We ask soldiers to show 'courageous restraint' which does not come naturally, and is intensely counter-intuitive when under fire. We ask them, in effect, to think through the consequences of their acts, which is difficult to do when others are trying to kill you. In the heat of battle it is very difficult to reflect. Reflection is easiest for the rear echelon officers behind the lines in command of all the facts, or so they tell themselves.

Secondly, the rules of war largely govern how we retaliate. They tell us what not to do (when and when not to show restraint). Or they govern how we should take out an opponent with force proportionate to the force used against us. The evolutionary benefit of retaliation lies in the probable adjustment to the future behaviour of others. Retaliation is intended to intimidate (in some cases to deter further attacks). It is asking a lot of any human being to show undue restraint, even a soldier, however well trained. (Yudowsky, 2001)

In effect, when we train soldiers not to automatically return fire, and to observe the distinction between civilians and combatants, we are teaching them the correct level of counter-attack (one that is part of the cultural grammar of war which also involves the cultural grammar of killing). We are training in different instincts. We work on the basis that all of our instincts are context-related. We always weigh up the consequences of act-ing in the context in which we find ourselves. For all of us life is context-related in a way that is not true for other animals. The problem is that the context, as soldiers know, can change quickly. You can be sent out on a mission and find you have been misled (you soon find that your senior commanders, contrary to what they may think, are not in possession of all the facts, a problem that the US soldiers found themselves in the famous fire fight in Mogadishu).

Green's crime also revealed, as cruelty often does, a striking absence of imagination. And it is imagination that should come into play whenever we contemplate doing something that the rules tell us we shouldn't. Imagina-tion is that most unique of human gifts: the capacity to imagine something that might exist beyond our ability to see it in front of us. It gives us the gift of insight, not sight. It is the ability to imagine suffering through represen-tations on stage or screen (which prompt us to cry during a film, even though we are suspending disbelief in the knowledge that the people on stage or screen are not actually suffering). Empathy in the broadest sense is concern for others beyond kin, family and even another species. It reveals what makes us most human.

But if listening to our conscience is difficult at the best of times and especially in the heat of battle, we have a conscience for a reason—it makes us fit for purpose. Indeed, the Greeks were the first to deduce what we now know scientifically, that morality is hard-wired into us.

The conscience of (talking) tools

We have met Socrates already, and will meet the real man again in the next chapter when we look at the extraordinarily quick thinking he showed at the battle of Delium, one of only two major land engagements that distin-guished the Peloponnesian War. In *The Republic* Socrates is most definitely Plato's spokesman, already with a developed theory of the mind at hand to share with us. In the *Meno*—the early dialogue that we will now discuss—Socrates is probably much nearer the man Plato knew in real life, the person who influenced him more than any other to pursue a philosophical career, to make up for the frustration of his own hopes of becoming a politician.

At times, Plato's dialogues can be pretty frustrating, particularly if you do not like the style of Socrates' relentless questioning. And Socrates always has the last word, as he probably demanded in real life. No wonder the Socratic method is used in American law schools. But what he was trying to instil in his listeners was the habit of an active mind—the rigorous questioning of everything that they had been told was the truth.

The dialogue called *Meno* is especially interesting because it features someone outside the 'political community' which excluded women and foreign residents, those who were not allowed to have political thoughts of their own. It involves a slave boy, one of Aristotle's 'talking tools', the graphic term the Greeks applied to those they enslaved. And what the dialogue shows is that even a slave was born with some rudimentary ideas that can be elicited through close questioning. Even the Greeks acknowledged that unlike a tool, a slave could have thoughts of his own.

The slave boy in question is the property of Meno, a young aristocrat from Thessaly. And in the dialogue Socrates asks him to solve a geometrical problem which requires him to undertake a series of steps in reasoning out the solution. Socrates leads the boy to the correct answer, establishing that since he had no previous training in mathematics, he must have had mathematical training in a previous life, and merely 'remembered' what he had once been taught. We call the ideal *anamensis*—certain knowledge is innate, and recollected by the soul with proper enquiry such as the Socratic method. (*Meno*, 81d) Socrates goes on to say that he will not 'take an oath' that the slave boy really had access to knowledge from a previous life; he is merely speaking metaphorically. But we now know that the mind is not a blank slate when we come into the world. Morality is already programmed into us by natural selection; we possess it for a reason—to exercise moral choices.

Plato was to develop this in a later dialogue, the *Phaedo*: 'When people are questioned, if you put the question well, they will always answer correctly; and yet, unless they have knowledge and the correct account already within them, they could not do this'. (*Phaedo*, 73)

He is arguing that the mind can puzzle out universal laws such as those that govern mathematics without prior training. On one level he is claiming that we can infer the laws of mathematics. He is actually claiming much more: he is claiming that knowledge (hence the 'memory of an earlier life') is involved. When it comes to morality we do not just infer that certain actions are bad, we instinctively know them to be so. Plato is arguing a very important point: that the origins of virtue are to be found in our own natures. Because Plato was not an evolutionary psychologist, he did not employ the terminology we do today, but he did use the concept of kinship that linked the Greeks to their distant ancestors. Kinship is actually a metaphor he uses in the dialogue (*Meno* 81C-D): 'Since all nature is akin, and the soul has learned all things, there is nothing to prevent her by recollecting one single thing, but covering all the rest'. (Allen, 1959, 165–74)

Now, to be sure Plato was not making a scientific claim. But remember that the scientific method derived from philosophy, and so it should not be surprising that sometimes philosophers stumbled upon a scientific truth through inductive reasoning and their close observation of human nature. Socrates begins the dialogue by asking Meno to define virtue. Influenced by the Sophists, the young man remarks with great self-assurance that virtue is relative to time and place—all conditions of life, young and old, male and female, bondsman and free citizen, have different virtues, for virtue is relative to the actions and ages of each of us in what we do. To which Socrates replies ironically, 'how fortunate I am, Meno, when I ask you for one virtue and you present me with a host of them'. Socrates then goes on to show his interlocutor that the virtues he is enumerating are all cultural constructions. We do indeed make our own rules, but virtue as a concept can be abstracted into an essence which applies to all people at all times, and even to slaves. Once you awaken to that philosophical insight you are not far from stumbling upon what we now know to be a scientific claim. Richard Tarnas puts it well:

The Platonic perspective … asks the philosopher to go through the particular to the universal, and beyond the appearance to the essence … Plato directs the philosopher's attention away from the external and the concrete, from taking things at face value, and points 'deeper' and 'inward', so that one may 'awaken' to a more profound level of reality'. (Ford, 2007, 59)

It took a long leap from Socrates' reasoning to the understanding that morality is biological as well as cultural, that we are hard-wired to be moral beings, but Plato was well on the way to getting there.

In other words, we are all born with a conscience. The notion of an innate idea, writes Julius Morasevik, is a claim that Plato makes not about the slave boy in particular, but about the human species. To contend that the concept is innate, he concludes, is to claim that it is not acquired by abstraction but pre-exists in the mind at birth, and can be utilised by everyone, even a 'talking tool', if the tool is allowed to talk. (Moravesik, 1971, 61) We all have the capacity to reason morally, writes Matt Ridley, because morality is innate. We do not have to learn it in the classroom, although it helps to be taught how to reason out moral principles, and it helps to have principles in order to theorise about the moral predispositions with which we are born. And Plato used the example of mathematics because it relies on a pre-cultural language of logic. The ability to reason logically, he correctly perceived, is not acquired. It is part of our nature as a species. The Pythagorean theorem which Socrates draws out of the slave boy is also 'above' all the culturally determined roles we play. And an intelligent slave is just as capable of logical thinking as his master.

The difference between Meno, the young aristocrat and his young slave illustrates the unfairness of life. Meno has had an education and even the chance to bandy words with Socrates, the first great Western philosopher. He had the unique opportunity to translate the innate ability with which he was born into a social capability, and by thinking more logically than others, to catch out his peers in debate. But even an intelligent slave, given an education, can make that journey, too.

Unfortunately, knowing 'right' from 'wrong' does not mean that we will always act upon the knowledge. We do not all have 'character', the strength of will to do the right thing in a crisis. Some of us are very weak vessels indeed, and Meno happened to be one of them. Even when Socrates knew him he was a rich kid from Thessaly who played with philosophy, but was incapable of putting what he learned to good use. He was a follower of fashionable opinions. His own definition of virtue as 'the power and desire of attaining things that are honourable' was plagiarised from a poet. His knowledge was entirely derivative. This is not to say that he was a fool. In the course of the dialogue we see him rediscovering the truth of the Pythagorean theorem, but he was quite incapable of taking this knowledge any further in later life.

We don't know what happened to his slave boy (if he existed at all) but we do know what happened to Meno in real life. He was among the Greek generals captured by the Persian King Artaxerxes after the battle of Cunaxa. He had joined Xenophon's famous band of freebooters who had been recruited by the King's brother to help him seize the throne. Two of our sources tell us that of the captured generals he alone was spared. Xenophon himself in his own account of the expedition, the *Anabasis*, claimed that he was executed a year later.

Virtue, Aristotle always insisted, relies on character, which is moulded from early childhood. But it is precisely because we have an innate ability to act well if we choose to, and badly if we choose not, that it has been so difficult for the military over the centuries to programme soldiers with a morality. We can try to programme human minds, but not human hearts. So, what is the difference? Shakespeare puts it well in one of his finest character studies. In the last act of *Macbeth* we find the King's wife plagued by a bad conscience as a result of first encouraging and then abetting her husband's murder of Duncan:

> Canst thou not minister to a mind diseas'd?
> Pluck from the memory a rooted sorrow
> Raise from the written troubles of the brain
> And with some sweet oblivious antidote
> Cleanse the stuff'd bosom of that perilous stuff
> Which weighs upon the heart?

Lady Macbeth may have steeled her husband to murder Duncan, the king whose crown he usurps, but she has not acted upon her heart, only upon her head. It is not her mind that is diseased. Her mind has given her a moral framework that she ignored at her peril. She is plagued with remorse. It is the connection between the mind and the heart which Mary Midgley calls 'the organised business of living', and it is something of importance to a soldier in the organised business of war. (Midgley, 2003, 3)

A conscience, in short, is a demand of our nature. It is embodied, and feeling comes first, then the thought. Wordsworth put it very well: 'our thoughts are the representative of our past feelings'. When we describe someone as being without a conscience, we are calling him or her—in Nietzsche's terms—a 'fragmented' man or woman: a one-dimensional person in whom we find a 'deficiency of feeling': a lack of imagination, an incapacity to empathise or be moved. Like a schizophrenic, a person can live in two worlds at the same time. We can be over-rational, always finding good reasons to justify abominable acts. Conscience, we have come to realise pretty late in history, relies on physical embodiment. Our instinct to betray our friends and so save our own lives or to stand our ground, in solidarity with those next to us, is not the product of reason or emotion. It is the product of both, but it is reflection after the fact which makes us feel guilty and weighs us down—hence the saying, to be 'burdened with a conscience'. A conscience is simply the reflection on our actions. In that sense, it can be considered a thoughtful reflection.

Or, to put it reductively, conscience is the product of reflection when our instinct for survival has trumped our sympathy for the plight of others. The Polish poet Zbigniew Herbert offers a delightful retelling of the story of Prometheus, who famously was punished by the gods for stealing fire and giving it to humanity. We find him, as in the original Greek myth, chained to a rock in the Caucasus. Except that in Herbert's version the story is only half true; the messenger god Hermes tells Prometheus:

'If the truth be told, the gods reconciled themselves easily with the theft of fire. It was quickly degraded and chased into kitchens. All it could achieve is to heat a pot, so it was not the heavenly Fire that consumed cities. By now, everyone has forgotten that the gods' ire was provoked by Prometheus' theft of memory'.

...

'And from memory, conscience is born', Hermes goes on, drawing out the vowels as if the word itself was delectable. 'At first inconspicuous, it grows like fire, and envelops the entire soul at moments of trial. Once awakened, it cannot be extinguished. It is what makes Orestes wander the roads seeking forgiveness. That's what you've made of man. The gods have no conscience'.

A cry from Prometheus.

Hermes departs. He has never come to know the charms of conscience, either.
(Herbert, 2010, 367)

In Herbert's tale, Hermes departs quite unmoved by Prometheus' plight. We, by contrast, are different. The memory of an uncharitable deed can haunt us for the rest of our lives.

The gods, of course, are not really embodied beings, even if the Greeks gave then human emotions, like anger and jealousy. Their immortality made them different from human beings. Our embodiment is on a plane with all other organic life—we live a cycle from birth to death. And as organic creatures we feel morality 'in our pulses' (to quote Keats) or we do not feel it at all. There can be no 'objective criteria', writes Michael Pritchard, that we can apply to discovering what is the right thing to do except through physical sensation. (Baumann, 1993, 36) We cannot strip ourselves of our moral sentiments the better to view them objectively, because what resources would we be able to call on to conduct such an examination? To do justice to morality we have to call on our sensibilities, including our sentiments. 'If it is to be of any practical use for us, moral philosophy must be "an inside job" however much one may wish otherwise'. We tend to put much more emphasis than ever, and certainly more than fifty years ago, on re-personalising morality, or anchoring it to what de Tocqueville called the 'habits of the human heart'. We have returned moral responsibility from the finishing line (to which it was exiled) to the starting point (natural selection): we now acknowledge that it is rooted in the way we humans are. (Baumann, 1993, 34) We feel instinctive sympathies and share an instinctive hatred of injustice. It is only because we are emotional creatures that we are also moral.

Meno did not attend a military academy, of course. He was not asked to sit an exam on the ethics of war. These courses are not intended to give us a conscience or to help us to think deeply; they are intended to encourage us to be more thoughtful (and the moment you are that, you are in a better position, of course, to challenge some of the lessons you are taught at school). This emerges clearly in one of the finest books to come out of the Vietnam war, Philip Caputo's *A Rumour of War*, a troubled and troubling meditation 'about the things men do in war and the things war does to them'. At the head of one of the chapters we find a quotation from Hobbes' *Leviathan*, the famous description of the state of nature, the war of all against all. Caputo and his friends found themselves fighting in the most unforgiving of environments. It was a war in which most soldiers felt only contempt 'for those who sought to impose on this savage struggle the mincing distinctions of civilised warfare—that code of battlefield ethics that seeks to humanise essentially inhuman war'. (Caputo, 1978, 27) It is those 'mincing distinctions' that so many soldiers find so difficult to apply in the circumstances in which they find themselves. It is not because of thoughtlessness that our ethical codes are problematic; it is because we think about them all the time. Reflection is dangerous for that reason. The real concern of the military is not that a soldier will act badly because he hasn't been instructed in moral reasoning, but that he may reach the conclusion—on reflection—that the laws of war have no place in the 'real' world.

In 2006, the Office of the Multi-National Force Iraq and Office of the Surgeon General-United States Army Command issued the first comprehensive Behavioural Ethics Report for the war in Iraq as part of its Mental Health Advisory Team IV (MATCH)-Operation Iraqi Freedom 05–07 Report. As the first of its kind, MATCH IV addressed some key areas of ethical concern. The results of this survey surprised and disheartened many. Let me quote just a few excerpts from the report.

1. Only 47 per cent of soldiers and only 38 per cent of Marines agreed that non-combatants should be treated with dignity and respect. Well over one-third of soldiers and Marines reported that torture should be allowed to obtain important information from insurgents (36 per cent and 39 per cent respectively). (Surgeon-General's office 2006, 35)
2. The most common behaviour soldiers and Marines reported engaging in was cursing and/or insulting Iraqi non-combatants in their presence (28

per cent of soldiers and 30 per cent of Marines). (Surgeon-General's Office 2006, 35)

3. The most likely battlefield ethics violations that soldiers and Marines would report included a unit member injuring or killing an innocent non-combatant, with 55 per cent of soldiers agreeing that they would report a unit member and 40 per cent of Marines agreeing that they would report a fellow Marine. Less than half of soldiers and Marines claimed that they would report a team member for unethical behaviour, with the Marines being less likely to report a fellow Marine than soldiers reporting a fellow soldier. (Surgeon-General's Office 2006, 36)

Ethical violations are as old as war itself, but what is interesting about the report is that it is consistent with a new attitude not only to battlefield ethics but ethics in general. Character is less prized than it once was because we have discovered—or believe we have—that we will always act badly if the wrong circumstances arise. Indeed, it is all a matter of *situation*—the circumstances and the context. And in the increasingly challenging environments in which we ask our soldiers to fight—in environments such as Afghanistan and Iraq where the enemy is ever present but not always visible, where lethal fire-fights have replaced traditional battles—we are asking a great deal of them. Are we asking too much?

The erosion of character

Let me take a famous passage from Virgil's epic poem, *The Aeneid*. Just as Greek schoolchildren were brought up on the moral lessons of Homer, so young Roman boys derived a great deal of their moral education from Virgil's national epic. It ends abruptly with the death of the great warrior, Turnus, at the hands of Aeneas, the founder of Rome. Aeneas is a recognizable 'modern' figure in a way that Achilles is not. Indeed, he has greater integrity, as William James called it, because he subordinates everything to the gods' will. His famous *pietas* (or piety) is a love-fulfilling duty, which brings him no personal pleasure but whose personal expression is justice. Justice is obtained the hard way, by a long, Pyrrhic victory of the human spirit.

There is no joy in Virgil's account of the final encounter between the two great warriors of his poem. Turnus, who is in every respect an admirable or worthy foe, lies wounded at Aeneas' feet, and in a brief speech asks for mercy. At first Aeneas is inclined to show it, but then he sees, gleaming on Turnus' shoulder, the sword belt he had stripped from the body of Aeneas' great friend, Pallas. Enraged, Aeneas strikes the fatal blow and avenges his friend's loss. He could have spared Turnus' life; he chooses not to. Aeneas inhabits a recognizably human world. We are all creatures of choice. Our agency is freedom, and the responsibility to choose which comes with it. And our character is judged by others according to the choices we make.

For Virgil's readers there would have been nothing wrong about Aeneas' reaction. Today, however, soldiers are not allowed to kill to avenge the death of their comrades. Indeed, we try to limit their choice by hedging them in with rules and conventions and legal protocols. Still, in the heat of battle and on a battlefield where there are no judges at hand, or police officers to enforce the rules, ultimately life and death is still a matter of choice. Some soldiers will calculate the odds and pull the trigger, others may be deterred by the thought of being caught and prosecuted on returning home.

A striking echo of this appears in a passage from Caputo's *A Rumour of War*:

> Out there, lacking restraints, sanctioned to kill, confronted by a hostile country and a relentless enemy, we sank into a brutish state. The descent could be checked only by the net of a man's inner moral values, the attribute that is called character. There were a few … who had no net, and plunged all the way down, discovering in their bottom-most depths, a capacity for malice they had probably never suspected was there. (Caputo, 1978, xx)

In a perceptive commentary on Conrad's morality tale *Heart of Darkness*, the literary critic Ian Watt similarly assesses the responses of the author's commercial agents in the Congo to their fear: 'There are those who succumb, like Kurtz; those who possess a 'deliberate belief' which enables them to survive almost every adversity; and then there are the fools—the 'hollow men' who do not respond at all because they simply do not notice'. (Herzog, 1992, 29)

In striking ways, this is also true of every soldier on a battlefield. Some will discover that they are heroes, others will be 'outed' as the cowards they have always been, and a few will be exposed as monsters. And many will survive the experience completely untouched by it. Often, tales of heroism find otherwise quite ordinary men and women thrust out of the shallows, and achieving unexpectedly a bit of depth. This idea runs through Western thinking. The warrior ethos places great emphasis on 'acting in character' in a way that enhances the reputation of the individual soldier.

What was acknowledged by Greek authors post-Homer is that we are only ethical beings because we have a character. The great characters in literature, like Aeneas, are defined by their moral qualities, their respective virtues and vices. If we were to remove ethical choices from a narrative like Virgil's epic we would still have to take a moral stand ourselves on the other characteristics of the hero, such as humour and intelligence. We would still have to ask, do our heroes laugh appropriately, or are they insensitive to the misfortune of others? Do they put their intelligence to good use? We the readers cannot help but evaluate them morally.

The warrior ethos is often called Aristotelian because of the importance that Aristotle attached to character. The military instructs its officers that a virtuous disposition will provide them with the required moral perspective on life. It seeks to weed out psychopaths, sociopaths and others whose dispositions cannot be moulded. For war is very much 'the human thing', and as with everything else that we dignify with the name, you can only be human—you can only become what you are—in dialogue with other people.

Aristotle's most famous observation is, of course, his remark that man is by nature a *zoon politikon*, a term nearly always rendered in translation as a 'political animal'. The Greek translates more correctly into 'a living creature designed by its nature to realise its full human potential'. The purpose of life, Aristotle insisted, was the pursuit of *eudaimonia*, which frequently is mistranslated as 'a happy life' when Aristotle actually meant a fulfilled one. A fulfilled life is not just a set of actions, it is a set of actions performed by someone who does them because they correctly see the point of doing them. The warrior's life is the life of a person who fulfils himself through war. But a fulfilled life needs an audience because it is a manifestation of character—truth is lived, not taught. Without an audience, no truths can be revealed. A warrior is a man who wants to be well thought of because of his good character, but the point is not to be seen to be himself, to be the good character that one wishes to be in the eyes of others, as well as his own. (Hughes, 2001, 26) As Plato recognised, if you are not at ease with yourself you will not be at ease with other people.

The point is that when a soldier goes to war, he enters a realm that will test him as no other probably will, and he has only the vaguest idea of what reaction it will provoke. All he knows is that he cannot possibly escape either the situation or himself. In Shakespeare's *Macbeth* there is a striking sentence from the hero of the play: 'To know any deed t'were best not know myself'. Macbeth cannot possibly predict what effect the murder of Duncan will have on his soul. He is as much surprised as everyone else at the changes that occur in the course of the drama. This is what makes Shakespeare's work one of the great tragedies in the literary canon. A man's moral psychology is not a mechanism that can be tinkered with at will; it can be meddled with only at great risk. Colin McGinn writes of a mismatch of character and situation. A person broken by war is not necessarily a flawed human being. In all other circumstances he might cope well enough, but the situation is not normal. The disintegration of a personality can occur when one finds oneself inadequate to the situation and its demands. (McGinn, 2006, 195) Circumstances really do matter. Indeed, some philosophers contend that few of us have really robust character traits. Human behaviour is far more sensitive to situational factors than one would suspect, even if we actually were to possess the sort of robust character traits that virtue ethics demand.

This biological explanation has tended in recent years to supersede the psychological one that was made famous by the experiments of Miligram and Zimbardo fifty years ago, but social psychology persists in weaving its spell over institutions like the military.

In a naïve moment some time ago, I once wondered whether in all of the United States, a vicious government could find enough moral imbeciles to meet the personnel requirements of the national system of death camps of the sort that was maintained in Germany. I am now beginning to think that the full complement could be found in New Haven.

A few days after beginning his famous 'obedience experiments' at the end of the summer of 1961, Stanley Millgram wrote these words in a letter to his fellow social psychologist, Henry Riecken. He informed Riecken that his students had been willing to administer what they thought was a fatal electric shock to actors playing the part of victims. Few had been deterred in the slightest by their screams. On the professor's instructions they had kept turning up the power. Most, though not all, did what they were asked to. The results, wrote Millgram, were 'truly terrifying and depressing'. (*The Times*, 2 December 2009)

Milgram's experiments, however, made him deeply unpopular with his colleagues. He was denied tenure at the top US universities, finding an eventual home at New York City College. He died a disappointed man, and a controversial one in the academic community, for his methodology was questioned throughout his life by others members of the profession who challenged his experiments on the grounds of their lack of 'external validity'. What does an experiment show if it cannot be replicated outside controlled conditions? Some critics went further and insisted that what Milgram had tested that day was not obedience but trust. None of his students, after all, had any reason to question his good intentions, and what someone is willing to do in an experiment may differ significantly from one's willingness to do the same thing in the field.

The problem was that Milgram himself seems to have doubted whether the situation itself always wins out. He conducted personality tests at the end of each of his sessions, collecting data on the education, religion and gender of his students because he himself suspected that their moral hinterland—what they believed or had been taught—might have influenced their actions. And in the end, we must always remember that 35 per cent of his subjects did not do what they were told. They defied their professor and put other factors (including their conscience) first. Social psychologists can never explain why people do that; they can only really observe aggregate behaviour. They cannot, writes Lauren Slater, tell us much about the exotic tendrils that curl off the mainframe and give sprout to something strange: 'To extend the metaphor ... (if) it was not the soil, it must have been something in the seed'. (Slater, 2004, 47)

Many social psychologists are still unwilling to accept this conclusion. They continue to place far too much emphasis on stressful conditions or factors that impair our ability to reason out what is right, and what is wrong. This is particularly true of Philip Zimbardo who gave evidence in the defence of those accused of cruelty in Abu Ghraib. Chip Fredericks, one of the chief characters involved, was represented by Zimbardo at his trial.

There is absolutely nothing in his record that I was able to uncover that would predict that Chip Fredericks would engage in any form of abusive, sadistic behaviour. On the contrary, there is much in his record to suggest that had he not been forced to work and live in such an abnormal situation, he might have been the Military's All-American poster soldier on its recruitment ads. (Zimbardo, 2007, 344)

The point Zimbardo was making is that social conformity tends to be hard-wired into us as a survival mechanism against in-group violence. Peer pressure to conform, to pass muster, to make the grade, to 'come through' for one's side is neurologically wired into us. What we fear most is rejection by our friends. To become an outcast (quite literally in the ancient world, to be ostracised from a community) can still be dangerous and often fatal. To be ostracised was often to be outlawed or excluded from the civic order. One such figure was Cain who was branded by God for killing his brother, Abel. The Septuagint or Greek version of the Hebrew Bible translated the mark as 'trembling and groaning', which would certainly have made him stand out from the crowd in the years of wandering that stretched out ahead of him. (Jacoby, 2011, 84)

The pain of rejection is there for a reason too. Like all pain it is a warning, a sign to draw back. The anterior singulate cortex in the brain is the area where we register the pain of rejection and ask the question, 'Why me?' It also happens to involve the same circuitry that induces the emotional content of pain. 'Evolution may have piggy-backed brain functions that regulate social interaction on top of the more primal system', writes Gary Stix; 'even the way we speak (I'm crushed) hints at just such a connection'. (Stix, 2010, 12)

But this is all a little too neat. For the other side of the coin is that in well functioning communities (and war requires team work) peer pressure acts in a different way: it encourages good behaviour. This comes out implicitly in an essay by John Stuart Mill: 'Though we cannot emancipate ourselves from the laws of nature as a whole, we can escape from any particular law of nature, if we are able to withdraw ourselves from the circumstances in which it acts. Though we can do nothing except through laws of nature, we can use one law to counteract another'. (Aiken, 1956, 152)

One law of nature involves peer conformity, the desire to live up to the expectations of our friends, rather than disappoint them because it is safer to do so. But we also get to choose our peer reviewers. We find ourselves members of teams each of which has its own honour codes and way of doing things. We have constructed those teams for a reason as a force multiplier. They maximise social capital which is the essence of all successful team-building. We may be constrained to act within the laws of nature, but team work allows us to change the context in which those laws apply. And because, James adds, we have more instincts than any other animal, we can use our portfolio of instincts: we can use one instinct to offset another. And we also have cultural instincts that are drilled and programmed into us. Those instincts made it particularly difficult for others to prevail upon us to act in a way inconsistent with the principles that define our character.

In fact there were many soldiers in Abu Ghraib, including some on the notorious torture floor, who showed enough character to say 'no'. Three US Navy (USN) dog teams led by Master-at-Arms William Kimbro refused to take part in any abuse and successfully resisted what they later called 'significant pressure' do so from the others. (Danchev, 2011, 212–213) Clearly, they were in a stronger position to resist because they worked as a team, and were superbly led, and they were from the Navy and not the Army, which created service rivalry and made it easier for them to stand out from the others. They found themselves in the situation but not of it—and that is where character really matters.

Character and circumstance; the two are conjoined. So are justice and mercy, truth and harm, desire and duty, expectation and result, the actual and the ideal. It is these very contradictions that give us a character in the first place. In his still well-regarded book, *Seven Types of Ambiguity*, William Empson argues that irony—in this case the ambiguity in not always playing the roles we would like—is central to our humanity. It is also central to most great literature. The greatest literature from the Greek tragedies to Ibsen's plays provides the most memorable moments when the main characters step abruptly and tellingly out of their roles. We can be two people at the same time. Ambiguity is not only a critical literary trope, it is a central human characteristic. We are judged most often by our acts—what we do—but we often judge ourselves by what we know we might have done had circumstances differed. To go to the assistance of a wounded man, or to press on and reach the objective in time—both are part of a soldier's character. 'Whichever they did', writes Empson, 'they will still have lingering in their minds the way they would have preserved their self-respect if they had acted differently; they are only to be understood by bearing both possibilities in mind'. Empson's point is that we live with two conflicting thoughts and two different images of ourselves, and this can further undermine our self-belief. We may be surprised by what we find out about ourselves. We may find ourselves changing in ways we cannot grasp. A situation is never more real than when it presents us with a test we possibly never expected to face.

Hence the term 'baptism of fire'; a soldier can be re-born again. Not only do we not know how we will behave in a given situation until we face it, we do not know what the behaviour will do to us. Having received the primary sacrament of war, the baptism of fire, their boyhoods were behind them, writes Caputo. 'Neither they nor I thought of it in those terms at the time. We didn't say to ourselves: "we've been under fire, we've shed blood, now we're men". We were simply aware, in a way we could not explain, that something significant had happened to us'. (Caputo, 1978, 127) But, of course, the same situations might undo others. Is a man to be judged bad simply because he is found to be inadequate to the situation in which he finds himself? Yes, if he is a soldier. To find himself inadequate to the challenge may have major implications, not only for himself, but for everyone else.

Situationism

Virtue ethics are coming under attack on another front—not only from social psychologists and biologists but from philosophers themselves. They are called 'situationists' and they argue that the human behaviour is primarily the result of the situation in which one finds oneself. In his book *Experiments in Ethics*, the Harvard Professor Kwame Appiah cites a number of examples of how inconsistent is our behaviour. One of his favourite examples is that of 40 students at a seminary at Princeton who were asked to give a sermon. Half were allotted a random series of biblical topics, and half were assigned the parable of the Good Samaritan. The seminarians worked together in a room and every fifteen minutes one would leave to deliver a sermon in another building on the campus. Their route required them to pass by an actor slumped in a doorway who was groaning in pain; twenty-four passed right by, including the students who were about to distil the lesson of the parable of the Good Samaritan.

We still talk of doing 'what comes naturally', yet we behave differently in different situations. Even if there are deep behavioural tendencies in our nature, they have evolutionary explanations that will not always be engaged in every possible environment. History, Appiah writes, is the environment we find ourselves in as a result of earlier social practices which shaped those environments, creating selection pressures that stabilised genetically inscribed behavioural dispositions. Human behavioural possibilities are the result, at least in part, of concepts which are a central dimension of culture. (Appiah, 2008)

And we just happen to find ourselves at another cultural turn in our history. We are able to ask a question that would never have occurred to the Greeks: what if we could programme a robot to act ethically, to exercise moral choices on our behalf? There is a wonderful line in Leo Frankowski's *Bolbo* series of science fiction books, when a young tank crewman is told about his artificial intelligence tank: 'Son, if your tank's loyal, you do not have to be'. In other words, the young man does not need to have 'character', still less waste his time in the classroom being taught the values of virtue ethics; the machine will come through for us every time.

But one of the points Appiah makes is that we admire heroes because they grow, they have potential. Some will realise their potential and actualise it in action. Others may never find an opportunity to do so. Human growth is one of the ennobling themes of war, as well as an explanation of its abiding human appeal. On the battlefield, we see the development arrested, or even reversed. We see people who are unable to rise above their circumstances. Whether we think their courage is innate, or the product of circumstance, does not matter. Some heroes join up to be heroic; others are conscripted and find in themselves deep and unsuspected wells of heroism. The idea of human growth is the narrative of a life: it is our story or biography. It is the realization of a human possibility; the realization of 'who', not 'what' I am. A robot is quite different. It cannot reveal itself through action. It will always be a 'what' because it does not have a story. There are no deeds to record or relate. There is just work but no experience, no growth in self-knowledge—no chance to imagine the unimaginable, think the unthinkable, let alone entertain self-doubt. Computer chips make no such journey. They do not die for their country; they do not take risks; they do not run the gauntlet. They do not demand anything of themselves, and nothing is demanded of them in turn except consistency of behaviour.

We live, however, in post-heroic times. We prefer to belittle our heroes. Biographers frequently diminish the heroic by emphasising the hypocrisies and inconsistencies of their subjects whose actions are neither consistent with the actions of others, nor internally consistent with their own. But it is inconsistency that constitutes our humanity. To be capable of virtuous acts is also to be capable of corresponding vices such as cowardice and meanness. Evil, as Aristotle reminded us, does not require any additional physical or mental properties. Compassion and cruelty are cut from the same cloth; both are grounded in our capacity for free will. Cruelty in most cases arises from a choice, often calculated and quite rational. Some vicious people have no other reason to act badly than the desire to do so—they know they are doing wrong. Like Private Green and his friends they elect to set conscience aside in the expectation that they will not be caught or punished.

Equally many people choose to act well. We are moral beings but we cannot always anticipate how we will react under stress. This is why we derive character from behaviour, not the other way around. There is a gnomic passage in the *Poetics* where Aristotle remarks that moral character is displayed when a person makes an 'unobvious decision'. (Nuttall, 2007, 238) What he means—we might conjecture—is that we cannot judge a person's moral character by his or her obvious actions. Ethical character is in inverse proportion to external motivation. A mother is biologically obliged to protect her own child. A soldier who throws himself on a grenade to save a friend is not. It is this unobvious decision that allows us to determine the ethical character of the people we study.

We do not admire consistency; we admire acts of courage or heroism, or striking examples of sacrifice in situations which would probably have overwhelmed the rest of us. And what we admire most is an act of courage that makes a difference. It enhances life because in contemplating it we find renewed pride in being human. Appiah quotes a passage from J.S. Mill's tract *On Liberty*: 'It really is of importance not only what men do, but also what manner of men they are that do it'. Mill was insisting that part of the moral vision of life comes from the contemplation of virtuous acts, and the acts we admire 'partake of the character of those that do them'. And interestingly, he actually alludes to the possibility of robots (or, since the term had yet to be invented, automata):

… supposing it were possible to get … battles fought by machinery—by automatons in human form—it would be a considerable loss to do so. Human nature is not a machine to be built after a model, and set to do exactly the work prescribed for it, but a tree which requires to grow and develop itself on all sides according to the tendency of the inward forces which make a living thing. (Midgley, 2006, 58)

It is those inward forces which constitute our humanity. As Appiah concludes, 'only a misguided theoretical parsimony would make us choose between considerations of character and considerations of consequence'. (Appiah, 2008, 67)

So, even if the situationists are right to argue that virtues are rarely if ever instantiated; even if there is no such thing as a totally courageous or virtuous person, this does not bring into question the status of heroism as an ideal. Natural selection has given us heroes for a reason: so that it can inspire us on to greater deeds. This is what Darwin wrote in *The Descent of Man*: 'Love of praise and the strong feelings of glory and the still stronger horror of scorn act together as a powerful stimulus in the development of social values'. Without the ideals of sacrifice and courage—without the individual pursuit of glory—our species might be less fit for purpose. We evolved because we found certain actions especially inspiring. We were often inspired to reprise them ourselves.

Can a robot have a conscience?

'With every technology that readily changed the face of battle, there was one war where it made its debut, and another where it showed its potential', claimed Major John Amiss who headed the Joint Robotics Detachment in Iraq in 2010. (*The Times*, 21 May 2010) The battle which saw the debut of the robot was Operation Desert Storm in 1991. Something happened at the very end of the campaign which, if only for its symbolism, ushered in the beginning of the robotic age. Five Iraqi soldiers successfully surrendered at Faylaka Island, at the very end of the Gulf War, to an unmanned vehicle. The system was not autonomous, it was controlled by a human operator; it was what the US calls a partially autonomous operating system (UAS) because its human operator was able to use the machine's optical sensor to identify the soldiers as potential Prisoners of War (POWs). Human observation, in other words, made it possible for them to surrender in the reasonable hope that they would not be mistaken for soldiers trying to disable the machine. (Coyne, 1992, 123) Had they but known it, those five Iraqi soldiers almost twenty years ago found themselves 'present at the creation'.

Most crucially of all, of course, the system to which they surrendered happened to be unarmed. What if it had been armed? What if it had been truly autonomous—able to make its own decisions? And what if those five Iraqi soldiers had been facing a combat unit with no human supervision, one that they might have had difficulty negotiating the everyday ambiguities we find on the battlefield? What if they had to deal with a system to which they could not appeal, one unable to empathise with their plight or feel remorse if, after opening fire, it had later found out that they had been trying to surrender?

All these questions may well be asked in a few years' time. For some years now the US Army has been interested in developing a 'lethal autonomous system' with an 'ethical control and reasoning' capability that will allow the robots of tomorrow to exercise ethical judgements. The scientist who is working on the design has been in the news since the *Economist* magazine first 'discovered' him back in 2007. Ronald Arkin thinks that it is possible to endow a robot with an 'artificial conscience' which will be able to govern its behaviour in a manner consistent with the rules and laws of war. In a technical report entitled *Governing Lethal Behaviour: Embedding Ethics in a Hybrid Deliberative-Reactive Robot Architecture*, Arkin writes:

The report has provided the motivation, philosophy, formalism, representational requirements, architectural design criteria, recommendations and test scenarios to design and construct an autonomous robotic system architecture capable of the ethical use of lethal force. These first steps towards that goal are very preliminary and subject to major revision, but at the very least they can be viewed as the beginnings of an ethical robotic war fighter. The primary goal remains to enforce the International Laws of War in the battlefield in a manner that is believed achievable, by creating a class of robots who not only conform to international law, but out perform human soldiers in their ethical capacity. (Arkin, 2011)

In his book Arkin goes on to propose that ethical Autonomous Weapons Systems (AWS) are likely to behave more ethically than human beings for a variety of reasons which he sets out very clearly:

1. AWSs do not need to act conservatively, that is, robots do not have the need to protect themselves in situations of uncertainty. A soldier who is unsure, but 'has a feeling that a terrorist was in 'that' window', may find himself facing either death or firing into a window where there is no enemy at best, and an innocent non-combatant at worst. A robot simply does not need to protect its existence in uncertainty, and although it seems unlikely that robots will be programmed to risk their functioning carelessly, there is nothing impossible in programming a robot to take chances which are dangerous for a human being, such as dismantling an Improvised Explosive Device or entering a room to clear it first.

2. AWSs will also have a variety of sensory devices which are superior to those of humans, allowing them to distinguish friend from foe in low-visibility environments, where humans may otherwise be paralysed into inaction or forced to take the risk of misidentifying non-combatants and friendly forces as enemies. (Beal, 2000 and Sparrow, 2007, 63)

3. Fear and hysteria are always latent in combat and can result in criminal behaviour (Wolfzer and Arkin, 2009, 30). Though some form of 'robot emotion' has been developed, emotions such as fear, anger and the desire for vengeance have no place in AWSs. In addition we can avoid 'scenario fulfilment' in robots, a factor which Arkin cites as playing an important role in the downing of an Iranian airliner by the USS Vincennes in 1988 by the ship's Phalanx Closed-In Weapons System, which mistook a commercial airliner for a military aircraft (Arkin, 2009, 30). 'Scenario fulfilment' is quite typical of human beings who tend to ignore or distort contradictory information in such a way as to fit pre-existing belief patterns.

4. AWSs will also be able to make use of information from more sources far faster than a human, allowing for more thorough deliberation before determining whether or not to apply lethal force. These sources could be a part of the system itself or a part of a wider 'system of systems' such as the Global Information Grid. (DARPA, 2007, 1–27)

The most important ethical advantage which a robot would possess, of course, is consistency—it would consistently obey the laws of war and relevant Rules of Engagement. (Anderson, 2009, 264) It is this unswerving commitment that for Arkin constitutes 'progress' in war. The human space may be diminished but our actions will be rendered more 'humane'.

To objections that a robot would not be able to display such human qualities as empathy and compassion, Arkin responds:

> No provision is made for these emotions at this time. The rationale is not because it is more challenging than other secondary emotions, but rather that humanity is legislated into the laws of war, and as such, if they are followed, the robot will exercise restraint consistent with societal norms. This may be inadequate to some, but the reduction of the inhumanity exhibited by a significant percentage of soldiers is believed to offset this loss and can potentially result in a fighting force that is more humane overall than the all-human one. (Arkin, 2009, 43)

In essence, Arkin is proposing that we should no longer rely exclusively on the consciences that have been hard-wired into us by natural selection—the moral heuristics that even a 'talking tool' like Meno's slave boy was found to embody. Instead, we should invest in mechanical systems that would have a different mental wiring. The 'conscience' in a robot would be instantiated in what Eliza Yudkowsky calls a 'retaliation logic' in place of our own hard-wired survival instincts. We run on instinct because natural selection has programmed us that way. When threatened, our adrenalin rises dramatically. We become more aggressive. Even if, she adds, we could consciously control our endocrine system so as to reduce the adrenalin rush, we would not be able to think fast enough to get us out of the situation in which we find ourselves.

Robots do not have instincts. They have a logical code: they have goals, and retaliation is merely a sub-goal of a larger goal. If the goal is to limit conflict, a robot could process a serial selection of ways to avoid retaliation; getting out of the way, rebuking the aggressor, or, if necessary, hitting back. But it would assess those goals on the basis of the ultimate mission. For humans, it takes too long to process information in the heat of battle, and as we are embodied beings, chemicals get us to react differently. We act instinctively because we are programmed to do everything we can to enhance our chances of survival. Here is Caputo: 'We learned what war was about ...we became more professional, leaner and tougher, and a callus began to grow around our hearts, a kind of emotional flak jacket that blunted the blows and stings of pity'. (Caputo, 1978, 90) The survival instinct was enhanced by a simple reality: 'the recognition that the body, which is supposed to be the earthly home of an immortal soul…is in fact only a fragile case stuffed full of disgusting matter'. (Caputo, 1978, 212)

Survival is tied in with another instinct, to avoid pain, and the pain of war is real enough. Like all pain it is there for a reason—to alert us to the danger we find ourselves in, and to concentrate our minds on what we are doing so that we may desist. We are driven 'mad with pain' when we cannot see a way of easing it, when—to use a scientific term—there is nowhere for the cognitive negative feedback to focus. The capacity to be driven mad by pain may have no adaptive function and may therefore be a surprising feature of our physiognomy, but then natural selection programmed a short life, not a long one. For most of our evolutionary history, someone in terminal pain would not have survived very long, hence the sanity of the person in pain would have little bearing on his reproductive history.

It is the fear of pain that makes it so challenging to deliberately put oneself at risk, even more so when we are bound by tough rules of engagement, and expected these days to show 'courageous restraint'. The courage not to act in terms of naked self-interest but with the well-being of others in mind, and to abide by rules learned in the classroom, is not natural. It asks a great deal of a soldier, for reasons that are fairly self-evident. The optimum way to avoid pain is to anticipate it. Evolution programmed us to avoid situations in which pain will most likely result. By the time we experience it, it will often be too late to act. As we have come to know more about the world, we have been able to avoid putting ourselves at risk. Culture has given us the means to achieve this: we teach children at an early age what is unsafe to eat; we teach soldiers what is the courageous thing to do—we encourage them to act with fortitude but not recklessly. But culture has arisen very late in history. Our autonomic negative feedback system is still what it was millions of years ago. It evolved in the absence of culture and in times of great danger, and it can still overrule everything we have been taught or learned from history.

Robots are different again, which is why they appeal to the military mind. One of the main reasons why soldiers commit atrocities in the heat of battle is that they suffer personal loss—the death of a close friend or 'buddy'. Caputo again: 'Asleep and dreaming I saw dead men living; awake I saw living men dead'. (Caputo, 1978, 190) The death of his friends, especially that of Lieut Levy, his Officer Candidate School (OCS) classmate, killed while trying to recover the body of a dead Marine, made him hate the enemy more than ever. 'No one was guaranteed immunity against the moral bacteria spawned by the war'. (Caputo, 1978, 313)

Likewise, one of the reasons why a soldier will throw himself on a grenade is to save the life of a friend. Friendship, in other words, cuts both ways. It can evoke remarkable acts of altruism and self-sacrifice; but it can also provoke acts of rage as it did in the case of Aeneas. And there is a much thinner line between the two than we are often willing to acknowledge. Both are products of our selfish genes. It is our friends who are in danger; our friends who must be avenged. Selfishness is the heart of our moral imaginary. Imagine any of our moral codes without it.

A robot with no sense of self could no more imagine our pain than it could empathise with our plight. Even the most advanced would see humans as moral units needing protection, not fellow creatures owed compassion. Conversely, if a robot 'dies' in an act of protecting a human being, this could not be explained in terms of altruism. Computer chips really do not make sacrifices for their country, only selfish genes do. Without a 'self', no robot would have an identity, or personality. It could never be a social being, which is why it would never misbehave in a social context. To invoke a point that Caputo makes in his Vietnam novel, *Indian Country* (1987): 'Wars do not end when the shooting stops ... they go on and on in the wounded minds of those who did the fighting'. (Caputo, 1998, 395) Unlike a human soldier, a robot would be in no danger of returning home a bad citizen or finding itself rejected as a 'baby killer' as happened many times in the course of the Vietnam war.

'That's Ulysses speaking', the psychologist said, resuming his seat. 'Wishing he'd died with his comrades instead of being cast adrift by Poseidon. 'I should have had a soldier's burial and praise from the Achaeans'. We didn't get either, did we, Chris? We survived the war, and instead of being praised, we got cursed. We were treated like shit, weren't we?' (Caputo 1988 335)

But a robot will not 'return home;' it will be stored away in a warehouse until the next time to be redeployed, or simply retired from service.

Can a robot be a Kantian?

A young woman once wrote to the great philosopher Immanuel Kant to ask him whether it was permissible to lie under certain circumstances, that is, when telling the truth might hurt someone else. Kant wrote back that we must always tell the truth in all circumstances, because to lie to another person means violating one's humanity. What he meant by this was that it would be irrational to do so. He believed that our lives should be governed by absolute maxims, or principles of action, one of which is to always tell the truth. To ignore such a maxim for a particular and very limited end would be to violate what is at the very centre of our concept of agency—practical reason. We should strive to treat others as we wish to be treated ourselves. Only we act on that understanding; practical reason is what makes us most human.

Also spracht Kant—the great sage of Königsberg, the minor university town in which he spent his entire life immured with his unbreakable convictions. Kant was undoubtedly a great philosopher, although he is not the easiest to read, let alone understand, even in his native language. German students often prefer to read him in translation since the first duty of any translator is to make a text intelligible to the reader. Kant also considered that he was a great humanitarian, as indeed he was, up to a point—the problem was that he was not an especially imaginative man.

For most of us the requirement to act morally is a demand of our character. For Kant it is a demand of logic. He was unusual for his time in arguing that moral laws were *a priori*—that is, they were independent of experience, and they were not there for any good that they did us as a species. In this, he broke with Aristotle who argued that morality is embodied—that is, programmed into us. In the *Nichomachean Ethics* he famously wrote that we do not need to be taught morality; we all know cruelty when we see it.

Kant would have none of this. There is a famous phrase at the beginning of *The Critique of Practical Reason* in which he talks of the 'starry heavens above and the moral law within us'. For Kant morality is a law; to act morally is to set aside all personal desire, interest and inclination and identify one's rational will with universal laws. The Categorical Imperative or Law that Kant outlines in his work, particularly *The Groundwork of the Metaphysics of Morals* (1785), is a moral necessity that arises *a priori*—prior to the evidence of the senses—in human reason: we must act out of duty and as if our action were at once to become a law of nature. 'If I feel like murdering someone, I have to ask, what would the world be like if everyone murdered everyone else on a whim?' Kant's law is as inflexible as a computer algorithm. The Categorical Imperative (or universal law) requires that I should not murder. But it also requires that I should not lie either; if I am asked by a policeman to reveal where a friend is hiding, I must comply (I must never lie). That is why Kantian ethics is so unpalatable to many thinkers who feel that in such circumstances not only would it be prudent to lie, it would even be morally indefensible not to. (Roberts, 2005, 99) He ignored the first requirement of humanity: we may well have a responsibility to tell the truth on the understanding that we ourselves would not wish to be lied to, but we also have a greater responsibility not to hurt others. The point is that there is no such thing as an absolute duty—we have to make choices which is why we are so inconsistent. We are condemned to be free.

There is actually something 'robotic' about his discussion of morality which is based on a code called Reason, which is grounded, in turn, in something called 'the will', independent of any human factors associated with it such as goodness. In the *Ground Work* he writes of qualities such as intelligence and judgement and consistency of purpose and courage. Intelligence and judgement he dismisses as a talent of the mind. Consistency of purpose he describes as a 'quality of temperament'. (Roberts, 2005, 55) But for Kant even this was not sufficient. We can see why he came to this conclusion. Courage, after all, can be put to many uses, some of them bad. A bad man can be resolute in his purposes. Intelligence can engineer the worst atrocities. Even the goodness of the human being's will cannot be allowed to depend on an outcome it produces, since so many factors outside our control may determine the eventual outcome. For Kant, 'goodwill is not good because of what it affects or accomplishes … it is good for its willing alone—that is, good in itself'. For Kant goodwill is the expression of the exercise of reason unadulterated by the passions, designs and inclinations that move us in life. Those passions and inclinations are not to be condemned—after all, they are human, all too human. But they cannot be a reliable guide to rightness of human behaviour.

We can see why Kantian morality appeals to roboticists. Kant's theory is essentially deontological (from the Greek *deos*—duty). It stresses duty, or what scientists call laws. Kant called them Categorical Imperatives, which he was careful to distinguish from hypothetical imperatives by which most of us lead our lives. When a soldier asks himself in the heat of battle: why should I do my duty? He is invoking a hypothetical imperative. Most soldiers need reasons for doing their duty:

1. I do my duty because it makes sense to do it.
2. I do it because of the consequences of not doing it (court martial).
3. I do it because I agree with certain humanistic principles that are grounded perhaps in my Christian faith and tested in circumstances in which I find myself.

But the moment we rationalise in this way is the moment the imperative becomes hypothetical (based on an 'if'—if I want such an outcome I must act in a particular way).

Categorical Imperatives are very different. They are absolute in their demands. Moral duties are categorical because they should be followed for the sake of duty. Duties are only categorical when we do not allow ourselves to ask the question: why should I do my duty? And to program a robot with a conscience is the only way that hypothetical imperatives could be banished from the battlefield altogether. War as a result might become totally instrumentalised. The Cartesian dream of making soldiers predictable units would be finally realised in the absence of human beings.

Why we break our own rules

'Oh, to vex me contraries meet in one:
Inconstancy unnaturally have begot
A constant habit'

John Donne, *Holy Sonnet XIX*

As Donne's sonnet suggests, inconsistency is a human flaw, or attribute—it all depends on one's perspective. And we are inconsistent for a reason—we find that not all problems have solutions. 'Deciding the un-decidable', adds Michael Frayn, is likely to be 'the last human skill to be surrendered to the machines'. (Frayn, 2006, 216) Unlike the computers we build we have been gifted with a bicameral brain that allows us to experience the world in fundamentally different ways. We are the only species that can stand outside our subjective experience. Our moral freedom lies in our ability to mix emotion and reflection, attachment and detachment, and that freedom is instantiated in out ability to make exceptions, to suspend our own rules.

Computers, by contrast, are programmed to be consistent because for them life is logical. They are supremely logical entities, which, of course, is why we design them. We build them so that they can arrive at a decision in the light of perfect logic, and we program them to do so on the basis of data or information that we submit to them in digital or logical form. If our minds were like that, we too would be able to be more perfectly logical beings, but our minds are not. We are rational (not logical), though we are capable of logic. We invented chess, which is a logical game, but that is also why a computer can now usually beat us.

So why are we so annoyingly inconsistent? It is all due to the curse of imagination. We are always reading people in the hope of guessing what they are thinking, and how they might react to us. We are always trying to judge them at the same time, to read beyond their facial expressions, to the true 'character' of the person behind the mask. Computers are much more limited in their capabilities. A computer programmer can build a complex algorithm which will enable it to recognise images caught on a security camera, and match them with that of an image held by the police. Police departments across the Western world are investing in neural network technologies for pattern-matching which can scan faces in a crowd and cross-reference them to known troublemakers. Pattern-recognition software can now alert police to suspicious behaviour before a crime has even been committed. Very soon we will be able to program computers to recognise patterns and relationships that we cannot observe with the human eye—the body language, if you will, that betrays anxiety. Dogs can pick this up quickly; we cannot. We have to rely on technology instead to 'read' people's intentions.

But we have capabilities that a computer does not, and this brings us back to 'character' again. A CCTV camera can do face recognition but we can do so much more. We can see facial resemblances (genetic codes which suggest that you look like your grandfather). We can 'see' the character of the person we knew forty years ago and are talking to now, despite the transformations that have occurred over the course of his or her life. We can 'connect' the face we see on the screen with a member of a family; we can recognise family likenesses or resemblances etched on a face.

Indeed there is no limit, writes Frayn, 'to the volume of analogical traffic that our thinking can bear'. (Frayn, 2006, 363) Perhaps once we understand the neurological mechanisms involved in seeing an analogy we might be able to program a computer to do the same. But so far, we cannot. And why would we want to? We draw analogies for a reason: to assign value. It is rule-making that allows us to exercise moral freedom, to draw up rules which we will also decide to suspend. In any moral decision one has to weigh the greater versus the lesser good; a judge may have to suspend a rule so that justice can prevail. Rationality allows us to make the choices we do. It allows us to draw up rules for the common good; it allows us also to suspend them in the name of justice. It is because 'the law is an ass' that we sometimes do not apply it.

The main reason we cannot program a computer with an imagination is very simple, writes Frayn: we would have to instruct it to see whether things are other than they should be. But when we look for differences in patterns that we expect to find we do not look for random differences, but differences that we find significant. Or, to use a particular word that is peculiarly human, we look for differences that are meaningful. Frayn offers a thought-experiment as an example: if we imagine that the Russian Revolution never took place (a favourite counter-factual for historians over the dinner table), we are not going to imagine it being replaced by a packet of corn flakes or the musical key of A Minor. We mean that things might have been different in some historically meaningful way (perhaps, there would have been no World War II, certainly no Cold War). We have to specify exactly in what way things are allowed to be different. But how could we program a computer accordingly, since we do not know in advance in what way they would be different? If we could do the latter, we would not need to imagine it.

Some scientists, Frayn concludes, would like life itself to be more like a computer program. They would like it to be analysable into a series of discrete steps suitable for the embodiment of rules; they would like life to be more consistent than it is, and thus more predictable. We can digitally model the weather, but the weather is not digital. We can store music on digital recordings, but our delight in it is purely emotional. A moving object, we can say, in digital language occupies a sequence of twenty-four varying static positions per second, but a sniper knows that his target does not run at twenty-four frames per second. 'The elegance and digitality of the computer is seductive. We are easily persuaded that human mental processes work in some similar way'. But the brain and the mind are different. Our brain circuitry may be entirely digital (as cyberneticists told us back in 1948) but most of the thinking we do with it (and all of the feeling) is in broad-based analogy. (Frayn, 2006, 418)

At the bottom of all of this is a more profound reality about human nature. Wendell Berry once predicted that in the future human beings would divide into two: those who thought of themselves as creatures and those who thought of themselves as machines. We are not machines, even though we may regret the fact. Consistency, of course, is the highest value in any mechanical system—inconsistency usually means the breakdown of the system itself. Machines break down frequently, often from overheating or overuse. Their component parts can fail over time and result in metal fatigue. As Charles Perrow writes, 'interactive complexity' and 'tight coupling' produce inevitable accidents which cannot be avoided at all, however hard we may try. And breakdowns are often dangerous, even cata-strophic. With complex interaction, a banal and even apparently incon-sequential failure can lead to a catastrophic breakdown of the whole sys-tem. During the near meltdown at the nuclear plant on Three Mile Island, a critical warning light could not be seen by an operator for the banal reason that a maintenance tag on another machine obscured his vision. (Hughes, 2004, 90)

Of course, the point about machine error (as opposed to human error) is that it can nearly always be accounted for. If it can be recovered, the black box with the flight recorder will usually tell us why a plane has crashed. Using computers, we can even model the likelihood of machine errors in the future. We can even 'calculate' when metal fatigue is likely to occur. The problem with human beings is that we cannot predict failures or errors of judgement and we cannot always explain (after the fact) why human beings acted as they did (at his court martial even a soldier may be unable to explain why he fled the field; as Pascal told us centuries ago, the heart has reasons that reason does not know).

Consistency of belief, of course, is important. We are enjoined to act in a way that makes us true to our beliefs. We are especially enjoined not to be hypocritical. The problem is that we apply our principles in context. We may, for example, be generous by nature, but that does not mean we will always be a soft touch. We may decide that people we help should be deserving of it, and we may know a great deal more about a person's per-sonal circumstances or qualities than an outside observer. We may calculate that someone to whom we have been generous previously has forfeited our sympathy by their wilfulness or fecklessness; the second time they ask for help we may be disinclined to give it.

We exercise such judgements all the time. Some may think of themselves as good Samaritans, but even the kindest of people cross the road to avoid strangers. We may conclude that a person is deserving of our charity, but also conclude that someone else is more deserving still. There are choices to be made because our resources are not limitless. Others may conclude that we are not quite as worthy as we think we are; they may even judge our choices to be wrong. But to ask us to be logically consistent is to ask too much. Consistency cannot be a sufficient condition for morality, precisely because it demands so little of humanity.

Asimov's Laws

Isaac Asimov was a Russian-born writer who studied chemistry at Columbia. Later he gave up the idea of becoming a chemist and decided to become a writer instead, principally of science fiction. He was inspired by the magazines such as *Amazing Stories* that were on sale in his father's sweet shop. He went on to pen nearly 400 books in the course of his life, including a guide to the Bible. He used to call himself a 'writing machine', rather than a writer. But his more substantial stories show imaginative flair and a high intelligence; they are the product of human creativity, not machine logic.

He is most famous today for elaborating the three basic laws of Robotics. Like most science fiction writers, even of the first rank, he was not a very compelling philosopher, but what he was good at was putting ideas to the test of present day experience. His robot stories do not dissolve the real world into that of the future—we can only experience the present. The reason why his Laws are so compelling is that they provoke us into rethinking the value of our own moral heuristics, and they get us to ask an important question—what would happen if logic were to replace reason as the basis of our moral codes?

Here are the Three Laws:

1. A robot may not injure a human being, or through inaction, allow a human being to come to harm.
2. A robot must obey orders given to it by human beings, except where such orders will conflict with the First Law.
3. A robot must protect its own existence as long as such protection does not conflict with the First or Second Law.

Asimov's robots are purely Kantian precisely because they prescribe absolute duties, and they reflect the three most important Categorical Imperatives that are to be found in the *Ground Work* (pp. 79—81):

1. 'Act as if the maxim of your action was to become through your will a universal law of nature'. Act, in other words, as if the maxim under which we act is a universal law that applies to everyone in all circumstances at all times. There can be no exceptions or appeals to self-interest, or special circumstances. There is only the absolute demand of the software program.
2. 'Act in such a way that you always treat humanity whether in your own person or in the person of any other, never simply as a means, but always

at all times as an end'. Asimov's robots have no interest other than in human well-being. They are not allowed to treat a human being as a means to their own well-being; they have a duty to put the aims of humanity first, and not to distinguish some humans from others on the understanding that some are more equal than others. They do not have racial prejudices or ideological beliefs that would allow them to draw such distinctions.

3. 'So act as if you were through your maxims a law abiding member of a kingdom of ends'. Asimov's robots are not slaves. They are not fully at the disposal of humans. They have a third law to preserve themselves where it does not conflict with laws 1 and 2. In other words, Asimov was envisaging a community shared by robots and humans alike. Robots have a right to life which is more than the Greeks accorded their human robots—their 'talking tools'. Ultimately, slaves have no rights because they are merely another person's property. They are not members of the kingdom of ends; they do not inhabit the same life world in which disagreements between themselves and their masters can be resolved rationally. It is senseless to enter into a conversation with a tool even if it can answer back.

The key to Asimov's world is that the three laws of robotics allow for none of the contradictions that constitute our life world. Take his first robot novel (and in many ways the best), *The Caves of Steel* (1954), in which we find humanity has been divided into two groups, the 'Spacers' who live on the outer planets, and the rest who were too frightened or too prejudiced to leave Earth. In the course of the novel a Spacer invites a robot to explain what it understands by the word 'justice':

> 'What is your definition of justice?'
> 'Justice is that which exists when all laws are enforced'.

(Asimov, 1987, 83–4)

The Spacer agrees that this is a good definition—for a robot. But it is not an adequate definition for a man. Humans have the ability to recognise that some laws—if enforced in certain circumstances—may simply be unjust. For the robot, an unjust law is a contradiction in terms. (*Caves of Steel*, 83–4) In stories such as 'Too Bad', 'Robbie' and 'The Evitable Conflict' Asimov sought to show how a robot once programmed with the laws would allow nothing to divert it from its mission. Its moral consistency stems not from nobility of vision (robots do not have one, they have only their programmer's), but from consistency in execution. Human beings, by contrast, may start off with a noble vision but they all too often succumb to stress. The point is that Asimov's robots are superior only because they are not motivated by our own instinct for self-preservation. It is because they do not feel fear that they will never put their own survival first. What we admire in them is their unflinching commitment (a certain ideal of the will). Such unflinching commitment, of course, can be dangerous. The reason why many fear robots is that we may not be able to argue them out of anything (because they cannot even argue themselves out of a proposed course of action). We might not be able to enter into a conversation with them.

Kant asks us, of course, to accept that moral law exists *a priori* independent of all inner and outer experience, and of all emotions and feelings. Indeed, in the *Foundation of the Metaphysics of Morals* he writes that the moral law 'must not be sought in Man's nature (the subject) or in the circumstances of the world (the object) … Nothing whatever can be borrowed from knowledge relating to Man, i.e., from anthropology'. (Rifkin, 2009, 33) So much for compassion. One of his fiercest critics, Schopenhauer, was on to something when he located morality within the human animal and particularly in the ability of all of us to feel the pain of others as our own. 'I feel your pain' is a dreadful cliché employed by politicians when trying to show their softer side, but it is—for most of us—real enough. And if biology has given us a capacity to feel the pain of others, culture over the centuries has extended its range. We really are more compassionate than our forebears thanks to the 18th-century novel, the 20th-century cinema and the 21st-century soap opera. In identifying compassion as the source of morality, Schopenhauer was on to something although he did not have the techniques or language to explain exactly what. He called it the 'great mystery of ethics', (Rifkin, 2009, 333) but it is a mystery no longer. We no longer look to Reason as a source of morality. We no longer think the brain regulates everything. Much of what we do, we now know, we do without conscious thought, such as forming opinions and taking decisions and making moral judgements. The brain makes those judgements on the basis of a variety of intuitive roots often bolstered by emotional responses. We use reason—more often than not—to justify those judgements after the fact: in other words to rationalise or legitimise them.

Why Captain Kirk was right

There is a well known episode in the early *Star Trek* series, 'The City on the Edge of Forever', in which Captain Kirk and Mr Spock find themselves back in New York in the 1930s. They have been sent to undo a disastrous change in history accidentally caused by one of their own crew members, Dr McCoy, who after accidentally falling through an alien portal in time saves a woman called Edith Keeler from being killed in a traffic accident. He subsequently discovers that if she lives, she will form an influential pacifist movement that will delay America's entry into World War II, allow the Nazis time to develop atomic weapons, and change the whole course of history. Kirk sets out to undo the damage. But after arriving in New York he too falls in love with Keeler; he too is inclined to save her life. Spock, with his usual irrefutable logic, concludes that the fate which history intends for her must be allowed to unfold. In the end Kirk comes to his senses and even restrains McCoy when he tries to save her once again.

Most viewers watching the programme on the night it was screened would probably have agreed with Kirk's decision. It would have been very different had Dr McCoy prevented the original accident not by pushing Keeler out of harm's way but by pushing a bystander under the car instead, or even if Kirk had decided to keep faith with history by pushing Keeler under another truck in another part of the city. The closer we are to the situation, the more we will feel the consequences of our acts. Our morality is embodied. This is the price of being human. And we are also much more inhibited about employing violence against women and children than we are about employing it against fat men.

What the *Star Trek* episode was exploring is what social psychologists call the trolley problem. There are a number of versions of the problem which have been explored by Joshua Greene, a philosopher turned cognitive neuroscientist at Harvard, who postulates that all human beings share an innate 'moral grammar'. The first version is the situation in which the conductor of a trolley has fainted, leaving the trolley heading towards five people walking on the track. The banks of the track are so steep that they will not be able to get off the line in time. A man is standing next to a switch which he can throw, turning the trolley onto a parallel side track and saving the lives of five people. But there is also a man standing on the other track with his back turned to the trolley. Is it morally permissible to make a calculation— to save five lives at the expense of one? A variety of studies have been conducted in different cultures which have asked the same question and found that most people agree that is morally permissible to take a life in order to save the larger number of people.

But here is another version with the same initial set of circumstances. A man is standing on a footbridge over the trolley track. He is next to a heavy object which he can shove onto the track in the path of the trolley, thereby saving the lives of five people. The heavy object just happens to be a fat man who is standing next to him. Should he push the man onto the track, stopping the trolley? Is it morally permissible for him to kill someone in order to save a larger number of people? Again, studies across cultures suggest most people do not consider it morally permissible to actually murder one man, even to save five others.

Here then we have two cases in which people arrive at very different moral judgements. Greene's research suggests that 'impersonal' moral dilemmas—such as trying to save more lives at the expense of one—are mainly a listed activity in areas associated with reason and conscious deliberation. Personal dilemmas, by contrast—pushing an obese woman on a track to save five people further along it—act on the areas of the brain associated with emotion. Greene casts moral deliberation as a tug-of-war between an intuitive, emotional aversion to causing harm, and a more deliberative rational, cost-benefit analysis: '… two competing voices inside our heads which in turn find themselves represented in different normative ethical theories of how the world should work. One speaks in cold, calculating, utilitarian terms; the other in the emotional language of prescriptions against violence'. (Jones, 2010, 65) In other words, we are finding out that Schopenhauer was right and Kant wrong. Our moral judgements are indeed embodied; they can be explained by differences in brain function. Our emotions are often in control, as David Hume surmised when he wrote that reason is often a slave to passion.

Well, yes and no. No, because it is wrong to claim that we are not being particularly logical in exercising our moral freedom, and making some of the moral choices we do. We actually use essential mathematical reasoning in most of the decisions we make, as a moment's reflection about the trolley problem will show. Let us invert it and put ourselves on the track of the oncoming trolley. In the first version, if I am a potential victim, I am five times more likely statistically to be one of the five as the lone person on the track. It follows that my death is five times more likely if you fail to pull the switch. In the second version I am also five times more likely to be numbered among the dead if our neutral observer does not push the fat man in front of the trolley. This principle was first put forward some years ago by John Harsani, a Nobel prize-winning economist who was struck by the fact that if one denies oneself omniscience—the perspective of the outside observer looking on—then most of us would be consequentialists in our moral reasoning.

And that is why our morality is not Kantian. Our moral codes cannot reflect some absolute moral code that transcends human experience. Our morality is based entirely on our own history, but we are born logical creations, not creatures of passion. We are able to logically reason out what is best for our survival precisely because we can refer back to experience. Reason usually kicks in somewhere along the line (no pun intended). We do the mathematics; we calculate the percentages; we are always evaluating the odds; we are born calculating machines with an eye to our own self-interest, and especially survival. Our moral codes do not ask us to forgo self-interest. Instead, they remind us that we are social creatures who can only thrive in a social setting; accordingly we are programmed (where possible) to marry our own interests with those of others. And the main reason why robots cannot exercise moral choices on our behalf is that they are not social units. As a result they would have enormous difficulty negotiating the moral hazards and ambiguities of our human-built world.

Secondly, as the neuroscientist Raymond Tallis argues forcefully, the trolley problem is not really an ethical problem at all, and therefore does not tell us as much about human nature as we might think. It is merely a thought experiment conjured up by social psychologists. It only tells us what people are likely to do, or how they are likely to behave on the basis of impulse rather than reflection. Like the social psychology experiments of Stephen Milgram, the trolley problem absurdly simplifies moral issues. It offers a grotesque simplification of social problems that we encounter every day. (Tallis, 2011, 346) The Milgram experiments were so simplified, in fact, that they were considered to be deeply flawed, and Milgram paid the price by being marginalised in the academic community for the rest of his life. He may still retain his cult status in the wider world—his name is remembered long after that of many other, better scientists have been forgotten. But he is remembered for the wrong reasons.

Finally, if our moral heuristics are deeply rooted in our embodied feelings (our moral sentiments) the 'mystery of ethics' persists. Neuro-imaging technology allows us to see how stimuli produce responses in the brain but it still tells us remarkably little of what is actually going on. We know the functions that relate to an emotion like compassion, but we also know that it cannot be located, as we once thought, in a specific part of the brain. When we use the term 'emotion' we are talking about a number of interlinked systems involving many different sensory and cognitive processes. We still find it impossible to distinguish compassion from other emotions such as sympathy. The neurology of empathy is still in its infancy.

Which is why we should still listen to what philosophers have to say—at least, those who still have the courage of their convictions, because many do not. Scholars like Mary Midgley are rightly appalled that philosophy itself has been surrendering the high ground to science for some time. Back in 1958 Elizabeth Anscombe, one of the most famous writers on virtue ethics, insisted in a famous article that modern moral philosophy should be 'laid aside' until an adequate understanding of the psychology of moral reasoning could be obtained. She also argued that concepts such as 'moral obligation' and 'moral duty' should be abandoned until psychology had done its work. Today, philosophers stand in less awe of psychology than they did, but they are awed by neuroscience.

But are emotions so easily scanned? As Martha Nusbaum adds, you can only measure a person's grief via a scan for a putative correlation with instances of emotions identified on other, experiential grounds. (Nussbaum, 2001, 58) Emotions actually cause physiological effects, so that it is extremely difficult to determine which effects are consequences and which are even plausible candidates for being parts of the experience itself. The question she asks is: should we include physiological information in the definition of emotions? For example, Steven Pinker argues that the functioning of the amygdala (an almond shaped organ at the base of the brain) is a necessary condition of normal emotional activity. All cognitive processes have their roots in brain function. But the fact is that we still know so little. We do not know how the plasticity of the brain with regard to some functions affects the 'location' of emotional functioning. As Nussbaum concludes, neuroscience has done much to enrich our understanding of our emotional lives, but it has not reached, and may never reach, the stage where we can explain emotional life in terms of purely neurological functioning. (Nussbaum, 2001, 119)

In the end, it is probably best to conclude that both philosophy and science should be responsive to the human experience and yet critical of the essentialist thinking that both sometimes contain. And philosophy itself has made great strides in recent years. The idea that emotions are intentional, that they are connected to our way of interpreting the world, was dismissed thirty years ago, for which philosophers too bear much of the blame. Ignoring Plato, they tended to marginalise emotions or dismiss them as 'unintelligent', or encouraged us to see them as animal impulses with no connections to our thoughts. Philosophy once even sidelined emotion from all ethical judgements. It now accords emotional intelligence an essential role in the moral life. (Nussbaum, 2001, 92)

Revisiting Asimov's Laws

If we were to succeed in programming a robot with a conscience, would we be able to control it? Or would it evolve its own moral convictions?

In all his stories Asimov tended to portray his robots in benign colours and agreeably reassuring hues. One of the reasons why Asimov's robots are not armed was that in his own vision of the future the world is largely conflict free. It was an extraordinarily optimistic conclusion for a man who lived through and survived most of the 20th century. In Asimov's world, war is evitable; only the rise of robots is inevitable. And in his story *The Evitable Conflict*, it is the machines that, acting in time, prevent humans from trying to switch them off. The story concerns a future federation of regional governments that has entrusted the management of the economy to master computers. The machines are soon found to have made some inconsequential mistakes which have demonstrable but not serious effects on economic growth. It later transpires that the machines have evolved an intelligence beyond human comprehension; at the same time they are anxious that humans should not know it. They are still obedient to Asimov's Third Law—a robot should never harm a human being—but quite independently, they have evolved a Fourth Law: that human beings should not harm them. And they have concluded that they are most likely to be at risk if Man should ever decide it is really obsolete as a species. In conformity with the Third Law they also suspect that if human beings were ever to succeed in switching them off, the world would quickly return to a state of internecine conflict. (Asimov, 1968, 183–206)

Capek's robots are very different and more recognizably human; they very quickly become deranged. 'Occasionally they seem to go off their heads. Something like epilepsy, you know. It's called Robot's cramp. They'll suddenly sling down everything they are holding …and go into the stamping-mill. It's evidently some breakdown in the mechanism'. (Pick, 1993, 206) When the robots are armed they turn their guns on their masters, and Capek makes the telling point in the play that it is only when they armed that they awaken to the realization that they can now escape their servitude, as human slaves usually have—by taking up arms in the name of justice.

And we are beginning to worry about just such a future. In July 2009 scientists attending an AI/robots conference in Monterey proposed that the kind of ethical and clinical trials that are applied to new drugs should be applied to robots too. They feared that those nightmare scenarios, so far limited to science fiction could come true. (*Sunday Times*, 2 August 2009) They feared the day when robots become autonomous. California Polytechnic State University (Cal Poly) researchers at the US Department of the Navy Office of Naval Research have produced a report that voices those concerns for the first time. 'There is a common misconception that robots would do only what we program them to do', remarked Patrick Lin, the report's chief author. 'Unfortunately, such a belief is sorely outdated, harking back to a time when … programs could be written and understood by a single person'. The reality is that modern programs include millions of lines of code and are written by teams of programmers, none of whom knows the entire program. Accordingly, no individual can accurately predict how the various portions of large programs will interact without extensive testing in the field, an option that may be unavailable or deliberately sidestepped by the designers of the machines in the search of a quick profit.

Autonomous military robots, he concluded, must be programmed to live by a strict warrior code. At the heart of the report is a stark warning that in future robots might turn on their human masters, especially when or if they develop cognitive skills far superior to our own. Once they are 'smart enough' to make decisions, will we always agree with the decisions they take? And what happens if robots malfunction and cause unintended and unlawful harm to one side or the other? What happens if our enemies hack into them and turn them against their designers? But the really important question, perhaps, is this: what happens if they are not 'on side' in another respect—if they refuse to carry out the orders we give them?

We are a long way from autonomy, but robots are learning all the time. Japanese consumers are already able to buy robots that 'learn' their owner's behaviour by observing it. Some can find electrical outlets and recharge themselves without human intervention. One high-tech US firm is working on a nurse-bot that will be able to interact with patients and even simulate empathy. And unlike a human nurse it will not have bad moods, or suffer from off days, or favour some patients more than others. It is the simulation of feeling that the scientists fear most. Patients could find this de-humanising if they ever felt they were at risk of becoming mere objects of sympathy, not subjects in their own story. Conversely, a nurse-bot is likely to be much less manipulative than a real one. Computer intelligence is not emotional intelligence—it is not Machiavellian, at least not yet.

The solution, Lin insists, is to mix rules-based programming with a learning period which will allow tomorrow's robots to 'learn' the rights and wrongs of war. A simple ethical code along the lines of Asimov's three laws will not be sufficient to ensure the ethical behaviour of autonomous military machines. Lin insists that 'these things are military and they cannot be pacifists, so we have to think in terms of battlefield ethics. We are going to need a warrior code'. (*The Times*, 16 February 2009, 35)

The Cal Poly study expressed particular concern about the bottom-up approach, which is why it wants to program in not only a conscience but a warrior ethos. But the challenge is this—whether a robot evolves rules and codes of conduct or is programmed with something like Asimov's three laws of robotics, it is going to face a world that is foreign to it; it is going to have to exercise moral choices that we have to take to make sense of a world we have built for ourselves. Man, according to Protagoras, was only the measure and not the creator of things, but the Greeks knew that this was only half true—we may not have created the world but we have refashioned it for our own needs. We may be at the mercy of natural laws but we have also imprisoned ourselves within a bizarre and infinitely complex set of social codes and conventions. It is asking a lot of any machine to make sense of the world we have built with all its illogical inconsistencies and moral ambiguities.

In the end, we always return to Asimov's laws of robotics. When you come to think of it they are not very different from the everyday rules of thumb we have been applying to moral questions at least since we emerged from the hunter-gatherer stage of development. Take the tale *Evidence* (1946) in which Asimov explored the ethical implications of the laws, putting these words into the mouth of a robot designer:

If you stop to think of it, the Three Rules of Robotics are the essential guiding principles of a good many of the world's ethical systems. Of course, every human being is supposed to have the instinct of self-preservation. That's Rule 3 to a robot. Also every 'good' human being with a social conscience and a sense of responsibility is supposed to defer to proper authority; to listen to his doctor, his boss, his government, his psychologist, his fellow man; to obey laws, to follow rules, to conform to custom—even when they interfere with his comfort and his safety. That's Rule 2 to a robot. Also every 'good' human being is supposed to love others as himself, protect his fellow man, risk his life to save another. That's Rule 1 to a robot.

'To put it simply, if Byerly follows all the rules of robotics, he may be a robot and may simply be a very good man'. (Warrick, 1982, 66)

But although the Three Laws are recognizably 'human' they are also encoded in very un-human logical structures of thought. The Laws are 'laws' only because they cannot be broken, unlike the moral heuristics which we employ every day and which we constantly transgress. Asimov's Laws are not moral heuristics; they are part of the engineering—they are central to the positronic-brain circuitry of robots themselves. They are intrinsic to their design. It would never enter their minds to break them, but that said, in his later stories they find it increasingly difficult to apply them.

For life is inconsistent and contradiction is central to it. It is a feature of complexity. And that is the point of Asimov's later tales in which, as they evolve their own intelligence, his robots find that exercising moral judgement is profoundly difficult.

By far the most intelligent exploration of this theme was by a computer scientist called Roger Clarke who published two articles in *Computer* magazine in 1993, a year after Asimov's death. Clarke set out a series of challenges that Asimov had to grapple with as his robots evolved in his own imagination; as they became more complex and sophisticated; as they became more intelligent over time. (Clarke, 1993)

Here are just a few of the dilemmas he identified. The first is the difficulty of defining an injury to a human being (Law One). Does the injury have to be life-threatening, physical or mental? Are we dealing with a soldier who has been wounded, or badly maimed, or one who is already near breaking point psychologically? Our conventions recognise two types of injury—one physical, the other mental. Torture is prohibited, for example, not only because of the physical harm that it involves, but because it shames us. Pain can be cultural. Human beings who have been broken under interrogation have a much diminished sense of self as well as a much diminished belief in humanity.

But this plays to a second problem of Asimov's Laws—how do we define what is human or not? And what if different societies were to program robots with different protocols that differentiated among common humanity? The Enlightenment discovered for the first time the inter-subjective nature of humanity in terms of what Karl Marx later came to call 'species-being'. It went much further than the Stoics in making man the object of scientific investigation for the first time: it invented the human sciences. 'Why should we not introduce Man as he is placed in the Universe? Why should we not make him the common centre?' asked Denis Diderot. (Todorov, 2000, 99) And once the human became the object of rigorous valid scientific knowledge, we looked at our humanity somewhat differently. To know scientifically that we come from the same species, and that all cultures share certain ideals—such as justice, if expressed in a different cultural grammar—is a demand on us to be less cruel to each other.

And yet, within the lifetime of the older readers of this book societies applied very different criteria. Political scientists, with their liking for a turn of phrase, spoke of 'objective criminality'. Certain peoples were deemed to be sub-human, or non-human, or not quite human, in other words, deficient in that common humanity that the Enlightenment had discovered. Some people were persecuted because they belonged to a 'criminal' social group, defined in terms of categories such as class, race or even ethnicity. Mercifully, today no government discriminates against its citizens in such terms, but some non-state actors still do. One is Al Qaeda. Bin Laden's *fatwa* in 1998 was against the American people as a criminal nation (not the United States as a criminal state). Terrorists target Israelis or Zionists on similar grounds.

Humanity is not simply a question of biological codes or DNA structures. We do not contrast ourselves with chimpanzees only on the basis of having a 1 per cent DNA difference. Humanity is the name we give ourselves as a species, that is true. But it is also the name we give to the qualities that the species is deemed to embody—at least by us. It is a product of cultural selection, and war is a definitively cultural activity.

But even biologically, we may have a much harder time defining humanity than we once did. This may be especially the case with the rise of the cyborg, an entity that can be seen as either a machine-enhanced human being or a biologically-enhanced machine. In Asimov's later stories, the prosthetization of humans leads inevitably to the humanization of robots; they become more familiar and less threatening. There is an entire cultural field called 'social robotics' devoted to giving thinking machines the sort of positive human qualities that would help them evolve into socially intelligent beings, capable of empathising with us. The work is being carried out by researchers at Hanson Robotics. But will they be able to empathise with cyborgs more readily than the rest of us?

And at what point does a robot that begins to attain human characteristics, such as the ability to learn from its environment (emerging behaviour), have rights that we human beings extend to each other? At what point will we be constrained in what we can ask a robot to do, such as the injury it should be expected to inflict on another human being?

Clarke's second set of problems involves the role of judgement in decision-making. Laws, like any ethical injunction, depend not only on the context in which they are originally drawn up, but on the context in which they are applied. A robot programmed with Asimov's Laws would still have to determine whether it is appropriate to carry them out, or whether it is safe to do so. Would it pose a risk to human beings, and what if a robot were to be given contradictory orders from two different sources? And what if it is necessary to injure one human being in order to save another? Here the Second and First Laws might well come into conflict. Would a robot be expected to exercise utilitarian criteria and think of the 'good' in terms of the greatest number? Most of our moral conundrums, indeed, prompt us to ask what is the price of an individual life? The 'greater good' has been the excuse for an innumerable number of cruel or unthinking acts (one cannot make omelettes without breaking eggs). But what for us is casuistry may for the robot be protocol.

And this raises another question. Could a robot be programmed to apply the Laws in all circumstances and at all times? The extent to which it will have to evolve its own judgement, which may require calculation of profit and loss, was actually addressed by Asimov when one of the human characters in his novels cynically re-phrases the First Law: 'A robot must not hurt a human being unless he can think of a way to prove it is for the human being's ultimate good, after all'. A character in one story thinks the First Law is fraudulent. In effect it really means that 'a robot may do nothing that to its knowledge would injure a human being, and may not, through inaction, knowingly allow a human being to come to harm'.

Clarke then adds the possibility of robotic deadlock. In essence, this is a response to the fact that life is indeed complex, sometimes irredeemably so. Asimov deals with this in *Robots of Dawn*. Two human beings are threatened with equal danger, but if the robot could only save one, whom would it choose? Under the Second Law, the two human beings might give contradictory orders of equivalent force, at which point in his story deadlock would set in:

What was troubling the robot was what roboticists called an equipotential of contradiction on the second level. Obedience was the Second Law, and [the robot] was suffering from two roughly equal and contradictory orders. Robot-block was what the general population called it, or more frequently, roblock for short … [or] 'metal freeze-out'. No matter how subtle and intricate a brain might be, there is always some way of setting up a contradiction. This is a fundamental truth of mathematics'. (Asimov, 1983)

Presumably, it might have to collect and process more data to resolve the dilemma, but there might not be time. Remember the android scientist in

Ridley Scott's film *Alien (1979)*? When asked by Ripley what is the nature of the creature they are dealing with, he replies that he is still 'collecting the data'. By then most of the crew of the *Nostromo* have been killed and those that remain have no reason to think they will survive much longer. Like many of us Ripley finds that she has to take a decision on the basis of the data at hand.

It was largely as a response to these dilemmas that towards the end of his life Asimov revised the Laws of Robotics, and put the 'good of humanity' before the value of individual human life. By the 1980s humanity had moved into the picture in ways that had not been true at the time he first formulated the Laws in 1942. Aristotle insisted that we can only discuss ethics on the basis of what is within our power. He could not imagine that humanity might one day engineer a change in the nature of matter by splitting the atom and creating an atomic bomb. Until that time all our previous injunctions to behave well were phrased in the present—not the future—tense. They were addressed to those still alive. The philosopher Hans Jonas spent much of his life trying to infuse morality with what he called 'the heuristics of fear'; the fact that what should frighten us most are the consequences of our actions. His departure point was Hiroshima (1945), for the survivors of the first atomic bomb were also victims too—many did not die from radiation sickness until years later, and many of the children born to the survivors came into the world with genetic defects. Morality can no longer be time- or place-bound in the human imagination. Technology has invested us with the power to foreclose the future. It was this challenge that prompted Jonas to formulate a Third Categorical Imperative: 'Act so that the effects of your actions are compatible with the permanence of genuine human life'. (Jonas, 1999)

Asimov's stories tells us that there is no inherent fault or failure in the robots or their algorithms. The problem is that moral life is not algorithmic. Asimov's robots as interpreted by Clarke are conflicted or confused because they live in a human-built world, not one that they have built themselves; they find themselves living in a contingent universe, our own. And all their problems arise from their knowledge that they are answerable to human judgement for their actions. A highly intelligent and science-literate writer, he could foresee that robots—however intelligent—would have a hard enough time operating, not in a real world but only in a computer simulation of it modelled on our somewhat recondite understanding of how the world works. How could literal-minded machines cope, as we have to do, with everyday ambiguities? How would they interact with other human beings who act in ambivalent, ambiguous and not always easy to read ways? So, perhaps, Lin and others are right to contend that we should be worried about arming robots, though it is not their recalcitrance that may be the problem. Even more misguided may be the trust we invest in them to negotiate successfully the moral ambiguities of the world we have created for ourselves.

Asimov's warning to the future

As noted, science fiction writers have never been very convincing philosophers. But the best of them, like Asimov, have been able to put ideas to the test by extrapolating the present to its logical conclusion. Asimov's laws of robotics do not radically challenge the rules of the real world. Instead, they get us to rethink the value of the moral heuristics we adhere to (recast this time as computer algorithms); they challenge us to think what might happen if logic were ever to replace reason and emotion as the basis of our moral life.

Are we worrying too much? Many of these works may not be science fiction, but they are not science, either. In the words of one writer, they are situated between the imagination and reality. (O'Mathuna, 2009, 22) When discussing the ethics of using robots, are we looking at science or science fiction? When we give any thought to robots, we are actually thinking forward to the future. When the general public understands science fiction it turns to the films and their monsters: the T-800 cyborg (the ultimate state of the art killing machine), though the rebels (the rump of mankind still fighting their corner) are depicted as being as emotionally sterile as the computer chips at which they blast away with such enthusiasm.

The decisions we take today are framed by our fears and imaginings, and may inevitably influence the technology we go on to build. Science influences science fiction, but science fiction also influences science, so we must be careful to discuss what is real. This is the problem many scientists have with science fiction—it often makes us fearful of the future by exaggerating the speed of change. 'When I pronounce the word 'future, the first syllable already belongs to the past': the words are those of a contemporary Polish poet. (Brand, 1999, 29) This is why science fiction tends to date quickly. It was born, wrote Asimov, when it became clear the world was changing within an individual lifetime, when thinking about the future was a demand of the times. But the world, though speeding up, is not always heading in the direction we think it is.

But the other problem is that science fiction writers often raise fears that are exaggerated. Alfred Nordmann has questioned whether we really are arguing ethically when discussing the possibilities of future technology, or whether we are merely making wild speculations. Nordmann is particularly critical of what he calls the 'if-and-then' argument which is used to invent a mandate for action. If you could argue, for example, that robots will eliminate most human risk in war, then we could say it is ethical to work on their design. But if you argue that such systems could turn on us at some undeclared date in the future, or be hacked into by terrorists and turned against us, we should be very careful what we design. The if-and-then argument takes future predictions as givens, and from that determines what is ethical today.

The Greeks asked themselves the same question—implicitly, to be sure, since the past for them was always more real than the future, and they assumed that the future would not be very different from the present. In Book Three of the *Nichomachean Ethics* Aristotle questions whether one can deliberate about the ethics of anything that is beyond our power to build or do. He was more forward thinking than most of his contemporaries; he could even anticipate a mechanised world:

For if every tool were able to complete its own task when ordered—or even anticipate the end—just as the statues of Daedalus supposedly did, or the tripods of Hephaestus which Homer says 'entered of their own accord the assembly of the gods', or shuttles that pass through the loom by themselves, or plectra play the harp, master craftsmen would have no need of assistants, and masters no need of slaves. (*Politics*, Book 1, Chapter 4)

Aristotle could imagine a spindle that operated independently of human action, but as the Greeks did not have an Industrial Revolution, they did not have steam power for economic use. Hieron of Alexandria actually invented the steam ship in the 1st century, but it was not taken seriously as an entity until the 18th century, 'a slow burn', writes Michael Frayn, 'almost as long as that of a jet engine, a forerunner of what he also invented'. (Frayn, 459)

Certainly, many robotic visions of the future are really fanciful—at least for now. The same is true of many other technologies. An independent review by the US National Research Council found that much of the work on molecular self-assembly was overly theoretical and based on unconvincing computer modelling. The potential of futuristic nano-technology could not be evaluated because devices would have to be built using tools that at the moment do not exist. Molecular manufacturing, it concluded, is 'currently outside the main stream of both conventional science ... and conventional engineering'. (O'Mathuna, 2009, 30)

But we have been given a creative imagination for a purpose. We invented fiction to help us think. It makes vivid or more real—it shows us aspects of reality that otherwise we would not see unless the author showed them to us, writes Harold Bloom. (Bloom, 2002, 647) George Steiner stakes out an even better claim in his own unique voice—fiction, like all great art, is an enunciation that 'breaks into the small house of our cautionary being, so that it is no longer habitable in quite the same manner as before'. (Steiner, 1990, 142–3) Yes, we should be responsible not only for what we do, but for what we collectively imagine, but imagination gives us 'presponsibility' as Per-a Johansson calls it (Casti, 1999, 76). It seems to me we are often not presponsible enough. Johansson quotes Rodney Brooks, an influential roboticist at the Massachusetts Institute of Technology (MIT), and a leading authority on 'subscription architecture' who writes that he is not interested in the philosophical implications of what will emerge over time, although he does not doubt that there will be significant implications. (Casti, 1999, 95–6)

Robots or replicants?

When describing a robot, Richard Sennett prefers the word 'replicant', a term he borrows from Ridley Scott's film *Blade Runner* (1982), perhaps the best of the screen adaptations of the stories of Philip Dick. A replicant, in his words, is a particular kind of machine, a 'mirror-tool' that invites us to think about our own humanity. (Sennett, 2008, 84) A simple example of a non-robotic machine is a pacemaker which provides the energy for the heart to function optimally. It reproduces a human function which because of defective biology cannot reproduce itself. A replicant, by comparison, enhances or enlarges an existing function. An example of this is the I-Pod, a memory robot capable of containing or memorising 35,000 minutes of music, or almost the entire opus of J.S. Bach. But its memory augments only what human beings want to hear; it has no musical appreciation. It does not engage with music itself, for music is not a matter of memory but the response to harmony and rhythm; it can move us to joy or to tears. A mirror tool refers back, in other words, not to its own standards of excellence but to our own. (Sennett, 2008, 85) In that sense, it amplifies our own humanity; at the same time it invites us to ask: what do we want to enlarge? Do we want, for example, to reduce the instances of war or do we wish to enlarge the scope of our ethical responsibility when waging it?

Ridley Scott's film discarded much of Dick's original tale, which was much more complex and rich in ideas. In the original story Rick Deckard is a lonely bounty hunter who hunts down escaping replicants (robots that look like humans in every respect, and even have human emotions, though they differ from us in one critical respect—they are programmed to live for only four years). Deckard terminates those who have escaped in the hope of surviving longer with little thought to their eventual fate. The only way of telling a replicant apart from a human being is to administer the Voight-Kapff Empathy Test which is designed to measure reflex responses in the subject being tested by posing a series of challenging tests. One includes showing the subject pictures of bull-fighting which in Deckard's world elicits immediate human revulsion because most animals have been wiped out, and only a few species have survived. The androids have no such species-consciousness, but the latest Nexus VI series has evolved an empathetic ability. One of them is Rachael Rosen, an employee of the company that manufactures the robots, who turns the tables on Deckard during an interrogation by accusing him of lacking empathy. It is he who has lost touch with his own basic humanity.

True empathy is something that as a species we alone experience. As E.O. Wilson explains in his aptly named book *Biophilia*, 'humanity is exulted not because we are so far above other living creatures, but because knowing them well elevates the very concept of life'. (Thayer, 2004, 266) We now acknowledge that animals can show feeling and have emotional lives: some like elephants can even mourn the loss of their own kind. But no other species can ask itself how its life impacts on the life of others of its kind, still less how it impacts on that of other species. Empathy has allowed us to evolve, admittedly pretty late in the day, a sense of responsibility for species far removed from us in time and place; we even have taken responsibility for the fate of a planet which we share with others, and which one day we may find ourselves sharing with robots too. In Philip Dick's tale what humans fear in the replicants they have made is that they have evolved a sense of empathy for each other independent of any programming, and what makes this so threatening to humans is that they have developed this at the very point at which humans have lost the ability to empathise with each other. Mary Shelley got there first, of course. For in her famous story it is not the monster's inability to deal with human indifference that makes him turn in the end on his creator and the human race as a whole. It is humanity's inability to empathise with its own plight that makes humanity—not the monster—the villain of the story. The fault lies very much in ourselves. (Wheale, 1995, 106)

To return to Sennett's book, the last question I wish to pose in this chapter is whether robots may one day enlarge the scope of our empathy or compassion for others whose existence enriches our lives. Will they unlock the possibilities of humanising war which we have not managed to realise so far, or in enlarging those possibilities will they get us to rethink whether we should still be in the war business? Sennett reminds us that the Greeks were the first to appreciate how technology over the centuries has made us wonder at ourselves—our own powers of creation, our ingenuity and intelligence. The Greeks embedded wonder in *poiein*, the root word for making. (Sennett, 2008, 211) In the *Symposium* Plato says, 'Whatever passes from non-being to being is a cause for wonder'. The problem is that we have also been provoked by our own actions into wondering at our capacity for sheer malevolence—at our technical ingenuity in inventing weapons that can kill a larger number of people in ever more lethal and inventive ways. But we have never been dissuaded from inventing the most lethal weapons, including the most lethal of all, the atomic bomb: 'There is no universal history that leads from humanity to humanitarianism, but there is one that leads from the sling shot to the megaton bomb', wrote Adorno at the beginning of the nuclear era. (Adorno, 1973, 320) Moral progress has never kept pace with technological evolution.

What we know is that robots will certainly be 'other'—more intelligent perhaps, than ourselves, but inferior in what we call humanity, the richness of their social, emotional and imaginative life. Of course, we have no real way of evaluating or measuring these elements that make up that world; they differ over time and from culture to culture. All we know is that the life-world is necessary for us. Without it we would not live or thrive, except in the very minimal sense of survival. And for us survival has never been enough, as it has been, apparently, for every other species.

But my students would add at this point, 'but Professor, here's the thing'. Aren't we changing too; aren't we beginning to resemble the robots we are designing? Will there be any great ontological chasm between the two?

Indeed, what would a robot make of a cyborg soldier with smart chips in his brain (which enhance his memory and muscular reflexes) and artificial sensory systems and communications devices embedded deep under his skin. (In the *Matrix* series of films the robots have taken over while deceiving mankind into thinking it is still in control, but even the rebels are cyborgs: in a famous scene Trinity is able to download the knowledge to fly a helicopter in the middle of a fire fight thanks to a computer chip in her brain.) The objective set by the Defense Advanced Research Projects Agency (DARPA), which is running a programme called AugCom—or Augmented Cognition—is to create 'a more adept human war fighter who uses microelectronics to achieve machine-like precision'. Would a robot see such a war fighter or what DARPA calls 'a synergistic blend of man/machine intelligence' as a fellow robot? (Talbot, 2005)

Cyborg warriors

'This is not a war', said the artilleryman. 'It never was a war, anymore than there's war between man and ants'. The words are to be found in one of the classic science fiction works of all time, H.G. Wells' novel *The War of the Worlds*, which tells a gripping tale of an invasion of Earth by the Martians. The artilleryman is right, but not for the reasons he volunteers. In Wells' novel, the Martians invade a world in which *Homo sapiens* is about to be displaced from its position on the food chain. Humans find themselves being exterminated like ants. Fifty years later, watching the newsreels of the war in the Pacific theatre, Theodor Adorno formed much the same impression. With their flame throwers and aerial bombardments the Americans were killing the Japanese like ants. What he saw on the screen reminded him not so much of war as a 'civil engineering project', a new type of combat whose remorseless logic put him in mind of the way we deal with ants. War had become 'fumigation and insect eradication on a terrestrial scale'. (Adorno, 1993, 56)

In the Pacific theatre technology was dwarfing the human dimension of war, and becoming more compelling than the everyday sacrifices demanded of the soldiers themselves, and it is the Martians' technology that the Artilleryman admires most. In a touch of genius, Wells has him enthuse: 'Just imagine this; ...... their fighting machines starting off—heat rays right and left and not a Martian in 'em, but men—men who have learned the way how ... behold: Man has come back to his own'. The future the artilleryman envisages is grim, indeed. For he foresees that one day men may become the machines they build.

Wells was attuned to the rhythms of his own age which were taking humanity forward into uncharted territory. In that sense, he was what Nietzsche called a 'posthumous' author, the true significance of his work being grasped only by readers who had not yet been born. And it is as a posthumous writer that Wells should be seen today. What he offered his readers was a glimpse of a future that was creeping up on them 'inaudibly'. It is a future that has now arrived; we are already living it today. Even the Martians' death-rays may soon be with us. One prototype is the US Navy's Free Electron Laser, built by Raytheon, a multiple-wavelength weapon that works like a particle accelerator, moving electrons around a racetrack to speed them up. Boeing has designed for the US Air Force (USAF) a directed energy gunship that would have the same effect as opening up fire with a 20mm Gatling gun, or a 105 howitzer. (http://www.wired/com/thedanger-room/2009/09/boeings-new-death-beam-zaps-vehicle/)

But the genius of Wells is that he gets us to imagine something much more challenging. For in the future that the Artilleryman envisions, the Martian tripods are not unmanned: they are not robots. It is the men in them that we need to be worried about, men who have effectively become 'Martians' themselves, indifferent to human loss and quite as uncaring about it as the aliens they eventually displace, at least for now. It is not a question of men 'coming back into their own' (taking back the earth which they have lost) but of men realising their destiny; evolving into the next stage of human existence, one in which there is no place, either in war or in the battle of life, for those human characteristics that once made war 'heroic' (that is, human). Once the artilleryman clambers into the machine and adapts to the new environment, he will be as far from a Greek hoplite soldier, or even an anti-artillery man in World War II, as the latter were from Achilles. Once we are integrated functionally and performatively into the machine, we will become something different. Were Thucydides to be teleported into the future he might well conclude that we had become cognitively indistinguishable from Wells' Martians.

To be sure, what the artilleryman grasps imperfectly is perhaps a demand of the future. In *The Gutenberg Galaxy*, Marshall McLuhan wrote,

Science fiction writing today presents situations that enable us to perceive the potential of new technology. Formerly, the problem was to invent new forms of labour-saving devices. Today, the reverse is the problem. Now we have to adjust, not to invent. We have to find the environments in which it would be possible to live with our new inventions'. (McLuhan, 1996, 121)

Wells' generation inevitably thought in terms of machines like Martian tripods, a mechanical environment into which a human being could easily fit (not so very different, really, from the land monsters he also foresaw—the tanks that first appeared in World War I). But our environments are less solid or fixed, and more liquid in their potential, and today's science fiction writers have a much greater ability to penetrate the future earlier and faster then before. Words like 'cyberspace', 'net-surfing', 'neural implants', 'virtual interaction', all of which originated in the science fiction of the 1990s, have penetrated the scientific mind.

But Wells' tale raises another prospect which we must consider. What will happen when man and machine are fused functionally, when they become cyborgs? And what then of our relationship with robots? As Rodney Brooks writes, the traditional distinction between robots and ourselves is gradually disappearing anyway as we continue to incorporate more and more technology into our bodies and immerse ourselves more fully in cybernetic worlds. (Laziz, 2008, 212)

At a US National Science Foundation/Department of Defense conference in Washington in 2003 the presenters positively enthused about the coming of a post-human age in which advances in semi-conductor devices, bio-electronics, nanotechnology and applied neural control techniques would facilitate a breakthrough in the emergence of 'hybrids of humans and machines'. Such a breakthrough, it was suggested, would represent 'a turning point in the evolution of human society', and by implication, too, in the evolution of war. (O'Mathuna, 2009, 159)

The term 'cyborg' was first coined in 1960 by two authors, Manfred Clynes and Nathan Kline, in a paper written for the Air Force School of Aviation Medicine in San Antonio, Texas. Clynes suggested the term would be a good shorthand for 'cybernetic organization' or 'cybernetically controlled organism'. Both authors were addressing the issue of space travel in the future and proposing that the best way to penetrate space would not be to build ever more sophisticated spaceship environments in which an astronaut could survive in a state of suspended animation, but to re-engineer the bodies we were born with. Space travel, they wrote, challenged our humanity not only technically but spiritually, in that it invited us to take an active part in our own biological evolution.

At the time, cybernetics was very much in fashion and Clynes envisaged not only a machine-man merger, but a self-regulating system. A body is just such a system which works non-stop (without us consciously being aware of it) to keep key physiological parameters within balance. As we labour harder and oxygenation falls, we breathe harder and our hearts beat faster, pumping more oxygen into the blood stream. By re-engineering the human body it might be possible to enable astronauts of the future to breathe in space. In an essay on the space race that it is not often read these days, Hannah Arendt claimed that seen from a sufficient distance—from the Archimedean point of space—human beings were beginning to look very different. She had no concept of a cyborg but she grasped nonetheless that something profound was underway. Seen from a sufficient distance, she wrote, 'the cars in which we travel … will look as though, as Heisenberg once put it, "as inescapable a part of ourselves as the snail's shell is to its occupant…". The whole of technology, seen from this point, in fact no longer appears 'as the result of a conscious human effort to extend man's natural powers, but rather as a large scale biological process'. (Arendt, 2006, 274)

Space travel, alas, has not realised its promise in the 1960s, the era which led Arthur C. Clark to imagine a base on the moon and regular space shuttles to a space station equipped with a Hilton hotel orbiting the Earth. The moon landing in 1969 was greeted at the time as 'the next chapter in evolution'. 'The Apollo landing', opined Clark, may be the only achievement of ours remembered in a thousand years time', (Cornfield, 2007, 27) except that there has not been another lunar landing since 1972. But what we have achieved on Earth is impressive enough. Fifty years later, neural implants and mergers have created the first cyborgs. Ten per cent of the population of the US has been upgraded with electronic pacemakers, artificial joints, drug implant systems, and implanted corneal lenses. A much higher percentage is wired into cybernetic worlds, for example a secretary who works on a computer keyboard, or a games player who spends hours a week fighting the *World of Warcraft*. All have 'terminal identities', a different subjectivity from their non-cyborg colleagues, friends and family members which makes them if not another sub-species, at least sufficiently different from the rest of the human race to be called by a new name—cyborgs. (Bukatman, 201) Much less recognised or even discussed are the psychological changes within us produced by this fusion of man and machine, which may change the way we think of ourselves as human beings. Those who have experienced the merger may even consider themselves different from those in whom the merger has not taken place. For we are morphing once again in our imagination into something more recognisably human but different. 'The human body', wrote Emerson, 'is the magazine of inventions, the patent office where are the models for which every hint was taken. All the tools and engines are only extensions of its limits and senses'. (Emerson, 1982, 84–5) But now the outer world is penetrating the body; we are interiorising the technology we use in ways that Emerson and his contemporaries could not have grasped.

One of the first films to explore what this might mean on the battlefield was Roland Emmerich's 1992 film *Universal Soldier*, which extrapolates from today's genetic research into a future that some of the military are actively working towards. In the film the protagonists are Vietnam veterans who have been cybernetically hollowed out and reprogrammed. They are part flesh, part machine: genetically re-engineered cyborgs, an elite force of warriors specially designed to deal with terrorists. In between missions they are suspended in flotation chambers where their bodies are pumped full of muscle enhancing steroids, and maintained at a constant temperature of 60° below zero. Informed by a doctor (or 'maintenance engineer') that one of his fellow soldiers is unaware he is actually alive, our hero replies, 'He's not. He's dead like me'. (Conrad, 1998, 641) There is a perverse pride in his defiance. He has the pride of an Achilles on steroids, devoid, of course, of everything that makes Achilles interesting as a man. And while soldiers today still dream of emulating the heroes of the Trojan war, no soldier in real life, unless dead to the world, would wish to emulate Emmerich's killer-machines. These post-human warriors are competing not with the Homeric heroes but with the idealised figures of the computer-game age, and it is clear, if you play such games, that it would be next to impossible to attain the morphology of these avatars without technological modification.

But the Universal Soldiers (or Unisols) are not unlike Achilles in one respect; they are difficult to kill because they are almost, but not quite, immortal. Achilles' only weakness is his heel by which his mother held him when dipping him into the river Lethe; it is this vulnerability which undoes him in the end when Paris fires an arrow into his heel. He dies, wrote André Gide archly, 'condemned by a mother's touch'. Emmerich's heroes have an invulnerability given to them by enhancement: they are essentially cyborgs (part machine, part human). But unlike Achilles, they inhabit a dead zone in which there is no moral struggle, and no personal choices to be made. To all intents and purposes, they really are dead to life. Indeed, on one reading they are not unlike those unfortunate human beings who suffer from a condition called Cotard's Syndrome. For the sufferer, nothing in the world has any emotional significance; nor for that matter does any tactile sensation or sound. The only way in which they can interpret this complete emotional desolation is to believe that they are actually dead. And strange though it may seem, it is notoriously difficult to argue them out of this conviction, however intelligent they may be (and their reason is not impaired by the condition). Rationally, they know perfectly well that if you are dead you cannot bleed. But whenever a doctor pricks them with a needle, they change the story and insist that dead bodies can bleed out. (Ramachandran, 2003, 107)

Of course, many of the Greek heroes were super-heroes, but they were all intensely human figures. A flawless Achilles would be a much impoverished and shrunken figure. His flaws may be huge, but they are also magnificent and all of a piece with his nature. What distinguished the Age of Heroes from all the others, wrote Hesiod, was that we know their names. Achilles has etched himself on our memory: 'Achilles and Hector fight and fight again in measureless memory', wrote the poet Edward Muir. The Trojan War is quite literally ageless for that reason. What links the modern world with the pre-modern past (what explains why the young Tom Swofford took Homer to the Gulf in 1990, and why the young Nate Fick was influenced by the classics to join up and fight the next Iraq War) is that the heroes are intensely human, which is why we keep a place in our heart for them still.

The question I wish to raise is this: will our post-human cyborgs be able to recognise themselves in Achilles? Will they still be in touch with the great tradition, or will they have moved on? Will Achilles and Hector still be fighting in the 'measureless memory' of anyone?

The Cyborg condition

'This is Pat', G.G. Ashworth said, his arm with ostentatious familiarity around the girl's waist. 'Never mind her last name! Square and puffy, lean, overweight, wearing his usual mohair poncho, apricot coloured felt hat, argyle ski socks and carpet slippers, he advanced towards Jo CHIP ... 'Pat, this is the company's highly skilled, first-line electrical type tester'. Coolly, the girl said to Jo CHIP, 'Is it you that's electrical, or your tests?' 'We trade off', Jo said.

Philip Dick, 5 Novels, 513.

Hollywood caught up with the idea of cyborgs quite early. Take the film *Robocop* (1987) which went on to spin several sequels, a TV series and several video games. The hero is a policeman, part human, part machine (reconfigured from what is left of his body after a hit by a drug gang leaves him on life support). A product of Omni Consumer products (OCP), Robocop patrols a devastated urban landscape of the near future, a city that is in receivership. Yet he triumphs at the end of the movie against a much less emotionally intelligent two-ton robot, the ED 209. Much earlier TV had launched the hero of the 1970s series *The Six Million Dollar Man*. A former astronaut who works for the Office of Scientific Intelligence as an agent in the field he derives his lethal efficiency from bionic implants with which he has been 'upgraded' after a near fatal air crash, all of which enhance his strength, speed and vision. His bionic eye, for example, has infrared vision that can detect movement in the dark and identify the heat signatures of those he finds himself battling against. He also has a Geiger counter in his arm (this was the time of the Cold War) and he eventually acquires a bionic girlfriend. And then there is *Firefox* (1982), a film in which Clint Eastwood plays an American pilot who steals a prototype Soviet jet fighter that can be partially controlled by a neurolink which allows it to be flown through the pilot's thought patterns and impulses. The fact that plane and pilot share the same cognitive space is the film's central theme.

Fictional renditions of the cyborg experience tend to explore three different aspects: Restorative (restoring lost functions, or replacing lost limbs and organs); reconfiguring (creating post-human possibilities by adapting humans to their environment); enhancing human abilities (the aim of most military research).

All three visions are at the heart of what DARPA calls 'neuro-engineering'. At a conference in Washington in 2003, hosted by the US National Science Foundation and the Pentagon, the presenters looked forward to the day when advances in semi-conductor devices, cognitive science, bio-electronics and applied neural control techniques would produce 'a turning point in the evolution of human society'. The conference report, 'Converging Technologies for Improving Human Performance', anticipated future progress in promoting synergies of neuro- and bio-technologies in genetic engineering, information technology and computer-cognitive sciences which would allow scientists to interface electronic devices with the human nervous system. Instead of being creatures of our natural abilities, we will become our own intelligent designers. (O'Mathuna, 2009, 159)

Let us take examples of all three:

Restorative functions are largely medical. Retinal implants are currently in use to combat macular degeneration (a disorder that affects the macula in the centre of the eye, and makes it difficult to see fine details). Contact lenses called 'eye-contact' already allow disabled people to interface with a computer and control cursor movements by sight. Quadriplegics will soon be able to use brain-computer interfaces (BCIs) to operate machinery without any physical connection between themselves and the machines they are operating. These are only a few of the significant medical breakthroughs in recent years that promise to restore or enhance the quality of life, and even to extend life itself to those previously considered to be 'disabled'.

Reconfiguring is where it all began with the work of Manfred Clynes and Nathan Kline on the hypothetical advantages of adapting humans to travel in space. Of particular interest to the military is the prospect of enhancing a soldier's physical strength, as well as mental capacities through brain-computer interfaces. The US National Aeronautics and Space Administration (NASA) already has an ongoing project, 'The Extension of the Human Senses'. One day it hopes it will be possible to insert into a soldier's brain tiny microchips that will give them seven-day access to data streams, and possibly even a complete overview of the battlefield. Before going into battle they will have scanned the battlefield like a CAT scan scans the brain. Satellite photos will be transformed automatically into 3-D landscapes stored in databases. Soldiers will be given greater situational awareness than the enemy they are fighting: they will have negotiated their way around a city on screen which has been mapped by a computer, building by building. They will know every alleyway and shortcut, every ridge and road before they have been deployed. They will know much more about the neighbourhood than the neighbours.

Enhancing human abilities is of even greater interest to military scientists. The Human Cognome Project in the US is designed to enhance the human mind. Soldiers at Fort Bragg are conducting ongoing research designed to make the 21st-century soldier a more effective instrument by augmenting his mental skills. The project buzz words are 'real time cognitive state assessment'; 'augmented cognition' and 'human-computer war fighting integrals'. Some of the programmes already begun include:

1. The Metabolic Dominance and Engineered Tissue Program, aimed at building up tissue muscle strength.

2. The Persistence in Combat Program: a combat self-treatment scheme which will allow soldiers to manage stress and deal with pain through the self-administration of drugs.

3. The Continuous Assisted Performance Program, which is intended to find bio-technological ways to push exhausted soldiers on without loss of performance.

Marrying brain cells with silicon chips is not difficult (neurons can be cultured on silicon as effectively as we do bacteria in a petri dish). We could also reverse the cochlear implants that turn sound into brainwaves, allowing us to turn brainwaves into sound: opening up the possibility of directly transmitting thoughts from brain to brain. Another area of interest to the military is sensory enhancement: enhancing those faculties we are all born with, or engineering in those we are not. We could re-engineer ourselves with the packages we program into computers for face recognition, so that we could subliminally detect reactions and responses such as lying. We might be able to detect the body language of another person which we might otherwise fail to pick up when interrogating prisoners. Other animals are good at instinctively reading our bodies (dogs can detect fear, we cannot). So why not a technological upgrade that would allow us to do that in the same way, as today night vision enables us to see in the dark.

What scientists are trying to go for is something not entirely dissimilar, except in its technological possibilities; they are aiming for neurosocial networking. So far, experiments with monkeys allow them to know which box holds the treat by conveying direct signals into their cerebral cortex. The next endeavour will be to get monkeys to share this information with each other purely through cerebral communication. (Nicoledes, 62) It is called the brain net, and if extended to humans it would enable soldiers to communicate with each other through thought alone. Social networking, after all, is now an accepted face of society in texting and Twitter. The idea is an upgraded version of online social networking to allow us to interact with others via the brain. Intel, Google and Microsoft all have their own brain-machine divisions working on this, and expect to make a breakthrough in twenty years' time. The immediate purpose of the research is to help future patients operate sophisticated robotic arms that can be attached to, or detached from, a biosynthetic torso as an eco-skeleton (very different from the prostheses that people now operate through physical exercise).

All this is going to be incredibly difficult. To realise the brain-machine interface will require a new generation of high-density micro-electronics, as well as custom designed neuro-chips. The first will allow long-term simultaneous recording of electrical activity of tens of thousands of neurons, distributed across multiple brain locations. The second will allow a disabled person's brain to condition and process its own electrical patterns into signals capable of controlling the eco-skeletons.

These new technologies are getting us to question our own ontology. A nanotechnology textbook proclaims: 'Many people ask themselves whether machines will ever have the ability to think. The answer is very clear and simple. There are machines that can think! The most elaborate one is called *Homo sapiens*'. (Gazit, 2007, 126) Once we are encouraged to think in these terms some challenging questions present themselves. Are we quite as unique as we thought: do we actually have a sense of self? Are we more than the technologies we invent? Is technology re-enchanting our humanity, presenting us with greater or fewer opportunities for self-fulfilment? And for the military there is another even more interesting question: will war still remain what Thucydides called it, 'the human thing', or will the 'human' mean something else altogether?

Cyborg warriors?

The Greeks were inveterate cataloguers. Aristotle insisted that systematic thinking starts with making distinctions, and he and his contemporaries went on to make the distinctions we take for granted today between time and space, quality and quantity, cause and effect, form and matter. They also drew rigid binomial distinctions within the social sciences as we call them today, between gods and humans, humans and animals, men and women and Greeks and barbarians. Some of those distinctions we have long discarded but two have persisted much longer and are being challenged only now. A cyborg, writes Donna Harraway, exists within two boundaries that we have taken for granted since the Greeks but which we have now crossed: that between animals (or other living organisms) and ourselves, and that between self-governing machines (automata) and organisms (or models of autonomy such as, and especially, our own). The cyborg is the figure born of the interface of automaton and autonomy. (Gray, 1995, xix) 'To be a cyborg is to experience a transformation of one's sense of existence in such a way that one cannot be fully human or fully oneself outside of the link to certain machines'. (Lazez, 2007, 61) This does not require a literal physical fusion. Anyone who uses a cell phone is a cyborg of sorts: without social

215

networking many of us would have no friends; without being wired into a worldwide web we would have no social identity.

One of the books much quoted in the community is an autobiography by Michael Chorost: *Rebuilt: My Journey Back to the Hearing World* (2006). The original subtitle read 'how becoming part computer made me more human', and the book is important because it is a reflection of what the author, in his own eyes at least, thinks he has become. Chorost was deaf until he was given a cochlear implant. A set of tiny electrodes were implanted deep inside his inner ear. They stimulated nerve fibres in the ear and transmitted messages to the brain (a functioning auditory nerve is necessary to allow people to detect sounds). Electrodes were attached to a receiver that was implanted under his scalp, along with a magnet which held a removable wireless transmitter to the scalp. The transmitter was attached, in turn, to a microphone that looked like an ordinary hearing aid. After undergoing this procedure Chorost was able to hear for the first time. He had become a cyborg.

He is not, he insists, either inhuman or post-human—just differently enabled, or 'differently human' (Chorost, 2006, 33). In an attempt to explain what he has become he invokes science fiction. He is not a Terminator, he maintains, but he worries that he is undergoing a Borg assimilation (a reference to the *Star Trek* franchise in which an alien race of robots assimilate everything in their path). The implant in his case allowed him to 'perceive the world by a programmer's logic and rules instead of the ones biology and evolution has given him'. But one science fiction genre he does not mention is cyber-punk and its technologically enhanced individuals (or cyborgs) who derive their sense of humanity from their technicity—not their natural talents, but their enhanced skills. In this world, the cyborgs are quite literally 'set apart'. Human experience has been transformed in ways that even they do not always fully comprehend, and that is important because their skill-set is such that it can transform the lives of others.

In William Gibson's short story 'Johnny Mnemonic' one of the principal characters has electronically upgraded vision and prostheticised fingers that house a set of razor-sharp, double-edged scalpels, myo-electronically wired into her enhanced nervous system. She is no longer what the Greeks would have considered a warrior to be, a specific human type; instead she is a customised, functional product of a cyborg culture and she has little respect for others who are not like her (she certainly has no affinity with the great chain of being—the genealogy that links today's all-too-human warriors with Achilles and his Myrmidons). She is a member of a special caste, one that is no longer a product of culture but of bio-engineering. And what she admires most in others like herself (even her enemies) is their technical virtuosity and operational speed, attributes which have been integrated directly into her prosthetic and genetic architecture. Her 'excellence' or what the Greeks called *arete* has morphed into what David Tomas calls 'a technological edge'. (Tomas, 1995, 180)

Chorost is particularly enlightening on this subject. He was concerned that the implants which he was given would mean that he would not be able to hear as the rest of us do; in effect, he would cease to be a person, and become a machine, 'a receptor of a flood of data'. (Lazez, 2007, 62) For we tend to take hearing for granted. We do not process data; we are the data we process, we are part of the world we hear. Chorost expresses it particularly well, 'The sense of hearing immerses you in the world as no other … Hearing constitutes your sense of being of the world, in the thick of it. To see is to observe, to hear is to be enveloped'. But Chorost soon discovered that his implant melded with his own neural network and that the implant 'reprogrammed him'. The implant ceased to be an implant and became fully incorporated into his body. His brain remapped itself to accommodate new inputs. It reorganised its structure by growing new connections between neurons.

[Do I have] a unitary identity? Not anymore, if ever: there are two minds in my skull, one built by genes, the other by a corporation. I am a walking collective, a community of least two. The x-rays of my head are riveting, a stark juxtaposition of sensuous biology and angular computational power. The computer invaded the sacred domain of my body, yet to my own astonishment we learned to work together as a total system, mutually changing each other in the process. I fed it lithium batteries; it fed me electrons. I altered its software; it re-patterned the dendrites in my auditory cortex. We have literally reprogrammed each other. (Chorost, 2006, 73)

Chorost concludes that he is now 'a cybernetic organism, or an organic creature whose body is controlled by algorithmic rules'. (Chorost, 2006, 71) He may indeed be differently enabled and, to that extent, not quite like the rest of us, but he also believes that he has become human, not superhuman; he has merely 'become' what nature intends for all of us but doesn't always deliver. His 'becoming' is merely a realization of his 'being'. And the point he is making is not to be underestimated, for the world of the deaf is different from ours. (O'Mathuna, 2009, 121)

There is a lot of white noise in this business; there are many absurd claims and alarmist visions, and promises of enhancing life when all people mean is offering the chance of a normal life. We resort to science fiction (the only thing we have recourse to) but we must be careful when invoking it. We may be moving ever closer to the cyborg era, but we have not reached it yet.

Perhaps it is fitting to give the last word to Clynes, who started us off along the journey on which it would seem we have embarked. His idea was to supplement the homeostasis by which man evolved physiologically only; to supplement it by his own imagination and creativity without changing his nature, to help him use his faculties without having to waste his energies, or adjusting the living functions necessary for the maintenance of life. He imagined that they would become automatic in the same way that we do not adjust our own blood pressure—it is self-adjusting. In other words, the technology that allows us to become cyborgs merely enlarges a human function. Like walking, it is a form of homestasis. A child learns to walk by trial and error. Once it has learned to walk it does not give it another thought (unless later injured or immobilised in some way). A child rides a bicycle, another difficult step into its development, but once learned it becomes second nature. Every human being in that sense can be called a cyborg. (Gray, 1995, 47)

Clynes will not talk of any change in emotional expression and experience. He insists that cyborgs will feel and think like the rest of us; they will have the same emotions, the same capacity for anger and joy. But he argues that in fifteen years' time we will know enough about emotional states from the physiological point of view, at which point we may be able to change our emotional world, too. We may be able to reduce the need for sleep, and therefore reduce the number of dreams. We may be able to do so by turning genes on and off. Our emotional world is formed by molecules like neuropeptides. Each emotion has its own neuropeptides (many of which have yet to be identified). In future the aim will be to produce a computer-designed molecule along the lines of naturally occurring molecules that will be able to change our emotional states.

Clynes insists that he is a realist. He insists that he is interested in real possibilities, not unrealistic dreams. And he gives some very modest as well as utilitarian examples of enhancement, getting us to remember digits (such as PIN numbers) without having to learn them or remember them: we will be able to implant them directly in the brain, thereby eliminating forgetfulness and one of the symptoms of ageing—short term memory loss. He is a romantic only when looking far into the future, to 2050 and beyond, for by then he suspects that we may be able to heighten positive emotions like joy, rather than merely eliminate negative emotions like depression. And if there is more joy in the world, there may be less anger, resentment or envy. In other words, mankind may find itself living in a world in which there is less conflict and, possibly, fewer wars.

Well, we can all make a bet on technological determinism, if we so wish.

6

DESIGNER WARRIORS

Socrates keeps his head

'If I have exhausted the justifications I have reached bedrock and my spade is turned. Then I am inclined to say: "This is simply what I do"'

Wittgenstein (Appleyard, 1992, 249)

It is difficult at this distance to evoke the experience of battle in the ancient Greek world, to recapture the atmosphere and intensity of the world in which Socrates moved. Even a philosopher could expect to don armour more than once in a lifetime and Socrates was called upon to serve his city three times, the last occasion being one depressing November afternoon at the battle of Delium. Delium made Socrates famous for his bravery and, especially and most importantly, his presence of mind.

The Peloponnesian War was a messy, asymmetrical struggle involving attritional campaigns, long sieges and ambuscades. It only saw two set piece encounters. We have discussed one of them, Mantinea; Delium was the other. It was the largest battle in which Athenian soldiers were involved since Marathon, where they had made history and defied the Persian advance. At Delium 15 per cent of the Athenian soldiers who were on the battlefield that day were killed in the space of a few hours. A larger number were probably wounded or captured.

The Athenians had used the interlude between two wars with Sparta (which we tend to lump together as one) to fortify the sanctuary of Apollo at Delium which lay in Boeotia, a territory dominated by another city-state, Thebes (then allied to Sparta). Finding himself isolated, the Athenian general Hippocrates marched home. The Thebans intercepted him the next day when both sides fought a pitched battle. Thucydides' account of the battle is vivid, if uncharacteristically brief. The Athenians soon found themselves in danger. Their right flank bested the Boeotian left, but very soon in the confusion of battle Athenian found himself killing Athenian. 'When a man stands face to face with the enemy, he is barely able to see what he needs to see', wrote the playwright Euripides, perhaps alluding to this very battle. (Lendon, 2005, 80)

The sights and sound of this fight, writes Lawrence Trittle in his history of the war, would have added to their panic. The battleground itself would have been littered with bodies of the wounded, dying and dead, making it difficult to walk and fight at the same time. Blood, and lots of it, would have made the ground slippery and the air foul. The noise and confusion would have been bewildering and disorienting, all at once: 'Killing with spears and swords is not easy—many more men would have been wounded than killed—and with thousands of men fighting, and pushing their way forward to replace the fallen—the duration of the hoplite battle would have been an affair that lasted hours rather than minutes'. (Trittle, 2010,101–33)

On the other flank, the Athenians were not so lucky. They found themselves pushed back. The enemy commander seized the moment to launch a cavalry attack, catching the Athenians by surprise. Thinking another enemy army had fallen upon them, the Athenians panicked, and fear being contagious, it was soon communicated to other parts of the front. The whole army broke and fled, and the fleeing soldiers were cut down by the Theban cavalry. Only a small number held their nerve, including Socrates who managed with his friends to escape the battlefield to safety.

Socrates had seen battle before; he was a veteran; he was middle-aged; he was well past forty, which was old for a 5th-century BC Greek. He knew from experience that it was unwise to succumb to emotions like fear; he knew the importance of mastering them.

In the *Symposium* Alcibiades gives a description of the orderly way in which Socrates behaved while everyone else was breaking ranks:

First off I noticed how much more in control of his senses he was than Laches, and how—to use your own phrase Aristophanes—he made his way there just as he does here in Athens 'swaggering and glancing sideways'. So he looked around calmly at both his friends and the enemy; he was clearly giving the message to anyone even at a distance that if anyone touched this man he would quickly put up a stout defence. The result was that he and his partner got away swiftly. For it is true that attackers do not approach men of this calibre but instead go after those fleeing headlong'. (Hanson, 2005, 9)

It is quite rational, of course, to want to flee a battlefield in the hope of escape, but an experienced soldier knows the danger of turning one's back on the enemy. He also knows that panic is contagious. The mood of the first soldiers to run was what psychologists like to call 'inherently reinforcing'— it made everyone else feel unhappy about themselves and their future. What makes this dangerous is what makes all mood swings dangerous; we do not always know that our moods have changed. We are looped unwittingly into mood shifts. The Athenians that day were seized by collective hysteria. Humans are given to hysterical moods precisely because they can imagine the world other than it is. They can ask themselves: what if? In that moment, they remake the world in their imagination, and once entertained, a thought will not go away. And the thought of what is to come can lead even the most experienced soldiers to making seriously bad decisions such as turning one's back on the enemy in the act of running away.

In *The Principles of Psychology* (1890), William James challenged the standard wisdom of his day in claiming that we have a far greater variety of impulses than 'any other lower animal'. (James, 1950, 389) It is those impulses that determine our fate. And each of us has different ones. When we say a soldier trusts to his instincts, we mean something very specific. We mean that he has instincts the rest of us do not: that is what makes him the professional he hopefully is. He has experience to rely on, of course, and training. But neither the sum of his experiences nor training, however good, is the ultimate factor in determining whether a soldier will hold firm or not. What makes a good soldier different from a bad one is not his training, it is his insight. He knows what is going to happen next; he can see beyond the immediate predicament in which he finds himself; he can analyse a situation and process information about it quickly. He knows instinctively when it is safe to leave the field and when it is not.

And there is a scientific explanation for this, which James was not aware of at the time. Dopamine, one of the key chemical transmitters in the brain, helps regulate all our emotions, from feelings of exhilaration to those of fear. It is the common neural currency of the mind, writes Jonah Lehrer in his book *The Decisive Moment*, the molecule that helps us decide among alternatives (the flight or fight response). By looking at how dopamine works inside the brain we can see why feelings are capable of generating deep insights. (Lehrer, 2009, 40) What a soldier needs to steel himself against most is surprise. We are all surprised in life, but I suggest no activity throws up more surprises than war.

The brain, writes Jonah Lehrer, is designed to amplify the shock of the unexpected. Nothing focuses the mind like surprise. The cortex immediately takes notice of what is not supposed to be there. Within milliseconds, the activity of brain cells creates an emotion like fear. This fast cellular process takes place in a tiny area in the centre of the brain, the anterior singulate cortex that is dense with dopamine neurons. It helps control the conversation between what we know and what we feel. If it is startled by some stimulus it can immediately focus on the relevant sensation, forcing us to take note of the unexpected event. It also sends signals to the hypothalamus which regulates crucial aspects of bodily function. Within seconds the heart rate increases and adrenalin shoots up. It is our emotions (manifest in a rising heart rate, as adrenalin pumps into the bloodstream) that force us to take note of a critical situation and respond immediately. A short-term feeling is translated into an experience. (Lehrer, 2009, 43)

And an experience has a biological basis, too. Every time we encounter something new, or make mistakes, our brain cells change themselves. One commonplace example Lehrer offers his readers is seasickness. We feel nausea not because a boat is pitching wildly, but because we expect the same motion as on land—solid unmoving ground—and are caught out by finding that things are not as we imagined. And it doesn't usually take long for the dopamine neurons to revise the models of motion, which is why seasickness is usually temporary. (Lehrer, 2009, 46) Every time, writes Lehrer, we make a mistake or encounter something new our brain cells change: 'Our emotions are deeply empirical'.

Dopamine is a key chemical transmitter. Parkinson's disease, a classic neurological condition, is due to the reduction in dopamine transmission; schizophrenia, the most classic case of madness, is partly characterised by over-activity of the nerve pathways that employ dopamine. And our dopamine neurons are central to everyday normal life more than we think, for they allow us to think at the unconscious level. The conscious mind takes time to assimilate information. It forces us to reason out our actions, to prioritise, to choose different courses of action. On a battlefield soldiers often do not have time to think through their actions. The very nature of battle—the speed at which a bullet flies to its target; the sheer volume of information that has to be processed about the environment in which a soldier finds himself—often makes thought impossible. If he spends too much time thinking about his predicament a soldier may not long survive. He depends on his instincts—the ability which his dopamine neurons give him to recognise patterns in the confusion of events, to predict what the enemy is likely to do next, and what would be the safest course of action: to flee, or to fight.

Ironically, for a philosopher, Socrates did not allow reason to win the day. Reason can be the enemy of the good. It is possible to over-rationalise. In a situation where you may be killed, it is not particularly sensible to think too much. Training works because it help us know instinctively what to do next. It gets the soldier to think about what he is doing—to aim accurately, to wait for the right moment to fire a gun (when the enemy is within range). Once the mechanics have been learned, however, analysing what is happening is not particularly useful. The brain already knows what to do next. When you start thinking about what you are doing, the part of the brain that monitors behaviour starts to interfere with decisions that are normally made without thinking.

Aristotle arrived at much the same conclusion without the benefit of modern science. He insisted that virtue is acquired by constantly repeating virtuous acts, and that those acts in turn, if regularly performed, were character-forming. There was a feedback process at work between the person we are and the actions we perform. And those actions will become second nature. Practice really does make perfect, as the old adage goes—whether it is a concert pianist who has put in hours of his or her life or a tennis player who has spent hours a day practicing on a tennis court. In his book *Straw Dogs* the philosopher John Gray, writing about the dangers of too much rationalism, warns that self-awareness is as much a disability as a power. The most accomplished pianist is not the one who is most aware of his or her movements when playing; the best craftsman may not know how he works. 'Very often we are at our most skilful when we are least self-aware'. (Gray, 2002, 62) He cites the example of archers in pre-modern Japan who were taught that they would hit the target only when they no longer thought of it, or themselves.

What Zen masters in Japan deduced by intuition we can now explain scientifically thanks to the recent discoveries of neuroscience. Consistency is a very human quality. For each skill reconfigures the brain in different ways. A substance known as myelin wraps itself around our neural pathways, making connections speedier the more they are used. We can indeed play a piano or game of tennis largely on reflex, bypassing the slow, deliberate circuits of the brain. This is particularly useful in the case of war. Drill is mechanical and rhythmic and designed to help soldiers cope with stress, which is why soldiers drill over and over again. It makes instinctive certain forms of behaviour. And morality is part of the process, too. It is quite literary drilled into them. Of course, in the heat of battle you cannot predict that a soldier will not go AWOL morally (any more than you can predict that a machine will not overheat or break down). We teach ethics to soldiers, however, to get them to behave in particular ways, to reconfigure their character so that they are no longer the people they once were, to engrave into them certain cultural instincts which we translate into behavioural codes. And far from being outmoded, Aristotelian ethics are deeply in tune with what neuroscientists have to tell us about human personality and character.

The advantage of an emotional brain is that it buys time to think through the situation and do the most reasonable thing. Socrates was able to think through his situation on that famous day at Delium. Imagination, though of course he did not know this, takes place in the pre-frontal cortex which is larger in *Homo sapiens* than in any other species. And it is in the pre-frontal cortex that we find the capacity for rational thought, the capacity to make sense of our emotions. We can master fear just as we can master anger. And this is essential when you encounter an experience you have never had before, when your dopamine neurons really do not have any idea what you should do next. For dopamine can also mislead, encouraging us to find patterns where none may exist; it can even encourage wishful thinking. Human beings are not machines; they make irrational decisions and act capriciously. We cannot always trust to our own feelings, which is why we have to place our trust in the right ones.

To keep emotions in check you need to focus on what is important. For Socrates, old campaigner as he was, this meant opting for a reasonable chance of survival. For that he had to process information about what was happening all around him. His brain did this by keeping some information in what Lehrer calls 'short term storage', in particular the part of the memory which can be accessed later, so that as other information streams in you can think of two thoughts simultaneously: you can see that you might not survive much longer unless you flee, but you may also see the danger of flinging away your armour and turning your back to the enemy in the urge to escape the battlefield. Studies show that neurons in the prefrontal areas will fire in response to a stimulus and keep on firing for several seconds after the stimulus has disappeared. This echo of activity allows the brain to make creative associations. It is why Socrates could probably think about fleeing while simultaneously thinking about standing his ground, in the hope that the enemy cavalry would choose a more tempting target. Once this overlapping of ideas occurs, cortical cells start to form connections that have never existed before, in the process wiring themselves into an entirely new network. (Lehrer, 2009, 128) Once an insight has been generated, the prefrontal cortex is able to identify it. Socrates would have been able to see his precarious situation in an entirely new light.

But it is important to stress that neuroscience does not tell us the whole story. Not all decisions are as spontaneous as we suppose. In fact, most have a non-spontaneous hinterland. (Tallis, 2011, 282) And Socrates in later accounting for his presence of mind was at pains to explain that by nature he was not given to panic either on the battlefield or at home. He was proud of his record in battle, especially at the battle of Delium. Not only is the battle mentioned three times in Plato's work, there are a number of veiled allusions in several others. And at the end of his life, on trial for corrupting the youth and not believing in the gods of the state, Socrates insisted that he was still a soldier, but one who served another master, not the people of Athens but Apollo, the god of wisdom and truth. He referred proudly to his bravery at Delium, his willingness to stand where the Athenian generals had put him, and not to break ranks as everyone else fled the field. But he went on to insist that just as the generals had commanded him to stand firm at Delium, so the gods commanded him to remain true to his conscience. And thus was born the founding myth of Western philosophy.

Socrates acted as much in character at the end of his life as he had in his last battle. If we want a similar figure in a modern setting, then look to Robert Jordan, the hero of Ernest Hemingway's novel *For Whom the Bell Tolls*. The novel tells how the young American remains behind to allow his friends to escape before the enemy arrives. His is no spur of the moment decision, either. It is who he is; he can do no other. As E.L. Doctorow writes, 'war is the means by which one's cultivated individualism can be raised to the heroic. And therefore never send to ask for whom the bell tolls; it tolls so that I can be me'. (Doctorow, 2007, 92)

None of this is very popular now, except with novelists. For the more we know about the brain's workings, the more we tend to think that all our actions can be explained away scientifically, and the more we explain them away the more tempting it is for scientists to see human beings as machines. The human gene itself is memorably described by Richard Dawkins as a 'survival machine'. As machines we can be retooled, and if necessary re-programmed. The metaphor goes back to Descartes, but the type of machine we think we are varies from age to age, the dominant technology at the moment being the computer.

We are told we should not ask fatuous questions, such as whether machines will ever have the ability to think for themselves, because the answer is already clear: there are machines that do. The most elaborate one so far is *Homo sapiens*: 'The brain is a very elaborate machine, but it is just a machine that obeys the rules of chemistry and physics'. (O'Mathua, 2009, 161) Kevin Kelly writes that human beings are no longer apes but 'machines with attitude'. We are merely, in other words, random ancestors of machines, and as machines we can be engineered ourselves. (Kelly, 1994, 14)

'We have invented inspiring and enhancing technologies', writes Sherry Turkle in her latest book, *Alone Together*, yet we have allowed them to diminish us. In the case of war, they are diminishing the idea of character. Turkle is a clinical psychologist as well as the world's leading expert on the social and psychological effects of technology, and her vision of the future is sobering indeed. We tend to see ourselves increasingly as automata, driven by chemical combinations that take decisions for us, all of which encourages us to think that we can be re-engineered by changing the neural pathways of our brains. Once you can decode what makes men 'heroic' you may also be able to produce 'designer-soldiers'.

Engineering emotions

In April 2002 two American F-16 pilots nearing the end of a ten-hour mission over Afghanistan mistakenly dropped a laser-guided bomb on a group of Canadian soldiers engaged in a training exercise. The attack killed four people and injured another eight. The incident was a case of 'friendly fire' based on mistaken identity. But the inquiry that followed found that the American pilots had been taking 'go-pills', an amphetamine issued by the US military as a 'fatigue management tool'. The Defense Advanced Research Projects Agency (DARPA) had been investigating the neurological causes of fatigue for some time. Its scientists have been trying to devise ways that soldiers could continue to function when deprived of sleep without running the risk of cognitive impairment (making wrong judgement calls). They are particularly interested in a class of drugs known as ampakines. Amphetamines act on the dopamine system, whereas recreational drugs such as ecstasy act on the serotonin system. And it is the dopamine system that the military have been interested in most ever since neuroscientists were able to identify how it works—how it allowed Socrates that afternoon in 429 BC to master his fear and fight his way out of an unenviable situation.

Long before pharmacology made an impact on war, alcohol was the preferred way of sedating soldiers, or rousing their passions. This was especially true by the late 18th century when for the first time courage was readily understood and acknowledged, more importantly, to be a bodily strength belonging to the nervous system rather than the mind. Alcohol might dull the mind, but it also dulled the senses, it calmed nerves.

Drugs were used widely for the first time in World War II. Amphetamines were widely used on all sides to keep soldiers ahead of the curve, though the Japanese preferred methamphetamines (a liquid form that could be absorbed by the body more quickly but which was also found over time to be more addictive). American servicemen used 'speed balls' in Korea, an injected ball mixture of amphetamines and heroin. The drug of preference in Vietnam was marijuana, though heroin became popular with the troops in the later stages of the conflict. But no less popular was alcohol, and both alcohol and drugs figure in Oliver Stone's movie *Platoon* in which the hard men get drunk and the more sensitive smoke pot, a typical 1960s trope.

Compared with the Vietnam era, drug use among the US military is now small. About 5 per cent of US soldiers self-medicate according to a 2005 report. As the situation in Iraq deteriorated that year soldiers went from taking ecstasy or marijuana to hard drugs including cocaine. Some insisted on taking two or three lines of coke before they would go into combat. (*Washington Post*, 16 February 2005) And at least 20 per cent of soldiers returning from campaign in Afghanistan or Iraq have substance abuse disorders (including alcohol). In today's military with a zero tolerance of drug use, soldiers self-prescribe in more basic ways: over the counter they buy cough and cold medications like Nyquil (Kan, 2008, 2). These drugs are self-prescribed precisely because soldiers think that they stimulate a person's will to fight rather than flee and hope to suppress anxieties engendered by thoughts of death or injury. They also fend off boredom, a state in which fear and anxiety tend to breed.

Drugs have not been favoured by the military, because of their long-term consequences, though they have been testing them on the troops (not always with their knowledge) since the mid-1950s. Morphine based drugs tend to sedate or relax the subject, reducing vigilance which is required of every soldier. Drug use tests in Western military forces also show the effects of drug use when not prescribed—when self-medication is dangerous. The US Marines in Fallujah (2002–4) were told to aim at the heads, not the bodies of the insurgents who, it was reported, were high on drugs. One Marine compared the operation to the George Romero cult classic *Night of the Living Dead* where it is almost impossible to stop zombies from rampaging across the countryside except with a well-aimed bullet through their heads. (Kan, 2008, 14) Zombies, we are told, have one great advantage over suicide-bombers; they are already dead.

What neuroscientists tell us is that drugs produce effects by prolonging or suppressing other effects and that these reactions can permanently damage the neural network. Minor short term gains can result in major long term losses. (Foley, 2011, 147–8) And the problem is that hard drug use does not remove fear, it actually increases it. Prolonged drug use can induce paranoia, agitation, and hallucinations. It can lead—as the Marines found when engaging drug high soldiers in Fallujah—to episodes of even greater unmediated (or psychotic) violence.

But none of this is likely to stop the military's experiments with drugs. DARPA has several new drugs under clinical trial which are intended to enhance performance. The 'Persistence in Combat Program' is well advanced and includes research into painkillers which soldiers could take before going into action, in anticipation of blunting the pain of being wounded. Painkillers such as R1624, created by scientists at Rinat Neuroscience, use an antibody to keep in check a neuropeptide that helps transmit pain sensations from the tissues to the nerves. The purpose is to ensure the soldier retains full motor and mental capability, which is not the case at present with morphine related drugs (DARPA). And then there are cognitive enhancing drugs which alter moods. The most familiar are Ritalin, which aids concentration for children suffering from Attention Deficit Disorder (ADD), and Adderall, which reduces stress and is often taken by students about to sit exams. And some would go further in the hope that one day it might be possible to pop a pill and display conspicuous courage under fire; one day it might even be possible to field an army of John Rambos.

All this lies in the future. For now the great hope is that drugs may help eliminate post-traumatic stress, the bugbear of today's professional militaries and the greatest cause of hospitalization in the American armed forces.

The traumatised soldier

In the 1950s the psychiatrist Aaron Beck conducted a series of experiments that changed his life, and that of his patients. Beck had completed his Freudian training and he was eager to test it out. He got his patients to dig into the past and relive their traumas. Then he encountered a problem. As the patients ventilated they began to unravel. There were suicide attempts. He found it difficult to put them back together again. Beck is the father of cognitive therapy which is intended to get patients to engage in positive thinking, let go of the past and gain 'closure'. Dostoevsky (arguably one of the first psychologists) got there first: 'A few good memories are all we need to find faith in the world'. Trauma is manifest when you lose faith in the world and cannot get it back.

Freud is even more important because he was one of the first writers to address what was then considered a new problem: post-traumatic stress disorder (or 'shell shock') in World War I. What made his analysis so compelling was that it was based on what was then considered to be a scientific principle: repetition. Neurosis was based on the repetition of nightmares and bad memories. Repetition, for Freud, was the basis of pleasure; clearly, nightmares brought none. Dreams were wish-fulfilments in the Freudian lexicon; clearly, no-one suffering bad dreams actually wishes to experience what is dreamed. Trauma, it followed, was a classical neurosis.

Freud is not as popular these days as he was in the 1950s. And the idea of a neurosis is not much in fashion, any more than hysteria (the diagnosis of trauma favoured by armies in 1915). Hysteria was dropped from the medical dictionary in the 1970s. The preferred terms are 'affective disorders' and 'syndromes' (every age changes the language it uses to describe conditions it does not fully understand). We do not even use the term 'mental' these days to distinguish conditions that are not physical, and anyway many mental disorders may have physiological explanations.

There is much that is physical in mental illness, and much that is cultural. Take addiction. Is it induced by weak character or by circumstances, or is it technically speaking a disease? Alcoholism was classified as a disease in the 1960s. Armies came across massive drug addiction for the first time a decade later in Vietnam, where men in the field self-prescribed. Instances of use were legion, but the interesting thing is that 90 per cent of those using heroin (one of the most difficult drugs to come off) stopped using it once they came home. And the majority never went back to compulsive use. Perhaps one explanation is that the veterans were never adopted by the counter-culture (including the habitual drug users at home); they were reviled and ostracised; they weren't 'encouraged' to remain addicts, and they didn't get any sympathy for the problem of addiction. No-one is saying that trauma is like an addiction, but it does seem that cultural factors may play some role in how it is structured and managed. One of the fascinating features of trauma in World War I was that officers were often left with a terrible stammer; enlisted men went mute; and the officers responded better to the then universal 'cure', electric shock aversion therapy, a technological solution typical of the times.

In part, how we treat illness or designate it depends a lot on cultural norms. The narrative of illness which is transmitted through culture and its impact on people is a dialectical one. Every culture, writes the sociologist Frank Furedi, has a set of beliefs about the nature of being which structures the way it encourages us to see the world and our place in it. Every culture frames emotional responses to life: permitting the display of some emotions and discouraging others. As we have seen Aristotle positively disapproved of soldiers weeping in public for the loss of their friends. And, of course, sometimes cultural traditions not only frame the way soldiers are expected to experience life; sometimes they can be an invitation to infirmity. The number and scope of recognised psychiatric disorders, syndromes and illnesses has increased exponentially in the past fifty years in all walks of life (even a child's temper tantrum is now defined as a 'temper-dysregulation disorder'). A veritable trauma industry has grown up in recent years with its own 'self-esteem educators', 'de-grieving professionals' and 'traumatologists', all busily measuring the damage that life does to the human psyche. The definition of mental illness is now so widely drawn that some psychiatrists clearly believe that if a soldier is not ill there is something wrong with him.

Every war now seems to produce its own syndromes. The more you read about syndromes in the press the more likely it is that you feel you should not have been at risk. 'We were not trained for this' is a common complaint. The problem of pathologising war in this way is to suggest that soldiers are as vulnerable as everyone else, indeed that there is nothing especially remarkable in being a warrior. (Furedi, 2004, 113) A soldier is much less likely to be traumatised if he is encouraged to see war as something other than as an emotionally scarring experience. Clearly, if suffering is deemed to be meaningless so will the pain and suffering that result.

So, what if anything do the Greeks still have to tell us about trauma? For they were under no illusion about war's horrors. The Homeric battlefield was one in which a soldier could expect to be drenched in blood from hacking, maiming and butchering away in face to face encounters that could last hours. In the *Iliad* there are at least 148 different ways in which a person can be killed, nearly all at close range. In an age before firearms the brutalities of war were up close and personal. The very first historian, Herodotus, tells of the Athenian soldier Epizelus at the battle of Marathon who was struck blind as he witnessed the man next to him cut down. Hysterical blindness is preserved in the Epidarian miracle lists which recall the names of soldiers who waited for years for arrowheads to work their way out of their chests and for spearheads to be dislodged from their jaws. (Trittle, 2007, 181) Hollywood shows us all too graphically the reality of the Greek battlefield in films such as *Troy* and *300* where the killing is unrelenting and remorseless. What the psychological effects would have been we can only imagine, as hour after hour warriors hacked away at each other with swords or axes—metal on fragile human flesh.

The thing of fear

> *'[War]: a sweet thing to him who does not know it*
> *But to him who has made a trial of it, it is a thing of fear'*
>
> Pindar, *Odes*, Fragment 120.5 in Hanson 1989, 18

The poet Pindar called war 'the thing of fear', for fear stalks every soldier, however brave on the day of battle. Fear can steel up upon a soldier and never leave him, for soldiers also live with the fear of returning home psychologically damaged. Remembrance has a colour of its own and its edges need no sharpening. For some the return home is not the end, but the beginning of a long and debilitating descent through deepening layers of horror.

Some historians would have us believe that in the past warriors had a different emotional register from those we produce today, and that fear and anxiety and the emotional commitment to battle would have been different. They almost certainly were not. As one historian of the early mediaeval era writes, we must never shut our ears to the differently pitched voices of the past, but no more should we close off our capacity for emotional engagement with humanity's common experience. The men who fought at Thermopylae, Cannae, Agincourt and Waterloo were not a different species, or from a different planet. Like us they also experienced grief, shock and awe. 'The de-humanised unemotional history of what some modern historians dream, the desire to assess the past as if it were data to be grasped and computed' is an inadequate response to the battles they seek to describe. Trauma is definitively human and we must assume that warriors over the centuries have experienced it, whether they were Greek hoplites at Delium or English infantrymen at Agincourt pole-axing Frenchman after Frenchman over a period of three hours. (Vincent, 2011, 50–51)

Modern war, of course, created a new challenge—long distance maiming, and worse still, the possibility of seeing a soldier's body blown apart. Fast forward to the mid-19th century and the Crimean War which witnessed the very first instances of industrialised killing. Trench fatigue was the big enemy. After ten months in the trenches, writes the historian Orlando Figes, soldiers became such nervous wrecks from living under constant bombardment that many of them succumbed to 'trench madness', a mixed bag of mental illnesses, as far as one can tell, from claustrophobia to what would later be called 'combat stress'. Suicides were not infrequent. (Figes, 2010, 374–5)

War is just as cruel today, especially when a soldier can be killed or maimed by an improvised roadside bomb. Here is a description volunteered by one US Army specialist who was one of the first men on the scene when a group of suspected insurgents were blown up on a Baghdad street in 2007, hit by 30mm bursts from an Apache helicopter: 'The top of one guy's head was completely off', he recalled. 'Another guy was ripped open from groin to neck. A third had lost a leg … their insides were out, and exposed. I had never seen anything like this before'. (Thompson, 2010, 22) Today quantitative electroencephalography now allows brainwave analysts to measure the extent of physical damage to the brain. Traumatic brain injury (TBI) is the technical term, and it has been a particular feature of the War on Terror. Bruised and battered brains can release stress hormones that trigger Post-Traumatic Stress Disorder. And because the brain and memory are intimately linked, molecules can change into memories, epiphanies and transformations, as well as nightmares. (Thompson, 2010, 22)

War has always been a demanding taskmaster and it has made different demands upon us at different times. The warrior is a human type, and over time our humanity changes subtly. Cultural selection—nurture not nature—has been powering our history almost exclusively for the past 10,000 years. And human attitudes change. Descartes thought that you could programme a soldier and thus predict an effect, all things being equal. He thought of the soldier as a machine that could be started up and sent off to its target (to kill another machine). But the problem is that the human mind always intervenes. As the historian John Lukacs contends, we can predict with some confidence at what pressure a bone will break; we can estimate the precise margin of intolerability, but we cannot do this for the human mind. For what a soldier finds 'intolerable' is simply what he thinks it to be, or what he is no longer prepared to tolerate. For him, tolerance is what he is prepared to undergo and some will go the extra distance, or master stress in ways that it is impossible for them or us to predict until the moment arrives and finds them equal or unequal to the test. The decisive event, adds Lukacs, is not the pressure itself but the lodging of that idea in the mind: 'And the mind is not a passive instrument, even though it can and will be strongly influenced by what others think'. (Lukacs, 2002, 114) A soldier can be 'shamed' into going the extra mile.

What a soldier thinks 'tolerable' will change over time. Would Achilles and his Myrmidons have survived more than a few hours on the first day of the Somme when 20,000 British soldiers went over the top to their death; would an English infantryman have survived a few hours of the harsh hand-to-hand fighting that Homer depicts on the killing ground before Troy? Would a young soldier from Antietam, one of the bloodiest engagements of the American Civil War, have been able to endure the relentless house to house and room to room fighting that both sides experienced at Stalingrad in 1942–43? The Pulitzer Prize author John Steinbeck was struck on a visit to the city four years later by the sight of children scavenging for food in the ruins of the city, their minds crazed by the relentless fighting that they had endured: 'We wondered how many more might be like this—minds that could not tolerate living in the twentieth century'. (Steinbeck, 1994, 121)

Theatre of war

If trauma has always been part of the psychological landscape of war, it is now so widespread that it is casting doubt on whether in future soldiers will be able to survive their circumstances. It has become an epidemic which the US Army is clearly under-resourced to deal with. Despite the fact that the Army Mental Health Corps has increased 60 per cent since 9/11, it is only able to cope at all because it is estimated that 50 per cent of soldiers who need help never seek it, for fear of being stigmatised by friends or colleagues, or losing their chances of promotion.

Since the Greeks were the first to identify 'combat stress' it is not surprising that the US military have gone back to the classics to help combat

235

veterans cope with their traumas. 'The Theater of War Project', a Pentagon funded production company, presents a reading of two plays by much the most popular of the three Greek tragedians, Sophocles. Two of his surviving plays, *Ajax* and *Philoctetes*, are now performed up and down the United States in front of veterans in an attempt to de-stigmatise psychological injury and help them come to terms with their own condition. The director, Bryan Doerries, was inspired by two seminal books by the psychologist Jonathan Shay, *Achilles in Vietnam* (1994) and *Odysseus in America* (2002), in which the author went back to Homer to explain why soldiers become traumatised and how they deal with their anguish. Shay was especially impressed by Greek theatre as the way in which in 5th century BC Athens battle veterans were folded back into Athenian society, and reintegrated into civilian life. (Carter, 2008) It was designed to offer a kind of psychic reintegration; a purging of violent emotions.

The point is that the Athenians took drama seriously. They rewarded authors they liked and punished others they didn't. An author could be fined if they found an interpretation too painful. And the theatre allowed the Greeks to interrogate themselves and their society through the refracting mirror of other places and times (the mythical past). It enabled them to 'recall' things they preferred to forget. On the stage everything was permitted. Actors spoke the unspeakable and represented the foreign. Attaining a certain psychological distance from events provided on occasion for a reflectiveness impossible in other public settings. (Euben, 2003, 32) The tragedies provoked strong emotional responses as well as negative emotions such as fear and pity which were released in the form of catharsis when the audience left the theatre, indelibly imprinting the message on their minds. According to Aristotle's analysis of tragedy, it is the message itself that creates the emotion and then reinforces it, and the same is also true of psychotherapy. Freud was drawn to the Greek myths for that reason.

The pain of trauma is an emotional experience before which words usually fail. As Ludwig Wittgenstein insisted, what can be said can be said clearly; whereof one cannot speak one must by default be silent. Given the immensity of the experience and the poverty of the vocabulary we have to describe it, the attempt to communicate the suffering of the traumatised soldier is rarely successful. Sophocles, however, comes near, indeed nearer than most to expanding the category of the 'sayable' by giving voice to the common but seldom articulated trajectory of post-traumatic stress. Sophocles himself was a general. Many of the actors would have served in the field, as would many members of the audience themselves. So it is not surprising that the tragedies have a certain appeal in military circles. Sophocles would have known about trauma at first hand even if he himself may never have experienced it. And Sophocles' characters are ones with which today's soldiers can relate, perhaps better than today's civilians.

Of the two plays the US military have adopted, the story of *Philoctetes* is the more powerful. The young man after whom the play is named was the only person who had the courage to light Heracles' funeral pyre as he lay dying (Heracles had asked to be burned alive so as to cut short an agonising death). In gratitude Heracles gave Philoctetes a magical bow whose arrows always reached their target. The bow made him a great warrior in the Trojan War, but it did not protect him from a serpent's bite. The bite festered, leaving him in perpetual agony. He personifies it as a beast 'in whose company he has been abandoned' by his former friends, 'a greedy animal that he has to feed'. Unable to endure either the stench of the wound or Philoctetes' cries of pain, his comrades, at the instigation of Odysseus, banish him to the island of Lemnos.

From the moment that Philoctetes is 'wounded' the play is an account of how he drags himself—just about—through the days and nights that follow. It does not make us admire the hero, nor are we meant to. He wallows in his solipsistic misery and yet somehow remains above it. He still retains our sympathy. He has imagination and a large heart. But he has become asocial. He has become 'the whole catastrophe', to borrow a striking phrase from *Zorba the Greek*. He has lost his trust in the world, as well as his faith in humanity. And it is the loss of trust that is one of the most tragic manifestations of traumatic illness:

Clearly there is no pharmacological panacea for the spectrum of psychological, biological, spiritual and existential injuries that can be sustained from combat or operational stress. No magic pill can erase the image of a best friend's shattered body or assuage the guilt from having traded duty with him that day. Medication cannot re-establish a person's trust in her mastery of her world, or restore her lost innocence. (Clayton, 2007, 219)

The serpent's bite is taken by the 'Warrior Theater' programme as a metaphor for Post-Traumatic Stress Disorder (PTSD), and this (mis)reading is not unproblematic. PTSD has quite a specific diagnostic meaning and there is no evidence that Sophocles was describing it in the play. Many bad things happen to men as a result of combat but they are not all PTSD, a particular problem of memory and arousal. Philoctetes is clearly distressed but great drama can be read in many ways including ones beyond the ken of the author; that is why we are still reading the Greek tragedies 2,000 years later, and what is striking about this particular play is that it is possible to read into it aspects of traumatic stress from our own privileged perspective.

The serpent, to begin with, is no ordinary serpent. It can be taken as symbolic of war itself, and the dire consequences that follow in its wake, not all of course leading to trauma. The wound is an affront to everything the heroes hold dear about war and themselves. They urgently need to remove Philoctetes so as to avoid confronting their own private demons, for his screams of pain echo the screams they would have heard every day on the battlefield.

An Athenian audience, many of whose members would have seen battle, might well have sympathised; many of them would have seen evils they would never forget. But at least they had not succumbed to them. In addition to his very real pain Philoctetes also has to endure another kind; the stigma of estrangement. He is stripped of his status as a hero and ultimately of his humanity, for in Greek thinking to be cast out and banished from the community was to be outlawed and stripped of everything that made one a *zoon politikon*. The hero's fate is a warning of the nothingness into which any human may descend if fate is against him. And the Greeks compound the hero's misery by not only expelling him but insisting that he deserved his fate. They cannot afford to acknowledge that any of them might suffer the same fate at any moment. That is why perhaps they have to put him out of sight and out of mind, and even strip him of his humanity to suppress their own fears that they too might already be damaged, but do not know it.

And then in the tenth year of the war, with the outcome still undecided but looking increasingly like a Greek defeat, Odysseus is ordered to accompany the young Neoptolemus, the son of Achilles, the greatest warrior of all, to the island to retrieve Heracles' bow. Without it, they have been told in a prophecy, they cannot hope to prevail. Odysseus and his young friend set out to Lemnos to wrestle the bow from Philoctetes by force, persuasion or craft. Naturally, Odysseus favours craft; it is in his nature. He tries to use cunning—what else does he have left? He is a calculating politician as well as a warrior. There has always been a crude utilitarian calculation in war which has appealed to the high command. Damaged minds and broken bodies may be regrettable, but what do they count when contemplating the greater good? It is this utilitarian philosophy which Odysseus embraces, and which made him even in the ancient world such a byword for cynical opportunism (notwithstanding his very real personal courage).

Neoptolemus, we must remember, is a mere boy; he is his father's son in name only. He is naturally in awe of Odysseus and wishes to impress him, but when he meets Philoctetes in person he immediately recognises in him an authentic, if flawed, hero. He sees him for what he is—a damaged human being, perhaps, a mere ghost of the great warrior he had once been, but a man, not a mere casualty of war: 'Is it just, or is it honourable', he asks Odysseus, 'to deceive a mortally wounded man?'.

Of course, the Greeks had no medical explanation for post-traumatic stress. Lacking such understanding they had to fall back upon character, the cornerstone of what was later to become Aristotelian virtue ethics. When Odysseus tells Philoctetes that his discomfort is affecting others, not merely himself, Neoptolemus—displaying a wisdom beyond his years—adds: 'everything is discomfort when someone acts out of character'. (902/4) When they finally leave the island, Neoptolemus remarks that 'a terrible compassion has fallen on me'. Aristotle calls compassion a painful emotion. (*Rhetoric*, 1305b, 13ff) Again, not having access to a neurological explanation, Aristotle could not locate our ability to feel pain in the body (mirror neurons). He attributed it instead to beliefs that fit the character concerned (that is, the victim has to be worthy of compassion, victim of a misfortune that he has not visited upon himself). Philoctetes does not deserve to suffer. And his comrades know in their hearts that they too may succumb one day to the same terrible 'lapse of character', which is perhaps why they have had to harden their hearts and expel him from their ranks. As Aristotle says, compassion involves those misfortunes which a person might expect to suffer himself. (*Rhetoric*, 1305b, 14–15) Mirror neurons spark only when we see events unfold every day. They do not spark when you read about them. And when they produce very real feelings of distress in ourselves, as observers we experience what Schopenhauer called 'pathological compassion'—a bodily reflex that 'arises from an instantaneous deception of the imagination [whereby] we put ourselves in the position of the sufferer and have the idea that we are suffering his pains in our person'. (Nussbaum, 2001, 327)

The Athenian audience would have known the main myths from Homer and the poets, and so when an author went 'off message'—when he gave a myth a novel spin, or particular twist (when he cast a traditional hero in a negative light or made a traditional villain a little more complex, and less villainous)—the audience would have picked this up immediately. At the end of the play Heracles makes an appearance and instructs Philoctetes to return the bow, and return with Odysseus to the war. But 'bear this in mind', he tells Odysseus and his young friend, 'When you lay waste the land [when you capture Troy] show piety. All else is less account in the sight of Zeus. Piety does not die with men; it does not perish whether they live or die'. (Morwood, 2008, 74)

The injunction may seem gratuitous, but Sophocles does not deal in idle remarks. He is reminding his audience that war is a savage business. Compassion can be fleeting, and war hardens men's hearts. The Trojan war will only end with the total destruction of the city. Even the qualities that make heroes what they are will evaporate quickly enough in the heat of battle. We do not know the fate of Philoctetes after Troy's fall, but we do know what happens to Neoptolemus. During the sack of the city he kills Priam, the old man whose life his father had spared when he visited his camp to recover Hector's body. And we know that Odysseus will spend ten years attempting to return home.

The main point that Warrior Theater is trying to communicate is that a soldier can only cure himself by facing his nightmares, not trying to escape them. In the play, Sophocles is particularly adept at drawing out the real ghosts which confront both Philoctetes and Odysseus: the comrade-less, abusive past that haunts both men. And Philoctetes does return to confront his comrades. The title of Seamus Heaney's adaptation of the play says it all, *The Cure of Troy* (2008). He cannot be cured in isolation. He can only be cured by returning home, by reintegrating himself in the community from which he has been banished, much as in the Great War the poet Siegfried Sassoon left the nursing home where he had been treated for post-traumatic stress and went back to the Front and his friends to honour his pact of friendship.

Losing oneself

'The biggest danger, that of losing oneself, can pass off in the world as quietly as if it were nothing; every other loss, an arm, a leg, $5, a wife, etc., is bound to be noticed'.

Soren Kierkegaard, *The Sickness Unto Death*, 1849, 62–3.

If you stop to think about it, there is extraordinary wisdom in Kierkegaard's words. A wounded soldier may lose an arm or a leg but still retain his sense of self. A traumatised soldier may lose the capacity to hold down a job, and lose his wife and family as a result, and in losing all of these he will be in grave danger of losing himself. This is why the phenomenon of trauma is so disturbing and why through therapy we try to reintegrate damaged minds, and even damaged souls.

But therapy takes a long time to work and Warrior Theater is for retired veterans, not men on active service. But what if we could deal with trauma by more radical measures still; what if one could pre-empt it or better still prevent its occurrence altogether by getting soldiers to pop a pill? Even today drugs are now the main way in which we deal with PTSD. Back in 2004, 80 per cent of all US patients suffering trauma received psychotropic medication; 89 per cent were given anti-depressants, 61 per cent anxiolytics, or sedative by-products, and 34 per cent anti-psychotics. (Kamienski, 2011, 12) All of these are designed to mentally sedate the patient, to suppress the bad memories that lead to sleeplessness and anxiety.

The problem is that the adrenalin rush which soldiers often experience when going into battle reinforces memory. It is the body's way of getting us to remember an event and to be better prepared for the next encounter. It is a natural defence mechanism. Adrenalin, scientists have found, when administered soon after a learning task reinforces the memory consolidation process, and the more significant an event, the more likely we are to remember it. As Arieh Shalev writes, traumatic events are traumatic for a reason. They are followed by a critical period of increased brain plasticity during which irreversible neuronal changes may occur in those who go on to develop traumatic stress disorders. (Shalev, 2007, 277) Simply put, the more the adrenalin, the stronger memories consolidate. As Roger Pitman argues, 'an excess of epinephrine release at the time of a psychologically traumatic event leads to overly strong emotional memory and fear conditioning that subsequently manifest themselves as PTSD symptoms'. (Pitman, 2002, 189)

So, one way of dealing with trauma is to switch off bad thoughts. Targeted memory erasure is the theme of Charlie Kauffman's film *The Eternal Sunshine of the Spotless Mind* (2004), which plays with the prospect of a neurotech company (Lacuna Inc) specialising in erasing painful memories by means of trans-cranial brain stimulation. The film taps into a contemporary phenomenon. The wish to lose painful memories is part and parcel of the other lifestyle choices we now make out of general dissatisfaction with the 'giftedness' of life—take botox injections, facelifts, and skin resurfacing, all readily available 'upgrades' or enhancements of the body. So why not erase painful memories if we could? In the film the science behind this is pretty minimal. 'Is there any risk of brain damage?' asks Joel who wants to erase the painful memory of a love affair which has gone sour; the answer is, 'Well, technically speaking the operation *is* brain damage, but it is on a par with a night of heavy drinking. Nothing you'll miss'. (Emphasis in original) Clementine, the heroine, opts for the procedure without giving it a further thought. 'Blessed are the forgetful, for they get the better even of their blunders'. (Nietzsche, *Beyond Good and Evil*) 'Found it in my Bartlett's', remarks one of her friends, somewhat archly.

For a popular film it is surprisingly scientifically savvy in treating memories as feelings. Traumatic memories of the kind soldiers re-experience over and over again are captured in two separate parts of the brain: the hippocampus (where memories centre) and the amygadala, one of the brain's emotional centres. In other words, memory is contained in both. Someone whose long-term memory is impaired by hippocampus damage may mistake someone he or she has met before for an apparent stranger, but may still 'feel' that he has met the man before, if the person concerned, for example, has harmed him in the past. Good memories are much harder to 'feel'. What we can do is re-write them. We used to think that once written they were stacked away on the shelf like a book in a library. It might be difficult to retrieve them; they might have been miscataloged and placed on the wrong shelf, but once on the shelf they would remain the same. We now know that once you access a memory, it can be re-scripted.

Memory is generally separated into four different stages: acquisition, consolidation, storage and retrieval, and specific molecules play a role in these various stages. In the case of experiments with transgenic mice, a research team in 2008 was able to manipulate the protein CaMKII (a calcium/calmodulin-dependent protein kinase 11 which plays a key role in brain cell communication). They soon found that what had made mice fearful in the past could be not only blocked, but erased ('US scientists perfect targeted memory erasure in mice', see http://afp.google.com/article/AleqM5jz18RUJtfJCgG44hosjxpbBrheknA) This phenomenon has been confirmed by other experiments with laboratory mice who are conditioned to fear certain objects or recall that they get fed when they perform certain actions. Every time they commit the procedure to memory, a protein synthesis is creating synaptic connections between two neurons, which is the associative link at the heart of all neuronal learning. If you block that synthesis, the mouse will forge a memory anew in a completely new associative context—that is, what before made it fearful may now make it happy. Could we do this for the human brain, too? In the case of mice, a drug called ZIP blocks the activity of a PKM# enzyme which plays a particular role in long-term memory formation. One dose and mice forget how to navigate their way through a maze. In theory, we could do the same to human beings, and we probably will.

Indeed, we are almost there. In 2008 Karim Nader, a neuroscientist at McGill University, discovered a process called 'memory reconsolidation'. Each time a memory, whether traumatic or not, is recalled it becomes vulnerable to change, depending on how we are feeling or what we are seeing at the time. And when we stop remembering the brain synthesises proteins to re-stabilise and restore the memory long-term. Research suggests that introducing Propranol before the memory has been stored into the brain can stop the production of the proteins that enable reconsolidation. The memory will then either fade or lose its emotional power. Normally, memories are simply put back into 'storage', but Propranol may disrupt the process. Factual elements of the memory would be retained but the negative emotions associated with it would be removed.

But as with all research on potentially personality-altering drugs, this too is fraught with problems. In the real world memories are not so easily erased; they often re-appear later. The trouble is that all the tests that have been conducted so far are largely inconclusive. The subjects of testing are tested only for a few days, not for months, let alone years. They are also given artificial fears—a favourite is electric shocks every time a subject is shown a picture of a spider. Once a subject is given the drug Propranol the shocks do not elicit the fear. But things may be very different if fears are not conditioned in a laboratory, but remain with one as the result of a real and very vivid experience—say, the experience of battle. A traumatised soldier may react every time he hears a loud noise that may conjure up in his mind the sounds of being under fire.

What makes the military so wary of prescribing drugs is their side-effects (and side-effects, as we know in our own lives, can be as bad as the original condition, or even worse) and they are particularly problematic for the military when they lower locomotive activity. They may well reduce anxiety levels, but they may also make us drowsy at the same time, and lessen our ability to focus on danger with the intensity it demands. They may also make us more reckless. Courage is not recklessness. As Aristotle tells us, it is doing the right thing in the right circumstances. Soldiers are trained to take risks, but only informed ones. But if you cannot forge a memory, how can you learn? You might forget the normal flight, or fear response. You might find yourself throwing yourself into battle without any thought of the consequences.

And then there is the third and perhaps greatest fear: moral pain. Dampen that, and you ask no questions or anything of yourself. You might find yourself acting in unexpected and disturbing ways without thought to the moral consequences. You might cease in the process to be a moral being, even though you may appear heroic to others.

All of this, as we shall see later, brings to mind Aldous Huxley's classic novel *Brave New World*. Not that in Huxley's world we meet any soldiers, for war has been abolished, together with everything else that gives us pain. And then there is the drug *soma*, an early and much more life-changing version of Prozac. Pop a pill and you are happier than ever. 'There is always *soma* to give you a holiday from the facts'. (Huxley, 1994, 217) Swallow two or three half gram tablets to remove anger, or the wish for revenge ('you can carry at least half your morality about in a bottle. Christianity without tears—that is what *soma* is'). One day we may be able to carry courage with us in a bottle, too and produce heroism without tears. It is the tears, of course, that are part of heroism: a hero has to confront his or her inner states of mind which cannot, as yet, be programmed out by scientists.

And there is the rub. For one result of eradicating a memory, however painful, is that we may be in danger of diminishing our own personhood. Indeed, the moral of Charlie Kaufman's film is that it is only through the process of loss that we discover what we had to begin with. In the wake of the psychopharmacological invasion of our day to day life, we might become 'neurochemical selves', beings who define our states of mind and emotions in terms of medical categories (such as the ratio of serotonin to dopamine transmitted in our brains). The Greeks called the human organism *physis*, nature, taking *bios* as its living expression. The spirit is the inside of the organism; it is the soul of all actions, the meaning of life itself. Were we to be rendered merely neurochemical selves, we would lead pretty soulless lives. We would forfeit any sense of responsibility for our actions. We might even cease to want to 'become' what we are. Steven Rosen puts it very well: when Francis Crick (the man who decoded DNA) said we were nothing but 'a bunch of neurons', he missed the whole point. We are a bunch of neurons, as well as other cells, but by virtue of possessing those neurons, we are agentive—we have the ability to change the world. (Rosen, 2005, 305)

DESIGNER WARRIORS

A conscience-less soldier?

In 1973 Tim O'Brien returned home from Vietnam and found what home-coming means for many soldiers. You add things up. You have lost a friend in battle and gained another in the field. You have learned that war is not all bad; it may not make a man, but it teaches you that manhood is not something to scoff at. Some stories of valour are true (though many are not). You have to pick the times not to be afraid, but when you are afraid, you must hide it. You realise that most men value their lives and try to stay alive. 'Anyone can die in a war if he tries' is his cynical observation. On his return, O'Brien took off his uniform and stuffed it into a suitcase, and put on a sweater and blue jeans. 'Much as you hate it, you do not have civilian shoes, but no-one will notice. It's impossible to go home barefoot'. (O'Brien, 2003, 203)

And that is the point of the story. No soldier returns barefoot, at least not metaphorically; he brings something of the army with him (his life is never the same again, and often he is not the same person who was seen off by family or friends). In the words of the most famous First World War poet, Wilfred Owen:

> Memory fingers in their hair of murders,
> Multitudinous murders they once witnessed…
> Always they must see these things and hear them,
> Batter of guns and shatter of flying muscles
> Carnage incomparable, and human squalor
> Rucked too thick for these men's extrication.

(Holden, 1998, 7)

PTSD is not the inevitable result of the things a soldier witnesses in battle; it is not the inevitable product of suffering, pain, violence or humili-ation. Many bad things, as O'Brien reminds his readers, happen to soldiers as a result of combat stress, and many of them may be affected by anti-androgenics but they are not all PTSD. But the military knows that when 'the multitudinous murders' become too many a soldier's capacity can be impaired; he may no longer be prepared to go the extra distance. Like Wil-fred Owen, he may even begin to question what the war is all about, though Owen never ceased to fight beside his friends and even went back to France in the closing days of the war, when he might have avoided it and lived on like Sassoon into old age.

It is tempting to suppress bad memories in the hope, perhaps, of producing 'cheerful robots'. Michael Sandel has written at length about the ethics of cognitive enhancement (the enhancement of memory) but he is also concerned about the suppression of memory, the possibility that memory-suppressing drugs might be administered to soldiers to dull the trauma that might otherwise plague them later in life. (Sandel, 2007, 15) This was the theme of Peter Marin's influential essay published in 1981. Marin revealed how difficult life becomes after experiencing war and its horrors, though one of the greatest difficulties of all is that civilians can never understand them, because they are most unlikely to suffer from anything as complex or extreme. For Marin:

The [Vietnam] veterans' situation is Oedipus' situation—not for the reasons Freud chose, but because it reveals to us the irreversibility of certain kinds of knowledge, the power of certain actions and perceptions to change an individual's life beyond any effort to change it back. Oedipus saw and was blinded, came close to the truth and lost the world of men, and once in exile he suffered not so much because of what he had done, but because of what he learned he had done: the terrible and tragic knowledge deprived him of the company both of men and of gods. (Marin, 1991, 46)

Remember that Oedipus came to power in Thebes because he alone was able to answer the Sphinx's riddle. The Sphinx asks, 'What creature alone among all who live on land or in the waters or in air has one single voice, one way of speaking, one nature yet goes on two feet, three feet and four feet—*dipous, tripous, tetrapous*'. The answer is Man. As an infant he moves on all fours; as a man he stands upright, and when he is old he leans on a cane to aid his uncertain, halting walk. Oedipus is fated to seek out the Sphinx; he is a man who interrogates life unrelentingly, quite unconcerned where his questions may lead; he is a man for whom the random adventure of thought is the adventure he craves most. But the same is true of a soldier. He goes off to war leaving everything behind; he risks all; he pledges himself to death. In combat he encounters himself and he will not always like what he encounters. He may prove unequal to the test, or overwhelmed, broken in spirit or body. Few of us are willing to interrogate ourselves as directly as this, or to confront the riddle of our own lives.

But then the answer to the Sphinx's riddle is so obvious that we may well ask why Oedipus was the only man to solve it. Oedipus, writes Anthony Burgess, is remarkable in retrospect, not for his wisdom in answering the riddle, but his courage in daring to come up with an answer. For as a member of the Chorus remarks, perhaps the riddle was not meant to be solved. We might well conclude that the punishment for not answering it (death) would have been better than the outcome (to kill one's own father and marry one's mother). (Sorensen, 2005, 3–5) As the Chorus remarks in Burgess' fine adaptation of Sophocles' drama, 'It's dangerous to answer riddles/but some men are born to answer them/it is the gods' doing. They hide themselves in riddles/we must not try to understand too much'. (Burgess, 72, 80)

Few of us (and fewer, perhaps, in the Western world than ever before) have the inclination to ask the question, or attempt to come up with an answer to the riddle of war. But we still rely on those who do it for us. The world is full of bad people—suicide bombers, terrorists, pirates, drug traffickers, religious zealots and ethno-nationalists who are only too willing to engage in ethnic cleansing. We still need those who are asked to delve deeply into the mysteries of the human heart, some of whom will be broken as a result. We ask people to plumb depths not meant to be plumbed, to answer questions not meant to be answered. And those questions—difficult enough at all times to ask—are much more difficult today when we feel deeply conflicted about killing, and when the US military can talk of giving medals for 'courageous restraint': when one can become a hero for not pressing a trigger.

No wonder many soldiers return home burdened with the memory of what they have witnessed, which will be not always result in nightmares—flashbacks of the past they have survived physically but not mentally. Many may return home with a bad conscience. But here too scientists have now found a possible way of easing the pain of guilt, and they have done so ironically as a result of experimenting with ways of enhancing memory. CREB is a molecule which is to be found in the nucleus of the brain cell, and its purpose is to switch on the genes needed to produce the proteins that facilitate permanent connections between the cells that forge long-term memories. (Slater, 2005, 215) But when scientists discovered how the brain produces long-term memories, they also discovered that is has mechanisms built with it that allow for forgetting. Essential to these is an enzyme called calcineurin. (Slater, 2005, 220) There is now already a drug in the works which could delete memory of trauma within twenty-four hours of suffering the first symptoms. Lauren Slater puts it poetically. Such a drug would effectively obliterate the diagnosis of Post-Traumatic Stress Disorder: 'Post Trauma would be a pill, a pharmacological capsule of water from the River

Lethe, where old souls in Hades go to erase their pasts'. (Slater, 2005, 221) And it is in Hades, we may recall, that Odysseus during his attempt to return home encounters Achilles once again, still resentful of his early death, still haunted by memories of the vital warrior he had once been but is no longer. For the Greeks Hades was not hell; it was certainly not a place of torment. It was a rather greying, twilight world in which men and women were mere shadows of their former selves. Odysseus finds that Achilles, so outraged by mortality in his lifetime, remains unappeased in the world of the dead. But he remains the hero he always was: he has chosen not to visit the river Lethe. Even if offered a pill, we may be fairly confident he would not take it. That, too, is part of his greatness of soul, one that the Greeks admired in him more than anything else.

For Achilles, war really was 'the human thing'. It defined his personality and gave him a reason for being. Even our most painful experiences teach us invaluable lessons; and the more extreme the experience the more important the lesson. Extreme experiences get us to re-evaluate our life goals, increase our self-reliance and aid our spiritual development. (Warnick, 2007, 37) Perhaps none of these were especially pronounced in Achilles (remember William James' interest in 'the integrity' of his pagan instincts, which rendered him to the modern eye less than a three dimensional figure), but even in Hades his zest for life is undiminished; he wants to remember what it was like to be alive. But what about us? After all, while Christians and Muslims still believe in the afterlife, very many of us in the West do not believe in it, only in this life, and go out of our way to avoid painful memories or moments. One of the most painful of all is to live with a bad conscience, but what if we could make ourselves much happier by blunting the pain of recalling our own actions where they threaten our self-esteem?

Conscience, of course, is embodied in our evolution. It is there for a reason—to promote our own fitness as a species. There are people who have none: we call them sociopaths, people who are irresponsible in their social decision-making, precisely because they put short-term satisfaction before long-term gain. Some lack cognitive empathy; they can understand another person's pain but not feel it. Others lack affective empathy; they can feel the pain but not understand it. The first live an entirely self-referential life and are incapable of making moral judgements. They are intelligent enough to know that there are moral laws; they just choose to ignore them. To be moral is to refuse to do something that has undesirable consequences not only for ourselves, but for others.

248

Our moral make-up is also very specific to our bodies. One could, argues Richard Joyce, go even further and claim that nothing can be said to have a moral sense unless it has an internalised emotional response. The reason why we have emotions wired into us is that they are adaptive mechanisms designed to aid memory in particular, so that we make the right decisions and carry them out. (Joyce, 2007, 101) And the choices we make define us as people. As Vilayanur Ramchandran adds, 'the sense of free will associated with the activity of these structures may be the proverbial carrot at the end of the stick that keeps goading the donkey in you into action'. (Ramachandram, 2003, 130) A monkey may grab a chocolate bar, but if we do the same we can also evaluate the consequences in terms of moral outcomes (what eating the chocolate bar is going to do to our diet, or whether we might be seen as being unconscionably greedy by those whose good opinion we crave, that of our friends). Disgust, guilt, shame and embarrassment are cultural too, which is why they have a history; we are disgusted by the violation of social taboos which differ significantly from culture to culture, and over time. But cultural instincts guide our moral conduct as internalised feelings. Disgust is more than just distaste. (Ramachandram, 2003, 96) Something tastes bad and we know instinctively it is bad for us: our brain warns us not to eat it. But something that tastes bad can also be un-harmful in itself; nevertheless, we may still feel contaminated or polluted by the thought of eating it.

We tend to feel guilt when we transgress a social taboo. Guilt is an emotion, but like every other emotion it is moulded by what we have been taught or brought up to believe. In the end, although anthropologists distinguish between shame and guilt cultures (seeing pre-Socratic Greece as the former, and post-Socratic Greece as the latter) the two emotions are actually inter-connected. We can feel both at the same time. Guilt happens to be more immediate; shame tends to creep up on us—the longer we get away with something, we fear eventually being found out and shamed. Guilt is a sense of transgression—we have failed to come through for others; it is not fear of punishment if we are found out. But as Freud was the first to recognise, the desire for punishment is a form of reparation. It is payback to the society that gives us our sense of self, for we are intensely social, not asocial creatures. To have a conscience is to give of yourself to others; to be conscience-less would be to cut oneself off from others, to live the life of a psychopath in a world without love.

And yet there is now great interest in finding ways to stem guilt and arrest bad thoughts generated by actions of our own making. Not everyone in the world of the military would be unhappy if Achilles did visit the river Lethe. The question is whether in real life one could bottle the waters and administer it to the troops. For what it is worth we are a long way from being able to do this. Even in the treatment of PTSD tests with Propranol show only limited evidence that the drug alleviates physiological response following a traumatic event. (Hogue, 2010) But we can be sure of one thing—the pharmaceutical companies, spurred on by military contracts, will continue looking for the magic bullet.

The destruction of the 'I'

> 'We possess nothing in the world ... but the power to say 'I'
> That is what we have to give God. In other words, to destroy.
> There is absolutely no other free-act which is given to us to accomplish—
> only the destruction of the 'I'".

Simone Weil, 1986, 79

Apparently, there is something of the vole in Man, and of Man in the vole. Prairie voles are among the few creatures on the planet that form monogamous relationships. Like us, they are intensely sociable creatures that prefer to mate for life and spend time with each other and their off-spring. All this is the result, scientists tell us, of two hormones called oxytocin and vasopessin which are released when they have sex. It is really no different from the conditioning which lab scientists go in for when they train mice or rats to navigate a maze, or press a particular lever in return for a reward. When prairie voles go to it they have their minds on each other for a reason; they just happen to have particular brains with receptors for the two hormones in those regions of the brain associated with reward and reinforcement. Montanes, another genus of voles, do not. They tend to follow the traditional animal pattern of mating with whoever comes along, and they do not form families. Sex, too, makes them feel good—that is part of all programming for the reproductive needs of the species. They experience a rush of dopamine in the reward centre of the brain, but contrary to prairie voles, they do not associate the feelings with any particular vole with whom they have mated.

We now know that sex stimulates the release of vasopessin and oxytocin in our brains, too. We too may be conditioned to love at certain times and to associate the pleasure we derive from sex with a particular partner. Unlike voles, however, we also experience intense feelings of love. Young adolescents get 'love-sick' (voles do not). Love-sickness has been celebrated for centuries; it was a theme of the famous *chansons de geste* and later the romantic poetry of the early 19th century, and it is very much central to today's teenage 'chick-lit'. And that too, we are told, has a neurological explanation. Two scientists at University College, London in 2001 found from brain scans of students who claimed to be madly in love with each other that the parts of the brain in which feeling could be identified included ones which generated euphoria on the back of other activities, including snorting cocaine. Love-intense adolescent cravings which blind the parties to everything else use the same neural mechanisms that are activated by other addictions.

None of this would be of much interest to the military but for the fact that it suggests that feelings and emotions can be manipulated. Scientists have managed to strengthen the relevant receptors in prairie voles (for some voles, like human beings, do cheat on their long-term partners from time to time), and they have even inserted the prairie vole receptor into mice who are notoriously promiscuous; they, too, over time have knuckled down and been 'domesticated'. What is more interesting is that they have even discovered that feelings derived from emotions like love have their own motivational system. Lust involves a very passionate sexual state which induces traceable chemical changes including increases in levels of serotonin and oxytocin which make love euphoric, immediate and deeply satisfying. The state of falling in love or being in love seems to share certain neurological characteristics with a manic-depressive state or Obsessive-Compulsive Disorder (OCD). Certainly the parties involved tend to obsess about each other, and often are blind to each other's faults (which are often clearly discernible to other people, even their friends).

The third form of love, parental bonding and friendships associated with partners who go through life's journey together, is much less manic, and probably much less open to manipulation. Obsessive love, after all, if it resembles OCD, might be treated by some drugs, at least in the early stage. It is doubtful whether this would apply to a more stable and long-lasting relationship.

All of which tends to miss the point that all three states of love are not mutually exclusive. A happily married woman can lust after another, usually younger, man. A faithful spouse can establish a long term liaison with a mistress or girlfriend with whom he is in love, but whom he would never consider to be a suitable life-term partner. It is the instability of our emotional states that makes us interesting and uniquely human—our ability to fall in and out of love, to remain friendly with ex-spouses, to share the parenting of children despite divorce, to go from adulterous liaisons, even in the most stable marriages (adultery is the stuff of literature—imagine the 19th-century European novel or the 21st-century soap, or for that matter Greek myths, without it as their primary theme).

The cultural construction of our most basic emotions is discussed in a book by Helen Fisher, *Why We Love: The Nature and Chemistry of Romantic Love*. Fisher carried out exhaustive behavioural research into the effects of two crucial chemicals—dopamine and norepinephrine, both of which quite literally 'fuel' such feelings as passion, jealousy and joy. And of the two chemicals, dopamine holds centre stage in her study. It explains the 'high' of manic love (rapture) and the 'low' of rejection. In the case of the first, dopamine levels rise significantly; in the case of the second, they fall dramatically. Her research, she is the first to admit, is highly speculative. It is just one of several hypotheses under discussion in the scientific community, but it carries conviction, and it has won general acclaim.

Most of us think of love as a feeling, but Fisher sees it as a drive that can render even the most heroic figure a fool, or drive him into reckless passion like Achilles' anger at the death of his friend Patroclus, which is evidence of his driven nature—the 'madness' that seizes him was something which Homer could describe but not explain away scientifically. He could appreciate that it was not adaptive, but dangerous (if very human). Only we, it would seem, are so pained by the death of a loved one that we would put our own lives at risk to avenge their memory, but then vengeance as we have seen is a human construct. The problem is that of many such reductionist works: sexual feelings and romantic love are not necessarily the same, and to think of Hector's love for his wife as 'romantic love' is to make nonsense of historical accounts that identify romantic love as a recent phenomenon, one less than 700 years old.

The problem with Fisher's approach is that she ignores the complexity of cultural selection; she traces romantic love back thousands of years before most historians recognise its appearance. And because romantic love is so deeply entrenched in our own perspective on the world, we tend to find it wherever we are looking for it, whether in the *Iliad* or *The Song of Solomon*. It is when we get beyond sexual attraction to bonding with the same partner in particular that culture kicks in. It determines the 'ideal' of partnership, and the 'ideal' of the partners we are selecting. It may involve mimicking behaviour we have observed on the screen, and trying to reprise it in socially appropriate forms. Our ideals will be influenced by many factors other than sex or sexual reproduction, such as social status or aesthetics. And it is quite extraordinary how we fall out of love so quickly when the balance shifts against us and how few—in reality—break out of their social constraints and marry 'unsuitable' partners. To fall out of love is not that difficult if we put our minds to it. Even forlorn lovers who are separated by force do not die of love denial. They may feel depressed for a time, but they usually recover. Life is not a grey pastiche of *Wuthering Heights*.

As Fisher herself remarks, states of love vary enormously. Some lovers are more blind than are others to the faults of those they love; some are less jealous of different things including their own reputation. Some are more forgiving if those they love choose to err; others are more obsessive or pathological in focusing on their own obscure, or not so obscure object of desire. Not all unrequited love leads to depression (it can produce a wry sense of humour). It is one thing to recognise how we feel, quite another to understand how that clouds our judgement, or influences our thinking. Love is the most difficult of concepts to pin down. To believe in love is not necessarily to be in love with the idea of being in love (which was common among the Romantic poets, and is still one of the central storylines of Hollywood films even in these aggressively unromantic times). Indeed, adolescent love is highly ideational; for many it is like watching a romantic film. And yet sexually active teenagers go in for casual sex which involves little that convention would call 'romantic'; they sleep with partners for pleasure, not because they have projected an emotion onto the person concerned. You do not need to even like a person to sleep with them. The attraction can be purely sexual and ephemeral, the classic one-night stand.

Neuroscientists are far too reductive in the conclusions they draw, especially in their eagerness to debunk the idea of free will. The fact is that we are free to choose our partners for life, or to remain single or remain promiscuous. And the choices do not end there. We can choose to live an intense platonic relationship (memorably depicted by Rostand in his play, *Cyrano de Bergerac*), or we can remain celibate even within marriage, or we can form lasting relationships that include a wife and mistress at the same time. There is wonderful French term, the *mauvais quart d'heure*, to denote the emotionally challenging fifteen minutes in which you tell your mistress of many years' standing that you are finally leaving her. If the English have no such expression it is because their experience is culturally different.

Although we have a natural constitution that we can scan scientifically, we also have a cultural constitution, too. We are the only species that is able to make a choice. Some prefer serial infidelity, others mate for life. No other animal is able to pick and mix as we do. We may be serially promiscuous one moment and celibate the next, like the renowned composer Franz Liszt. We may marry a childhood sweetheart and remain faithful to the relationship for ever. The biological constitution which we are given is no obstacle to making choices. It is so formed that it actually forces us to choose (in Sartre's famous words, we are all condemned to be free).

What is free will? There is a passage in Rousseau's *Declaration on the Origin of Inequality* (1755) which I would like to quote:

I see in every animal merely an ingenious machine to which nature has given senses to keep it going by itself and to protect itself up to a certain point, from everything likely to distress or annihilate it. I see precisely the same thing in the human machine with the difference that nature alone brings everything to the activities of a beast, whereas man contributes to his own, in his capacity as a free agent. The beast chooses or rejects by instinct, meaning that it cannot deviate from the rules prescribed for it, even when it might benefit from doing so, whereas man often deviates from such laws to his own detriment. (Ferry, 2010, 106–7)

What Rousseau was saying is that free will is hard-wired into us. We are the animal that makes choices, including bad ones, like falling in love with the wrong person, or putting at risk a perfect marriage for a passing moment of sexual pleasure. We do not think of animals as machines any longer, for they too have a complex set of emotions and feelings. An animal that experiences pain will be able to experience pleasure as well. Some animals derive great pleasure from playing with each other, such as dolphins and apes, others can even bond with us (through millennia of breeding, dogs have a basic emotional intelligence—they can read us far better than we can read them). Dogs are particularly adept at 'reading' human expressions and picking up human moods. They know when to be submissive and when to be assertive. We interact with each other in subtle ways. Wolves, by comparison, from whom dogs trace their descent, cannot read us at all, but then they have not networked with us through the millennia.

What makes humans the intractable species they are, wrote Rousseau, is that other animals' instincts usually work to their advantage; this is not always the case with us. We frequently succumb to instincts that predispose us to make bad choices. An example of one is that some of us are in danger of becoming obese. And only we get drunk because alcohol can dull the pain of being a man (as Dr Johnson retorted when a woman reproached him for drinking to excess). We even make a style out of our excesses (Humphrey Bogart: 'I do not drink too much. The rest of the world is three drinks behind me'). But style can be fatal, as it was in Bogart's case.

But the same 'free agency" as Rousseau called it, that allows us to excess also allows us to exercise imagination. We can spare our enemies in the way a lion would never spare its prey. We must recall what Rousseau was writing about: it was not the difference between humans and all other animals, but human inequality. It is, he maintains, the very fact that we are not condemned to the life in which we are born that makes equality possible. To be born poor does not mean you are condemned to die in poverty. You may become very wealthy indeed if you have a talent for making money. To be born a woman does not condemn you to motherhood; a woman can choose to marry but not have children, or even to forgo sex altogether. All other animals are programmed to act to obey their natural instincts; we are not. And as we have evolved culturally our choices have grown more complex. Lions have not changed since they first preyed upon us back in the African savanna, but we are very different from our ancestors who once lived there. Above all, we have a very unusual inclination to sacrifice ourselves for others beyond the immediate family group, or for our artificial families—or, in the case of the military, for a particular fraternity, Shakespeare's 'band of brothers'.

And it is a very remarkable form of love because it is almost entirely a cultural construction. Here is one witness to it, a soldier who served in the Pacific theatre in some of the most brutal campaigns of World War II: 'War is brutish, inglorious and a terrible waste. ... The only redeeming factors were my comrades' incredible bravery and their devotion to each other'. (Ellis, 1993, 369) And here is another American voice, that of a soldier who was wounded at Okinawa but discharged himself from hospital as soon as he could to return to his unit: 'It was an act of love. Those men on the line were my family, my home. They were closer to me than I can say, closer than any friends had been or ever would be'. (Ellis, 1993, 369)

Courage is a form of love, writes Sebastian Junger. When you find yourself under fire all you have is each other. You cannot rely on rear echelon officers behind the lines, or the public at home who are often fickle. You cannot even rely on your own training. You rely on each other. And he adds, the:

shared commitment to safeguard one another's lives is un-negotiable and only deepens with time. The willingness to die for another person is a form of love that even religion fails to inspire, and the experience of it can change a person profoundly. What the army sociologists … slowly came to understand was that courage *was* love. In war, neither could exist without the other, and in a sense, they were just different ways of saying the same thing'. (Junger, 2010, 242) (emphasis in original)

In *Leviathan* Thomas Hobbes writes of 'the privilege of absurdity to which no living creature is subject, but man only', the human predisposition to put life at risk for others, especially in war. Hobbes did not disparage war as such—he recognised it as human, all too human—but he did disparage sacrifice (as did Jeremy Bentham over one hundred years later). Sacrifice is not unique to human beings, of course. But war is, and sacrifice in war is distinctly human. What makes us distinctive as a species is not our tendency to band together in groups or the willingness to kill those outside the primary group. What makes us different is the 'privilege of absurdity'—the unique practice of sacrificing ourselves for others who are not related to us by family or kin, those with whom we identify, often intensely, simply because they are members of the same group.

The rare privilege of absurdity

The very earliest inscription on a monument to the 'Fallen' in battle to have survived was published only very recently, in the summer of 2010. It commemorates the Athenians who fell at the battle of Marathon, and it is 2,500 years old:

ERECHTHEIS

Fame, as it reaches the furthest limits of the
… sunlit earth
Shall learn the valour of these men; how
they died
In battle with the Medes, and how they
garlanded Athens
the few who undertook the war of many
Drakontides
Antiphon
Aphsephes
Xenon
Glaukiades

The survival of the Marathon casualty list is due entirely to the historical interests of an Athenian millionaire, Herodes Atticus, who lived in the 2nd century AD, and was a tutor to the Emperor Marcus Aurelius. He had the monument installed in his country house in the eastern Peloponnese. What is striking about the inscription is that it is a 'first'—the first to enumerate the death of perfectly ordinary men, some aristocrats, others artisans or peasant farmers, who died that day side by side fighting a common enemy. We are so used to such inscriptions from the lists of the Fallen which commemorate the sacrifice of millions of soldiers in the two world wars that it is easy to miss the novelty of this approach. The Athenians thought it worth recording the deaths of the lowliest as well as the highest; it was a celebration of sacrifice by the strong for the weak, the poor for the rich—by men equal in the eyes of the enemy, and equal in their own eyes in battle despite being very unequal in status and wealth back at home. And in this case the word 'few' really does mean 'few'. No-one knows how many Persians (Medes) died at Marathon, but we do know how many Athenians—only 192, but they made a difference. Marathon was truly one of the decisive battles of history and the Greco-Persian wars changed its course decisively. (Thonemann, 2011, 10)

The Greek author Plutarch recounts how the poet Isocrates once said that those who had faced death at the battle of Marathon had fought as if their lives did not belong to them but their friends. Sacrifice is the supreme gift, a recognition that life is not just our own. And yet here—wrote Plutarch—was Isocrates now, aged 90, frightened of death, regarding his passing, as he was the first to confess, as the greatest of evils. Plutarch presents us with a portrait of a man who clearly had lived too long: 'For he had not grown old honing a sword, sharpening a spearhead, burnishing a helmet or playing a part in the army or the navy, but stringing together and composing antitheses, clauses, balanced in length, words whose endings in rhyme and almost polishing and shaping his clauses with chisels and files'. (Plutarch, 1992, 165)

Plutarch's point is that to serve one's country is the highest good, and to die for it the ultimate sacrifice. But his argument is not informed by the crude *pro patria mori* mentality that led millions to their death on the Western Front. Instead, he insists that sacrifice through the centuries has inspired great writers and artists. To be inspired by the sacrifice of others is to live more intensely ourselves. To be awed, or moved, by sacrifice is to celebrate our own humanity. It allows us to respect ourselves more (and occasionally to see ourselves in the person of our heroes). And the poet, in turn, will go on to inspire others through his rendition. It is the vivid images that get into our head which move us. Posidonius, the Stoic philosopher of the 1ˢᵗ century BC, called an image of this kind an *anazographesis*, or a mental picture, and stressed its importance in influencing our actions.

For the Western world, the iconic sacrifice will always be that of King Leonidas and his 300 (or to be precise, 299) Spartans holding the pass at Thermopylae against the Persians. Many readers will know the battle from Zach Snyder's film *300*. The film was panned when it came out by the critics, and it offended many scholars who thought it bordered on the kitsch. The Greek government feared that its homoerotic content might mislead the audience into thinking Sparta was the gay superpower of the age; the Iranian government, no less irked by the depiction of the Persians, lodged a formal complaint with UNESCO complaining that their forefathers had been depicted as a bunch of off-the-shelf grotesques led by a sexually ambivalent Xerxes. But when it came out the film was a great box office earner for the studio. The general public identified with Leonidas and his men, and they were sometimes more in step with reality than the critics, writes Victor Davis Hanson who was invited to write an introduction to the official book that accompanied the film. He is also quick to remind us that some of the corniest lines in the movie were actually spoken by the historical protagonists, or so Herodotus and Plutarch would have us believe. 'Come and take them', the Spartans respond when ordered to lay down their weapons; 'Then we will fight in the shade' is their response to the threat that the sun will be obscured by Persian arrows. Perhaps, concedes Hanson, this may be poetic license, but if so blame it not on the screenplay writers but on the ancient historians. (Hanson, 2011, 53)

Of course, the Spartans had a different concept of life from ours. Theirs was a warrior society whose young men were expected to die young. What was important was how one disported oneself on the battlefield. Spartan mothers really did demand of their husbands and sons that they return home either on their shields (borne aloft as heroes), or with them (so that they might fight another day). Spartan honour required them to place their lives at the service of their community. But are ethnographers right to claim cultural incommensurability, to insist in other words that cultures do not travel, that tribal norms are untranslatable into any language that we ourselves can ever hope to understand? The popularity of Herodotus' tale across the centuries would suggest quite the opposite. Sacrifice is readily translatable into the language of any age; it is also what we seem to consider among the most admirable attributes of our species.

And is there a biological explanation for this? Darwin's research on evolution demonstrates that natural selection favours social animals including humans who, as we have seen, have by far the strongest social instincts. Frans De Waal, a 21st-century disciple of Darwin, writes that 'the profound irony is that our noblest achievement—morality—has evolutionary ties to our basest behaviour—warfare. The sense of community required by the former was provided by the latter'. (De Waal, 2009, 858) Darwin himself was fully aware that selflessness was the key to social success, which is why it is admired in all cultures. He was also aware that natural selection could not explain the willingness of a few brave men to sacrifice themselves for others, to go beyond the call of duty, to ask more of each other than others asked of them. 'The bravest, most sacrificial people', he wrote in *The Descent of Man*, 'would on average perish in larger number than other men'. A noble man would often leave no offspring to inherit his noble nature. It seemed impossible, he added, that 'virtue could be increased through natural selection, that is by survival of the fittest'. If evolution really is the struggle to survive, then there can be no place for altruism or nobility.

Yet altruism has always been admired. Those who make sacrifices for others may lose their lives, but they win in return universal esteem:

A tribe including many members who, from possessing in a high degree, a spirit of patriotism, fidelity, obedience, courage and sympathy, were always ready to give aid to each other and to sacrifice themselves for the common good, would be victorious over most other tribes, and this would be natural selection. (Sacks 2009, 96)

How to get from the individual to the group was 'at present much too difficult to be solved'. Darwin solved the paradox, at least to his own satisfaction, by admitting that if natural selection works at the level of individuals genetically (we do indeed struggle to pass on our genes) society works at the level of the collective. The challenge, in other words, is to turn selfish genes into selfless people. The challenge is met in culture.

What Darwin was describing is the survival of the social:

'Individuals who took the greatest pleasure in society would escape various dangers, while those that cared least for their comrades and lived solitarily would perish in greater numbers'.

But social animals survive in larger groups whilst solitary animals, even assuming that they might survive just as well, tend to survive in smaller numbers. And over time social animals have come to outnumber the solitary ones in the gene pool purely by virtue of the law of natural selection:

An instinctive impulse if it be in any way more beneficial to a species ... would be rendered the more potent of the two through natural selection, for the individuals which had [social instincts] most strongly developed would survive in larger numbers ... the social instincts, which must have been acquired by man in a very rude state ... still give impulse to some of his best actions'. (Darwin, 1985, 13)

Evolutionary psychologists will not admit to any explanation except evolutionary ones in accounting for human practices such as war. Yet they have particular difficulty in explaining the seemingly non-Darwinian human characteristics which are universal (sacrifice most of all which is to be found in every time and every culture). They try to get round this by hypothesising kin-selection based on a concept called 'inclusive fitness' (the ability to pass on one's genes from one generation to the next) and they argue this can be accomplished through close relatives such as cousins, and not merely through the direct line (through children). Thus to sacrifice oneself for one's kin is one way of proving one's fitness. As Steven Rose writes, thus apparently disinterested behaviour in reality is only a way of enhancing genetic success either directly, by increasing our social posterity and hence reproductive attractiveness to sexual partners, or indirectly, by improving the life chances of those to whom we are generally related. (Rose, 2006, 98)

The Greeks too were tentatively aware of this biological explanation. In some Greek societies armies were organised by tribes; sometimes grandfather, father and son might all fight within sight of one another. In the heat of battle, soldiers would fight, quite literally, to protect each other's kin. In time, as city states developed and the concept of citizenship evolved, *philia* (love) extended to the citizen body. Aristotle tells us in the *Politics* that citizenship was most likely to motivate unit cohesion. The Spartans are an interesting case of a society that chose to anchor itself to a more distant past by socialising familial and tribal bonds. They did this by making the city quite literally into an extended family at the expense of the actual nuclear family. Boys were removed from parents at the age of seven. They ate meals together and slept in dormitories, so that they would learn to put the public good before that of their families.

So Leonidas' band of brothers, even for the Greek world, was the product of a rare social experiment. Quite literally, one could say that altruism, or the spirit of sacrifice, was biologically grounded in Sparta. Elsewhere in the Greek world *philia* was transformed in the course of time into *eros*—the erotic love of country and the military unit; it is a particularly vivid example of cultural selection at work. Because love of the family was neutralised, the city produced a male collective. As Paul Ludwig writes, *eros* in the Greek original (compared with its English rendition) can refer beyond the human—to love of learning, for example, or even more strongly lust for learning, or lust for civic consciousness. (Ludwig, 2007, 213)

And not to display this love could be fatal. Take the two Spartan soldiers who missed the battle of Thermopylae, for 301 men should have been guarding the pass. One was Pantites, who was away from battle on a diplomatic mission; he is said to have hanged himself on his return home because he felt dishonoured. In a shame culture, dishonour is triggered by the thought: 'I am a bad person'. In a guilt culture it is induced by the thought, 'I committed a bad action'. It is very difficult to redeem past failures with regard to the former but far easier in the case of the latter, and there is something else which is different. Shame induces a tendency to hide or disappear precisely because it is beyond redemption. Guilt tends to get us to confess, or make reparations; to confess our misdeeds can even be seen as heroic.

The other, more famous figure was Aristodemus, who was considered to have dishonoured himself twice—first, by loitering with intent out of either cowardice or insufficient zeal and thus missing the battle, then when he tried to redeem himself in the eyes of his fellow countrymen in the last major engagement of the war, Plataea (479 BC). Ostracised by the community and dismissed as 'the trembler' (*tresas*), he attempted to redeem his reputation by breaking ranks and charging into the enemy, deliberately seeking death. The Spartans, unbending as ever, still refused to honour him for he had broken ranks and disobeyed the order to stand firm. He had gone berserk. As Max Weber wrote, the Spartans did not hold in high regard a soldier who had chosen to fall in battle in order to redeem an earlier failure. They prized the whole character which 'in the Spartan example, would be an habitual temper of heroism'. They knew that Aristodemus did not display it.

In normative terms the Spartan concept of sacrifice was most certainly different from our own. But this is beside the point. It survives in the collective memory because it can be readily translated into the language of any age. Herodotus was not a Spartan; he was from a much more cosmopolitan society, Halicarnassus, and came from a quite different cultural tradition. He recognised bravery when he saw it and he thought Aristodemus had been a brave man, and says as much in his *History*. He recorded his name as he did the names of the Persians whom he thought worthy of mention for their bravery; he saw him as a hero, not someone who had gone berserk. It is true, too, that Pericles too contrasted Athenian bravery with Spartan in terms we also understand—the Athenians decided voluntarily to be patriotic, the Spartans were socially conditioned. But we still understand well enough what the Spartans did at Thermopylae; they translated a tactical disaster into a moral victory. There is no irony, writes Paul Cartlege, when the novelist William Golding wrote after visiting the battlefield that 'a little of Leonidas lives in the fact that I can go where I like and write what I like. He contributed to set us free'. (Cartledge, 2006, 213)

What still redeems war in the eyes of the public is the love that is manifest in sacrifice, and what makes sacrifice so important culturally is that it is sacramental. Behind the meaning of sacrifice—the consecration of life for one's friends—there is a religious element. As an ideal sacrifice has connected the idea of war with the impulse to endow human life with more than worldly significance. This is not to say Westerners are willing these days to die for God, though others elsewhere in the world are still willing to consecrate their life to an intelligent designer ('We owe God a death', Henry V reminds his men in what was an intensely religious age). It *is* to say that in many cultures war has drawn upon and amplified the experience of what forms the bedrock of religion, and in so doing, has offered a secular vindication of a sacred view of life. The basic idea in religion is that human life possesses a value that cannot be translated into purely temporal terms. Life continues after death, and so it does in war, for Achilles and Hector who fight in measureless memory still.

In the presence of sacrifice as opposed to a mere death we often find ourselves in the presence of something vastly more significant than our present interests and desires. Every soldier who is killed by an IED, or falls victim to a sniper, is worthy of respect, and we honour him as a hero. To sacrifice one's life actively, and quite deliberately, is however to go beyond the call of duty. What makes it sacred is that it is a gift, it consecrates friendship. It is a vindication of faith not in God but in our own humanity.

There is no more moving testament to this than the remarkable account by an American writer, Sebastian Junger, who was embedded for the best part of a year with the Second Platoon Battle Company, the Rock Battalion, 503rd Infantry Regiment, 173 Airborne Brigade Combat Team, and witnessed at first hand the kind of war on the ground that had become increasingly rare for the majority of American soldiers, but which would have been familiar to Alexander's soldiers fighting in the same area of Afghanistan. Cut off from the rest of the country in a hilltop razor-wired enclosure in the Korangol valley, a rift a few miles' donkey-ride from the Pakistan border, the unit found itself in a literal hellhole where temperatures were unbearably hot during the day and almost sub-arctic at night. Here, adds Junger, was fought a raw, primal struggle of the kind that we can read about in the pages of Homer.

And here what kept men sane, and the unit together, was their common humanity. The world, wrote Hannah Arendt, is not humane because it is made by human beings. And it does not become humane just because the human voice sounds in it. Humaneness is achieved in the discourse of friendship, or what the Greeks called *philanthropia*: 'love of man since it manifests itself in a readiness to share the world with other men'. And such love is made manifest in shared combat—what Junger rightly calls its 'religious element'. (Junger, 2010, 239) The willingness to die for another person is a form of love that even religion fails to inspire. Junger quotes Glenn Gray, the author of one of the oldest and most insightful studies of warrior culture: 'The coward's fear of death stems in large part from his incapacity to love anything but his own body. The inability to participate in others' lives stands in the way of his developing any inner resources sufficient to overcome the terror of death'. (Junger, 2010, 191)

There are different kinds of strength, reflects Junger, and overcoming the terror of death may be the most profound, the one without which armies could not function, and wars could not be fought. The containment of fear is key to successful combat. It is what makes a professional soldier, and what—when circumstances deteriorate—distinguishes the warrior from an ordinary soldier. And it is the front line 'grunts', whom Junger clearly came to admire, who have the most to fear. The excerpt is worth repeating:

… They are real soldiers, the only ones conducting what can be considered war' in the most classical sense and everyone knows it. I once asked someone in Second Platoon why front line grunts aren't much admired.

'Because everyone thinks we're stupid', the man said.

'But you do all the fighting'.

'Yeh', he said. 'Exactly'. (Junger, 2010, 226)

The members of Second Platoon were certainly fearful. What made them special was their ability to master it. At the heart of Junger's book is Lord Moran's distinction between cowardice and fear. Everyone will experience fear but the veterans will not show it, and they will not allow it to influence or direct their actions. 'By cowardice, I do not mean fear', Moran wrote in *The Anatomy of Courage*:

Fear is the response of the instinct of self-preservation to danger. It is only morbid, as Aristotle taught, when it is out of proportion to the degree of danger. Invincible fear (fear stronger than I am) the soldier has to struggle with a flood of emotion. He is made that way. Fear, even when morbid, is not cowardice. That is a label we reserve for something a man does. What passes through his mind is his own affair. (Junger, 2010, 3)

It is what passes through soldiers' minds, however, that is increasingly of interest to many in the military. The idea of a gift—the sacrifice soldiers are willing to make *in extremis*, the determination to overcome fear and stand firm with one's friends—is as old as war itself, but it has less appeal than it did in an age when we think we can upgrade the gifts with which we are born.

Engineering in courage

Extraordinary bravery requires extraordinary risk taking. It is not a passive act of fighting back, but the positive act of putting oneself in a position where one is very likely to be killed. To go 'beyond the call of duty' is what the military calls it, and it is a revealing term. Some soldiers are naturally fearless; they will always pick a fight in a bar if they feel that their honour is on the line. Others discover, in the heat of battle, wells of courage which they themselves never knew they possessed. In both cases they need a trigger to release them. Battle, in that sense, is quite literally cathartic. And then there are those who are trained, or conditioned. The army becomes a home; the unit a family. They will experience levels of friendship they have never experienced back at home. To throw oneself on a grenade for them is a personal gift, and as such cannot be patrolled or policed. A soldier cannot be court martialled for not doing so.

No one can be drilled into extraordinary acts of bravery (any more, so we are told, than a subject can be hypnotised to carry out an act, such as murder, if it is not in his or her nature). Extraordinary courage is one of the great dimensions of military life that has escaped instrumentalisation. It remains beyond all but scientific explanation, and therefore—for the non-scientist—retains its mystique.

So, why have so few Medal of Honor awards been conferred in recent years? Some time ago, the *New York Times* ran a story about a long-standing debate about bravery in the American armed forces. Acts of heroism are so many that the highest award that the US has to offer—the Medal of Honor—has been awarded sparingly since 9/11. Since the War on Terror was declared, only six have been awarded (at the time of writing, in 2010). The medal is cherished in the military because it rewards extraordinary acts of bravery that go 'beyond the call of duty' and involve great risk to life. By contrast, 464 Medals of Honor were awarded for service during World War II, and no less than 246 during the Vietnam War. From a larger historical perspective, the paucity of awards since 2001 is even more striking. Between 1917 and 2001 the number of recipients per 100,000 averaged between 2.3 (Korean War) and 2.9 (World War II), but since the terrorists struck New York and Washington they have averaged 0.1 per cent (or 1 in 1,000,000). (Zoepf, 2010)

There are hundreds of acts of private bravery in war, a great many of which, of course, never get reported. But are there fewer opportunities for bravery on today's battlefields? In a war among the peoples, is not the overwhelming need to avoid collateral damage, to engage in what the American military in Afghanistan calls 'courageous restraint'. Does the military now take courage for granted in an all-volunteer force? Or has it raised the bar? It seems unlikely. Intensely image conscious, the military tries its best to avoid accusations of being deceived by the testimonials of soldiers. It has made the whole process of receiving an award more difficult than previously. The Medal of Honor, like many others, is awarded for what the recipients nominated were seen to have done. In the past, eye witness testimony was enough, but today, the US military is particularly careful to validate eye witness accounts, ever mindful of its embarrassments in the past, when it tended to promote figures who, even by its own lights, were not particularly heroic. One person who comes to mind is Jessica Lynch, a media heroine of the hour who was captured by Iraqi soldiers after being ambushed on a road. Suffering a broken arm, a broken thigh and a dislocated ankle, she was hospitalised and later rescued by a special squad. In fairness, Lynch never claimed to be heroic; she had not chosen to place herself in harm's way for some greater purpose, an act which used to distinguish the true hero from the rest of us. Yet she soon became a media sensation. *Saving Jessica Lynch* became a television film, produced to order by a former assistant to Ridley Scott who had directed the film *Black Hawk Down*. Later, in testifying to Congress, she complained she had been falsely portrayed as 'a little girl Rambo from the hills'.

Rambo is an interesting figure in his own right. Ever popular with the grunts, he is undoubtedly a warrior. He is extraordinarily violent but he is clearly not a psychopath. He is a psychologically damaged man whose attachment to life requires a strange form of aversion therapy, unadulterated violence. Fifty years ago, Rambo would simply not have been an authentic American hero. Back in 1961 40 per cent of those who joined the US Marines claimed they had been inspired to do so by the great hero of the day, John Wayne, for his role in films like *The Sands of Iwo Jima*. (van Creveld, 2008, 314) Different times, different heroes.

The Greeks had their Rambos too—the heroes of Homer's epic. And what they all share is an unusual degree of courage, which the Greeks understood to be the property of lions. Diomedes' destructive violence is compared to that of a lion breaking the neck of a bull calf, or of a grazing heifer. The mere sight of Hector like 'a fine-maned lion' is enough to terrify the Danaans. And Patroclus, though destined for an early death, fights at the end with 'the force of a lion which in attacking a farmstead is wounded in the chest and is undone by its own strength'. (Sassi, 1988, 36) But the point about a lion is that it is brave by nature. So are some men; courage is gifted them by nature, but even the bravest warrior can fail the test. And human behaviour is complex; even a brave man has to know when to cut and run when the odds turn against him. In one episode the great Ajax, second only to Achilles in bravery, is forced to flee the battlefield but obstinately insists on turning round to taunt his pursuers. Homer uses two animal images to capture the scene—the noble one of a defeated lion, and the comic one of a stubborn mule that can barely be pushed out of a field.

But what if courage could be pre-programmed? What if we could produce Rambos to order; what if we could despatch an army of killing machines who were utterly fearless, because deficient in imagination, all potential Medal of Honor winners because they were all willing to engage in unthinking, near-suicidal acts? What if we could programme soldiers to go the extra distance, whether it was in their nature to do so or not?

Courage for the Greeks was not only a physical attribute but a quality of mind—the dictionary definition is that courage enables us to face a difficulty or danger without fear. There are lots of people who are asked to display courage: crusading journalists who 'speak truth to power'; ordinary men and women who speak out, or have the moral courage to bear witness. For some courage becomes habitual (Emerson: 'a great part of courage is the courage of having done a thing before'). And that is especially true of soldiers who go into combat time and again on ever longer tours of duty. Emerson talked of courage as 'self-possession at the cannon's mouth'. For him the self was vital to preserve for courage was not a 'what', but a 'who'. Take Louis Zamperini, a B-24 bombardier in World War II. He was born to be an Olympic mile runner, but the war intervened and he had to channel his enormous fortitude—the courage to push himself to the limit—in quite different circumstances. He survived the crash of his Army Air Corps plane and 47 days at sea. He survived the cruelty of a Japanese Prisoner of War (POW) camp on the Marshall Islands where his spirit attracted the unwelcome attention of a psychopathic commandant who tried, and failed, to break it. The experience left him a physical wreck, and put paid to his Olympic career. What strikes the reader of Laura Hillenbrand's biography, *Unbroken*, is that there is no psychological explanation that can satisfy our curiosity as to why Zamperini struggled to survive, when death would have been easier and possibly preferable. Was he a hero, or a hostage to his own will to live? The kind of courage he showed under an unrelenting regime of humiliation, starvation and slave labour would defeat most of us, but it is clear that to have buckled under pressure would have been to surrender his own sense of self. (Hillenbrand, 2010) 'We possess nothing in the world … but the power to say "I"', wrote Simone Weil. 'That is what we have to give God. In other words to destroy. There is absolutely no other free-act which is given to us to accomplish—only the destruction of the "I"'. (Weil, 1986)

Take the gift of courage out of war—its giftedness, and the gift of giving back—and what do you have? Something a little more akin to a trade, but even those who fight wars for private contract security companies can be courageous and often are. Steven Fainaru, a Pulitzer Prize winner, writes about one such young warrior, Jon Cote, a mercenary at the time he knew him, working for a company called Crescent Security Group. He had been trained as an Army Paratrooper and had served with distinction in Afghanistan and Iraq; he had then left the army but found he missed the thrill of combat. He went back to Iraq for that reason. He became a mercenary.

Mercenaries come in all forms; not a few are warriors, even if they are suspect in the eyes of the professional military; in taking money from whoever hires them they are considered to have dishonoured themselves. In fact, war has always been, as Aristotle understood, 'a form of acquisitive activity', and until recently it has usually been self-financing. Honour (or reputation) and cash have been conjoined from the beginning. 'I am so thankful for the war', Fainaru was told by another private security contractor. He had not known that Iraq was available to him. To many mercenaries it was simply a calculus of risk versus the reward, but Fainaru soon came to realise this was far too simplistic an explanation for what it meant to work as a mercenary in Iraq: 'The mercs had a saying … come for the money, stay for the life'. (Fainaru, 2007, xv) Cote undertook two tours of duty—one in Afghanistan as a soldier, the other in Iraq as a mercenary. In Iraq there were no orders and no rules, no shifting political rationales. 'It was just a sleek ride and an envelope full of cash'. It was an existential ride with money at the end of it.

Warriors are seeking some agency and autonomy in their life, translated into the currency of authenticity. We all want to authenticate our lives, to become what we are. What made Cote distinctive as a human type was his appetite for war. The friends he had made in the military were the ones he valued the most: 'It was America's post-millennial wars that had infused his life with meaning and given him the adrenalin rush he craved'. Fainaru, who got to know Jon Cote well, and even came to admire him, puts it better than anyone else. Cote told him that he had seen 'a hidden part of the war', one with its own rules, language, subcultures and secret battles. Then he adds tellingly, 'to me, in many ways, it summed up what Iraq was about. War without pretext. War without ideology. War without planning. War as a payback'.

It is payback, not the pay, which is important for many warriors: it is the actualization of their own personhood, an affirmation of their own authenticity as a human being. The warrior is a human type. And the warrior needs war far more than war today needs warriors. Cote was to die a terrible death; he was kidnapped and later decapitated, a scene videotaped on camera. Fainaru clearly admired Cote as a person, but despised his job as a mercenary. But that is the point. What is important is not the pointlessness of his life, or the terrible death in a far away country about which most Americans knew little and cared even less. It is the fact that war made him alive in a way nothing else could. Warriors, Fainaru reminds us, live outside the world the rest of us inhabit. Cote claimed that he had found in mercenary service what he had not in uniform: an existential side that had been suppressed: 'I felt like I had seen a hidden part of war'. (Fainaru, 2007, 124)

Can we really allow a man like Cote to become a mercenary in order to find himself, or rediscover what he had found? The warrior stands in the line of a great tradition, linked to those who came before him. To become a mercenary, for many, is to break the covenant. It is to share the illusion of Coriolanus—the greatest warrior in the Shakespearean canon—who acts 'as if a man were author of himself/and knew no other kin'. (Coriolanus, v.3)

No-one is, of course, an author of himself, as Coriolanus is later condemned to find out. For the ancestors are part of our neural network. To become a mercenary, perhaps, is to betray them the most.

Such a conclusion is unlikely to impress the scientists. For the Greeks, war was an example of the tragic nature of life against which even the Homeric heroes struggle, sometimes successfully, sometimes in vain. For the scientists the elements of the tragic in our lives can be mediated through pharmacology; we can even be given uplifting states of mind. It is not very heroic, is it? Indeed, cognitive scientists, neuroscientists and evolutionary psychologists seem intent on stripping away the 'hidden part of war', its existential appeal, and leaving us only with the chance of programming men and machines to do our bidding. So why bother with the story behind war that so fascinates most of the readers who want to learn more about how human beings confront the challenges that war throws up? Take away the soul and what have you left? Just a series of just-so stories that we tell ourselves and in which, if we are honest, we no longer believe.

Giftedness

The poet Pindar appreciated the giftedness of bravery. He wrote a series of Odes celebrating the courage of the great warriors and the accomplishments of the great Olympic athletes of his own day. The *Olympian Odes* have survived because they stress the joy of victory, and the exultation of competition. But victory is always fairly won and what the poet celebrates is human striving within the limits set by the athlete's humanity.

Take the 14th Olympian song for Asopichos Orchomenos, who won the boys' stadium race, though sadly in the absence of his father who had died a few days earlier. It is quite moving in its simplicity, for it allows fame fairly won to even penetrate the Underworld:

> Go, Echo, now, down to the dark-walled
> House of Persephone. Take the true word of his
> Fame to his father,
> Find Kleodamos and tell of the son who in
> Pisa's famed valley has fixed in his hair
> Wings that were won in a crown contest.

(Pindar, *14 Olympian Song* 2010).

Even in today's world of steroids and stamina-enhancing drugs, we still insist in the Olympics on human striving within the limits set by nature.

What makes sport so human is the striving for what the Greeks called *ta kala* (high principles), the high principles that victors espouse without a knowledge of which we could not aspire to test their mettle. 'It is the struggle with the givens of human nature that defines humanity, not the progressive effort to transform that nature', writes Bryan Appleyard. And we have been struggling against those givens since we set out on the road to becoming human. (Appleyard, 1999, 35)

The 'givens' of nature are those we have always been striving to enhance through artifice. The battlefield of *The Iliad* is more natural, because the soldiers have only the virtues they are given, which they can only augment by very rudimentary tools of death and destruction. And you needed to be physically strong to kill an enemy in hand-to-hand combat. The Trojan War involved what the Greeks called *ergon* (work): hacking and maiming, often for hours at a time. How long would each soldier have survived, not only physically, but mentally in such conditions? And which of the two, we might ask, is considered more natural, and which more artificial?

> Idomeneus stabbed Erymas in the mouth with the pitiless
> Bronze, so that the brazen spearhead smashed its way clean
> Below the brain in an upward stroke, and the white bones
> Splintered
> And the teeth were shaken out with the stroke and both eyes
> Filled up
> With blood, and gasping he blew a spray of blood through the
> Nostrils
> And through his mouth.

(Lendon 2005, 25)

What are the givens of nature for a warrior like Achilles? One, certainly, is swiftness of foot. But what does swiftness of foot benefit a man when he cannot outrun a spear? Polydoros is forbidden by his father Priam to fight, but he is a young blood like his brothers and he wishes to emulate them. Like them he is naturally brave and has a horror of being belittled in the eyes of others. So he leaves the safety of the city and runs across one of the battlefields to show off his excellence as a runner, and is immediately killed for his bravado by Achilles. The great hero does not even deign to outrun him. Instead, he casts a spear—for spear-throwing is another skill in which Achilles just happens to excel. By the age of gunpowder being fleet of foot mattered for little, for a musket could take out a man at a much greater distance than a spear.

Death in battle takes place within a killing zone of which, perhaps, No-Mans-Land in World War I is the best known example. The depth of each killing zone is determined by the effective range of the prevalent weapon, which in infantry battle is comparatively short and in hand-to-hand combat, like that portrayed by Homer, is only a few feet or an arms' length. (Keegan, 2004, 104) With area killing systems such as the machine gun depth became much greater and battle more lethal. Cut to the Korangor valley in Afghanistan and you find an intensity of combat as great as any Homeric hero had to endure. But though just as lethal, it was framed by a totally different technological environment. Soldiers today enhance their physical and mental strengths through arduous training; they are also more disciplined, and hedged in by rules of engagement, than they were in the past. They have soft porn and heavy metal music to dull the senses. They are every bit as heroic, but their world, compared with that of Achilles, and even the soldiers at Antietam, is much more artificial. Their fate is much less genetically defined than it was in the age of Achilles, and all the time man and machine are becoming fused.

But the cybernetic and cyborg condition is one thing; pharmacological enhancement another. At national sporting events athletes with prosthetic limbs can now compete with today's professionals for the first time; they are not all hived off to demonstrate their sporting prowess in the Paralympics. But drug taking is still rigidly policed in both worlds. It is becoming an uphill struggle as human ingenuity threatens to outpace policing. One example is the injection of Erythropoitin (EPO) produced by the kidney that stimulates red blood cell production. EPO is officially banned at the Olympics, but a new form of EPO gene therapy may prove more difficult to detect before long (Sandel, 2007, 33). Genetically modified distance runners may be able to generate higher than normal levels of their own natural EPO for an entire season or longer. Athletes could also use new medicines for anaemia to boost their blood; and further down the line another drug will come onto the market to counter muscle wastage which could allow an athlete to build up her muscle strength.

Drug enhancement in sport is banned for one overriding reason: it is considered to devalue the idea of human excellence. It also devalues the honour code that is central to sport; it rewards cheating (allowing the second best to win). It also threatens to transform sport into a mere spectacle, and spectacles require spectator-feats (not a demonstration of ability).

For some years the philosopher Michael Sandel has admonished us to treat human nature in the same way we are now urged to treat nature: not to exploit it for our own ends. He urges us to respect what he calls the 'gifted' power of human achievement. We have gifts such as excellence to celebrate a cultural construct called 'achievement'. We are a species that wishes to compete, to show off, to gain a reputation, but one honestly won. To upgrade our naturally endowed abilities would be to sacrifice our 'elective affinity' with the natural world (including wonder with the giftedness of humanity itself). For the moment that achievement becomes the pharmacist's, not the sportsman's; indeed, once records begin to be broken with predictable regularity, the very ideal of sport would be in danger.

Surprisingly, Sandel takes issue with those who criticize enhancement on the understanding that it diminishes human striving. He faults it on somewhat different grounds: it diminishes human excellence. (Sandel, 2007, 26–7) For however hard a woman may strive she will never realise the attributes with which she is not born. A great concert pianist is not just technically proficient at playing the piano; he or she must also have 'soul'. A great Olympic athlete is not just someone who excelled at running at school. We are what we make of the gifts we are born with. As Plato insisted we have a *telos*, a goal that requires us to realise our potential. Artificial enhancement, writes Sandel, represents a kind of 'high-tech' striving as opposed to an ethics of excellence which the Greeks placed at the centre of life. (Sandel, 2007, 29)

But, of course, the stakes in sport are very low. Umberto Eco puts it well, explaining how pent up aggression is often best expressed through sport rather than on the battlefield:

I am in favour of soccer passion as I am in favour of drag racing, and competition between motor cycles on the edge of a cliff, and wild parachute jumping, mystical mountain climbing, crossing oceans in rubber dinghies, Russian Roulette and the use of narcotics. Races improve the race, and all of these games lead fortunately to the death of the best, allowing mankind to continue existence serenely with normal protagonists of average achievement. In a certain sense I could agree with the Futurists, that war is the only hygiene of the world, except one little correction. It would be if only volunteers were allowed to wage it. But unfortunately, war also involves the reluctant, and therefore, it is morally inferior to spectator sports. (Eco, 1994, 168)

Irony aside, where life itself is at issue, and when the issues really matter, is not winning everything? I am often asked by soldiers, is not war different? Shouldn't a soldier be given every chance to upgrade his skills when it can make the difference between life or death? And you can see why, at first glance, the question seems to admit of only one answer. Unlike sport, war demands that we take the lives of others, not only hazard our own. But Eco is arguing that even in sport we have a duty to observe the limits. To be sure, entertainment counts. It offers value, but it does not add to the social value of the sportsman involved, whose time might be more usefully spent in doing socially more useful activities such as carpentry or salesmanship. Many athletes even squander their most productive years in an activity that may entertain but confers little that is actually useful to others. Professional footballers retire very young and usually remain socially unproductive, which is fine for them, but not for society as a whole. Olympic medallists do not make any real difference to anyone's life. War makes all the difference in some cases, and some difference in most. And although a life sacrificed is a life less, it is not necessarily a life squandered.

So, should we not go the extra mile? Should we not aim to win at all costs? And if a soldier's life is important, too (and if we value it much more than we once did), should we not give them every advantage? Sport might hold out against the pharmaceutical industry; I am pretty sure that war will not. In our instrumental world, functionality will determine everything. Indeed, it is difficult to say what is the essence of war if it is not winning. The warrior may inhabit an existential world, like the young John Cote, but he is only of use to the rest of us for the instrumental end to which he can be put. Except that even in war, it matters how you win. Breaking the rules or being seen to do so by the enemy can entrench attitudes, and encourage further resistance. Moreover, if breaking the rules means acting in morally dubious ways, this matters for the rest of us. When an Olympic athlete forfeits his gold medal for cheating, his fellow countrymen are unlikely to share vicariously in his disgrace. In war, guilt by association is important. The modern battle space is shared. Soldiers share it with embedded journalists and TV crews and NGO workers and humanitarian organizations, and one day soon they may find themselves sharing it with robots, too. Any of these, through their actions, can disgrace themselves, but only the man or woman in uniform can bring the mission itself into disrepute by their behaviour. This is why we ask so much of them. We ask them to display character.

In the end it is all a matter of reputation, and reputations, though difficult to win, are very easy to lose overnight. Pindar sang the praise of both athletes and warriors because they competed with each other for reputation by pushing themselves to the limit. Reputation has always been the currency of the Olympic athlete, and unlike medals it does not tarnish over time. It has also been a key factor in legitimising the use of force. I find it difficult to imagine a time when we will ever esteem anyone who is pharmacologically enhanced, soldier or athlete. If we did we would become geeks ourselves, indifferent to the genetic stain (the term is Philip Roth's) that in the Western imagination still links today's warriors to the heroes whose exploits Pindar celebrated in incomparable lyric verse.

Can warriors be cloned?

The issue of genetics and war has a long history. Like so much else, it can be traced back to the Greeks. The point about domestication, wrote Darwin in *The Origins of Species*, is that of selective breeding: 'When a race of plants is once pretty well established, the seed-raisers do not pick out the best plants but merely go over their seed beds and pull out the 'rogues' as they call the plants that deviate from proper standard'. (Dennett, 2006, 167)

And in essence, this was the point of departure for Plato in his engagement with Homer. Achilles was probably past reasoning or rehabilitating, but the worst could be weeded out as societies continued to do ever since. Richard Wrangham has suggested that the domestication of animals usually works by slowing down components of the developmental timetable—a process called pedomorphy. Domestic strains and species tend to be less aggressive. Domestication reduces the pay-off for aggression, a process he believes occurs in humans as well, and may still be taking place. (Pinker, 2011, 616)

But the challenge of our own domestication remains: a soldier is no use to society if he is not aggressive enough. The problem of mutualism—making fitness-enhancing mutually beneficial to both parties (for example, to animals and farmer alike)—is that the animals become more stupid and physically weaker. Dogs, though more intelligent than wolves, are far less aggressive. Over the millennia, sheep have evolved smaller brains relative to body size and weight. It is precisely because they do not need to defend themselves against natural predators or forage for food that they do not need to be as intelligent as they once were (Dennett, 2007, 170). We might consider that being slaughtered at the end is a high price to pay for other aspects of 'fitness', observes Dennett, but from the point of view of reproduction, the sheep get the better of the bargain.

Human beings are different again, of course. But we have occasionally entertained the hope of even getting warriors to 'breed true'. In the *Repub-

lic, in one of the sections singled out by Karl Popper for its intimations of totalitarianism, Plato briefly discusses the idea of breeding a warrior. The best of the warriors will get to mate with the best of the females. Those who prove themselves worthy in battle will get to copulate with more females as a reward, a form of what we might call (though Plato certainly did not) 'recreational sex'. Implicit in the first suggestion is that a better kind of warrior will be produced by genetic inheritance. It is the first example we have in literature of sexual breeding.

Nothing was to come of this Utopian scheme, of course, and it is by no means certain that Plato ever thought it would, or should. It is just a thought experiment, like the *Republic* itself; at this stage in time it is impossible to know for certain whether Plato was actually suggesting to his readers to implement many of the proposals he floated. But we have reached a stage in history when it is possible, at least in theory, to attempt to design a warrior caste, not through sexual reproduction but through genetic engineering. In theory we could create a caste of Auxiliaries if we could identify what Felipe Fernandez-Armesto calls the 'combat gene', a genetic abnormality that leads to high levels of adrenalin release. (Fernandez-Armesto, 2004, 161)

With so much genetic information available on every human being from simple single gene disorders to complex polygenic moods and behavioural traits, it is becoming attractive for employers to use genetic data to select prospective employees. As early as the 1970s the discovery of the sickle cell anaemia trait prompted the US Armed Forces to use genetic screening for the first time. Carriers of the recessive gene—most of them, as it happened, African Americans—were denied entrance to the US Air Force Academy for fear that they might suffer the sickling of their red blood cells in a reduced oxygen environment. (Bowring, 2003, 12) The military purportedly went further in 1992 when it launched an ambitious programme to collect several million DNA samples from military personnel. The exercise was intended to help identify more accurately men and women lost in combat. But in the legal battle that ensued when two Marines refused to give blood under the Fourth Amendment right to privacy, a fear was voiced that the same genetic samples might be used for biomedical research to identify soldiers with the best military genes, or to weed out those with the worst: those most susceptible to fear. (Rifkin, 1998, 164) And if it is possible to isolate genetic traits then it should also be possible to enhance personality traits like risk-taking that are rated highly by Special Forces, and even to produce above average levels of emotional stability for pilots in the virtual spaces that they occupy with computers.

But what if we could go further and one day clone ourselves? For cloning would only be a taking further of experiments we have been conducting for thousands of years, beginning with the domestication of plants and animals, and later the taming of our own savage mind, and the discovery of ways to maximise social intelligence through artificial means such as education and training.

Genes have been central to our world view since the 1990s when we came to realise that only 1 per cent of the genetic code separated us from apes. The gene, we are told so often, is what represents the very essence of our humanity. We are what our genes make us; they are more important than half a million years of evolution, tool use and even language acquisition. In the end, we tell ourselves that everything is genetically determined, an idea that Thucydides would have difficulty in grasping, not only because he did not know about genes but because like most Greeks he put an emphasis on culture, not nature.

Hollywood, as usual, tackled the question of cloning quite early. In the film *The Boys from Brazil*, Josef Mengele carries out his experiments in a remote Latin American jungle outpost in the hope of cloning Adolf Hitler. The film is more absurd than most, especially the final dénouement when a successfully cloned Hitler—a young boy of 9—turns his father's rottweilers not on the famous Jewish Nazi hunter Simon Wiesenthal (played by a particularly hammy Laurence Olivier) who has managed to track him down, but on Mengele himself (played equally self-consciously by a much less talented but seasoned screen actor, Gregory Peck). I suppose that the Hollywood script writers should be allowed some licence, including a surprise ending—even the most perfect clone would not necessarily behave like the person from whom he has been cloned. Cloning, if ever possible at the human level, will have unintended consequences (culture will always find a way). But at the most profound level, the screenplay is misleading. At one point, Mengele is shown to have succeeded in cloning orphan Indian boys with blue eyes. What could be simpler than that? The problem is that in real life, most properties are affected by many genes, and most genes affect many properties. And owing to polymorphism, properties which are similar in living individuals may be produced by different combinations of genes. The effect of a given gene can vary greatly, too, according to the influence of other genes that combine with it. Even properties which might seem no more complex than eye colour are normally impossible to change without a large number of other changes. (Midgley, 2006, 47)

In reality, we have probably claimed too much for the gene, which is not a thing so much as a cluster of information-carrying material. Its unity is given by the nature of the information it carries; it does not exist independent of the chain of 'instruction' in which it functions. We may know the genetic pattern, but not always precisely which piece of information or instruction is carried by which element in a recurring cluster or sequence of DNA. The gene is only part of the evolutionary story; it is not its sole motor. Many scientists, in fact, have begun to come round to the view that many genetic effects are produced not by a particular individual gene, but by genes working together in indeterminate ways, just as they have discovered that in the immune system, individual cells have more than one role to play. Engineering is not just a matter of finding which gene controls which quality and checking what other effects these genes have. It requires us to find a whole range of inter-linked qualities, each controlled by its own indefinite complexity of genes.

We know, for example, that psychiatric problems are unlikely to be caused by a single gene or a single neurotransmitter (such as serotonin or dopamine) any more than they may arise from a single traumatic event. They are most likely to be the result of a complex inter-action of genes and the environment. Psychology is wrestling with the challenge that pill poppers of the future will be able to self-medicate away depression, anxiety or phobia. Given ready availability, people will always take a pill. But most studies suggest that while drugs work for some people, and therapy for others, it is the combination that works best for most. And therapy has one distinct advantage over drugs: it allows you to learn about your condition and, even more important, about yourself. At the end of it, you are often a wiser person; you may have gained in self-knowledge, part of the human ambition to 'become' what we are. And intensive learning is biological, too. It produces changes in gene expression which can, in turn, change the strength of synaptic connections and structural changes that alter the pattern of inter-connection between nerve cells and the brain. The neurologist Alvaro Pascual-Leone has shown that the brains of professional musicians, for example, undergo functional and structural changes as they train (something which has been documented by neuro-imaging).

Perhaps the British philosopher Alfred North-Whitehead was right after all. Focusing on single entities, especially the gene (whether we regard it as selfish or selfless), is fundamentally inappropriate to the study of life, which must be about processes. Everything is in the connections, in the synapses (if you are studying how brains work), or the networks (if you are studying connections between the individual and the environment), or the dialectic between nature and nurture (if you are a biologist). And we are very far from understanding or mapping the genetic or neural networks on which we are counting so much.

Pharmaceutical companies regularly claim that drugs tend to be effective for all but 30 per cent of users. In other words, they work 70 per cent of the time, a success rate which, if true, would be truly impressive. But the figure needs to be looked at more closely. It is true that 70 per cent of people who take medications will respond to them, but less than one-third will respond robustly. The rest are likely to experience only a modest release from their symptoms, and two-thirds will develop in time drug tolerance which mitigates against the treatment they are receiving. (Slater, 2005, 242) In future, of course, psycho-chemicals may be specifically tailored to a person's individual geno-types, which will alleviate or even eliminate many of the side-effects that usually arise from taking them. But for the time being, that day is far off. It is quite likely that identifying the relevant genes to engineer would not address the larger question of gene combinations interacting with the environment. It would also be incredibly expensive to tailor a drug to a particular person. The advantage of Huxley's *soma* was that it was mass produced and universally applicable—it worked on everyone, every time.

The cruel truth is that the central objective of our research programmes in neuroscience remain beyond reach: 'there is only the most shaky understanding of how the brain, and the human brain in particular, engenders mind—the capacity to reflect on past events, to think and to imagine'. (Maddox, 1998, 276) We are a long way from being able to genetically profile, for example, a warrior class or manipulate a 'combat gene', even if 'everyone knows that … adrenalin is nature's lubricant for combat'. (Fernandez-Armesto, 2004, 161) We are unlikely to be able to profile an auxiliary class genetically suited for war. Genetic engineering, in the end, is likely to be defeated by human complexity.

Conclusion

In writing this book I have been at pains to challenge what I consider to be especially 'geekish'—the idea that science can explain away everything. It cannot. Perhaps one day it will, but I very much doubt it. Wiser minds like Darwin's respected the 'ineffable' such as the sacrifice men and women make for each other in combat, the 'love' they bear one another in the field. Wiser minds like William James accepted the giftedness of life without which we could never celebrate 'excellence', a quality we arrogate for ourselves.

This is why language still matters. It is fascinating and possibly telling that even the most reductionist of biologists cannot explain evolution to the rest of us without a degree of anthropomorphic talk. Scientists use the terms 'advantage', 'adapt', and 'fit for purpose' and 'survival of the fittest' (though in the information age many more prefer to speak of the survival of the best informed). Darwin himself mixed metaphor and science, which is why *The Origin of Species* sold so well. His constant bedside companion on *The Beagle* was a copy of Milton's epic poem *Paradise Lost*, the ultimate poem of evolution, our escape from a state of nature into civilization. The central character was Satan, God's chief protagonist, who was pictured so favourably that another poet, William Blake, was prompted to claim that Milton was 'of the Devil's party without knowing it'.

Language matters, otherwise one becomes like Hardy's Jude, who thought that you could understand Greek if you cracked a simple code in the professor's safe keeping: 'Don't you see? These [biblical phrases] are code words. 'Temple' is code for body. 'Heaven' is code for mind. 'Jacob's Ladder' is your spine. And 'Manna' is this rare brain secretion'.

As Terry Eagleton maintains, little new light is cast by this knowledge. To talk about Penelope's 'mate selection' in the *Odyssey* merely diminishes the art. It is now routine to explain everything in terms of neural connections. Literature itself is devalued into a kind of evolutionary handbook or manual for survival in which human beings cease to be characters and instead become 'complex thermostats fabricated out of carbon chemistry'. (Rosen, 2005, 297)

Richard Dawkins may leap up as high as any romantic poet as he beholds a rainbow, but he takes issue with Keats' complaint that when scientists unweave a rainbow, they spoil it. Conversely, Kant thought the Psalms of King David were inadequate praise of Creation, since its wonders had only been revealed by Newton. Mike King ripostes: Dawkins is trying to arrogate to science what is the domain of a quite different human impulse, the poetic and mystical. (King, 2009) And a given interpretative vocabulary is at its most disputable when it appears to privilege one way of representing reality when depreciating others. Both ways of interpreting rainbows are moving and equally valid. As King writes, it is unlikely that anyone but a scientist would be 'moved' by a scientific explanation of a rainbow, in the same way that only mathematicians are moved by the beauty of prime numbers. To be moved is to be awed. Awe is not a scientific criterion, it is a sense of the grandeur of life evoked by a rainbow, and it is properly the domain of spirituality or what Paul Ricoeur, the philosopher, has called an 'openness to the manifestation' of truth in the rites, symbols, prophetic sources and narratives of religion.

This is a demand of our nature. It does not demand a religious language, but we are by nature a religiously minded species in a way that other species are not. When a chimp engages in a threat display when sheltering from a thunderstorm it may be doing many things, but it is not railing against God. But then, unlike chimps we are 'the god species'; we are the only animal on the planet to worship a god and at the same time to arrogate his power. For sometimes the thunder is of our own making.

7

WARRIOR GEEKS

Warriors and the transcendent

A New Theory of Biology *was the title of the paper which Mustapha Mond had just finished reading... 'The author's mathematical treatment of the conception of purpose is novel and highly ingenious, but heretical, and as far as the present social order is concerned, dangerous and potentially subversive, not to be published'. He underlined the words ... it was a masterly piece of work. But once you began admitting explanations in terms of purpose—well, you didn't know what the result might be. It was the sort of idea that might easily de-condition the more unsettled minds among the higher castes—make them lose their faith in happiness as the Sovereign Good and take to believing instead that the goal was somewhere beyond, somewhere outside the present human sphere: that the purpose of life was not the maintenance of well-being, but some intensification and refining of consciousness, such enlargement of knowledge.*

The controller, meanwhile, had crossed to the other side of the room and was unlocking a large safe let into the wall between the bookshelves. The heavy door swung open. Rummaging in the darkness within, 'it's a subject', he said, 'that has always had a great interest for me'. He pulled out a thick black volume. 'You've never read this, for example' ... The Varieties of Religious Experience *by William James.*

'And I've got plenty more', Mustapha Mond continued, resuming his seat. 'A whole collection of pornographic old books. ...

'But if you know about God, why don't you tell them?' asked the Savage indignantly. 'Why don't you give them these books about God?'

'For the same reason that we don't give them Othello, *they're old; they're about God hundreds of years ago. Not about God now'.*

'But God doesn't change'.

'Men do, though'.

'What difference does this make?'

'All the difference in the world', said Mustapha Mond ...

'Then you think there is no God?'

'No, I think there quite probably is one'.

'Then why?'

Mustapha Mond checked him. 'But he manifests himself in different ways to different men. In pre-modern times, he manifested himself as the Being that's described in these books. Now ...

'How does he manifest himself now?' asked the Savage.

'Well, he manifests himself as an absence, as though he weren't there at all'.

Huxley, 1994.

Doing without God—without faith in the transcendent—is certainly one way of translating humanity back into nature: we get the natural by subtracting the supernatural. And we can go even further and subtract the metaphysical as well. But it would seem that we cannot do without artifice. The vision of a future in which our emotional life would be enhanced not through religious belief but by drugs was first conceived by Aldous Huxley in his dystopian novel *Brave New World*. In Huxley's vision of the future life is emotionally flattened but people are essentially happy and for them happiness is a pill called *soma*.

The novel is set in an imagined 27th century world which is peopled by human beings with a stunted humanity. In this future everything that the Greeks encouraged us to feel central to our humanity is almost entirely absent. Huxley's characters do not read, or think, or write. They do not even love, they fornicate. They do not spin their lives in artistic representations because they have no literature, and they do not believe in God because life has no transcendental dimension.

It is not a particularly repressive world, of course. It is not Orwell's *1984*. Sexual promiscuity is positively encouraged; people are offered the 'feelies'—3-D pornographic films which will be reaching our own TV screens quite soon. All of this is intended to offer real pleasure, though society regularly has to work at it to keep the pleasure levels up. 'Happiness is a hard master', observes Mustapha Mond, one of the World Controllers, 'especially other people's happiness'. (Huxley, 1994, 207) And Mond is not an entirely unappealing figure. He has enormous self-knowledge and reads Shakespeare, one of the forbidden works. For in Huxley's world, as in Plato's, some writers are banned for the good of society.

Soma is not Prozac, but the kinship between Huxley's bio-engineering projects and our current experiments is undeniably disquieting: 'All the more so since our technologies of bio-psycho-engineering are still in their infancy, and in ways that make all too clear what they may look like in their full maturity'. (Kass, 2001, 265) The irony is that Huxley later turned to drugs as the only way in which the sublime could be captured in the modern age. He quite literally found his own *soma* in what was on hand: LSD. Abe Hofmann, the man who brought LSD and Psilocybin into the world, compared his discovery to that of nuclear fission. Just as the latter threatened our fundamental physical integrity with the threat of blowing us to kingdom come, so psychedelics, he warned, might undermine the spiritual centre of the personality, of the self. (Horgan, 2003, 156) Hofmann's friend, the veteran warrior Ernst Junger (twice awarded the Iron Cross), also experimented with LSD in later life. Finding no other outlet for the sublime in the nuclear battlescape of the second half of the 20th century, he looked for a route to self-enlightenment, a road that only resulted in amplifying his already pronounced narcissism. You can read about Huxley's own experiments in LSD in *Doors of Perception* (1954), the title of which inspired Jim Morrison to name his band. (Morrison later died of a drug overdose, taken purely for sensational ends; Huxley took his drugs to see God when he was dying of cancer.)

Huxley's personal case history illuminates a fundamental truth about transcendence. We only get out of life what we put in, and transcendence offers a release from self so that a person can become detached from action. Intensive consciousness leads to unconsciousness, but the paradox is that only those fully in possession of a self can fully surrender it. (Foley 2010, 151) We are back to character again. The stronger the sense of self, writes Michael Foley, the greater the rapture in escaping it. Those with a strong sense of self-worth and self-belief have to escape from time to time the terrible burden of self-consciousness. Those with no character will find the only way to transcendence through drugs at some cost to their mental well-being. Huxley had character in spades, but towards the end of his life he began to experiment with LSD in the hope of amplifying the experiences to which he had already surrendered. So did Ernst Junger in old age, but remember that his first epiphany came during World War I in a moment of intense fighting. 'As I came down heavily on the bottom of the trench I was convinced it was all over. Strangely, that moment is one of the very few in my life of which I am able to say I was truly happy. I understood, as a flash of lightening, the true inner purpose of my life'. (Junger, 2004, 373)

In today's world drugs are already a short cut to happiness and gratification. On tomorrow's battlefields soldiers may well be prescribed drugs, but the drugs will not be putting them in touch with God, or the numinous. For what is most important, Mond remarks at one point in the novel, is God's absence. This is what permits the world to be without pain, fear and anxiety. And if all these can be eliminated from war too, they will destroy the essence of combat as self-revealing truth. In one of the essays constituting his collection *Prisms*, Adorno came up with an interesting observation on *Brave New World*, particularly on the value of death and what he called 'interiority'. In the novel a wild man is brought back from an Indian reservation. The Savage reports that he once stood on a cliff with arms outstretched in the burning heat in order to feel what it was like to be Christ, or to be crucified. Asked for an explanation of his behaviour, he gives a curious reply. He simply felt unhappy at the time. If, like the Savage, one can find no other justification for his 'religious adventure' than the wish to experience suffering, then one might as well take *soma*. 'Irrationally hypostasised, the world of ideas is demoted to the level of mere *existence*. In this form, it continually demands justification according to merely empirical norms'. (Adorno, 1995, 112) In other words, even the Savage has not really escaped the rationale of Huxley's world. Even he has been touched by the same logic. Everyone finds themselves locked into a world of pure sensation in which there is nothing 'higher' than bodily experience. A world in which people would want to experience pain to feel alive would be no better than one in which you take a drug to feel happy; it wouldn't be better, only different. It reminds me of the world conjured up in the film *Fight Club* where the violence its characters visit on each other in order to feel more alive is tellingly described by the film's schizophrenic protagonist as a 'near-life experience'.

Most drugs do not put people in touch with the transcendent. In the end, they merely confirm its absence, and the drugs that military scientists may one day design are different altogether. They are designed not to transcend fear, but to remove it, just as amphetamines are taken by some pilots to suppress fatigue. There is no metaphysics involved. For the transcendent is not about changing behaviour, but changing the *thinker*. As William Broyles, a US Vietnam veteran, writes, 'If you come back whole, you bring with you the knowledge that you have explored regions of your soul that in most men will always remain uncharted'. It is the only way in which men can 'touch the mythic domain of their soul'. (Mueller, 2010, 4) Sean Nelson, an American soldier who found himself in the famous fire fight in Mogadishu in 1993, said that when close to death, he had never felt more alive. He felt a state of complete mental and physical awareness. He felt that he would never be the same when he went home. The presence of death can makes one feel more alive—it is one of the many paradoxes of war. (Nelson refers to the fact that he had faced death once before in a near-fatal car collision, but combat was different; it was not ephemeral. For him, his combat experience was lived minute by minute over a period of three hours.) Or take a rare woman's voice from the battlefield, a veteran of the Israeli War of Independence in 1948: 'You cannot imagine the edge of the edge, of what we are going through here'. You had to be '"inside"'. (Harari, 2008, 9)

That is precisely the point. It is what Wittgenstein tells us in *The Tractatus 6.4ii*. Life is actually 'endless' in the sense that our visible field is without limits. There is only 'what we see', and with imagination we can see a lot more. While other animals have sight, we have foresight. Even more important, we have insight. Warriors like Broyles are indeed representative of a human type for that reason, but the journey they make is not one that most of us would wish to make. Most of us embark on very different voyages of self-discovery. For the great majority war is not fundamental in terms of any reality larger than the here and now, and many of us, perhaps most, will never experience a transcendent moment in the shape of God, or the actualization of a religious impulse. War, for some, is a terminus; it is where the warrior ends up. It is no help, of course, if you are trying to get somewhere else.

All of these strategies put us in touch with the ineffable, or inexpressible, which Aristotle also said is within us, but cannot always be expressed in language. 'Whereof one cannot speak, thereof one must be silent': Wittgenstein's dictum is now probably his most famous remark. Warriors do not always write about war—how can you communicate an experience that others cannot even begin to imagine? They do not often talk about their experiences, either. But when they do, it is worth hearing. What they are trying to express in words is what cannot be spoken; language will always be inadequate to the occasion. All writing on war is ambiguous for that reason; most of it contests its own possibility.

Yet this is what is important. The experience a warrior finds in war is inexpressible, and almost impossible to translate into the language he will speak in everyday life. An experience can be transcendent precisely because it transcends language; indeed, to transcend language is to look into the face of God. It is an inexpressibility which is akin to a religious experience. It communicates a truth, the ineffable which is beyond the mundane. It is this experience that can, in a very real sense, be labelled 'mystical'.

Now, remember that religion is banned in Huxley's Brave New World. One of the books locked away in Mustafa Mond's safe is Cardinal Newman's *Apologia Pro Vita Sua*. Newman's conversion to Catholicism was still a *cause célèbre* in the Victorian world into which Huxley himself was born. And Newman dashed off the book very rapidly; at times, he found himself writing 22 hours at a stretch, often in tears. It was a highly charged, emotional autobiographical account of his epiphany. For him just the writing of his autobiography was a religious experience. Mond does not dislike religion, he dislikes the religious impulse, and explains how *soma*, as we have seen, has replaced the religious impulse altogether: 'It's Christianity without the tears'. Another banned book to be found in Mond's private collection is William James' *Varieties of Religious Experience*. James was a self-confessed atheist, but what he liked about religion was not the faith (which he could not share) but the religious experience. What is striking about his approach is that he saw religion in largely existential terms. Just as one can translate war into the existential features of courage, physical endurance, and above all heroic recognition, so James examined such spiritual phenomena as conversion, repentance and martyrdom, or what we might call the heroic features of the religious experience.

There was something of the mystic about James: 'We and God have business with each other, and in opening ourselves to his influence, our deepest destiny is fulfilled'. As James confessed to his students, he had no such faith himself. He could claim no personal experience of the Almighty, but he recognised even in himself 'the mystical germ'. He did not believe in any instrumental purpose in religion, for example, in faith as the road to a concrete end, such as redemption from sin. His starting point was the 'will to believe', and the fact that his book has never been out of print suggests that he put a powerful case, not for religion so much as for religious belief, and not so much for belief as for the will to believe, to bet on a chance. He moved from the right to believe to the right of everyone to take a chance on salvation. 'No fact in human nature is more characteristic than the willingness to live on a chance. The existence of chance makes the difference between a life of which the keynote is resignation and a life of which the keynote is hope'.

Mond dislikes James for insisting that we are creatures of our impulses, and that what makes us distinct as a species is not that we tame those impulses or control them, but that we have many more than any other animal. And here we come to the heart of *Brave New World*. It features a world without pain, despair and hardship; a world full of positive sensations, such as fun, pleasure and ecstasy (induced pharmacologically, of course, or through social conditioning). But it is a world in which the 'sublime' is totally absent. The missing element is described in an essay Huxley wrote in 1931:

> How shall we define a god? Expressed in psychological terms (which are primary—there is no getting behind them), a god is something that gives us the peculiar feeling which Professor Otto has called the 'numinous'. Numinous feelings are the original god-stuff, from which the theory-making mind extracts the individuated gods of the pantheon. (Roberts, 2005, 162)

Rudolf Otto had shown in the treatise *The Idea of the Holy* (1917) that the concept of the 'holy' had not always had its modern implication of moral goodness. In its primordial form the 'holy' represented what he called the 'numinous'—a sublime force that inspired terror and dread, or 'an awful majesty'. (Wright, 2009, 176) In Huxley's dystopia there is no experience of the sublime or numinous, which Huxley defined in aesthetic terms as 'beauty' and Tolstoy, writing from his own experience of war, called the 'truth' which he also tried to reduce to the 'human differential', a mathematical equation that would explain why men were prepared to fight on when all was lost, or why some were willing to go the extra distance and others were not. In this he failed, for the 'truth' about humanity is even more elusive in war than it is off the battlefield, and those who discover it are usually the first to be surprised. Take a British Paratrooper in the Falklands War, shouting to a journalist in the midst of combat, 'I've just learned more about myself in the last ten minutes than I knew in my whole life before'. (Harari, 2008, 2)

Otto believed that the numinous could be explained scientifically. He believed that awe was originally 'designed' by natural selection for some non-religious purpose. Nicholas Humphrey is just one scientist who speculates—although he is the first to admit it is a hypothesis that is impossible to prove—that human consciousness itself might be a 'conjuring trick' designed to fool us into thinking that we are in the presence of an inexplicable mystery. Natural selection may have put consciousness beyond the reach of rational explanation. We may never be able to grasp how it really works. But this particular form of consciousness—what Darwin called the grasp of the ineffable—may have an adaptationist design. When faced with an awesome challenge chimpanzees either go into the threat mode or crouch in submission. The primatologist Jane Goodall has observed chimps reacting to a rainstorm or a waterfall by making a threat display. She speculates that the 'awe' underlying belief in God may be grounded in such 'primeval, uncomprehending surges of emotion'. (Wright, 2009, 482)

The need for transcendence is probably hard-wired into all of us. Even science is actually a by-product of it (not a refutation). It is our attempt to understand what Stephen Hawking calls 'the mind of God'—an attempt which must fail inevitably by its very nature, because it will never remove the mystery from life, or end our quest for communion with something larger than ourselves. But this has not stopped scientists from trying to figure out the physics of transcendence. In their book *The Mystical Mind* (1999) Andrew Newberg and Eugene D'Aquali, both professors at University of Pennsylvania argue that there are two kinds of mystical experience that can be induced: top-down methods such as meditation and prayer, and bottom-up techniques, including dancing and chanting. Such methods, they claim, tap into different components of the body's autonomic nervous system which regulates heartbeat, respiration and metabolism. Top-down methods limit the body's expenditure of energy; bottom-up methods pump adrenalin into the bloodstream, causing in some cases hyperventilation, or a boost in the heart rate and respiration. (Horgan, 2003, 74) Transcendent experiences, they maintain, are therefore not imagined, but are neurologically quite real, and it is possible to study the neurological basis of mysticism with the assistance of new techniques of magnetic resonance imaging and positron emission tomography which can detect neural activity in the brain with much higher resolution.

The chief subjects have been people who claim mystical experiences, particularly nuns. In the case of any religious experience, those who recount them seem to consider them more real than the everyday realities they meet in real life. And the brain scans conducted on nuns would suggest that these subjective states correlate with observable brain states. Our two authors are convinced that they are there for a reason; they have been programmed into us by natural selection. In short, they have adaptive value. They lead to higher states of self-esteem and lower levels of anxiety, as well as a higher than average level of overall psychological health. (Horgan, 2003, 78)

But this is scientific reductionism at its worst. In the case of nuns, the experiments happen to be far from conclusive. For one thing, scanning is not as accurate as often thought. Secondly, fMRI scanning overlooks the networked or distributive nature of the brain's workings. It tends to emphasise local activities when it is the communication between regions that is most critical to mental functioning. (Tallis, 20211, 81–3) The spatial resolution of scanners is improving all the time, of course, but this still does not address the real problem. An fMRI scan will allow you to work out what a subject is looking at, but that is very different from understanding the experience that the subject is experiencing. We cannot scan feelings yet.

Of course, you can parcel up the brain into cubes of tissue—three-dimensional pixels, each with hundreds of thousands of neurons. And this is what scanning does. But human behaviour is not allocated to bits of the brain. Tallis cites the example of love, which involves emotions, intentions, motor actions (buying flowers) and even imagined conversations, all of which involve different areas of the brain. (Tallis, 2011, 82) Even more telling, he adds, Positron Emission Tomography (PET) scans have revealed that even the ability to associate the word 'chair' with another, the vital concept—'sitting'—involves not only the language centre in the left hemisphere, but extensive stretches of so-called 'silent' areas of frontal lobes and the parietal cortex.

And anyway, even if it were possible to conduct experiments which could actually locate the 'spot' on the brain which explains why nuns have intense spiritual experiences, or why warriors may feel the presence of the 'sublime' on the battlefield, what would such experiments prove? They would bring into question not only what we understand to be awe in religion and war, but what we think makes us the human beings we are. We have awe for a reason, because it puts us in tune with the importance of the present moment—the moment which is a turning point in a soldier's life, a moment that is very short when compared to the whole length of a human life but one that shapes the definitive image of a man and which, as an epiphany or encounter with the self, may determine the nature of his entire subsequent life story.

When a warrior is awed in battle, he is attributing meaning to an experience that is quintessentially human; and that meaning is not susceptible to scientific explanation alone. Such transformations will affect very few, to be sure. Most soldiers merely wish to survive. In wartime, most remember the by-products—such as friendliness, loneliness and boredom. But those who are genuinely transformed by the experience often undergo a profound change in their world view.

And so do we, and that is the adaptionist value. After all, although many mystics live a solitary life some have gone on to found world religions and some, less usefully, have incited their followers from time to time to violence. A mystical vision can be shared with those who have not experienced it. Even within the military profession, 'mystics' like Lawrence of Arabia and Orde Wingate (to mention just two British 20th-century figures) have been a source of inspiration for many soldiers. As James maintained, a mystical vision is to be assessed not by its neurological roots, but its consequences. Who cares whether it is real or not (in the objective sense) if it inspires others?

In his day, there were no scans or positron scanners, but there was much speculation about what was called 'medical mysticism', the predisposition of some writers to explain away St Paul as an epileptic and St Joan's visions as the hallucinations of a cross-dressing schizophrenic. The validity of a vision, James insisted, could not be explained in such narrow terms. Its importance stemmed from its consequences. St Joan may indeed have been a schizophrenic, but she inspired her countrymen to continue the fight. St Paul may have been an epileptic, but he almost single-handedly defined Christianity as we know it today in his writings. We could talk about the madness of poets, too, or comment on the alcoholism of many mainstream American novelists, but neither detracts from or, more important, explains the creative spark. The problem is that our neurological explanations appear to devalue the experience of the mystics. It is our heroes, the human types, the mystics and warriors, whose stories we still want to hear because the characters concerned usually made a difference. We are still inspired by extraordinary stories of self-sacrifice. And it is because many of us still see sacrifice as the ultimate affirmation of our humanity that war still has an emotional appeal.

In every war, writes Broyles, there are two kinds of soldiers: those who find God in battle, and those who, for one reason or another, are rendered soulless. There are those who are overwhelmed when peering too deeply into the abyss; those who possess what Joseph Conrad called 'a deliberate belief' which enables them to survive all adversity; and the hollow men who do not experience any sensation because they are dead to the world. And one such soldier is brought to the fore by Michael Herr in *Despatches*, his critically acclaimed account of his Vietnam War experience. At one point he recalls a soldier he knew as Robert 'Blowtorch' Komer. Komer was an instrumentalist to the core who spoke the war's language and employed its absurd euphemisms such as 'protective reaction' (counterattack), 'free fire zones' (battlefield), 'collateral damage' (civilian casualties), 'hostiles' (enemy combatants), 'air support' (bombing) and 'accidental delivery' (friendly fire). 'If William Blake had "reported" to him that he'd seen angels in the trees', Herr writes, 'Komer would have tried to talk them out of it. Failing that, he'd have ordered defoliation' (a reference to the widespread practice of using Agent Orange to clear the countryside of enemy combatants). (Herr, 1979, 42)

This is where we stand today. Some wish to purge war of its existential and metaphysical elements and render it wholly instrumental. They are the real 'geeks', quite irrespective of whether they spend their day behind computer screens. Others wish soldiers to remain in touch with their 'humanity' and the spiritual dimension of 'being'; they continue to look back to a tradition that goes back to the Greeks. The pity of it all, of course, is that anyone should think that it is an either/or.

Geeks or Greeks?

Whether or not the post-human fantasies discussed in this book are realised—or how long they come to fruition—is not the point. It is a future others are dreaming for us, especially many of the scientists on contract to the military. For that reason I think Ray Kurtzweil—perhaps the most famous post-humanist today—is right to claim that 'the primary political and philosophical issue of the [21st] century will be the definition of who we are'. (Graham, 1998, 1) Kurtzweil is one of the most famous analysts of the post-human condition, and he was writing about the 'singularity', the moment when computers become self-aware and evolve their own consciousness. Before the end of the century human beings may no longer be the most intelligent entity on the planet. And long before then war may be conducted by machines of our own invention, some of which, once they become autonomous, will be able to make decisions and even exercise difficult ethical choices on our behalf.

We should not be carried away by the post-human vision. Take the prospects of genetic engineering. The possibilities of cloning are as difficult as the possibilities of using the latest discoveries in neuroscience to change the way we think and act. So far genomics has generated more questions than it has answered—about how genes interact with each other, about the role of the long stretches of 'non-coding DNA' in between the genes, about the effects of having too many or too few copies of a gene, about changes in the genes that can occur during an individual lifetime. None of these complications were anticipated by the pioneers who launched the Human Genome Project. We are discovering the complexity of life as we go along, as we continue to discover more and more. The DNA code does not tell us how we can re-engineer human beings successfully; the gene itself is not even a necessary key. It is the combination of genes and their inter-action with the environment that is—and this would be far too complex for us to decipher for many years yet.

Deciphering the neural code is more challenging still; the language whereby brain cells gather, store and communicate information is at present beyond our understanding. Indeed, some scientists suspect that unlike the DNA code, there may be no single neural code to decipher. Even autonomous robots are a long way off, though these different fields are not bracketed off from each other, at least in the artistic imagination. In the film *The Matrix* robots have cracked the neural code and are able to fool the human population of the planet into thinking that they still live in a relatively benign, pre-robot world, when, in reality, they have been enslaved long ago and become little better than helots.

What I have tried to do in this book is to examine the likely impact of early 21st-century technologies—digital, cybernetic and bio-medical—upon our understanding of how war and our humanity will continue to co-evolve. And it is we who are likely to change faster than ever before in observed human history, from the time that Thucydides wrote the first work of military history. We are being asked not only to come to terms with the cultural impact of the new technologies—something that Thucydides would have understood, even if he would have had difficulty grasping the scale of the technological changes involved. We are being asked what this means for questions of our own ontology, especially the fixity of human nature which Thucydides took for granted: the difference between man and artefact, the organic and inorganic.

Throughout this book I have been sceptical of the direction in which we are taking war. I am concerned that if soldiers are denied their private thoughts and are embedded in a cybernetic web they may be denied the chance for personal development, the chance to think for themselves. I am concerned that if we were ever to subcontract responsibility for ethical decision-making to robots, however sophisticated, we might forgo our right to live by the choices we make. I am concerned that if we could ever engineer courage or blot out a conscience through drugs we would severely compromise what we value most—our individual free will.

And with these changes war will change too, for as I have argued, the relationship between war and humanity is symbiotic. War may no longer be sacred as we continue to hollow out sacrifice which has always been at its core, at least in the stories we tell ourselves. It may no longer offer even the warrior the transcendent experience of battle. War may instead transcend the spiritual realm altogether and become just a 'routine'.

Can life be called 'life' if it is lived on other than heroic terms? To render war itself entirely post-heroic is probably possible; we can remove much of its pain and much of the effort, at least for ourselves. We can demand no sacrifices from our own soldiers, or ask that they take risks for us or each other; we can hollow out the existential dimension of war until we reach the point where it delivers for them fewer and fewer emotional rewards. If this were to bring about the end of war, the changes would be welcome. But it will not; all we will succeed in doing is to render war even more 'inhumane'.

That is the moral of Don DeLillo's short story, 'Human Moments in World War 3', which anticipated the world of the drone pilot long before drones appeared over the skies of the Middle East. Happiness, our hero is told, is outside the crew's frame of reference. The crew of the spaceship certainly seem dead to the world and each other. They could almost be mistaken for machines (say, androids) because of the flattening of affect. Affect is an old word but it was seized upon by psychoanalysts at the turn of the 20th century to describe an emotional value within the individual psyche, the inward disposition to feel the pain of others, and therefore display compassion. Allied to affect is another word: empathy. Through empathy we know and feel another's pain. It is the most recent development of the pre-frontal cortex; it is what makes us most human (dogs show it too, but only because they have co-evolved with us over thousands of years). It is doubtful whether in DeLillo's story the crew members feel anything towards the enemy.

And what of robots? Once we can design autonomous machines that can think for themselves, why not contract out war to machines entirely? In

Douglas Adams' novel *Dirk Gently's Holistic Detective Agency* there is a robot, the Electric Monk, a labour saving device which you can buy 'to do the believing for you'. The deluxe model is advertised as 'capable of believing things they wouldn't believe in Salt Lake City'. Of course, the point about Adams' joke is that believing is not something you decide to do when you wake up one morning. Belief is a truth that has been revealed often as a result of conversion or revelation. We only have the right to choose our secular beliefs, not our mysteries.

The point Adams is implicitly making is a criticism of Kantian morality which tells us what is right and what is wrong independent of our desires. The hard work of morality consists in the transformation and taming of our desires so that we aim at the good. As Aristotle said, morality is in the striving (*orexis*). In other words, the truth is not something fixed that we can discover if we look hard enough for it; it is rather a certain kind of procedure concerning the way we approach moral problems. (Hawthorn, 2005, 52) The problem with the Electric Monk is that it is the product of a society in which people are no longer required to strive for anything. Getting others to do the hard work for us will make us not bad characters, it will simply make us characterless, with no interest in matching desire to the good of anything larger than ourselves.

Character is at the heart of this change; and it is being relentlessly challenged by the march of science. It is being undermined by genetics (the idea that behaviour is determined by genes); by evolutionary psychology (the idea that behaviour is determined by evolved survival mechanisms); and by neuroscience (the idea that behaviour is determined by modules of a hard-wired brain). And it is under challenge from robotics, the belief that machines can do the things we do much better, if only they are properly programmed. The Geeks are coming into their own and in the process threatening to displace the Greeks from our imagination.

The problem with the Geeks is the problem of foreshortened historical perspectives: the idea that we live in the most interesting times, that everything we have discovered about ourselves is newly discovered in the laboratory. The Greeks may not have had a scientific language, or even the techniques—they had no PET scans, etc.—but they were able to deduce a great deal from human observation. And they were able to speculate a great deal more about our origins.

We have history for a reason; the past should never be distant from our present thoughts. As a result, it is important to be linked back to our past which is also part of the neural network into which we are wired. The problem with many scientists is that they think everything is of importance in this brave modern world of ours that they themselves have forged. They situate us in an entirely material world in which there is no place for the human spirit. Locked behind their screens and PET scans, they have a one-dimensional view of life, and only a half-formed understanding of phenomena such as war in all its bewildering complexity. When I attack geekishness I am attacking a particular and distinctive attitude to life.

But then there is really no need to choose between Greek and geek; between the humanities and science. Unlike science, philosophy does not seek to discover new facts about the world, but it does get us to see what we know for the first time, to see through appearance to the inner reality beyond. Science supplies us with new facts about reality and thus enlarges our field of vision. Philosophy seeks to get us to see the world anew, including those features of the world that science reveals for the first time. We should be engaging with the Greeks in a contrapuntal dialogue. Their insights into humanity and war and the relationship between the two are still essential to acknowledge if war is to remain humane.

The fact is that the post-humanists are a small but growing group, happy to make a wager on the future. They are at one with Shakespeare's Cassius, who with blind confidence in the verdict of the future, looked forward to 'states unborn and accents unknown'. Behind this fear is that the scientists are giving themselves over to a questionable neo-Lamarckism which demands we give ourselves over to the future as an act of blind faith. The billboard for bio-technology, claims Bill McKibben, is 'lose yourself to the future!', which suggests that we simply become 'programmed to do what we are supposed to do'. (McKibben, 2003, 135) Post-humanity may be our fate. But, in the end, 'fate' is only a word we use to describe a choice, not a destiny. Our continued survival will depend on the choices we make.

And we should always remember that we have been here before. At the end of the First World War the cultural critic Irving Babbitt, taking stock of his own age and its hubristic hopes of remaking humanity, of improving the human strain and bringing forth Nietzsche's Superman, waxed ironic: 'The world, it is hard to avoid concluding, would have been a better place if more persons had made sure they were human before setting out to be superhuman'.(Appleyard, 1992, 118) It is a warning to those writers who are carried away by their enthusiasm for the post-human future and to those in the military who seem intent on bringing it nearer with every day.

BIBLIOGRAPHY

Abramson, Jeffrey, *Minerva's Owl: The Tradition of Western Political Thought*, Cambridge, MA: Harvard University Press, 2009.

Adams, James, 'Future Warfare and the Decline of Human Decision Making—Weapons Automation', *Parameters*, 31:4, winter 2001. See http://findarticles.com/p/slash/article/mi_m01BR/is_iv_31/ai_82064206/

Adorno, Theodor, *Minima Moralia: Reflections from a Damaged Life*, London: Verso, 1993.

———— *Dreamnotes*, ed. Christoph Godde, (trans. Rodney Livingstone), Cambridge, Polity, 2007.

———— *Prisms: Essays*, Cambridge, Mass.: MIT Press, 1995.

———— *Negative Dialectics*, London: Verso, 1979.

Aiken, D.H., *The Age of Ideology: The 19th Century Philosophers*, New York: Mentor, 1956.

Alberts, David, *Network-centric Warfare: Developing and Leveraging Information Superiority*, Washington: Department of Defense, CCRP, 1999.

Albucher, Ronald, 'Psycho Pharmacological Treatment in PTSD: A Critical Review', *Journal of Psychiatric Research*, 36, 6, September–November 2002.

Allen, R.E., '*Anamnesis* in Plato's *Meno and Phaedo*, *The Review of Metaphysics*, 13:1, September 1959.

Almond, Peter, 'Managing Unmanned Air Vehicles: Fighter Pilots and Geeks', *RUSI Defense Systems*, 12:1, 2009.

Alvarez, Al, *Risky Business*, London: Bloomsbury, 2007.

Andrew, Laurie B., *The Clone Age: Adventures in the New World of Reproductive Technology*, New York: Harry Holt, 1999.

Andriev, Kora, 'Sorry for the Genocide: How Public Apology can Help Promote National Reconciliation', *Millennium*, 38:1, August 2009.

Ansell-Pearson, Keith, *Viroid Life: Perspectives on Nietzsche and the Trans-Human Condition*, London: Routledge, 1997.

Appiah, Kwame, *Experiments in Ethics*, Harvard University Press, 2008.

Appleyard, Brian, *Understanding the Present: Science and the Soul of Modern Man*, London: Picador, 1992.

———— *The Brain is Wider than the Sky: why Simple Solutions don't Work in a Complex World*, London: Weidenfeld and Nicholson, 2011.

Arendt, Hannah, *The Human Condition*, University of Chicago Press, 1998.

———— *Between Past and Future*, London: Penguin, 2006.

Arkin, Ronald, *Governing Lethal Behaviour in Autonomous Robots*, Boca Raton: Taylor & Francis Group, 2009.

Asimov, Isaac, *Caves of Steel*, London: Grafton, 1987.

———— *Robots of Dawn*, London: Grafton, 1983.

———— *Robot Visions*, New York: New America Library, 1990.

———— *The Evitable Conflict*, Reprinted in *I, Robot*, London: Grafton, 1968.

Asimov, I. and R. Silverberg, *The Positronic Man*, London: Victor Gollancz, 1992.

Bailey, Ronald, *Liberation Biology: The Scientific and Moral Case for the Bio-tech Revolution*, Amherst, NY: Prometheus, 2005.

Baker, Dewleen *et al.*, 'Post Traumatic Stress Disorder: Emerging Concepts of Pharmacotherapy, an Expert Opinion', *Emerging Drugs*, Volume 14, 2, 2009.

Baldick, Chris, *In Frankenstein's Shadow: Myth, Monstrosity and 19th Century Writing*, Oxford: Clarendon, 1990.

Barnes, Julian, *Nothing to be Frightened of*, New York: Knopf, 2008.

Barnet, Corelli, *The Sword Bearers: Studies in Supreme Command in the First World War*, London: Penguin, 1966.

Barrow, John, *The Artful Universe Expanded*, Oxford University Press, 2005.

Bateman, Robert, *Digital Soldiers: A View from the Front Lines*, Novito, Cal.: Presidio, 1999.

Bauman, Zygmunt, *Living on Borrowed Time*, Cambridge: Polity, 2010.

———— *Cultural Damage: Social Inequalities in the Global Age*, Cambridge: Polity, 2011.

———— *44 Letters from the Liquid Modern World*, Cambridge: Polity, 2010.

———— *Post-Modern Ethics*, Oxford: Blackwall, 1993.

Bell, Jennifer, 'Preventing Post Traumatic Stress Disorder or Pathologising Bad Memories?' *The American Journal of Bioethics*, 7:9, September 2007.

Bering, Jesse, *The God Instinct: The Psychology of Souls, Destiny and the Meaning of Life*, London: Nicholas Brearley, 2011.

Best, Steven and Douglas Kellner, 'The Apocalyptic Vision of Philip K Dick', *Cultural Studies* 3:2, 2003.

Betz, David, 'The Mystique of Cyberpower and the Strategic Latency of Network Social Movements', Unpublished draft, 14 May 2011.

Birkerts, Sven, 'Into the Electronic Millennium', in Craig Hanks (ed.), *Technology and Values*, Oxford: Wiley-Blackwell, 2010.

Blinn, James, *The Aardvark is Ready for War*, New York: Anchor, 1997.

Bloom, Harold, *Genius*, London: Fourth Estate, 2002.

Bloom, Harold (ed.), *Thomas Pynchon's Gravity Rainbow (Modern Critical Interpretations)*, New York: Chelsea House, 1986.

Borges, Jorge Luis, *Other Inquisitions 1937–1952*, Austin: University of Texas Press, 1964.

Borgmann, Albert, *Holding Onto Reality: The Nature of Information at the Turn of the Millennium*, University of Chicago Press, 1999.

Bowden, Mark, *Black Hawk Down*, London: Bantam 1995.

Bowring, Finn, *Science, Seeds and Cyborgs: Bio-technology and the Appropriation(?) of Life* London: Verso, 2003.

Bousquet, Antoine, *The Scientific Way of Warfare: Order and Chaos on the Battlefields of Modernity*, London: Hurst, 2009.

Brand, Stewart, *The Clock of the Long Now: Time and Responsibility*, London: Weidenfeld & Nicholson, 1999.

Brodsky, Josef, *On Grief and Reason: Essays*, London: Hamish Hamilton, 1996.

Bronowski, Jacob, *The Ascent of Man*, London: Causton and Sons, 1973.

Brown, John Seely and Paul Duguid, 'The Social life of Information' in Craig Hanks (ed.), *Technology & Values: Essential Readings*, Oxford, Wiley/Blackwell, 2010.

Burgess, Anthony (trans. and adapted), *Sophocles: Oedipus Rex*, Minneapolis: University of Minnesota Press, 1972.

Burridge, Brian, 'Post-Modern War Fighting with Unmanned Vehicle Systems: Esoteric Chimera or Essential Capability?' *RUSI Journal*, 150:5 (2005).

———— 'UAVs and the Dawn of Post-Modern Warfare: a Perspective on Recent Operations', *RUSI Journal*, 148:5 (2003).

Burleigh, Michael, *Moral Combat: A History of World War II*, London: Harper, 2010.

Caputo, Philip, *A Rumour of War*, London: Macmillan, 1978.

Carter, Chelsea, 'Greek tragedies offer modern lessons on war's pain', *USA Today*, 14 August 2008, http://www.usatoday.com/news/nation/2008–08–14–3840 8159_x.htm.

Cartledge, Paul, *The Greeks: A Portrait of Self and Others*, Oxford University Press 2002.

———— *Alexander the Great: The Hunt for a New Past*, London: Macmillan, 2004.

———— *Thermopylae: The Battle that Changed the World*, London: Pan, 2006.

Carr, N., 'Is Google Making us Stupid?' in J. Lundberg, *From the Return of Religion to the New Narrow-Mindedness*, Stockholm: Axess Institution, 2009.

———— *The Shallows: How the Internet is Changing the Way we Think, Read and Remember*', London: Atlantic Books, 2011.

Casti, John, *Paradigms Regained: Unravelling the Mysteries of Modern Science*, London: Abacus, 2000.

BIBLIOGRAPHY

Casti, John *et al.*, *Mission to Abisko: Stories and Myths in the Creation of Scientific Truth*, Cambridge, Mass.: Perseus, 1999.

Chandor, A. (ed), *Penguin Dictionary of Computers*, London: Penguin, 1985.

Chesneaux, Jean, *Brave Modern World: The Prospects of Survival*, London: Thames & Hudson, 1992.

Chorost, Michael, *Rebuilt: My Journey Back to the Hearing World*, Boston: Mariner, 2006.

Christian, David, *Maps of Time: An Introduction to Big History*, Los Angeles: University of California Press, 2005.

Christakis, Nikolas and James Fowler, *Connected*, London: HarperPress, 2010.

Clark, Andy, *Natural Born Cyborgs, Technology & The Future of Human Intelligence*, Oxford University Press, 2003.

———— 'Cyborgs Unplugged' in Susan Schneider, *Science Fiction & Philosophy: From Time Travel to Super-Intelligence*, Oxford: Wiley-Blackwell, 2009.

Clarke, Roger, 'Asimov's Laws of Robotics: Implications, Information Technology', *Computer* 26, 12 December 1993 and 27 January 1994. http://www.rogerclarke.com/SOS/asimov.html.

Clastres, Pierre, *Archaeology of Violence* (trans. Jeanie Herman), Los Angeles: Semiotext, 2007.

Clausewitz, *On War* (ed. Michael Howard, Peter Parritt), London: Everyman, 1993.

Clayton, Nancy M. and William P. Nash, 'Medication Management of Combat and Operational Stress Injuries in Active Duty Service Members' in Charles Figley and William P. Nash (eds), *Combat Stress Injury: Theory, Research and Management*, New York: Routledge, 2007.

Cochran, Gregory and Henry Harpending, *The 10,000 Year Explosion: How Civilization Accelerated Human Evolution*, New York: Basic Books, 2009.

Coker, Christopher, *Humane Warfare*, Routledge, 2001.

———— *Warrior Ethos*, Routledge, 2008.

Coliaco, James, *Socrates Against Athens: Philosophy on Trial*, London: Routledge, 2001.

Conrad, Joseph, *Heart of Darkness*, London: Penguin, 1995.

Conrad, Peter, *Modern Times, Modern Places: Life and Art in the 20th Century*, London: Thames & Hudson, 1998.

Coombs, Alan, 'The Making of Colossus', *Annals of the History of Computing*, 5:3, 1983, http://www.ivorcatt.com/47d.htm.

Cornford, Penelope, *Time and the Shape of History*, New Haven: Yale University Press, 2007.

Coyne, James, *Air Power in the Gulf*, Arlington, Va.: Aerospace Education Foundation, 1992.

Crane, Stephen, *The Red Badge of Courage* (ed. Donald Pizer), New York: Norton & Co., 1976.

Cummins, Mary, 'Supervising Automation: Humans on the Loop', *Aero Astro* number 5 (2007–8) http://www.web.mit.edu/aeroastro/news/magazine/aeroastro5.pdf.

Damasio, Anthony, 'Self Comes to Mind' *Wired Science*, 8 November 2010, http://www.wired.com/wiredscience/2010/11/self-comes-to-mind.

——— *Looking For Spinoza: Joy, Sorrow and the Feeling Brain*, New York: Vintage, 2004.

Danchev, Alex, *On Art and War on Terror*, Edinburgh University Press, 2011.

Darwin, Charles, *The Moral Sense of Man and the Lower Animals*, The Great Books: Reading and Discussion Program, 1985.

Davies, Tony, *Humanism*, London: Routledge, 1997.

De Landa, Manuel, *War in an Age of Intelligent Machines*, New York: Zone, 1991.

De Lillo, Don, 'Human Moments in World War III', *Esquire*, July 1982.

——— *Running Dog*, London: Picador, 1999.

——— *Underworld*, New York: Scribner, 1997.

——— *End Zone*, London: Penguin, 1986.

Dennett, Daniel, *Consciousness Explained*, London: Penguin, 1991.

——— *Breaking the Spell: Religion as a Natural Phenomenon*, London: Penguin, 2006.

Detienne, Marcel, *The Greeks and Us: A Comparative Anthropology of Ancient Greece*, Cambridge: Polity, 2007.

De Waal, Frans, *Primates and Philosophers: How Morality Evolved*, Princeton University Press, 2009.

Diamond, Jared, *Guns, Germs & Steel: the Fate of Human Societies*, New York: Norton & Co., 2005.

Dick, Philip, *The Gun*, New York: Citadel, 1987.

Dipert, Randall R, 'The Ethics of Cyberwarfare', *Journal of Military Ethics*, Vol. 9, No. 4 (2010).

Doctorow, E.L., *Creationists: Selected Essays*, New York: Random House, 2007.

Dower, John, *Cultures of War*, New York: Norton, 2010.

Dunnigan, James, *Digital Soldiers: the Evolution of High-Tech Weaponry and Tomorrow's Brave New Battlefield*, London: St Martin's Press, 1996.

Eco, Umberto, *Travels in Hyper Reality*, London: Picador, 1994.

Economist, 'I Get a Kick Out of You', 12 February 2004. http://www.oxytocin.org/oxytoc/love-science.html.

Edwards, Paul, *The Closed World: Computers and the Politics of Discourse in Cold War America*, Cambridge, Mass.: MIT Press, 1996.

Ellis, John, *Social History of the Machine Gun*, London: Pimlico, 1993.

——— *The Sharp End: The Fighting Man in WWII*, London: Pimlico, 1993.

Emerson, Ralph Waldo, *Selected Essays* (ed. Larzer Ziff), London: Penguin, 1982.

Empson, William, *Seven Types of Ambiguity*, New York: Lightening Source Inc., 2008.

BIBLIOGRAPHY

Etzione, Amatai, 'Unmanned Aircraft Systems: The Moral and Legal Case', *Joint Force Quarterly*, number 57 (2010).

Euben, J. Peter, *Platonic Noise*, Princeton University Press, 2003.

Evans, Michael, 'Stoic Philosophy and the Profession of Arms', *Quadrant* 54: 1—2 (2010)   http://207.57.117.110/magazine/issue/2010/1.2/ stoic-philosophy-and-the-profession-of-arms.

———'The Second Horseman: The Philosophy of War in Blood Meridian', *Quadrant* 55: 4, April 2011.

Fainaru, Steve, *Big Boy Rules: America's Mercenaries Fighting in Iraq*, New York: Da Capo Press, 2009.

Faulkner, Robert, *The Case for Goodness, Honourable Ambition and Its Critics*, New Haven: Yale University Press, 2007.

Fernandez-Armesto, Felipe, *So You Think You're Human? A Brief History of Humanity*, Oxford University Press, 2004.

Ferrari, G.R.F. (ed.), *Cambridge Companion to Plato's Republic*, Cambridge University Press, 2007.

Ferre, Frederic, *The Philosophy of Technology*, Athens: Georgia University Press, 1995.

Ferry, Luc, *Man Made God*, Chicago University Press, 1996.

——— *Learning to Live: A User's Manual*, Edinburgh: Canongate, 2010.

Feyerabend, Paul, *The Tyranny of Science*, Cambridge: Polity, 2011.

Figes, Orlando, *Crimea: The Last Crusade*, London: Allen Lane, 2010.

Finch, Shannon, 'Code of the Warrior' in Russell Parkin (ed.), *War Fighting and Ethics*, Canberra: Land Warfare Studies Centre, 2005.

Finkelkraut, Alain, *In the Name of Humanity*, London: Pimlico, 2001.

Finley, Moses, *Ancient History: Evidence and Models*, London: Pimlico, 2000.

Fisher, Helen, *Why We Love: The Nature and Chemistry of Romantic Love*, New York: Henry Holt, 2004.

Foley, Michael, *The Age of Absurdity: why Modern Life Makes it Hard to be Happy*, London: Simon & Schuster, 2011.

Ford, Dennis, *The Search for Meaning: A Short History*, Los Angeles: University of California Press, 2007.

Foster, Charles, *The Selfless Gene: Living with God and Darwin*, London: Hodder, 2010.

France, John, *Perilous Glory: the Rise of Western Military Power*, New Haven: Yale University Press, 2011.

Frayn, Michael, *The Human Touch: Our Part in the Creation of the Universe*, London: Faber & Faber, 2006.

Fredericks, Tim, *Black Hearts: One Platoon's Descent into Madness in Iraq's Triangle of Death*, London: Macmillan, 2011.

Frohm, Erich, *The Dogma of Christ and Other Essays on Religion, Psychology and Culture*, 1963, London: Routledge, 2004.

Furedi, Frank, *Therapy Culture: Cultivating Vulnerability in an Uncertain Age*, London: Routledge, 2004.

Fussel, Paul, *The Bloody Game: An Anthology of Modern War*, New York: Scribeners, 1991.

Gallie, W.B., *Philosophers of Peace and War: Kant, Clausewitz, Marx, Engels and Tolstoy*, Cambridge University Press, 1978.

Galison, Peter, 'The Ontology of the Enemy: Norbert Wiener and the Cybernetic Vision', *Critical Inquiry*, 21:1, Autumn 1993.

Gardner, Dan, *Future Babble: Why Expert Predictions Fail and Why We Believe Them Anyway*, London: Virgin, 2010.

Gazit, E., *Plenty of Room for Biology at the Bottom: an Introduction to Bio-nanotechnology*, London: Imperial College Press, 2007.

Geyer, Felix, 'From Simplicity to Complexity: Adapting to the Irreversibility of Accelerating Change', Paper presented at the 14th World Congress of Sociology, Montreal, 26 July–1 August 1998, see http://critcrim.org/redfeather/chaos/022adaptations.htm.

Ghamari-Tabrizi, *The World of Herman Kahn: The Intuitive Science of Thermonuclear War*, Cambridge, Mass.: Harvard University Press, 2005.

Gibson, William, interviewed in *No Maps for These Territories* (Director Mark Neale) 89m, Mark Neale Productions, 2000.

Gillespie, Michael, *Hegel, Heidegger and the Ground of History*, Chicago University Press, 1984.

Gillingham, James, *Violence: Reflections on our Deadliest Epidemic*, London: Jessica Kingsley Publishers, 2006.

Glannom, Walter, 'Psychopharmacology and Memory', *Journal of Medical Ethics*, 32:2, February 2006.

Glenny, Misha, *Dark Market: Cyberthieves, Cybercops and You*, London: Bodley Head, 2011.

Goody, Jack, *The Domestication of the Savage Mind*, Cambridge University Press, 1995.

Goetz, Stewart and Charles Taliaferro, *A Brief History of the Soul*, Oxford: Wiley-Blackwell, 2011.

Goldman, Daniel, *Social Intelligence: The Revolutionary New Science of Human Relationships*, New York: Bantam, 2006.

Gottschall, Jonathan, *The Rape of Troy: Evolution, Violence in the World of Homer*, Cambridge University Press, 2008.

Graham, Elaine, *Representations of the Post-Human: Monsters, Aliens and Others in Popular Culture*, Manchester University Press, 2002.

Gray, Charles Hables, *Postmodern War: the New Politics of Conflict*, London: Routledge, 1997.

Grey, Charles Habbles (ed.), *The Cyborg Handbook*, London: Routledge, 1995.

BIBLIOGRAPHY

Grey, John, *Straw Dogs: Thoughts on Humans and Other Animals*, London: Granta, 2002.

Groves, Eric (ed.), *The Antiwar Quotebook*, London: Quirik Books, 2009.

Greenfield, Susan, *Tomorrow's People: How 21ˢᵗ Century Technology is Changing the Way We Think and Feel*, London: Penguin, 2003.

—— *You and Me; the Neuroscience of Identity*, London: Notting Hill Editions, 2011.

Gudkin, Lee, *Almost Human: Making Robots Think*, New York: Norton, 2006.

Hanson, Victor-Davis, *The Father of Us All: War & History, Ancient & Modern*, London: Bloomsbury, 2010.

—— *A War Like No Other: How the Athenians and Spartans Fought the Peloponnesian War*, London: Methuen, 2005.

—— *The Western Way of Warfare: Infantry Battle in Classical Greece*, Oxford University Press, 1989.

Harari, Yuval Noah, *The Ultimate Experience, Battlefield Revelations and the Making of Modern War Culture 1450—2000*, London: Palgrave, 2008.

Harris, Marvin, *Cannibals and Kings: The Origins of Culture*, London: Collins, 1978.

Harvey, A.D., *Collisions of Empires: Britain in Three World Wars*, London: Phoenix, 1994.

Hawkings, Stephen, *The Grand Design*, London: Bantam, 2010.

Hayles, Kathleen, *How We Become Post-Human: Virtual Bodies, Cybernetics, Literature and Infomatics*, Chicago University Press, 1999.

Hazlitt, William, *An Essay on the Principals of Human Action* (ed. John Nabholtz), Gainesville, Florida: Scholars, Facsimiles and Reprints, 1969.

Healey, Dennis, *The Time of My Life*, London: Michael Joseph, 1989.

Heaney, Seamus, *'Creating Poetry' Nobel Lectures from the Literature Laureates*, New York: New Press, 2007.

—— *The Cure at Troy*, New York: Farrar, Straus & Giroux, 1991.

Heilbroner, Robert, *Visions of the Future: The Distant Past, Yesterday, Today and Tomorrow*, Oxford University Press, 1995.

Heim, Michael, *The Metaphysics of Virtual Reality*, Oxford University Press, 1993.

Heims, Steve, *Jon Von Neumann and Norbert Weiner, From Magic to the Technologies of Life and Death*, Cambridge, Mass.: MIT Press, 1980.

Heller, Joseph, *Catch-22*, London: Vintage, 1994.

Hennessey, Philip, *The Junior Officer's Reading Club: Killing Time and Fighting Wars*, London: Allen Lane, 2009.

Henry, Michael *et al.*, 'Propranolol and the Prevention of Post Traumatic Stress Disorder: Is it Wrong to Erase the Sting of Bad Memories?' *The American Journal of Bioethics*, 7:9, September 2007.

Herr, Michael, *Despatches*, London: Picador, 1979.

Herbert, Zbigniew, *The Collective Prose 1948—1998* (ed. Allasa Valles), New York: HarperCollins, 2010.

Hertzog, Toby, *Vietnam War Stories:; Innocence Lost*, London: Routledge, 1992.

Hill, Charles, *Grand Strategies: Literature, State Craft and World Order*, New Haven: Yale University Press, 2010.

Hillenbrand, Lauren, *Unbroken: a World War 2 Story of Survival*, New York: Random House, 2010.

Hobbs, Angela, *Plato and the Hero: Courage, Manliness and the Impersonal Good*, Cambridge University Press, 2000.

Hobbes, *Leviathan*, London: Penguin, 1971.

Holden, Wendy, *Shell Shock: The Psychological Impact of War*, London: Macmillan, 1989.

Holmes, Richard, *Acts of War: the Behaviour of Men in Battle*, London: Cassell, 2004.

Horgan, John, *Rational Mysticism: Spirituality Meets Science in the Search for Enlightenment*, New York: Houghton Mifflin, 2003.

Hughes, Gerard, *Aristotle and Ethics*, London: Routledge, 2001.

Hughes, Thomas, *Man Made World*, London: Michael Joseph, 1989.

Hurley, Elisa, 'The Moral Costs of Prophylactic Propranol', *The American Journal of Bioethics*, 7:9, September 2007.

Huxley, Aldous, *Brave New World*, London: Flamingo, 1994.

Ignatieff, Michael, *Virtual War: Kosovo and Beyond*, London: Chatto & Windus, 1999.

Jacoby, Russell, *Blood Lust: On the Roots of Violence from Cain and Abel to the Present*, London: London Free Press, 2011.

James, Clive, *The Revolt of the Pendulum, Essays 2005—2008*, London: Picador, 2009.

James, William, *Varieties of Religious Experience: A Study of Human Nature*, New York: Signet, 2003.

Jantzen, Grace, *Foundations of Violence*, London: Routledge, 2004.

Jarvis, Jeff, *Public Parts: how Sharing in the Digital Age Improves the Way we Work and Live*, New York: Simon & Schuster, 2011.

Jaspers, Karl, *The Way to Wisdom*, New Haven: Yale University Press, 1954.

Jay, Martin, *Permanent Exiles: Essays on the Intellectual Migration From Germany to America*, New York: Columbia University Press, 1985.

Johansson, Per-A., 'Algorithmic and Ascetic Storytelling: Alternative Approaches to the Imagination and Reality' in John L. Casti and Anders Karlqvist, *Mission to Abisko: Stories and Myths in the Creation of Scientific Truths*, Reading, Mass.: Perseus, 1999.

Johnson, Paul, 'Head Above the Clouds', *The Times Literary Supplement*, 17 December 2010.

Jones, Dan, 'Unpacking the Brain', *Prospect*, March 2010,

Jonas, Hans, *Mortality and Morality: A Search for the Good After Auschwitz*, Evanston, Ill: Northwestern University Press, 1999.

——— 'Cybernetic and Purpose: A Critique' in Hans Jonas (ed.), *Phenomenon of Life: Towards a Philosophical Biology*, Evanston, Ill.: Northwestern University Press, 2001.

Jordan, Tim, *Cyberpower: the Culture and Politics of Cyberspace*, Durham, NC: Duke University Press, 1999.

Joyce, Richard, *Evolution of Morality*, Cambridge, Mass.: MIT Press, 2007.

Junger, Ernst, *Storm of Steel* (trans. Michael Hoffman), London: Penguin, 2004.

Junger, Sebastian, *War*, New York: HarperCollins, 2010.

Kail, P.J., 'Restless, Unquiet Reason', *The Times Literary Supplement*, 21 October 2011.

Kaku, Michael, *Physics of the Future: How Science Will Shape Human Destiny and Our Daily Lives*, London: Allen Lane, 2011.

Kagen, Donald, *Thucydides: The Reinvention of History*, London: Penguin, 2010.

Kamienski, Lukasz, 'Helping the Post-Modern Ajax: Is Managing Combat Trauma Through Pharmacology a Faustian Bargain', Unpublished paper, 2010.

Kassimeris, George, *The Barbarisation of Warfare*, London: Hurst & Co., 2006.

Kateb, George, Hannah, *Arendt, Politics, Conscience, Evil*, Totowa, NJ: Rowman and Allanhead, 1984).

Kam, Paul, *Intoxicated Irregular Fighters: Complications, Dangers and Responses*, Carlisle, Pa.: Strategic Studies Institute, U.S. Army War College, 2008.

Kelly, Kevin, *Out of Control: The Rise of Neo-Biological Civilisation*, New York: William Patrick Books, 1994.

——— *What Technology Wants*, New York: Viking, 2010.

Keegan, John, *Face of Battle: A Study of Agincourt, Waterloo and the Somme*, London: Pimlico, 2007.

Keltner, Dacher, *Born to be Good*, New York: Norton, 2009.

Kierkergaard, *The Sickness Unto Death*, Radford, VA: Wilder Publication, 2008.

Anthony King, Anthony, *The Transformation of Europe's Armed Forces: from the Rhine to Afghanistan*, Cambridge University Press, 2011.

Knox, Bernard, *Essays: Ancient and Modern*, Baltimore: Johns Hopkins University Press, 1989.

Krishnan, Armin, 'Automating War: The Need for a Regulator', *Contemporary Security Policy*, 30:1, April 2009.

——— *Killer Robots: Legality and Ethicality for Autonomous Weapons*, Farnham: Ashgate, 2009.

Kristeva, Julia, *Hannah Arendt*, New York: Columbia University Press, 2003.

Kroker, Arthur and Marie Louise, *Digital Delirium*, London: St Martin's Press, 1997.

Kundera, Milan, *Encounter: Essays*, London: Faber & Faber, 2010.

Kurtzweil, Ray, 'Superiority and Singularity' in Susan Schneider (ed.), *Science Fiction and Philosophy: From Time Travel to Superintelligence*, Oxford: Wylie-Blackwell, 2009.

Landes, David, *Revolution in Time*, Cambridge: Bell Knapp Press, 1983.

Landsburg, Steven, *The Big Questions: Tackling the Problems of Philosophy with Ideas from Market Economics and Physics*, London: Pocket Book, 2009.

Lanier, Jaron, *You Are not a Gadget*, New York: Penguin, 2011.

Larkin, Marillynn, 'Can Post Traumatic Stress Disorder Be Put on Hold?' *The Lancet* Volume 354, 18 September 1999.

Leaio, Matthew *et al.*, 'Neuroethical Concerns About Moderating Traumatic Memories', *The American Journal of Bioethics*, 17:9, September 2007.

Lear, Jonathan, *Aristotle: the Desire to Understand*, Cambridge University Press, 1988.

Le Blanc, Steven, *Constant Battles: Why we Fight*, New York: St Martin's Griffin, 2003.

Le Doux, Joseph, *The Emotional Brain: the Mysterious Underpinning of Emotional Life*, London: Weidenfeld and Nicolson, 1998.

Lehrer, Jonah, *The Decisive Moment: How the Brain Makes up its Mind*, Edinburgh: Canongate, 2009.

Lendon, J.E., *Soldiers and Ghosts: A History of Battle in Classical Antiquity*, New Haven: Yale University Press, 2005.

Leonard, Miriam, *How to Read Ancient Philosophy*, London: Granter, 2008.

Leslie, Ian, *Born Liars*, London: Querous, 2011.

Levidow, Les, *Cyber Worlds: The Military Information Society*, London: Free Association Books, 1989.

Lewis, C.S., *The Abolition of Man*, Grand Rapids: Zondervan, 2001 (original publication 1943).

Lin, Patrick, 'Blowback from Emerging Technologies', *Journal of Military Ethics*, Vol. 9, No. 4 (2010).

———— 'Military's killer robots must learn warrior code', *The Times*, 16 February 2009.

Logue, Christopher, *Kings: An Account of Books One and Two of Homer's Iliad*, London: Faber & Faber, 1991.

Low, David, *Lion Rampant: Studies in British Imperialism*, London: Frank Cass, 1973.

Ludwig, P., 'Eros and The Republic' in G.R.F. Ferrari (ed.) *The Cambridge Companion to Plato's Republic*, Cambridge University Press, 2007.

Lukacs, John, *At the End of an Age*, New Haven: Yale University Press, 2002.

———— *The Future of History*, New Haven: Yale University Press, 2011.

MacGregor, Neil, *History in a Hundred Things*, London: British Museum, 2010.

MacIntyre, Alisdair, *After Virtue: A Study of Universal Theory*, London: Duckworth, 2002.

––––– *Dependent Rational Animals: Why Human Beings Need Virtues*, London: Duckworth, 2009.

MacKay, Sinclair, *The Secret Life of Bletchley Park: The World War II Codebreaking Centre and the Men and Women who Worked There*, London: Aurum, 2010.

Maddox, John, *What Remains to be Discovered: Mapping the Secrets of the Universe*, New York: Simon & Schuster, 1998.

Magnuson, Stew, 'Debate over Legality of Robots on the Battlefield', *National Defense*, 94, number 672 (2009).

Marin, Peter, 'Living in Moral Pain', *Psychology Today*, November 1981, in Walter H. Capp (ed.), *The Vietnam Reader*, New York: Routledge, 1991.

McCarthy, Cormac, *Blood Meridian*, New York: Vintage, 1992.

McGinn, Colin, *Shakespeare's Philosophy: Discovering the Meaning Behind the Plays*, New York: Harper, 2006.

McGrath, Alister, *Why God Won't Go Away: Engaging With the New Atheists*, London: Society for the Promotion of Christian Knowledge, 2011.

McKibben, Bill, *Enough*, New York: Henry Holt, 2003.

McLean, Maureen, 'Literate Species: Population Humanities and Frankenstein', *English Literary History*, 62, 1996.

McLuhan, Marshall, *The Gutenberg Elegies: The Fate of Reading in an Electronic Age*, New York: Fawcett Columbine, 1996.

McNeil, William, *Keeping Together in Time: Dance and Drill in Human History*, Cambridge, Mass.: Harvard University Press, 1995.

Manguel, Albert, *A Reader on Reading*, New Haven: Yale University Press, 2010.

Martin, James, *The Meaning of the 21st Century*, Oxford: Riverhead Books, 2006.

Marx, Karl, *The German Ideology*, London: Lawrence and Wishart, 1996.

Mayer, Jane, 'The Predator War', *The New Yorker*, 28 October 2009, http://www.newyorker.com/reporting/2009/10/26/09106FA_fact_mayer?printable=true.

Mazis, Glen, *Humans, Animals, Machines: Blurring Boundaries*, Albany: State University of New York Press, 2008.

Meir, Christian, *Athens: A Portrait of the City and the Golden Age* (trans. Robert/Rita Kimber), London: John Murray, 1998.

––––– *A Culture of Freedom: Ancient Greece and the Origins of Europe*, Oxford University Press, 2011.

Midgeley, Mary, *Science and Poetry, Hearts and Minds*, London: Routledge, 2003.

––––– *Beast and Man: The Roots of Human Nature*, London: Routledge, 2006.

––––– *Evolution as Religion: Strange Hopes and Even Stranger Fears*, London: Routledge, 2006.

Mill, John Stuart, *On Liberty*, Oxford: Oxford World Classics, 1998.

Miller, Gray, 'Neuro-Science: Reflecting on Modern Minds', *Science* 308, May 2005.

Mitchell, Ben *et al.: Biotechnology and the Human Good*, Washington: Georgetown University Press, 2007.

Morasevic, Julian, 'Learning as Recollection' in Georgy Vlastos (ed.) *Plato: A Collection of Critical Essays Volume One: Metaphysics and Epistemology*, New York: Doubleday, 1971.

Morrie, Jacquelyn Ford, Josh Williams, Aimee Dozois and Donat-Pierre Luigi, 'The Fidelity of Feel: Emotional Affordance in Virtual Environments', www.dtic/cgi-bin/GetTRDoc?Location_U2&doc.pdf.AD=ADA459193.

Morris, Ian, *Why the West Rules for Now: The Patterns of History and What They Reveal About The Future*, London: Profile, 2010.

Morwood, James, *The Tragedies of Sophocles*, Bristol: Phoenix, 2008).

Moskos, Charles and Frank Wood (eds), *The Military: More than a Job?* Washington: Pergamon Brassys, 1988.

Mosovici, Serge, *The Invention of Society*, Cambridge: Polity, 1993.

Mount, Ferdinand, *Full Circle: How the Classical World Came Back to Us*, London: Simon & Schuster, 2010.

Mullen, Mike, *Text of Admiral Mullen's Prepared Testimony* 3 December 2009, accessed at http://www.nytimes.com/2009/12/03/us/politics/03mullentxt.html?pagewanted=1.

Muller-Doohm, Stefan, *Adorno: A Biography*, Cambridge: Polity, 2009.

Mumford, Lewis, *The Myth of the Machine: Vol 2, The Pentagon of Power*, New York: Harcourt Brace Jovanovich, 1970.

Munton, Alan, *English Fiction of the Second World War*, London: Faber & Faber, 1989.

Nash, Christopher, *World Post-Modern Fiction*, London: Longman, 1993.

Newberg, Andrew and Eugene D'Aquili, *The Mystical Mind*, Minneapolis: Fortress Press, 1999.

Nietzsche, Friedrich, *On the Genealogy of Morals* (ed. Keith Ansell—Pearson), Cambridge University Press, 1995.

Nuttall, A.D., *Shakespeare: A Thinker*, New Haven: Yale University Press, 2007.

Nussbaum, Martha, *Upheavals of Thought: The Intelligence of the Emotions*, Cambridge University Press, 2001.

O'Brien, Tim, *If I Die in a Combat Zone*, London: Flamingo, 2003.

———— *The Things They Carried*, London: Belgrave, 1991.

O'Connell, Robert L., *Of Arms and Men: History of War, Weapons and Aggression*, Oxford University Press, 1989.

———— 'Origins of War', in Robert Cowley and Geoffrey Parker(eds), *The Osprey Companion to Military History*, London: Osprey, 1996.

O'Connor, T.J. and Joseph Dotty, 'We Need Teams of Cyber Warriors', *Army Magazine* (USA), 60:1, January 2002, available at http://www/ausa.org/publicaton/armymagazine/archive/january2010.

BIBLIOGRAPHY

O'Mathuna, Donal, *Nano Ethics: the Big Ethical Issues with Small Technology*, London: Contiuum, 2009.

Origo, Iris, *The Vagabond Path: An Anthology*, London: Chatto & Windus, 1972.

Outka, Paul, 'History, the Post-human and the End of Trauma: Propranol and Beyond', *Journal of Traumatology* 15:4, 2009, http://tml.sagepub.com/content/15/4/76.full.pdf+html.

Paret, Peter, *The Cognitive Challenge of War*, Princeton University Press 2010.

Perkins, Henry, *The Third Revolution: Professional Elites in the Modern World*, London: Routledge, 1996.

Pfohl, Stephen, 'The Cybernetic Delirium of Norbert Wiener' (2009), http://www.project.cyberpunk/su/idb/cyberinc_delerium.html.

Phillips, Michael, *The Undercover Philosopher: A Guide to Detecting Shams, Lies and Delusions*, Oxford: One World, 2009.

Pick, Daniel, *War Machine: The Rationalisation of Slaughter in the Modern Age*, New Haven: Yale University Press, 1993.

Pickering, Andrew, *The Cybernetic Brain: Sketches of Another Future*, University of Chicago Press, 2010.

Piette, Adam, *Imagination at War: British Fiction 1939–45*, London: Papermac, 1995.

Pindar, *Odes For Victorious Athletes* (trans. Anne Pippin-Burnett), Baltimore: Johns Hopkins University Press, 2010.

Pinker, Stephen, *The Blank Slate: The Modern Denial of Human Nature*, London: Allen Lane, 2001.

——— *The Better Angels of our Nature* (Allen Lane, 2011).

Pitman, Roger, 'Pilot Study of Secondary Prevention of Post-Traumatic Stress Disorder with Propranolol', *Biological Psychiatry*, 51:2, January 2002.

Plato, *Selected Dialogues* (ed. Benjamin Jowett), New York Modern Library, 2001.

——— *Meno*, Incomplete Works (ed. John M. Cooper), Indianapolis: Hackett Publishing, 1997.

Plutarch, *Essays* (trans. Robin Raite), London: Penguin, 1992.

Poirier, Richard, 'Rocket Power' in *Thomas Pynchon's, Gravity's Rainbow: Modern Cultural Interpretations* (ed. Harold Bloom), New York: Chelsea House, 1986.

Postman, Neil, *Technopoly: The Surrender of Culture and Technology*, London: Vintage, 1993.

Price, Simon and P. Thonemann, *Birth of Classical Europe: History from Troy to Augustine*, New York: Viking, 2010.

Pynchon, Thomas, *Gravity's Rainbow*, London: Picador, 1972.

Quintana, Elizabeth, 'Debate: Robots and Robotics', *RUSI Defense Systems*, 12:3 (2010).

——— 'The Ethics and Legal Implications of Military Unmanned Vehicles', Occasional Paper, RUSI, 2009.

Radine, Lawrence, *The Taming of the Troops: Social Control in the US Army*, Westport, Conn.: Greenwood Press, 1977.

Ramchandran, Bilayanur, *The Emerging Mind*, London: Profile, 2003.

Ridley, Mark, *Nature via Nurture: Genes, Experience and what Makes us Human*, New York: Harper, 2003.

———— *The Origins of Virtue*, London: Penguin, 1996.

Rifkin, Jeremy, *The Emphatic Civilisation: The Race to Global Consciousness in a World in Crisis*, London: Penguin, 2009.

———— *The Biotech Century: How Genetic Commerce Will Change the Mind*, London: Orion, 1998.

Rizzo, Albert *et al.*, *Human Emotional State and its Relevance for Military Virtual Reality Training*, see DTIC.mil/cgi-bin/GetTRDOC?location=u2&doc.pdf&ad=eda45916.

Roberts, Adam, *The History of Science Fiction*, London: Palgrave, 2005.

Roland, David, *The Stress of Battle: Quantifying Human Performance in Combat*, London: TSO, 2006.

Rorty, Richard, *Contingency, Irony, Solidarity*, Cambridge University Press, 1989.

———— *Philosophy and Social Hope*, London: Penguin, 1999.

Rose, Mark, *Alien Encounters: an Anatomy of Science Fiction*, Cambridge, Mass.: Harvard University Press, 1981.

Rose, Michael, *Taking Darwin Seriously*, Oxford: Blackwall, 1986.

Rose, Steven, *The 21st Century Brain: Explaining, Mending and Manipulating the Mind*, London: Vintage, 2006.

Rosenbaum, Ron, *How the End Begins: The Road to Nuclear World War III*, New York: Simon & Schuster, 2011.

———— *The Shakespeare Wars: Clashing Scholars, Public Fiascos, Palace Coups*, New York: Random House, 2006.

Rowlands, Mark, *The Philosopher and the Wolf: Lessons From the Wild on Love, Death and Happiness*, London: Granter, 2008.

Royakkers, Lamber and Renie van Est, 'The Cubicle Warrior: The Marionette of Digitalised Warfare', *Ethics Information Technology*, number 12, 2010.

Sacks, Jonathan, 'Darwin pointed the way to an unselfish evolution', *The Times*, 28 March 2009.

Safranski, Rüdiger (trans. Shelley Frisch), *Nietzsche: A Philosophical Biography*, London: Granter, 2003.

Sagan, Eli, *The Lust to Annihilate: a Psychological Study of Violence in the Ancient Greek World*, New York: Psychological Press, 1979.

Samman, Jean-Luc, 'Cybercommand: The Rift in US Military Cyberstrategy', *RUSI Journal* 155:6, 2010.

Sandel, Michael, *The Case Against Perfection: Ethics in the Age of Genetic Engineering*, Cambridge: Bell Knapp Press, 2007.

Sandywell, Barry, *The Beginnings of European Theorising: Reflexivity in the Archaic Age, Logological Investigations, Volume 2*, London: Routledge, 1996.

Sardar, Ziabddin and Jerome Ravetz, *Cyber Futures: Culture and Politics on the Information Superhighway*, London: Pluto Press, 1996.

Sassi, Maria, *The Science of Man in Ancient Greece* (trans. Paul Tucker), University of Chicago Press, 1988.

Schulz, Kathryn, *Being Wrong: Adventures in the Margins of Error*, London: Portobello Books, 2011.

Sennett, Richard, *Craftsmen*, London: Penguin, 2008.

———— *The Corrosion of Character*, New York: Norton, 1998.

Shankman, Steven and Stephen Durrant, *'The Siren and the Sage: Knowledge and Wisdom in Ancient Greece and China*, London: Cassell, 2000.

Sharkey, Noel, 'Cassandra or False Prophet of Doom': AI Robots and War', *IEEE Intelligent Systems 23/4*.

———— 'Grounds For Discrimination: Autonomous Robot Weapons', *RUSI Defense Systems*, 11:2 (2008).

———— 'A Matter of Precision', *Defense Management Journal*, number 47 (Winter 2009).

———— 'Saying 'No!' to Lethal Autonomous Targeting', *Journal of Military Ethics*, Vol. 9, No. 4 (2010).

Shalev, Arieh, 'Biological Responses to Disaster', *Psychiatry Quarterly*, 17:3–4, 2000.

Shipley, Graham and John Rich *War in Society and the Greek World*, London: Routledge, 1993.

Siegfried, Tom, *The Bit and the Pendulum: From Quantum Computing to M Theory*, New York: Wiley, 2000.

Singer, Peter, 'Gaming the Robot Revolution: A Military Technology Expert Weighs in on Terminator: Salvation', *Slate*, 22 May 2009, in http://www.slate.com.toolbar.aspx?action=print&id=2218834.

———— *Wired For War: The Robotics Revolution and Conflict in the 21ˢᵗ Century*, New York: Penguin, 2009.

———— 'The Ethics of Killer Applications', *Journal of Military Ethics*, Vol. 9, No. 4 (2010).

Slack, Gordy, 'Why We're Good: Mirror Neurons and the Roots of Empathy' in Alex Bentley (ed.), *Edge of Reason? Science and Religion in Modern Society*, London: Continuum, 2008.

Slater, Lauren, *Skinner's Box: Great Psychological Experiments of the 20ᵗʰ Century*, London: Bloomsbury, 2005.

Sorensen, Roy, *A Brief History of Paradox: Philosophy and the Labyrinths of the Mind*, Oxford University Press, 2005.

Sparrow, Robert, 'Do you need us HAL? Robot Warriors, Moral Machines and Silicon that Cares,' *Journal of Applied Philosophy*, 24:1 (2007).

Starr, K., *21: Strategic Technologies for the Army of the 21ˢᵗ Century*, Washington: Technology Forecast Assessments, 1993.

Starr, Paul, 'The Easy War', *The American Prospect*, 14, number 3, 2003 http://www. prospectorg/cs/articles?article=theeasywar.

Strathern, Oona, *A Brief History of the Future: How Visionary Thinkers Change the World and Tomorrow's Trends are Made and Marketed*, London: Robinson, 2007.

Steiner, George, *Grammars of Creation*, London: Faber & Faber, 2004.

Steinbeck, John, *A Russian Journal*, London: Minerva, 1994.

Sterling, Bruce, 'War as Virtual Hell', *Wired*, March-April 1998 www.wired.com/ wired/archive/1.01/verthell.html?pg=1&topic=p7.

Stix, Gary, 'Social Analgesics', *Scientific American*, September 2010.

Stock, Gregory, *Redesigning Humans: Our Inevitable Genetic Future*, Boston: Houghton Mifflin, 2002.

Surgeon General's Office, Mental Health Advisory Team (MHAT, iv), *Operation Iraqi Freedom 05–07*, Final Report, 17 November 2006.

Swofford, Tom, *Jarhead: A Marine's Chronicle of the Gulf War*, New York: Scrivener, 2003.

Talbot, David, 'The Ascent of the Robots Attack Jet', *Technology Review*, March 2005.

Tallis, Raymond, 'Screwing Up, Being Wrong: Adventures in the Margins of Error', *Times Literary Supplement*, 18 March 2011.

———— *Aping Mankind: Neuromania, Darwinitis and the Misrepresentation of Humanity*, London: Acumen, 2011.

———— *Michelangelo's Finger: An Exploration of Everyday Transcendence*, London: Atlantic Books, 2010.

Tancredi, Lawrence, *Hard Wired Behaviour: What Neuro Science Reveals About Morality*, Cambridge University Press, 2005.

Tarnas, Robert, *The Passion of the Western Mind: Understanding the Ideas that Have Shaped our World View*, New York: Ballantine Books, 1993.

Taylor, Robert, *Human Automation Integration for Supervisory Control of UAVs* (Report, DSTI Air & Weapons System, 2006), *see* http://www.ffp.rta.nato.int/ public/PubFullText/RTO/MP/RTO-MP-HEM-136/MP-HFM-136–12PDF.

Taylor, Timothy, *The Artificial Ape: How Technology Changed the Course of Human Evolution*, London: Palgrave, 2010.

Teng Oyang, 'Video Games and the Wars of the Future', *Executive Intelligence Review*, 10 August 2007, *see* http://www.larouchepub.com/lyon/2007/34?1video-wars_future.html.

Thayer, Bradley, *Darwin and International Relations: On the Evolution and Origin of War and Ethnic Conflict*, Lexington: University Press of Kentucky, 2004.

Theroux, Paul, *The Tao of Travel*, London: Hamish Hamilton, 2011.

Thompson, Mark, 'An RX for the US Army's wounded minds', *Time*, 16 August 2010.

BIBLIOGRAPHY

Thucydides, *The Peloponnesian War*, London: Penguin Classics, 1954.

Tightman, Andrew, 'I came over here because I wanted to kill people', *Washington Post* Sunday edition 30 July 2006, http:///www.washingtonpost.com/wpdyn/contents/articles/2006/07/28/AR2006072814.

Todorov, Tzvestan, *In Defence of the Enlightenment*, London: Atlantic Books, 2000.

Toffler, Alvin and Heidi, *War and Anti War: Human Survival at the Dawn of the 21ˢᵗ Century*, New York: Warner Books, 1994.

Tomasello, Michael, *Why We Co-Operate*, Cambridge, Mass.: MIT Press, 2009.

Tonemman, Peter, 'Light Armies', *Times Literary Supplement*, 18 March 2011.

Toulmin, Stephen, *Return to Reason*, Cambridge, Mass.: Harvard University Press, 2003.

Tritle, Lawrence A., *A New History of the Peloponnesian War*, Malden, MA: Wiley-Blackwell, 2010.

———— 'War and Peace Among the Greeks' in Kurt Raaflav (ed.), *War and Peace in the Ancient World*, Oxford: Blackwell, 2007.

———— 'Xenophon's Portrait of Clearchus: A Study in Post-Traumatic Stress Disorder' in Christopher Tuplin (ed.), *Xenophon and his World: Papers From a Conference Held in Liverpool in July 1999*, Stuttgart: Franz Steiner Verlag, 2004.

Turkle, Sherry, *Along Together: Why We Expect More From Technology and Less From Each Other*, New York: Basic Books, 2011.

Urso, Carmello, 'An Inquiry On Philoctetes' Disease', *American Journal of Dermatopathology*, 18:3, June 1996.

Van Creveld, Martin, *The Culture of War*, London: Ballantine, 2008.

———— 'Culture of War' in *The Strategy of the Axis Powers in the Pacific War International Forum on War history: Proceedings*, March 2011, Tokyo: National Institute of Defence Studies.

Vest, Hugh, *Employee Armies and the Future of the American Fighting Force*, Montgomery, Alabama: University Lab Press, Maxwell Air Force Base, 2002, see http://www.dtic.mil/cgi/bin/GetTrdoc?location=u2doc=getdrocc.pd.ada420759.

Virilio, Paul, *Speed and Politics*, New York: Semiotext, 1986.

Vlastos, Georgy (ed.), *Plato: A Collection of Critical Essays, Volume 1, Metaphysics and Epistemology*, New York: Doubleday, 1971.

Von Neumann, John and Oscar Morgernstern, *Theory and Games in Economic Behaviour*, Princeton University Press, 2004.

Voorhoeve, Alex (ed.), *Conversations on Ethics*, Oxford University Press, 2009.

Wallace, Wendell and Colin Allen, *Moral Machines: Teaching Robots Right from Wrong*, Oxford University Press, 2008.

Warnick, Jason, 'Propranol and Its Potential Inhibition of Positive Post Traumatic Growth', *The American Journal of Bioethics* 7:9, September 2007.

Warwick, Patricia, *The Cybernetic Imagination*, Cambridge, Mass.: MIT Press, 1982.

BIBLIOGRAPHY

Waugh, Evelyn, *Unconditional Surrender*, London: Penguin, 1964.

Weil, Simone, 'The Self' in Miles Sian (ed.), *Simone Weil: An Anthology*, New York: Grove Press, 1986.

Wells, H.G., *War of the Worlds*, London: Penguin Classics, 2005.

Wiener, Norbert, *The Human Use of Human Beings, Cybernetics and Society*, New York: Doubleday, 1950, (with introduction by R.M. Young) New York: Free Association Books, 1989.

———— *Cybernetics: On Control and Communication in the Animal and the Machine*, Cambridge, Mass.: MIT Press, 1961.

Williams, Bernard, 'The Liberalism of Fear' in G. Hawthorn (ed.), *In the Beginning Was the Deed: Realism and Moralism in Political Argument*, Princeton University Press, 2005.

Wilson, A.N., *The Victorians*, New York: Norton and Co., 2003.

Winner, Langton, 'Artifice and Order' in Craig Hanks (ed.), *Technology and Values*, Oxford: Wiley-Blackwell, 2010.

Wolf, Maryanne, *Proust and the Squid: The Story and Science of the Reading Brain*, London: Icon, 2008.

Woolfe, Bernard, *Limbo*, New York: Random House, 1952.

Wright, Robert, *The Evolution of God: The Origins of Our Belief*, New York: Little and Brown, 2009.

———— *Non-Zero: The Logic of Human Diversity*, London: Vintage, 2001.

Yudowsky, Elizer, *Creating Friendly AI* (2003) available http://www.singinst.org/CFAI/index.html.

Zimbardo, Philip, *The Lucifer Effect*, New York; Rider, 2007.

Zoepf, Katherine, 'What happened to valour?' *New York Times*, 5 October 2010, see http://www.nytimes.com/2010/05/30/magazine/30medals-t.html?pagewanted=2&hp

INDEX

Achilles: 102, 111–12, 166, 207, 210–11, 235, 250, 252, 266, 270, 274; character of, 47–8, 51, 144; death of, 46, 49, 210, 248; family of, 49, 238; heroic image of, 39

Adams, Douglas: *Dirk Gently's Holistic Detective Agency*, 294

Adams, Thomas: view of evolution of warfare, 26

Adorno, Theodor: 17, 20–1, 23, 25–7, 31, 118, 205–6; background of, 15–16; correspondence with Max Horkheimer, 16; *Minima Moralia: Reflections From Damaged Life* (1951), 16–18; *Prisms*, 284

Afghanistan: 120, 128, 135, 150, 166, 267; borders of, 263; ISAF presence in, 95; Korangor Valley, 271; mercenary activity in, 267–8; Operation Enduring Freedom, 124, 229; use of drones in, 18, 118–19, 122–3

Alexander the Great: 92

al-Qaeda: 128, 198; members of, 123; online presence of, 113

Amiss, Major John: head of Joint Robotics Detachment in Iraq, 175–6

amphetamines: use in Second World War (1939–45), 229; use for fatigue management amongst US military personnel, 228

anamensis: concept of, 160

Appiah, Kwame: 174–5; *Experiments in Ethics*, 173

Apollo moon landing (1969): philosophical discussion arising from, 209

Arendt, Hannah: 209

Arkin, George article in *Governing Lethal behaviour: Embedding Ethics in a Hybrid Deliberative-Reactive Robot Architecture*, 176–7

Aristodemus: *History*, 261–2

Aristotle: 50, 57, 60, 97, 103, 215, 243, 285, 294; concept of '*zoon politikon*', 168; ideal of warrior ethos, 144, 168, 232; *Metaphysics*, 142; *Nichomachean Ethics*, 58, 202; *Poetics*, 174; *Politics*, 40, 260; *Rhetoric*, 57–8; 'talking tools', 160; view of language, 35; virtue ethics of, 115

artificial intelligence (AI): 173; current limitations of, 11–13; fictional

317

depictions of rogue AIs, 9–11,
13–14, 140; proposal for ethical
and clinical tests of, 194–5; use of
means-ends analysis in development of, 154
Artaxerxes: 162
Asimov, Isaac: background of, 187;
Evidence (1946), 196; *Robots of
Dawn*, 199; *The Caves of Steel*
(1954), 188; *The Evitable Conflict*,
194; Three Laws of Robotics, 187,
194, 196–7, 199–201
Asquith, Herbert: British Prime Minister, 141; family of, 141
Asquith, Robert: family of, 141
Athenians: 221, 257; military of, 67,
122, 124, 222, 238; role in Battle
of Mantinea (418 BC), 67; role in
Battle of Marathon (490 BC), 256
Attention Deficit Disorder (ADD):
use of Ritalin for treatment of, 137,
230
Attention Deficit Hyperactivity Disorder (ADHD): genes associated
with, 45
Atticus, Herodes: background of,
256–7; casualty list of Battle of
Marathon (490 BC), 256
Auden, W.H.: view of role of writing
in human development, 61
Ausonius: poetry of, 78
autonomous system: 152; approaches
for development of, 153–4; characteristics of, 153
autonomous weapons systems (AWS):
potential for greater ethical behaviour than humans, 177–8

Balchin, Nigel: deputy Scientific
Advisor to British military, 84; *The
Small Back Room*, 84
Battle Zone (1980): gameplay of, 128

Bavaria: military of, 78–9
Beck, Aaron: development of cogni-
tive therapy, 231
Belyaev, Dmitry: experiments on
domestication of animals, 44
Bentham, Jeremy: 256
Betz, David: cyberwarfare evolution-
ary model proposed by, 114
Birkerts, Sven: 94
Blinn, James: military career of, 96;
writings of, 95
Bloom, Harold: 47
Bohr, Nils: 95
Bonaparte, Napoleon: 22, 110
Bosnian War (1992–5): use of drones
in, 120
Bowden, Mark: 120
brain-computer interfaces (BCIs):
potential use by quadriplegics, 213
bravery: 264–5; Greek concept of,
266
Brecht, Bertolt: *Refugee Dialogues*, 16
Breda Academy: 80
Brodsky, Joseph: 57
Bush, Vannevar: scientific advisor to
Franklin D. Roosevelt, 27
Butler, Samuel: 9; *Erewhon: or, Over
the Range* (1872), 6–7

Cameron, James: *The Terminator*
(1984), 11, 13, 150, 201
Canada: military of, 228
Capek, Karl: 194; death of, 20;
R.U.R. (1920), 19; *The Absolute
at Large* (1922), 20; use of term
'robot', 19; *War with the Newts*
(1936), 20
Caputo, Philip: *A Rumour of War*
(1972), 165, 167, 172, 178–9;
Indian Country (1987), 180
Card, Orson Scott: *Ender's Game*
(1985), 127; *Xenocide* (1991), 127

INDEX

Three Mile Island accident (1979): 186
Thucydides: 12, 49, 56–7, 68, 70, 84, 95, 123–4, 131, 148–9, 215; *History* 122; observation of Battle of Mantinea (418 BC), 65–6
Tolstoy, Leo: 68, 287; *War and Peace*, 130
traumatic brain injury (TBI): prevalence in War on Terror, 234
Trojan War: 102, 122, 211, 233, 240; *ergon* in, 270; heroes of, 210, 237; Trojan Horse, 26, 111–12
Trotsky, Leon: 3
Turing, Alan: 12; background of, 4–5; role at Bletchley Park, 116; Turing test, 13–14
Turner, Frederick Winslow: 82; *The Principles of Scientific Management*, 141
Turkle, Sherry: *Alone Together*, 126, 228

de Unamuno, Miguel: 'Mecanopolis', 6–7
United Kingdom (UK): Bletchley Park, 4, 10, 116–17; Defence Operational Analysis Establishment, 84–5; London, 15–16, 23; military of, 81, 84, 92, 109, 287; Royal Air Force (RAF), 108
United Nations (UN): Educational, Scientific and Cultural Organization (UNESCO), 258; World Citizen's Award, 6
United States of America (USA): 6, 16, 23, 88, 135; 9/11 attacks, 135, 235, 265; Air Force (USAF), 5, 96, 99, 118–19, 125, 129–30, 132, 136, 140, 207, 275; Army Mental Health Corps, 235; Atomic Energy Authority, 2; Central Intelligence

Agency (CIA), 125; Civil War (1861–5), 12, 72, 74, 85, 92, 110, 235; Congress, 265; Constitution of, 275; Department of Defense, 208; Department of Homeland Security, 71; Department of the Army, 93; Department of the Navy, 195; economy of, 149; Federal Bureau of Investigation (FBI), 16; Las Vegas, 118; Marine Corps, 127, 129–30, 230, 266; military of, 84, 89, 93–4, 99, 106, 116, 128, 149, 152, 155, 157, 159, 165, 172, 176, 228, 234–7, 247, 262–3, 265; navy of, 96, 139, 171–2, 207; Navy SEALS, 128; Navy Special Projects Office (SPO), 5; New York, 265; Pentagon, 212, 236; role in development of Stuxnet, 113; Washington DC, 208, 212, 265
University of Southern California: Brain and Creativity Institute, 137; Institute for Creative Technologies (ICT), 131
unmanned aerial vehicle (UAV/drone): 120, 139–40; 'death TV', 135; pilots of, 134–5; use in Afghanistan, 18, 118–19, 122–3; use in Bosnian War (1992–5), 120; use in Pakistan, 18
unmanned autonomous system (UAS): examples of, 176
Unmanned Effects: Taking the Human out of the Loop (2003): conclusions of, 150
US National Aeronautics and Space Administration (NASA): 'The Extension of the Human Senses', 213
US National Research Council: 202–3
US National Science Foundation: 208, 212
USS *Vincennes*: role of in downing of Iranian airliner (1988), 177